ALEXANDER THE GREAT

ALEXANDER THE GREAT

A LIFE IN LEGEND

RICHARD STONEMAN

YALE UNIVERSITY PRESS
NEW HAVEN AND LONDON

For information about this and other Yale University Press publications, please contact:

U.S. Office:	sales.press@yale.edu	yalebooks.com
Europe Office:	sales@yaleup.co.uk	www.yaleup.co.uk

Set in Bembo and Meridien by J&L Composition, Filey, North Yorkshire
Printed in the United States by Sheridan Books

Library of Congress Cataloging-in-Publication Data

Stoneman, Richard.
    Alexander the Great: a life in legend/Richard Stoneman.
       p. cm.
    Includes bibliographical references and index.
    ISBN 978-0-300-11203-0 (alk. paper)
    1. Alexander, the Great, 356–323 B.C.—Romances—History and criticism. I. Title.
    PN687.A5S76 2008
    809'.93351—dc22
                                                                                         2007022903

10 9 8 7 6 5 4 3 2 1

CONTENTS

ILLUSTRATIONS

Colour Plates

PREFACE

I first began thinking about the legends of Alexander in 1984, when I was compiling an anthology of travel writing about Greece.[1] This led me to the legends, folk-songs and spells that feature Alexander in the modern Greek tradition, and prompted me to ask where they had come from. The quest has occupied me now for more than twenty years. (Alexander conquered the east in thirteen.) The first step was to achieve some understanding of the *Alexander Romance*. Beginning from a translation of the Greek version, and translations of several related texts in Greek and Latin, I have explored various aspects of the legends of Alexander in a series of articles (listed in the bibliography). A short textbook on the historical Alexander was another stepping-stone; a rather larger one was an edition and commentary on the Greek and Latin recensions of the *Romance*, completed in 2001, which is being published in three volumes by the Fondazione Lorenzo Valla. The present book builds on these and, while it could never be definitive, it aims to present my understanding of the material I have studied for so long, in the hope that it will prove at least a map for others who find the subject of interest. These are wonderful stories, and they have lasted because they have something to say.

In the course of this long investigation I have incurred many debts, and made many friends, both among the living and among the long dead, and cannot hope to name them all here. I think with pleasure of time spent in the company of audiences who have listened to and commented on portions of my researches. They include seminars at the University of Sydney, Brown University, Loyola Marymount University, the University of Glasgow, Newcastle University (Australia), Miami University (Oxford, Ohio) and meetings of the Classical Association, the Groningen Colloquium on the Ancient Novel, the International Society for the Classical Tradition, and the Ancient India–Iran Trust. I was able to shape some of my thoughts in a contribution to the British Library lecture series, 'The Mythical Quest', in 1996.

The resources of the London Library, the Institute of Classical Studies, the British Library and the Bodleian Library have been indispensable to my research. In addition, I have pursued manuscripts, both illustrated and otherwise, through the Bibliothèque Nationale, Paris; the Staatsbiblotheke of Berlin and Munich; the University Library in Leiden; the Royal Library in the Hague and the Rijksmuseum, Amsterdam; the Chester Beatty Library, Dublin; the John Rylands Library, Manchester; Trinity College Library, Cambridge; the Pierpont Morgan Library, New York; and the New York Public Library. Their librarians have been unfailingly helpful and efficient in supporting my quest.

Portions of the book have appeared in different form as articles in journals and have benefited from the scrupulous comments of those journals' readers. The Press's readers for the book have been of inestimable value. I am grateful to all of them, and to my editor, Heather McCallum, for giving the book the best home I could have hoped for.

Richard Stoneman
University of Exeter

NOTE ON PROPER NAMES AND LANGUAGES

The choice of linguistic forms in a work that ranges over so many cultures is bound to be problematic. I have always borne in mind Eduard Fraenkel's dictum that those who reject the familiar Latin forms of Greek names (Herodotus not Herodotos, Thucydides not Thoukydides) are 'guilty of widening the gap between their readers and the classics'. I have tried to extend this principle, no doubt inconsistently, to a text which includes names from Egyptian, Syriac, Arabic, Hebrew, Persian, Chinese and Sanskrit as well as most modern languages. Accordingly, I have chosen to use the forms that have become familiar through the Latinate tradition of western writing (Roxane not Rowshanak, Nectanebo not Nekht-hor-heb). A writer of a different background might choose another system, but I think at least we will all know whom we mean.

Of the languages that feature in this book, I read English, Latin, Greek (including modern Greek), French, German, Dutch, Italian and Spanish with ease, and Middle English, Middle High German and Old French with help. I have used translations, and the best scholarly advice available, for all texts in Egyptian, Hebrew, Arabic, Persian, Armenian, Sanskrit and Urdu (not to mention Mongolian and Malay): I beg the indulgence of fluent users of these languages for any errors and misunderstandings that may have crept in, and hope that they will nonetheless grasp what I was driving at.

ABBREVIATIONS AND MAJOR CLASSICAL TEXTS CITED

AJAH	*American Journal of Ancient History*
ANRW	*Aufstieg und Niedergang der römischen Welt,* eds H. Temporini and W. Haase
Byz. Neugr. Jahrb.	*Byzantinisches und Neugriechisches Jahbuch*
BZ	*Byzantinische Zeitschrift*
CQ	*Classical Quarterly*
DK	H. Diels and W. Kranz, *Die Fragmente der Vorsokratiker*
EETS	Early English Text Society
FGrH	F. Jacoby, *Die Fragmente der Griechischen Historiker*
GaR	*Greece and Rome*
GRBS	*Greek, Roman and Byzantine Studies*
HP	*Historia de proeliis*
HSCP	*Harvard Studies in Classical Philology*
JHS	*Journal of Hellenic Studies*
JNES	*Jounal of Near Eastern Studies*
JRAS	*Journal of the Royal Asiatic Society*
JSJ	*Journal for the Study of Judaism*
JSS	*Journal of Semitic Studies*
MusHelv	*Museum Helveticum*
OTF	Oriental Translation Fund
Pack^2	R.A. Pack, *The Greek and Latin Literary Texts from Roman Egypt* (Ann Arbor 1965)
PCPS	*Proceedings of the Cambridge Philological Society*
PG	*Patrologia Graeca*, ed. J. P. Migne
PGM	*Papyri Graecae Magicae*
PL	*Patrologia Latina*, ed J. P. Migne
PMLA	*Proceedings of the Modern Language Society of America*
POxy	*Oxyrhynchus Papyri*

PSBA	*Proceedings of the Society for Biblical Archaeology*
REA	*Revue des Etudes Antiques*
RhMus	*Rheinisches Museum*
SS	*Secretum secretorum*
TAPA	*Transactions of the American Philological Association*
ZDMG	*Zeitschrift der deutschen morgenländischen Gesellschaft*
ZPE	*Zeitschrift für Papyrologie und Epigraphik*

Aeschines, *Speeches*
Arrian, *Anabasis* and *Indica*
Curtius Rufus, *Historia Alexandri Magni*
Diodorus Siculus, *Bibliotheca*
Josephus, *Antiquities of the Jews (AJ), Against Apion (Ap)* and *Bellum Judaicum (BJ)*
Justin, *Epitome of Pompeius Trogus*
Pliny, *Natural History*
Strabo, *Geography*
Xenophon, *Education of Cyrus*

For other abbreviations the reader is referred to the *Oxford Classical Dictionary* (OCD) and the Liddell–Scott *Greek–English Lexicon* (LSJ).

All quotations from the *Alexander Romance* are from Richard Stoneman, *The Greek Alexander Romance* (Harmondsworth, Penguin Classics, 1991).

HISTORICAL TIMELINE

Historical Timeline
(all dates BC)

356, July	Birth of Alexander III to Philip and Olympias, rulers of Macedon
336, summer	Assassination of Philip; accession of Alexander Accession of Darius III in Persia
335	Alexander campaigns in Balkans; sack of Thebes
334, spring	Alexander's expedition leaves for Asia
334, May	Battle of the Granicus. Alexander visits Troy
334–333	Conquest of Asia Minor
333, Nov.	Battle of Issus
333–332	Conquest of the Levant
332, Jan.–July	Siege of Tyre
332–331	Alexander in Egypt; visit to Oracle of Ammon; foundation of Alexandria
331	Alexander marches into Mesopotamia
331, 20 Sept.	Eclipse of the moon
331, 1 Oct.	Battle of Gaugamela: final defeat of Darius Alexander enters Babylon
331–330, winter	Macedonian army at Persepolis
330, summer	Darius assassinated by his own courtiers. Alexander assumes title of Great King
330–327	Elimination of pretenders
329, spring	Crossing of Hindu Kush
329–28	Foundation of Alexandra-the-Furthest
327, spring	Marriage of Alexander and Roxane, daughter of a Bactrian chieftain

326, spring	Arrival in Taxila. Encounter with the 'Naked Philosophers'
	Battle on the Hydaspes: defeat of Porus, who is re-established as a vassal king
326, Nov.–spring 325	Alexander turns back and voyages down the Indus
325, Sept.–Nov.	March of the army through the Gedrosian desert and arrival in Carmania
324, Feb.	Marriages at Susa
324, Oct.	Death of Alexander's closest friend, Hephaestion, at Ecbatana
323, spring	Alexander arrives in Babylon. Omens
323, 10 June	Death of Alexander
323, Aug.	Birth of Alexander and Roxane's son, Alexander IV
317, Sept.	Murder of Alexander's half-brother, Philip III, by Olympias
316	Execution of Olympias by Cassander, king of Macedon
311	Execution of Alexander IV by Cassander
308	Murder of Alexander's sister Cleopatra on the orders of Antigonus, king of Macedon
296	Murder of Alexander's half-sister Thessalonike, wife of Cassander, by her own son Antipater

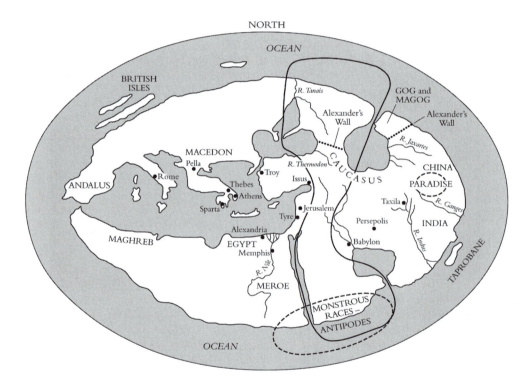

The world of Alexander's legendary adventures

INTRODUCTION

Sultan Iskander sat him down
On his golden throne, in his golden crown . . .
And cried, 'O Lord of my ships that go
From the Persian Gulf to the Pits of Snow,
Inquire for men unknown to man!'
Said Sultan Iskander of Yoonistan.
'Daroosh is dead, and I am king,
Of everywhere and everything . . .
And stay! Impress those learned two,
Old Aflatun, and Aristu,
And set your prow south-western ways
A thousand bright and dimpling days,
And find me lion-hearted lords
With breasts to feed Our rusting swords'.

James Elroy Flecker, 'The Ballad of Iskander'

Alexander the Great was born in the summer of 356 BC and died thirty-three years later in the month Daisios (June) 323 BC. Setting out from his native Macedon, a kingdom lying in the northern part of the Greek peninsula, he pursued the plan of conquest of the Persian Empire, ancient enemy of the Greeks, which had been mooted by his father Philip before his premature death by murder in 336 BC. The twenty-year-old Alexander, whose education had been at the hands of the greatest philosopher of his age, Aristotle, led an army of Greeks and Macedonians further east than any Greek had ever been. In three spectacularly successful battles he demonstrated his brilliance as a general and comprehensively defeated the might of Persia, declaring himself Great King in succession to Darius III and making himself ruler of the largest empire the world had yet known. But he succumbed to fever (many said poison) in the humid lowlands of Babylon in the summer of 323 BC and the empire he had created quickly fell apart as his generals engaged in twenty years of warfare before the outlines of the Hellenistic world emerged.

Even in his lifetime contemporaries were overwhelmed by the military achievement that took him 'beyond the borders of the known world'. The news that percolated back to Greece took on the quality of legend. Alexander himself abetted this development by his overt emulation of the ancestral heroes of the Macedonian kingdom, Heracles and Dionysus, and by his mysterious visit to the Oracle of Ammon at Siwa in the Egyptian desert, where he may have been told that he was the son of the god (who was identified by Greeks with Zeus). Contemporary historians such as Callisthenes and Cleitarchus encouraged the growth of legend by retailing fantastic stories about his achievements; but even the information given by soberer historians like Chares (the court chamberlain) had an otherworldly quality about it, with its tales of the wealth and magical accoutrements of the Persian court; while another historian, Onesicritus, made a set piece of Alexander's encounter with the philosophers of India that was to echo through the literature of antiquity.

A central feature of Alexander's personality, emphasised by the historian Arrian (who wrote several hundred years after Alexander but made use of contemporary, now lost, historians, notably Ptolemy and Aristobulus), was his *pothos*, a quasi-religious longing that led him to push himself, and his army, to ever greater feats of exploration.[1] This, coupled with his passion for the poetry of Homer and the heroic ideal represented by Achilles, ensured that his personality seemed always larger than life. Yet there were ambitions that Alexander was never able to fulfil: the exploration of the Nile, for example, and the conquest of Rome and Carthage.

Some time after his death, probably within a generation, a work of popular literature was produced which latched on to Alexander's dreams and longings and treated them as if they had actually happened. This was the *Alexander Romance*, a work which went on being rewritten, expanded and modified throughout antiquity, and which formed the basis of an enormous literature on Alexander that was produced in the Greek east and penetrated Arabic and Persian traditions, medieval and modern Greece, and, via two Latin translations, the romances of western Europe. The story of Alexander's legends is the story of the metamorphoses of this extraordinary (and, to be sure, rather shaky from a literary point of view) historical novel.[2] In the *Alexander Romance* the historical Alexander is almost entirely overlaid by another Alexander, a protean character who is able to embody some of the deepest fears and longings of the human condition. It is the purpose of this book to explore these legends, to find out where they came from and to trace some of their developments in different cultural milieux. It is remarkable that such a scrappy and unsatisfactory book as the *Alexander Romance* became so influential and inspired much greater works of literature, including the Persian *Shahnameh,* the French *Roman d'Alexandre* and the modern Greek *Phyllada tou Megalexantrou.*

James Elroy Flecker's poem, quoted above, is one of the most recent to revisit the legend of Alexander, and it focuses entirely on the orientalised Alexander and his wise companions Aflatun and Aristu (Plato and Aristotle), so important in the Arabic and Persian traditions. It encapsulates the type of the Alexander who will concern us in this book: not the world-changer who died with his task half done, but the world-ruler who converses with sages and whose desire is endless.

The legendary material is vast and a lifetime would not be sufficient to explore it completely, or even to acquire the languages in which it is purveyed, which range from Icelandic to Malay and from Spanish to Mongolian, as well as the core texts in Greek, Latin, Syriac, Armenian, Hebrew, Persian and Arabic. (Fortunately, almost all the versions have been translated into at least one modern language.) The picture that emerges is of an Alexander who is able to absorb the colour of the world around him (from jihadist Islam to crusader Christianity) and to be a bearer of meaning for pagan philosophers and Jews to boot. The religious categories are not accidental. This Alexander faces questions – how to live, why we die – which will never have a final answer. He can speak for Everyman.

The organisation of such a huge body of material offered various possible approaches, and the one I have chosen is structured around the biography of the hero, from birth to death and beyond. (An alternative method, by groups of texts, would have been very repetitive, but the texts are tabulated in the appendix for reference). In each chapter a period or episode is treated, from which broader themes emerge. The order of chapters is determined by the events in the *Alexander Romance,* which sometimes coincides with historical developments, but more often does not. But it is very notable that many of the legends emerge from a historical nugget, or from an ambition that Alexander expressed (to see the source of the Nile, to see the end of the earth, to be a philosopher, to live for ever). At the same time, each chapter adds a further layer to the legendary complex, each one building on the preceding ones to take the legend's ramifications further.

Chapter 1 covers the birth and inheritance of Alexander and also the origins of the legend itself in its Greek–Egyptian milieu. Both book and hero have an Egyptian parentage. Chapter 2, on Persia, covers the hero's career of conquest and the legend's first stages of development in the Persian context. Chapter 3 considers Alexander's city foundations, which are enmeshed with the origins and motivation of the Jewish traditions. Chapter 4, in which Alexander's historical trajectory continues to India, introduces the geographical material with which he was most widely associated in the medieval west, in Sir John Mandeville and the *Mappae Mundi*. Chapter 5, the encounter with the Brahmans, is the moral heart of the *Romance* and, perhaps, of the legend itself. The many related texts that emerged from this encounter show how pregnant the contrast between the man of action and the contemplative man was to become in later literature, both western and eastern. Chapter 6 concentrates on some of the most widely known stories of Alexander in the Middle Ages: his diving bell and flying machine, and his role as a sage. Here it is easy to trace the roots of his reputation for wisdom to his education by Aristotle, and to show how the story of his flight brings together the themes of exploration and restless ambition that dominated earlier chapters. Chapter 7, on Alexander's relations with women (never a major feature in the historical character's life), begins to show his limitations as a hero and by the way offers the first opportunity to explore the modern Greek tradition. The search for immortality, the subject of Chapter 8, is, with the philosophical aspirations of Chapter 5, the central theme of the legend. It develops first in the Arabic tradition, which is outlined systematically here for the first time, though some of its roots are planted in Jewish and Persian soil. The enclosure of the Unclean Nations (Chapter 9), a late accretion to the legend from the seventh century AD, is important in both eastern and western traditions, and brings a return to the geographic theme from an Arab point of view. With the death of the hero and the portents that surround it (Chapter 10), the history of Alexander's life on earth ends and his legendary career begins. So the last two chapters (11 and 12) are devoted to his 'afterlife' and sketch some of the lines along which the figure of Alexander developed in the western Middle Ages, and in medieval and modern Greece. In showing how Alexander meshes with contemporary concerns and ideas for a thousand years, I hope to have gone some way to answering the question of why Alexander's name has continued to resound through the centuries, why his story was translated more often in medieval Europe than any work except the Gospels, and why he reverberates in the politics and iconography of modern Greece.

Cameo portrait of Alexander the Great, the two-horned. Naples Archaeological Museum.

1

NATIVITY

Egyptian Origins (356 BC)

On the night before [Philip and Olympias] were to be locked into the bridal chamber together, the bride had a dream in which, following a clap of thunder, her womb was struck by a thunderbolt; this started a vigorous fire which then burst into flames and spread all over the place before dying down. And later, after they were married, Philip dreamt that he was pressing a seal on his wife's womb, and that the emblem on the seal was a figure of a lion . . . Moreover, a snake was once seen stretched out alongside Olympias' body while she was asleep, and they say that it was this incident more than anything that cooled Philip's passion and affection.

Plutarch, *Alexander* 2.3–6[1]

[Nectanebo said to Olympias] 'You must have intercourse with an incarnate god, become pregnant by him and bear his son and bring him up. He will be your avenger for the wrongs Philip has done you.' . . .
[Olympias said to Nectanebo] 'I had a dream and saw the god Ammon whom you spoke of. I beg you, prophet, make him make love to me again, and be sure to let me know in advance when he is coming, so that I may be better prepared for the bridegroom.'

Alexander Romance I. 4 and 6

And as the child fell to the ground at the moment of birth, there were great claps of thunder and flashes of lightning, so that all the world was shaken.

Alexander Romance I. 12.9, cf. Justin 12.16.4

The birth of a hero is generally an occasion when the gods show their involvement in human affairs by celestial portents, dreams and other remarkable phenomena. The birth of Alexander the Great in 356 BC was no exception. Even before his birth, both his father and his mother had, we are told, exceptional visions. In the *Alexander Romance* the magician Nectanebo used his astrological arts to ensure the correct moment of birth for a world-conqueror; and historians duly recorded the miraculous cosmic signs that accompanied his arrival in the world. An important precedent for Alexander, being an ancestor of the Macedonian royal house, was the baby Heracles, who a few hours after his birth was already able to sit up and strangle the two snakes that his enemy Hera had sent to kill him and his twin brother in the cradle. So it is no surprise to find snakes involved in Alexander's birth too. The historian and philosopher Plutarch knew a number of stories that went back to the time of Alexander but were omitted by the other historians. He also knew that Eratosthenes was the source for 'the secret of his birth' – presumably the story about Olympias and the snake. The information about Olympias' interest in snakes has a good chance of being true. There is evidence for snake-handling cults in Molossia, where Olympias came from, and in Macedonia in her own time:[2] snakes could be bought very cheaply at Pella, according to Lucian.[3] So the idea that Olympias might have been seen in the 'embraces' of a serpent is not absurd, though perhaps the thing did not take place with quite the melodrama that the *Alexander Romance* attributes to it:

> Suddenly Nectanebo turned himself into a serpent . . . and crept into the dining room, hissing in a most fearsome way, so that the very foundations of the palace shook. When those who were dining with the king saw the serpent, they leapt from their places in fright; but Olympias, who recognized her special lover, extended her right hand to him. The serpent raised himself up and placed his head on her lap; he then coiled himself up and lay on her knees, popping his forked tongue in and out to kiss her, which the onlookers took as a sign of the serpent's affection for her. (*AR* I. 10)

The story of Alexander's being fathered by a serpent became established enough to find imitators. The Roman general Scipio Africanus was said to have been born in precisely the same way, as was the child who was to become the Emperor Augustus.[4]

But if a serpent is enough to mark the birth of a hero, in the tale told in the *Alexander Romance* there is more to the serpent than that: for this serpent is in fact an incarnation of the god Ammon. Ammon is the Greek name of the Egyptian god Amun-Re, the sun god who commonly took the form of a ram. He had been known, and even worshipped, in Greece since at least the fifth century BC, and the Oracle of Zeus at Dodona was said to

have been founded by two doves that flew from the Oracle of Ammon at
the oasis of Siwa in Egypt's western desert. Alexander in his youth was well
aware of the stories circulating about his mother's divine lover, and the first
major detour of his expedition of conquest was to visit the Oracle of
Ammon at Siwa to consult the god about his putative divine parentage. No
one – of course – knows what the god said to him, but the historians tell
us that he 'received the answer he wanted', and he seems in later years to
have believed that he was the son either of Ammon or of Zeus, of whom
Ammon was in Greece taken to be a manifestation.[5] He used sometimes to
dress up as Ammon,[6] and it was also possible to drive him into a fury by
mocking his divine parentage.[7]

One reason why the story about Ammon was important to Alexander,
and to the author of the *Romance*, was that it made the former a legitimate
Pharaoh of Egypt. All the Pharaohs were the incarnation of Re[8] and in
direct linear descent from the previous Pharaoh. Alexander became ruler of
Egypt by conquest in summer 332, but none of the historians makes any
mention of his having been crowned as Pharaoh, and it is usually assumed
that no formal ceremony took place, even though documents soon began
to be dated by his regnal years[9] and Alexander appears on temple reliefs
making sacrifice to the gods in the normal manner. The *Romance* is unique
in referring to a coronation ceremony for Alexander (I. 34), and it may be
closer to the truth in doing so,[10] though it is also true that it was important for the author of the *Romance*, who was certainly living in Egypt, to
make Alexander the legitimate ruler of the country and founder of the
Ptolemaic dynasty.

The birth of a god is a rarer event, even in legend, than the birth of a
hero. Heracles did manage to become a god, though he was born a mere
hero (son of a god); no other mortal became a god in antiquity before the
fourth century BC, though the fashion was just beginning with the posthu-
mous dedications to the Spartan general Lysander on Samos after his death
in 395 BC. When Alexander demanded worship as a god in 324 BC, it came
as a shock to the Greeks, though some affected to be blasé: 'Let him be the
son of Zeus, and of Poseidon as well, if he wants to' (Demosthenes,
Epitaphios 21). The impact of his claim was considerable, and Hellenistic
kings regularly expected, and received, worship as gods on earth: the title
Epiphanes, used by several Ptolemies and Seleucids (following Pharaonic
practice), indicated that its holder was a 'manifest' god.

The word 'Epiphanes' is, evidently, from the same Greek root as
'epiphany', the word which in the church calendar denotes the manifestation of the baby Jesus to the world as God. Much ink could be spilt
over the matter of whether the stories of the birth of Christ are directly

1 Alexander as Pharaoh paying homage to the god Min. Relief at Luxor.

influenced by Greek stories of the birth of gods and heroes. Certainly there are many details in common, though theologians tend to dismiss any parallels with the Gospel story as irrelevant.[11] So it is perhaps not surprising that when medieval artists came to illustrate the birth of Alexander in manuscripts of the numerous vernacular retellings of the Alexander story, they used an iconography which is in effect indistinguishable from that familiar to us from Nativity scenes of several centuries. In a typical illustration from the fifteenth century,[12] the new mother is shown seated frontally in a bed covered with a coverlet of the deep blue associated with the Virgin Mary. Were it not for the crown on her head, the figure of Olympias cradling and presenting her child could be that of Mary.

2 The Birth of Alexander. From Jean le Bon, *Miroir des histoires*, c. 1345. Leiden, MS Voss 44F. 3a. f. 157v.

3 The birth of Alexander portrayed on a mosaic from Soueidié, Lebanon. Drawing after the photograph published by Chéhab 1957.

4 The Birth of Alexander. From the Armenian translation of the *Alexander Romance*, John Rylands Library, Manchester, MS Arm. 3 f. 11v.

The birth of Alexander was portrayed in a very different way in anti-quity. We have two representations of this event from this era. The first is a late antique mosaic pavement from Lebanon, probably of the 3rd century AD.[13] On the left, a woman (Olympias) sits with her right arm extended: a snake crawls up it and extends its head towards her mouth (this is hard to see in reproductions). On the right the midwife (*nymphe*) washes the baby in a bowl of water. In the background sits Olympias, with a maid (*therapaena*) behind her along with a standing figure labelled Philip. The scene is a normal one of everyday life, though the subject was clearly deemed of sufficient importance for Alexander's birth to be the centrepiece of a room's décor. The second image is not itself antique but belongs to a series of illustrations which, from the details of costume and the general style, go back to late antiquity, perhaps the fourth or fifth century AD. These occur in several of the illustrated manuscripts of the Armenian translation of the *Romance*, which was probably made in the fifth century AD, perhaps by the Armenian national historian Moses of Khoren.

The manuscripts themselves are of the fourteenth century and the beau-tiful and highly coloured pictures, of which there are over one hundred, depict the whole story of the Armenian *Romance*.[14] One of the earliest portrays the birth of Alexander. Olympias sits on the birthing stool as in the text, while Nectanebo observes the heavens to identify the most opportune moment for the birth.[15] The manuscript illustrations are a precious witness of the way the story of Alexander was told and envisaged in antiquity, though even this moment is separated by more than seven hundred years from the birth of the god himself.

In late antiquity Alexander acquired a talismanic significance for the pagans who were fighting to preserve their culture from encroaching Christianity.[16] No Christian iconography of Christ's birth had yet arisen, but the pagans had no need to base their depiction on anything Christian: they had a culture of their own with a much longer tradition than anything the Christians could offer. It was only centuries later, when Christianity had won the day, that artists could as a matter of course adopt Nativity motifs for the birth of a pagan hero. Nonetheless, Alexander was of particular significance for medieval Christians, as we shall see in a later chapter, so perhaps the adoption of this iconography was not entirely fortuitous.

Nectanebo's Role

5 Nectanebo at the feet of his protecting falcon. Basalt sculpture, Metropolitan Museum, New York.

The birth of Alexander in a manner befitting a hero, or even a god, and the paternity of a god, perhaps Ammon or Zeus, are regular elements of the tradition known to Plutarch and other ancient authors. The *Romance* adds a further dimension which complicates matters considerably, namely the role of Nectanebo.

Nectanebo II (Nekht-hor-heb) the last Pharaoh of Egypt (r. 360–343 BC), was ruler when the Persian king Artaxerxes Ochus attacked Egypt in 350 and again in 343. Resistance was unsuccessful: Nectanebo fled from Egypt to Nubia and was never heard of again.[17] Except, that is, in the

Alexander Romance. In this work Nectanebo, being an expert magician, divines through his magic arts that the gods are on Persia's side and that resistance is useless. Like Amenophis in Manetho's account of the Pharaohs,[18] written in the middle of the third century BC, he declines to 'fight the gods' and retreats. In the *Romance*, he flees, not to Nubia (or to Memphis like Amenophis), but to Macedon. He takes refuge at the court of King Philip, falls in love with Queen Olympias, and uses his cunning, as well as his magic arts, to become her lover.

6 Nectanebo arrives at Pella. On the left, he assumes the form of a dragon and kisses Olympias. From a fifteenth-century History Bible. Koninklijke Bibliotheek, The Hague, 78 D 38 II, f. 69r 6.

He tells her (in the passage quoted at the head of this chapter) that she must have intercourse with the god Ammon, who has 'hair and beard of gold, and horns growing from his forehead, these also made of gold'. After collecting some desert herbs, he 'made an infusion with them, then moulded a female figure of wax and wrote on it the name of Olympias'. Uttering the appropriate incantations, he causes Olympias to have an erotic dream about just such a figure, which makes her eager for the visit of the god in person.

The next stage shows Nectanebo in the role not of magician but of trickster. He

> Procured a fleece of softest sheep's wool, with the horns still attached to its temples. The horns shone like gold. He also procured an ebony

sceptre, a white robe and a cloak resembling a serpent's skin. Wearing these, he entered the bedroom, where Olympias was lying under the coverlet, just peeping out. She saw him come in, but was not afraid, because he looked just as the god had done in her dream. The lamps were lit, and Olympias covered her face. Nectanebo, putting aside his sceptre, climbed on to the bed and made love to her. Then he said, 'Be calm, woman, in your womb you carry a male child who will avenge you and will become king and ruler of all the world.' Then he left the room, taking the sceptre with him, and hid all the pieces of his disguise. (*AR* I. 7)

What is going on here? What begins as a story about a great magician turns into the tale of a seducer's trick. The noble Pharaoh becomes a sleazy Don Juan. The story is one of the best-paced narratives in the *Romance*, but its significance is thoroughly ambiguous. How can we clarify its intent? Or must we say that the author is confused, trying to do too much at once?

Certainly two well-established story patterns are interwoven here, the first about Nectanebo the magician, the second what has been dubbed by the anthropologist Wendy Doniger 'the Bed Trick'.[19] Nectanebo has an impeccable pedigree as a magician, which is in itself unusual in a Pharaoh: magic was the province of priests, though magicians were not a special class at all in ancient Egypt.[20] Perhaps Nectanebo was as a matter of historical fact interested in magic. An elaborate magic stele bears his name (Koenig 1994, 101–5), and a drawing of his face adorns one of the magic papyri.[21] His competence in magic and divination is presented as fact in the *Romance*: he divines that the Persians are going to win the war by examining wax figures which he floats in a bowl of water, a widespread magical practice in antiquity,[22] as is the idea that a woman should seek a dream in order to conceive.[23] His method of bringing a dream to Olympias, using a wax figure, is a standard one,[24] and later in the *Romance* he sends a prophetic dream to Philip by casting a spell on a 'sea-hawk' and sending it off to speak to him.[25] (This is a Greek 'Homeric' type of dream where the divine figure makes a pronouncement to the hearer, in contrast to the vision of the god in action that Olympias receives which seems more folkloric.)

Nectanebo's magic arts and his unhappy fate seem to have made him a vehicle for popular stories in Egypt in the third century BC. Martin Braun argued that a putative 'Nectanebus-Romance' lay behind the story of Amenophis told by Manetho:[26] it is at least curious that the thirteen years which elapse between Amenophis' flight and his return correspond neatly to the thirteen years between Nectanebo's flight and the 'return' of his 'son'

Alexander to reclaim the throne.[27] Nor was this the only story of Nectanebo in circulation at this time. As Ben Edwin Perry says,[28]

> When, after the flight of Nectanebus [*sic*], the hated Persians once more took over in Egypt, the heart of the people was crushed, and only hope and fond memory could sustain their spirits. They thought of Nectanebus with sorrow and affection as the last of their native Pharaohs, and in him all their hopes for the future came to be focused. He had gone, no one knew where. Perhaps he was only sleeping for the present, like Frederic Barbarossa in the great Kyffhäuserberg; but, like Frederic and other famous champions of old, he was destined to return again in the person of a younger and more vigorous king, who would drive out the enemies of Egypt and liberate the people.

This sentiment is apparent in the *Demotic Chronicle*, a series of prophecies written in the third century BC and describing the events of the fourth.[29]

The fragmentary text known as *The Dream of Nectanebo*[30] also tells of how Nectanebo saw that the gods were abandoning him. They appear *en masse* in a papyrus boat, and the god Onuris complains to Isis that work on his temple has remained incomplete. Nectanebo awakes and orders completion of the works; but the papyrus is incomplete and we do not know how the story ended. Another papyrus contains a story about Nectanebo pursuing priests who desert from the temple of Asclepius.[31] All these Egyptian stories, like the *Alexander Romance*, portray a Pharaoh whose kingdom is collapsing about him.

The second element in the *Romance* is a story about a seduction trick. Though Nectanebo has begun by casting spells to bring a dream to Olympias, the 'dream' he brings is not a magic one but simply himself in disguise, satisfying his passion for her. There are some indications that Olympias knows perfectly well what is going on. The next morning, when he asks her how the night went, she replies, 'I am amazed that you do not already know about it, prophet. But will the god come to me again? For it was very sweet with him' (*AR* I. 7). Nectanebo now persuades Olympias to let him have the key to her room, so that he can come to her as often as he wants. 'And all the time she thought it was the god Ammon who came to her . . . . In this way Olympias was taken in by the magic powers of Nectanebo' (ibid.). The author of the *Romance* preserves the ambiguity of the magic/deception throughout the narrative.

However, in the earliest surviving recension of the *Romance* (A) there is no such ambiguity. Nectanebo simply turns himself into a representation of Ammon (with no mention of his obtaining the disguises), as he does later (I.

10; p. 14) into a dragon. It seems that we have here a rationalising rewriting of a simple magic tale, in such a way that the trick is at odds with the religious dimension. But is it really so simple? Even by magic, Nectanebo does not become the god Ammon; he is himself in disguise, by whatever means he adopts. The rationalism of the later versions penetrates only to the means, not to the substance of the trick. Nectanebo is still a crafty seducer.

The pattern is a common one that goes back to the dawn of storytelling. It is familiar in more modern literature from Boccaccio (*Decameron* 4.2, 'Gabriel'), and the story of Nectanebo and Olympias is told by John Gower in his *Confessio Amantis* VI. The exiled Pharaoh falls in love with Olympias as he sees her riding in the city, for all the world like a dame of chivalry:

> The lusty quene in good array
> Was set upon a mule white,
> To seen it was a great delite
> The joie that the citee made.
> With freshe thinges and with glade
> The noble town was all ehonged   [hung]
> And every wight was fore alonged
> To se this lusty lady ride . . .
> Nectanabus came to the grene
> Amonges other and drough him nigh.   [drew]
> But whan that he this lady sigh
> And of her beaute hede toke,
> He couthe nought witholde his loke   [could]
> To se nought elles in the felde,
> But stood and only her behelde.

He makes himself known to her as in the *Romance* and promises her a vision of Ammon ('Amos'), as we have seen. He then prepares his herbs and the wax figure inscribed with her name:

> And therupon he gan conjure,
> So that through his enchantement
> This lady, which was innocent
> And wiste nothing of this guile
> Met, as she slepte thilke while,
> How from the heven came a light,
> Whiche all her chambre made light.
> And as she loketh to and fro,
> She sight, her thought, a dragon tho,   [there]

Whose scherdes shinen as the sonne [scales]
And hath his softe pas begonne [pace]
With all the chere that he may
Toward the bed there as she lay.

Nectanebo's deception on the night following the dream is again achieved by simple magic and not by dressing up:

The night come, and the chambre is weived, [closed]
Nectanabus hath take his place,
And whan he sigh the time and space, [saw]
Through the deceipt of his magique
He put him out of mannes like
And of a dragon toke the forme,
As he, which wolde him all conforme
To that she sigh in sweven er this. [dream]

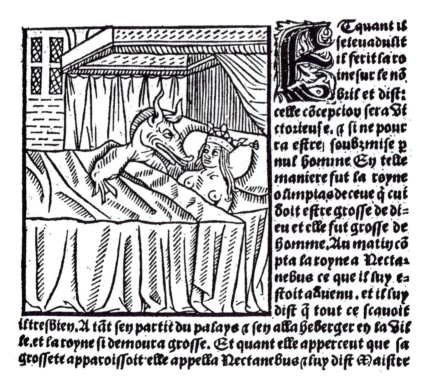

Tquant il seleuaduft il ferit sa roine sur se nõ bril et dist: celle cõcepciou sera victorieuse. q si ne pour ra estre soubzmise p nul homme Ey telle maniere fut la royne osimpias deceue q cui doit estre grosse de di= eu et elle fut grosse de homme. Au matiy cõ pta la royne a Necta= nebus ce que il suy e= stoit aduenu. et il suy dist q tout ce scauoit istresbien. A tãt sen partit du palays q sen alla hebergter ey la vil= le. et la royne si demoura grosse. Et quant elle apperceut que sa grossete apparoissoit·elle appella Nectanebus q suy dist Maistre

7 The Begetting of Alexander. From the *editio princeps* of the French Prose Alexander, *Alixandre le Grant*.

Where did Gower get this story from? The *Alexander Romance* was a popular and familiar work in the European Middle Ages. The earliest Greek version (A), known to us from a single MS in Paris, was considerably expanded and adapted in its later Greek versions. Another version of the tradition represented by A (the alpha recension) was translated into Latin by Julius Valerius soon after AD 300 but seems not to have been well known, though it was copied a number of times in the Middle Ages. (See the appendix for an account of the numerous versions of the *Romance*.) Much more influential was a second Latin translation, again of an alpha version of the Greek, made by Leo the Archpriest of Naples in the tenth century AD. Leo was in the service of Duke John III of Naples, of whom Domenico Comparetti wrote:

> It is not without surprise that, in the gloom of the tenth century, we encounter in this medieval Naples, of which we know so little, a duke such as John III, who, full of noble instincts, appears, like a miniature Charlemagne, as the patron of letters, and even Greek, collecting together from every place, even from Constantinople, works both sacred and secular in both languages.[32]

Leo was sent by John to Constantinople for the specific purpose of collecting Greek manuscripts, and when he returned he translated some of them into Latin. Among them was the *Alexander Romance*. The MS he worked from was of much better quality than the one surviving MS of alpha, which is slightly later than Leo's translation: it is highly corrupt (in places there are mere strings of letters without meaning) and now in places illegible. Would that we still had the Greek MS from which Leo worked! Leo's translation follows the Greek original faithfully in an approachable Latin with simple syntax and several features of contemporary speech (notably vocabulary items such as *caballus* for *equus*, 'horse').

Two copies of Leo's translation survive (see Appendix I), but it was the adaptations of his work that spread the *Romance* all over Europe. These go under the title of the *Historia de Proeliis*, 'the History of [Alexander's] Battles',[33] and three versions were made between AD 1000 and 1236. The first version, known as the First Interpolated Version (I^1 or, usually, J^1) was translated into every vernacular language of Europe between about 1100 and 1400. (See further Chapter 11 and Appendix I.) The second was nearly as popular, and the third, besides existing in numerous MSS, was printed several times from 1486 onwards.

From Icelandic to Romanian, from Irish to Italian, from Russian, Serbian and Czech to English and Spanish, there is no language that does not have

at least one *Alexander Romance* in its portfolio. No other work, apart from
the Gospels, was more frequently translated in the Middle Ages.[34] Any of
these might have been known to Gower. It is not at all unlikely that the
book was also known to Boccaccio, who may have adapted the Nectanebo
story consciously for his own story 'Gabriel'.

There were good classical and Egyptian precedents for the seducer
disguised as a god. The familiar story of Alcmena being impregnated by
the god Zeus disguised as her husband Amphitryon is not quite the same
(it really is a god, and the virtuous lady thinks her paramour is her
husband). Likewise the Germanic story of Siegfried sleeping with
Brünnhilde in disguise as Gunther, and the Celtic one of Uther engen-
dering Arthur while disguised as Gorlois, the true husband of Ygerna,
depend on the wife expecting the person she thinks she sees. But Josephus
(*AJ* 18, 65ff.) tells a story, set in Egypt, in which Paulina is tricked into
having intercourse with Mundus in a temple on the pretext that he is the
god Anubis. (The story was made into a Roman mime, *Anubis Moechus*:
Tertullian, *Apologeticus* 15.171–4.) Plutarch makes it clear that it was a
common Egyptian belief that someone might be the offspring of a mortal
woman and a male god (*Quaest. Conv.* 8.13).

The story pattern is in fact fundamental to the Egyptian kingship myth
that the Pharaoh is the son of Amun or Amun-Re,[35] begotten by him on
the wife of the Pharaoh.[36] An inscription in the Temple of Amenhotep III
at Luxor, and another in Hatshepsut's mortuary temple at Deir el-Bahari,
tell the tale:

> Words spoken by Amun-Ra, Lord of Karnak, pre-eminent in his harem,
> when he had assumed the form of this her husband, King Menkheperura
> (Tuthmosis IV), given life. He found her as she slept within the inner-
> most part of the palace. She awoke on account of the divine fragrance,
> and turned towards his Majesty. He went straightway to her, he was
> aroused by her. He allowed her to see him in his divine form, after he
> had come before her, so that she rejoiced at seeing his perfection. His
> love, it entered her body. The palace was flooded with the divine
> fragrance, and all his odours were those of the land of Punt.[37]

From an Egyptian perspective, it was vital that Alexander, as a ruler of
Egypt, should have been conceived in the proper manner for a Pharaoh. So
Nectanebo ensures that his intercourse with Olympias is carried out in the
proper manner. True, Nectanebo is setting out to satisfy his own desires, and
there is humour in the story; but the net result is a child properly engendered both by the preceding Pharaoh and, by his magic arts, by the god

Amun-Re. The story is of a piece with other aspects of the *Romance* that emphasise Alexander's Egyptian credentials (see Chapter 3 below).[38] If the story as told still retains some ambiguity, that may be due to the artistry or the irony of the author rather than to his supposed incompetence.

Nectanebo and the Stars

The story of Nectanebo is not finished when he successfully makes love to Olympias. Their union has its natural consequence and a son is born. Nectanebo brings his arts to bear to ensure that the son will be a ruler of the world. This time it is Nectanebo not as magician, but as astrologer, who comes into play. On his first encounter with Olympias he produces his credentials in the form of a folding writing tablet (rather like a travelling chess set) constructed of ivory, ebony, gold and silver. It is engraved with three circles, on the first of which are the thirty-six decans,[39] on the second the twelve signs of the zodiac, and on the inner one the sun and moon. One may imagine a layout something like the Zodiac of Osiris from the Temple at Dendera (c. 50 BC), now in the Louvre.[40] In a separate ivory box Nectanebo carries images of the heavenly bodies made of precious stones, which can be positioned on the zodiac like chess pieces. The sun is of crystal, the moon of diamond, the Mars of haematite, the Mercury of green stone (perhaps serpentine), the Jupiter of something called *aitheritos*, which ought to mean air-stone, the Venus of lapis lazuli, the Saturn of ophite.[41] In addition there is a pointer of white marble ('the ascendant'), to mark the moment of birth (*AR* I. 4).

Nectanebo uses this equipment to cast the horoscopes of himself, Olympias and Philip. He then makes his pronouncement that the son she bears by the god will be her avenger for the wrongs Philip has done her. Later, when Nectanebo sends the dream by the sea hawk to Philip, the god he sees in his dream addresses Olympias: 'Woman, you have conceived a male child who will make you fruitful and will avenge the death of his father' (*AR* I. 8). Given the corruptions in the text where it relates to astrology, one might suspect that the earlier reference to revenge might also have said something like this: for it is a common piece of Egyptian theology that the incoming Pharaoh is the 'avenger of his father', sometimes against the destructive god Seth. The new Pharaoh annihilates the death of his predecessor and picks up his father's responsibilities.[42] This piece of the 'royal ideology' of the Pharaohs was adopted by the Ptolemies, for example in the title Philopator ('father-loving') adopted by some of them.

When the time comes for Olympias to give birth, Nectanebo is in attendance with his ivory horoscope. 'She sat down on the birth-stool and

went into labour. Nectanebo stood by her, measuring the courses of the
heavenly bodies: he urged her not to hurry in giving birth' (*AR* I. 12).
Nectanebo is forcing her to time the birth so that the astrological
conjunctions will be as auspicious as possible.[43]

Unfortunately the text in A is extremely corrupt, and the authors of the
later versions, when faced with what are often mere strings of letters ('the
scribe scarcely understood a word of what he was writing'),[44] simply gave
up and omitted the whole passage, so that we have no check on the text to
help us to elucidate it. I believe that in its original form this text did make
sense and represented a genuine horoscope for Alexander. The critical work
of F. Boll has done much to bring order out of the chaos, but there are
insufficient data preserved in intelligible form to construct the horoscope
intended.[45] Alexander was probably born in early July 356 BC. When
Olympias goes into labour, Scorpio is in the ascendant, which at the present
time would occur at about 6 or 7 p.m. Nectanebo tells her to wait, and we
then hear that Cancer is in the ascendant, which would take place about
eight hours later, around dawn. (We are now told that the moon is setting.)
Aries is therefore in the *mesouranon* or mid-heaven, but the important point
is that Jupiter is now in Aries, and it is on this that Nectanebo bases his
prophecy that the child will be a world ruler. (Aries is the Ram, i.e.
Ammon, and is a sign of kingship, according to the astrological authority of
the fourth century AD, Firmicus Maternus, II. 10.) A number of negative
influences are also present, but it is impossible to determine how Nectanebo
deals with these. His speech concludes with a resounding pronouncement:

'Jupiter, the lover of virgins, who was pregnant with Dionysus in his
thigh, is now high in the clear heaven, turning into horned Ammon
between Aquarius and Pisces, and designating an Egyptian as world ruler.
Give birth NOW!' And as the child fell to the ground, there were great
claps of thunder and flashes of lightning, so that all the world was shaken.
(*AR* I. 12, end)

Philip in the *Romance* continues to be uneasy about this son who, as he
finds, in no way resembles him; but he permits him to be raised on the
grounds that 'he is the seed of a god and his birth has been signalled by the
heavens' (*AR* I. 13). Twelve years later, he is still suspicious of Olympias and
she fears that she has something bad in store for her. Alexander, who is now
taking school lessons from Nectanebo, accompanies his teacher to observe
the stars outside the city. As soon as they have reached the hill, Alexander
seizes the magician by the hair and pushes him into a deep pit, where he
breaks his neck. This act is never adequately explained, and Alexander's

8 The Death of Nectanebo. The pages narrate the events in cartoon strip fashion: Nectanebo shows Alexander the stars, the dying Nectanebo tells Alexander he is his father, Alexander carries the body home to Olympias. From MS Venetus (D), Hellenic Institute, Venice, Codex gr. 5

excuse is singularly feeble: 'Blame yourself . . . because, although you do not understand earthly matters, you investigate those of heaven' (*AR* I. 14).[46] The dying Nectanebo, however, takes the opportunity to reveal the truth of Alexander's birth. When Alexander realises he has killed his own father, he is grief-stricken. He shoulders the body and carries it back to the palace. When Olympias hears his story, 'she was astounded, and berated herself for having been made a fool of by Nectanebo's magic and tricked into adultery' (*AR* I. 15). Is this, then, the sense in which Alexander has become avenger of his father, in that he has killed the man who cuckolded his legal father Philip?

Garlic and Golden Eggs

Alexander has grown up fast, and will soon be ready to embark on the major enterprise of his life (though it is but a small part of his legend), the conquest of the Persian Empire. Before we leave the story of his birth, there is another, radically different version of events to consider. This might be called the Persian version.

The *Shahnameh*, or Book of Kings, of the Persian poet Firdausi is a vast work, comprising 50 books.[47] The national epic of Persia, it is an account of Persian history from legendary times to the reign of Yazdigird III (AD 632–42), the last Shah before the Arab conquest. The story of Alexander (Iskander) and Dara occupies Books 18–20. Firdausi wrote in the tenth century AD but for most of his account of Alexander drew on the *Alexander Romance*, which he knew through the Syriac translation of the sixth century, or a derivative (see Appendix I). He probably also made extensive use of oral tradition (see Chapter 2).

Though the narrative of Alexander's reign by Firdausi contains many of the episodes which will become familiar to us later in this book – such as his education by Aristotle, his military cunning, his search for the Water of Life, his building of a wall against the Unclean Nations, and his letters to his mother – the story of his birth takes a quite different form in his poem.

The Shah of Persia, Darab, is at war with Filicus the King of Rum. Darab is a fictitious personage, invented to differentiate him from his son Dara, who is Darius III and will become Alexander's opponent. Filicus is Philip II of Macedon, and Rum is the name the Islamic nations gave to the Roman Empire, by which they meant the Byzantine Empire of the Greeks. The nomenclature betrays the date at which the story took its final form, after the Arabs and Byzantines had already come into contact in the seventh century AD.

After three ferocious but inconclusive battles, Filicus sends messengers to Darab inviting him to a parley. Darab consults his ministers, who advise him as follows:

> 'Let the king choose the action he knows to be best. That famous monarch has a daughter of cypress stature and beautiful as the spring. No idol-adorner in China ever saw her like; she shines forth like a jewelled ring among other beauties. If your Majesty saw her he would approve of her. Let this lofty cypress be transplanted to your garden.'
>
> The Shah summoned the messenger from Rum and repeated to him what he had heard . . . . Filicus and his courtiers rejoiced that he should have a son-in-law like the Shah, but discussion ranged back and forth about tribute and taxes and how much the king of Rum should bear. It was agreed that each year the Shah should be paid a hundred thousand eggs of gold, in each of which there was to be a royal gem, each of the gems a jewel of price. The Caesar then commanded that all the learned men and men of substance prepare for the road and accompany the royal lady to the Shah. (Firdausi, 1967, 229)

Honour seems to be saved and further hostilities averted. But

> One night, as the princess lay by the king's side, she suddenly exhaled a pungent breath at which the monarch conceived disgust. He twisted about and turned his face into the bedclothes . . . . Wise physicians were summoned and seated themselves beside the princess. One perspicacious and shrewd physician pursued researches until at last he produced a remedy. He pounded up a herb which burned the mouth – in Rum it is called Sekandar – and applied it to the mouth of Nahad [the princess], who shed tears. The evil odour departed, though her mouth was burned, and once more her cheeks resumed their glowing colour. (Firdausi, 1967, 229ff.)

Alas, it is all too late. The king is permanently put off his bride and sends her back to her father, 'sad and pregnant'. When the baby is born, it is a boy and she names him Sekandar, after the remedy that had cured her illness. Sekandar is of course Alexander: the syllable al- is taken by Islamic writers to be the Arabic article, so that the name in Persian (which does not use the article) becomes Sekandar or Iskander (the spellings vary). The herb is, as likely as not, garlic (Greek *skandix*), though its use to cure bad breath is in contradiction to its usual reputation.

Darab, meanwhile, marries again, and his new Persian wife bears him a son called Dara, who at the age of twelve inherits the throne of Persia. It is

Dara who is the opponent of Alexander or Sekandar and who is eventually defeated by him. The two kings are half-brothers, and thus the Persian myth that the Empire had never been conquered by an invader is preserved intact. The war between them was merely a civil war, and Sekandar is a legitimate king of Persia. As such he is one of the most prominent heroes of Persian legend, in a league with Sohrab and Rustum, with Kai Ka'us and Kai Khosrow.

The Persian version of Alexander's birth became most influential in the east, and the Arab historians from Tabari onward adopt the same tale. For the Arabs, it has the additional advantage that it avoids the story of the divine birth by Nectanebo, which to the Muslim Arabs was as much a blasphemy as the virgin birth of Jesus.

But what of those golden eggs? These were not an invention of the Persian poet, but appear also in the Greek *Romance*. Though they are not in its earliest version, A, they occur in the later recensions, all of which predate the composition of the *Shahnameh*. The Greek version, however, has a mere 100 eggs, each weighing 20 pounds, of solid gold (*AR* I. 23). When the Persian ambassadors arrive on one of their annual visits to collect the tribute, they find Philip away on campaign and Alexander in charge. Alexander dismisses them, saying: 'It is not right for Philip, the king of the Macedonians, to pay tribute to the barbarians: one cannot rule over Greeks just by wanting to . . . . As long as Philip was alone, he paid tribute to you, but now that he has sired a son, Alexander, he will not pay tribute, but I myself shall come and take back from you in person all that you took from us' (*AR* I. 23). His reply in Firdausi is even more succinct: 'Go to Dara and tell him that all the glory has now departed from our tribute, for the bird which laid the golden eggs has died and so our tribute is made valueless' (Firdausi 1967, 232). The envoys are filled with panic and flee; Sekandar, who in this version has already succeeded to the throne, promptly sets out on campaign to conquer the Persian Empire. Which brings us to a new stage of the story.

GOLDEN VINES, GOLDEN BOWLS AND TEMPLES OF FIRE
The Persian Versions

[Darius speaks]: 'When I am dead, Alexander, bury me with your own hands. Let the Macedonians and Persians carry me to my grave. Let the families of Darius and Alexander be one. I commit my mother to you as if she were your own, and I ask you to sympathise with my wife as if she were one of your relatives. As for my daughter Roxane, I give her to you for a wife, to start a line of descendants that will preserve your memory . . . .' With these words, Darius laid his head on Alexander's breast and died.

Alexander Romance II. 20

When Alexander was right upon them, Satibarzanes and Barsaentes wounded Darius, left him where he was and escaped themselves with 600 horsemen. Darius died of his wound soon after, before Alexander had seen him. Alexander sent Darius' body to Persepolis, ordering it to be buried in the royal tomb, like the other kings who ruled before him . . . . This was the end of Darius . . . No man showed less spirit or sense in warfare; but in other matters he committed no offence . . . even if he had had the will, he was no longer free to play the tyrant to his subjects, as his position was more dangerous than theirs. His life was one series of disasters, with no respite, after his accession.

Arrian, *Anabasis* III. 21.10–22.2

Alexander becomes King of Persia

Alexander's conquest of Persia took just four years (334–330 BC). Once Darius was dead Alexander could regard himself as rightful king by conquest, and from this point the legendary tradition regards him as such, ignoring the historical complications.

One of the most recognisable scenes in Persian manuscript painting represents the death of Darius (see colour plate 1). The dying King Darius rests his head on Alexander's lap, his eyes closing as the conqueror Iskandar strains to hear his last words. A groom holds Alexander's horse, and to the left the two murderers of Darius, their heads shaved, are brought in by a Macedonian soldier. All the participants wear medieval Persian battle dress, a long robe, mail over the shoulders and a helmet that rises in an ogee to a point. Darius' eyes are closed and a look of grief suffuses the conqueror's face. Related scenes occur in most MSS of the *Shahnameh* and of the *Iskandarnameh* of Nizami: sometimes the whole Macedonian army is present; sometimes the murderers are not.[1] Another *Shahnameh* shows the crowd encircling the *pietà* group,[2] this time under a tree, and the murderers are not present.

The image of Alexander succouring, and hearing the last words of, Darius might seem to belong purely and simply to a Persian version: Darius' words make Alexander the legitimate successor of the dying king, who mourns him truly and carries out all proper funeral rites before marrying his daughter to continue the royal line. In the *Shahnameh* Dara's last words are 'See to my children and my loved ones whose faces are veiled. Marry my pure-bodied daughter and maintain her in security in your palace. Her mother named her Rowshanak and with her provided the world with joy and adornment. It may be that by her you will have a noble son who will restore the name of Esfandiyar to glory, bring lustre to the fire of Zoroaster and elevate the Zand and the Avesta. He will treat the great as great and the lesser men as lesser, and the Faith will flourish and prosper' (Firdausi 1967, 236). Yet this Persian version takes all its details, except the points about the Zoroastrian religion, directly from the Greek *Alexander Romance*.

The narrative is in flat contradiction to all that we know of the final moments of Darius from the Greek historians. We can be fairly sure that his death followed more or less the course described by Arrian: Darius was in flight with his nobles when two of them, Bessus and Nabarzanes, turned on him, struck him down and left him for dead beside the road. Bessus declared himself king under the name Darius IV and fled to Bactria to continue the resistance. Alexander's army came upon the body of the king, dead and degraded beside the road. It was a victory, for Alexander could freely enter Babylon and be received as king, but he had to devote two more years to hunting down Bessus to eliminate him. Alexander did not, as the *Romance* describes, find Darius still alive and receive the mantle of kingship from him. Furthermore, Alexander did indeed marry a girl called Roxane (Persian: Rowshanak), though not until spring 327, nearly three years after the death of Darius in summer 330; and she was not the daughter of the Persian king, but of a Bactrian chieftain named Oxyartes.

The story that makes Roxane the daughter of the Persian king suits the Persian writers, but it is unclear how the author of the *Romance* came to invent it in the first place. The simple answer may be that it is one of the many glorious 'historical muddles' that the Greek author perpetrates, on a par with the debate in Athens (*AR* II. 1–5) where the sixth-century BC philosopher Heraclitus is made to pronounce on the opinions of the fourth-century BC orator Demosthenes, who in any case is given views opposite to those he in fact held; or with the geographical confusion that puts the kingdom of Meroe somewhere in the region of India, and has the conqueror cross the Taurus range to Troy before reaching Thebes (*AR* I. 42). It is easy to make sport of such howlers, worthy of Hollywood, and one may conclude that the author did not remember all he should have from his school lessons; but from a dramatic point of view there is a real fitness in Alexander's marrying the daughter of the Persian king. Often the author of the *Romance* represents Alexander carrying out expeditions that he only dreamed of (such as the exploration of Egypt to the source of the Nile);[3] here he seems to act as he (historically) ought to have done, whether he wished or no. Roxane becomes the Persian princess, and her name remains a familiar personal name in modern Iran. It is as if the history of the Roman Empire had constructed itself in accord with the plot of *Gladiator*. The celluloid Commodus, whose death is quite unhistorical, or the fictional Alexander, carry more resonance than their historical counterparts because of a certain poetic fitness – as Aristotle might have called it.[4] The Persian author adopted the Greek fiction because it suited his grand design.

It is Alexander's entry into the Persian legendary record of its kings that established him as a major figure of Persian literature. Firdausi's *Shahnameh* (Book of Kings) is the first to develop the story (see p. 24 above).[5] Many details of the campaign against Darius stick closely to the version in the Greek *Romance*, including the episode when Alexander in disguise goes as his own ambassador to the court of Darius: both the Greek author and Firdausi devote a paragraph to elaborate description of the Persian king's clothing and regalia, and the episode continues with Alexander's attempt to steal the cups from the table on the grounds that he thought they were a gift; recognised, he makes his escape across the River Stranga, which remains frozen as he rides across and then obligingly breaks up so that the Persian pursuers cannot catch him.[6] The campaign in Firdausi involves three major battles where the *Romance* only has that of Gaugamela, the final defeat of Darius; the historical detail is probably taken from the Arab historian al-Tabari (AD 839–923),[7] but the battles are not identifiable as the three known from the Greek historians, and in both Tabari and Firdausi are entirely generalised.

After the death of Darius, Firdausi's account of Iskandar wanders increasingly far from the Greek original. The divergence can be explained by the fact that Firdausi used the Syriac version of the *Romance*, which adds a number of episodes that are not in the Greek. For example, the Syriac tells of Iskandar's visit to the Emperor of China,[8] which is not in any of the Greek versions, and also of his battle with a dragon in the land of the Narmpai (Ethiopia). [9] Other adventures that loom large in Firdausi are the

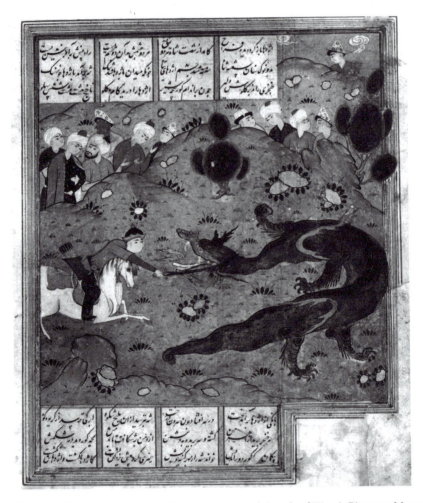

9 Alexander fights a dragon. From Firdausi, *Shahnameh* (Book of Kings). Pierpont Morgan Library, New York, MS M. 847 f. 1.

meeting with Queen Qaidafa (Candace: Chapter 7); the search for the Water of Life (Chapter 8) and the building of the wall against Gog and Magog (Chapter 9).

The Syriac *Romance* and Tabari are not the only sources on which Firdausi drew for his narrative. Alexander's pilgrimage to Mecca comes from the ninth-century Arab author al-Dinawari (d. AD 891), who also included the detail, not found elsewhere, that Alexander was buried in Jerusalem. And following Alexander's death in Firdausi there is an episode where the philosophers gather around his bier to make moralising comments on his fate. This does not occur in any of the extant versions of the *Romance*, but is known as a free-standing Syriac text of the sixth century and subsequently became a popular set piece in Arabic accounts of Alexander.[10]

Alexander in Persian Tradition before Firdausi

How far back in Persian literature can we trace Firdausi's sources? There certainly was an oral tradition going back to perhaps the second century BC. The Parthian *gosan* or minstrel stands at the beginning of a long history of storytelling in Persia which extended up to modern times when a reciter, known as a *naqqal*, might tell in a tea-house a story lasting up to ninety minutes, emphasising the turns of the plot with taps of his wand.[11] Firdausi used stories from the oral tradition in his *Shahnameh*, but he also used books, such as Dinawari's, and even popular romances.[12]

Were the stories of Alexander among those that survived in oral tradition?[13] It is perhaps more likely that the Greek tales became known to the Persians as a result of the interest of the Sassanian king Chosrow I Anushirvan (Chosrow of the Immortal Soul, AD 531–79) in Greek learning and philosophy. An important medical school was founded at Gundeshapur in the fifth century by Nestorian refugees from Byzantium, and a nice story tells that Chosrow gave refuge to the distinguished Athenian philosopher Damascius and his companions following the closure of the schools of philosophy at Athens by Justinian in 529.[14] Paul the Persian wrote a compendium of Aristotle's philosophy in Syriac for Anushirvan, and the Indian classic *Kalila wa Dimna* was translated into Persian in his reign.

These traditions concern Greek science and philosophy, and it is a moot question whether the effort of translation would extend to works of entertainment. It must be remembered, however, that the story of Alexander was more than just entertainment for the Persians: it was regarded as history. It may be that the Syriac *Alexander Romance* was also prepared under the patronage of Chosrow. It is at least curious that Xerxes in the Syriac version is invariably referred to by the name of Chosrow – hardly flattering to the king, but it indicates the dominance of his presence in the translator's mind.

Theodor Nöldeke[15] argued forcefully that the Syriac translation was made via a Pahlavi (Middle Persian) intermediary, but this has now been disproved by Claudia Ciancaglini:[16] the mangling of the proper names is to be explained, not by transmission through Pahlavi but as a result of dictation, or more likely self-dictation by a scribe as he worked from the Greek. The Syriac preceded any Persian translation, which must therefore have been made in the late Sassanian period.

We know very little about the literature of Sassanian Persia.[17] Crucially, we do not have the *Khuday-nameh* or 'Book of Lords', which was compiled for the last Sassanian king, Yazdigird III (ruled AD 632–42, murdered 651) by his vizier.[18] Following the Arab conquest of Iran, the Arabs set about learning Persian and absorbing the culture of their more cultivated subjects: like Greece under Roman rule, the captured people took its fierce conqueror captive.[19] In the eighth century AD Ibn al-Muqaffa' (a converted Magian Persian) translated into Arabic a great deal of Pahlavi literature, including the *Khuday-nameh* – a substantial achievement – before his execution for heresy in AD 757.[20] By the tenth century Pahlavi was not well understood; contemporary Persian was being used as a literary language, and the translation by Muqaffa' was retranslated into Persian in AD 957. This prose version may have been Firdausi's source, and much of what we know of it must be deduced from Firdausi. It may have included the tale of Iskandar, and perhaps it was the source for the 'nationalist' version of Iskandar's birth.[21]

After Firdausi

Firdausi's work was reprised in the twelfth-century prose *Darabnameh* of Abu Taher Tarsusi, but Tarsusi has some interesting differences from Firdausi. For example, 'Iskandar's mother abandons the baby on a mountain not far from Aristotle's dwelling. An old woman has her goat suckle the child and has Aristotle teach him dream-interpretation and wisdom till he is ten. Alexander eventually marries Darius' daughter (this time called Purandukht) but only after she brings an army against him several times and loses.'[22] Much of the plot seems to be free invention: his account of the birth of Alexander, for example, is clearly modelled on the traditions about the birth of Cyrus the Great.[23] Alexander has not one but three guides in his search for the Water of Life – Luqman, Elijah and Khidr – and he ascends Mount Qaf on a talking horse which recalls that of Muhammad.

His character, too, is far different from the *javanmard* (knightly hero) of Firdausi: he is an average man, lacking courage, who has difficulties with women, and succeeds by wits and good looks rather than bravery.[24] (In this he presents one aspect of the Greek *Romance*'s trickster hero at the expense of the others.)

The influence of Firdausi's epic was such that writers of secondary epics borrowed episodes wholesale to attach to their own heroes. A notable example is the *Garshasp Nameh* of Asadi Tusi (999/1000–1072/3; poem completed 1058) in which Garshasp, like Alexander, travels extensively and has an interview with the Brahmans.[25] (On Alexander's encounter with the Brahmans see below, Chapter 5.)

Firdausi was one of the key figures in the transmission of the story of Alexander to central Asia and beyond. The Great Mongol *Shahnameh* of the 1330s (of which detached plates are scattered through the world's libraries since the MS was broken up in the early twentieth century) is just the culmination of Mongol interest, which even went so far as to make Genghis Khan a direct descendant of Olympias.[26] Nestorians had brought his story eastwards, in a form of the 'Christian Legend' (see Chapter 9 below, and appendix), even before this date,[27] and this was translated into Mongolian in the fourteenth century.[28] Nestorians also brought living knowledge of Alexander to China: epitaphs from the early fourteenth century have been found at Zaytun (Quanzhou) which give the date according to the era 'of Alexander the Ilkhan, the son of Philippos the Khan from the city of Macedonia'.[29]

Nizami

The legend of Iskandar was expanded by later Persian writers,[30] of whom the most notable is Nizami (1140–1203). The poet and mystic Abu Yusif Nizami Ganjavi spent his career among the golden domes of Qom, and came at the end of his life to Azerbaijan, where his patron was the Atabeg Nusrat-ud-Din, to whom he dedicated the revised version of his *Iskandarnameh* (the first had been dedicated to the Atabeg of Mosul). The *Iskandarnameh* is one of the five works that comprise Nizami's *Khamsa*, the others being *Layla and Majnun*, *Makhzan al-Asrar* (The Treasury of Secrets), *Haft Paykar* (Seven Portraits) and *Khosrow and Shirin*. The *Iskandarnameh* is a massive work, divided into two parts, of which the first, the *Sharafnameh* (Book of Honour) covers the life of Iskandar and his adventures; the second, the *Ikbalnameh* (Book of Fortune) or *Khiradnameh* (Book of Wisdom) is a 'Mirror for Princes', a common genre in medieval

Persia, presented as discussions on statecraft between Iskandar and the philosophers assembled at his court. [31]

The narrative is too long to summarise other than in the most sketchy fashion.[32] Alexander is here the son of Philip (not Dara) and is educated by Nicomachus, the father of Aristotle. He is a loyal vassal king of Darius until he mounts an expedition to Egypt against the Zangis, in the course of which he founds the city of Alexandria. He sends plentiful booty to Darius, but gets no thanks, we are told, because of the envy of the Great King. Alexander now observes two partridges fighting and takes the event as an omen of his coming conflict with Darius. In the bizarre translation of Captain H. Wilberforce Clarke (1881), he:

> Saw, on a stony place, two mountain-partridges
> In battle, according to the habit of fighting partridges.
> Sometimes this one wounded with his beak the other's head
> Sometimes that one broke with his claws this one's wing.
> The king urged his steed towards that contest,
> And kept being a spectator as to both birds.
> From the fierceness with which the partridges grappled together,
> They fled not at the sight of the king.
> The monarch remained astonied at that matter,
> Saying: – 'How is this malice in the brain of birds!'
> On this one – he made the name his own name;
> Established on it the omen of his own end (the issue of the battle with Dara):
> On the other bird – he made the name Dara;
> Placed his eyes open on that lot (-casting) . . . .
> In the end, became victorious that very bird
> On which the monarch had cast the omen of his own name.
> When he beheld the state victorious, like that,
> He regarded that omen, the proof of victory.
> The partridge, strutting, victory-gained,
> Flew from the partridge defeat suffered.
> Flew towards the knoll of a mountain;
> An eagle came and split his head.

From this omen the king knew that he would defeat Darius but that he would not live long to enjoy the victory. Alexander refuses to continue to pay the tribute of the golden eggs, and goes to war with Darius. The diplomatic exchanges between the two kings follow quite closely the exchanges in the *Alexander Romance*, including a series of letters and an exchange of insulting gifts. (See further Chapter 6.) After this Nizami's plot diverges from the Greek and Syriac original. Iskandar wipes out the Zoroastrian religion, to the author's approval (there is nothing of this in Firdausi, in whose work the Islamic point of view is only infrequently evident), and then sets off for Mecca, and thence to Armenia and to visit Nushaba, the queen of Barda' (who replaces the Candace/Qaidafa of other authors). He visits a number of hermits, sits on the throne of Kay Khosrow, and proceeds eastwards to make war on the Indian *kayd* or king, named Fur (i.e. Porus): the latter sends him his daughter, a ruby cup, a philosopher and a physician. (What more could a man need than health, wealth, wisdom and love?)

The next stop is China. It is possible to trace the origin of this rather surprising stage of the itinerary. The Byzantine historian Theophylact Simocatta (*c.* 580–post-641) is the earliest source to mention activities of Alexander in China, which he calls Taugast, after the name of the ruling Mongol dynasty of the 560s.

> This Taugast in fact, the barbarians say, was founded by the Macedonian Alexander when he enslaved the Bactrians and Sogdoane and burnt twelve myriads of barbarians. In this city the ruler's wives have carriages made of gold, each of which is drawn by one bullock lavishly decorated with gold and precious stones . . . and there is a report that Alexander also founded another city a few miles away, which the barbarians name Chubdan . . . . (VII. 9.6.)

This information came to the Byzantines from a letter of the Khaqan of the Turks to Emperor Maurice. The compression of the geography results from the fact that the To'pa Mongols, who conquered China, also conquered western Turkistan, so that from the point of view of those further west the two districts were the same.[33] Chubdan is perhaps Ch'ang-an, the capital of China at this date, though the location on two rivers better suits Hsien-gang, the old capital.

The story of Alexander's foundation of these cities is reported from Simocatta by the Arab historian Qudama, with a date corresponding to 349 BC; perhaps the synchronism encouraged the link with Alexander.

At the Chinese court, Nizami describes an interesting episode.[34] Alexander oversees a competition between a Greek and a Chinese painter, who are set to portray an identical subject without looking at each other's work.

> In secret, the workers sate
> In that two-fold arch like the double arch (of the eyebrows).
> In a little while, they finished the work;

They cast up the veil from those two forms.
Of the two arzhangs (the two bepainted wall-surfaces), the form was one;
Both as to drawing and colour – no difference.
At that work (of exact) similarity, the beholder remained astonished;
Was altogether dejected at the wonder.

The king is unable to choose between the two identical depictions for beauty, and escapes from the quandary only when the sage Balinas (Apollonius of Tyana) hangs a veil between the two pictures.

When that veil intervened between the two walls,
One was desponding (obscure), and the other was gleaming.
The delineations of the Rumi departed not from water (lustre) and colour;
Blight (obscurity) fell upon the mirror (the polished wall-surface) of the Chini.

(Nizami, transl. Clarke 1881)

The secret is out! While the Greek has made a painting, the Chinese artist has simply erected a mirror. The story is a parable about the role of the artist in relation to God's creation. Nizami was wont to call himself 'a mirror of the invisible' and to see his vocation as 'an experience of illumination by the irradiance of the divine'.[35] But does the artist have the right to depict the real world in competition, as it were, with God? The origin of the idea is Platonic: only the world of the Forms is true, and everything we see is a pale reflection or shadow of the Forms.[36] Conversely, mirrors symbolise the presence of God, because they reflect his creation. Platonic thought is adapted to express the Islamic quandary about representational art.

The quandary provides the central theme of Orhan Pamuk's 2001 novel about medieval painters in Istanbul, *My Name is Red*, where the European practice of drawing from life is represented as 'satanic': Master Osman goes so far as to blind himself in order to see 'as Allah sees'. Painting is always from memory, because of the split second that elapses between the artist's looking at his subject and his putting brush to paper. In a view like this, painting must always be a false representation and only the mirror is true. So Nizami hopes to mirror the truth rather than simply to describe it. So, too, he makes Alexander a representative of *i'tidal*, balance or symmetry, a word which also denotes the symmetry between the mirror image and its object. Alexander is in fact the inventor of mirrors, in an earlier episode of the *Iskandarnameh*; so this odd story becomes a central symbol of spiritual kingship.

The adventures continue with no fewer than seven campaigns against the Rus, Alexander's introduction of veiling among the Qipchaq women (Nizami's wife was a Qipchaq, so he knew they were unusual), and the quest for the Water of Life.

The second part of the *Iskandarnameh* was, perhaps mercifully, not translated by Wilberforce Clarke, but is accessible to western readers in the complete German translation by J.C. Bürgel. Focusing on his conversations with the philosophers Aristotle, Thales, Apollonius, Socrates, Porphyry, Hermes and Plato, it includes several intriguing episodes which became

10 The Invention of Mirrors. From Nizami, *Iskandarnameh*. Walters Art Gallery, Baltimore, W. 613 f. 16v.

popular themes for painters: an interview with a shepherd,[37] discussions
with Aristotle on magic stones, and a visit to Plato,[38] who has invented a
musical organ to enchant the beasts and trees: 'From the dry wood Plato
conjures notes which with their liquidity draw down the spheres. When he
moves his finger on a certain note, all beasts fall immediately asleep. But if
he moves to another note, he brings the sleeping creatures back to reality.'[39]
Again, the episode alludes to the power of Platonic philosophy to lead from
illusion to reality.

After an account of how Alexander built a wall to protect the world from
the Unclean Nations, Gog and Magog (Nizami probably believed that this
was the so-called 'Wall of Alexander' in the Caucasus, not far from his home
in Azerbaijan),[40] the book concludes with his death, and also the deaths of
all the philosophers who have kept him company, with disquisitions on the
meanings of each death.

Nizami created a harmonious unity from the diverse traditions about
Alexander in Persia: this king, who represents balance, equipoise and
moderation, overthrows the evil King Darius and destroys the religion of
the Zoroastrians. By his nature as well as his actions he establishes the rule
of Islam in Iran. His destruction of the Unclean Nations, his invention of
the mirror, his patronage of philosophers and his role in the episodes that
exemplify the power of Plato's philosophy, as well as the morals that are
drawn from his death, all make him a mirror for princes, a portrait of a ruler
that a living ruler would be flattered to have dedicated to him.[41]

Jami and beyond

A further development takes place in Jami's (d. 1494) 'Logic of Alexander',
which picks up Nizami's theme of the symposium of the philosophers at
Alexander's court. It begins with sermons and praises, and proceeds to
recount the advice given to Alexander by a group of philosophers
consisting of Aristotle, Plato, Socrates, Hippocrates, Pythagoras, Asclepius
and Hermes. It concludes with his consolatory letter to Olympias about his
imminent death and funeral orations. It exhibits a preoccupation with
death, which seeks consolation for the evil of a world that condemns all
living beings to death in the idea that this world is merely vanity:[42] 'if death
could be repulsed with arms and soldiers, here are the armies of the whole
world; and if it could be repulsed with prayers and rosaries, here are the sufis
and sheikhs of the whole world . . . and if it could be bought off with riches
and treasures, here are all the treasures of the face of the earth'. Yet Iskandar
dies. He bids his companions: 'Leave one of my hands outside the coffin,
and place a piece of rough cloth in my palm and say, "Iskandar conquered

the whole world and made it his realm from one extremity to the other, but when death came upon him he was vanquished by dust and, relinquishing his dominion over the face of the earth, he took away with him only this piece of rough cloth".' It is a theme that we shall encounter many times in the legends of Alexander, across the world.

For Jami, Iskandar is not only a conqueror and sage, but a prophet of God. Alexander has now been thoroughly Islamicised as a result of cross-fertilisation from the Arabic tradition, which we shall consider in Chapter 8.[43]

Besides these 'literary' works there are other popular romances on Alexander, not only in Persian but also in Turkish. The thirteenth-century Turkish *Oghuz-name*[44] tells the story of Alexander's journey in the Land of Darkness and his search for the Water of Life, while the *Iskandar-nameh* of Ahmedi (1407) and the 'Wall of Alexander' by the Chagatay poet Neva'i (d. at Herat 1485) also bring episodes of Alexander's legendary career to a Turkish readership. Mehmet II, the conqueror of Constantinople, liked to read of the deeds of Alexander, and probably learnt of them from one of these versions.[45] Selim I in 1518 also read tales of Alexander and aimed to emulate his achievements.[46]

The most substantial of the Persian popular romances is the anonymous fourteenth-century *Iskandarnameh*:[47] this starts off with the stories of Alexander's birth and campaigns against Dara, much as in Firdausi, but thereafter drifts into a land of fantasy more or less unrelated to other narratives. Some familiar characters appear, including Fur (Porus), who is now at odds with the greater Indian King Kayd, and the Emperor of China.

The whole work runs to some 770 pages and has only been translated in part, as it is very repetitive. The manuscript is unfinished, leaving one to speculate on how many similar episodes might have followed the portion we have. Its geography makes that of the Greek *Romance* look like a gentle stroll, as the hero races from Iran to Ceylon, Kashmir, Mecca and Yemen before visiting Andalusia, which becomes the setting for the Candace episode. Pretty soon he ends up in the Land of the Fairies, where he marries their queen, Araqit – one of an enormous number of wives he acquires in the course of the story – and continues to the Land of the Sunrise via that of the Rus, and thus reaches the Zangi (black Ethiopians) with whom he fights a series of campaigns. Sometimes the narrative is interrupted for characters to tell long stories, in the manner of *The Arabian Nights*; some of the most intriguing parts are the 'parables' where strange series of events have apparently purposive conclusions: Alexander's pursuit of a wild zebra leads him to discover a princess who has been imprisoned in a box by an evil Zangi who has since died from a snakebite: he releases

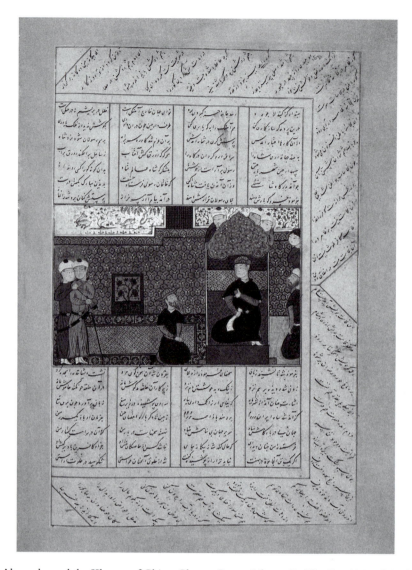

11 Alexander and the Khaqan of China. Chester Beatty Library, Dublin, Per. 124. I. f. 240b.

her from her plight to much gratitude, and the ways of God are shown to be unfathomable. As usual, the dominant theme is Alexander's search for the secret of immortality, but he is interestingly aware of his future fame: 'my life story will become a science in the world. They will read and write my life story until Resurrection Day.'[48]

Alexander the Destroyer

Against all these popular and elevated images of Alexander as a Persian culture-hero is set a very different view of Alexander. It is encapsulated in the *Zayn al-akhbar* of the historian Gardizi, written in the mid-eleventh century AD (after Firdausi but before Nizami). As Julie Scott Meisami writes, 'Gardizi . . . connects the transfer of learning with that of power. This is most clearly exemplified in his account of Alexander's conquest: Alexander devastated Iran and burnt the Zoroastrian books; he had the Persian books of learning translated into Greek, sent the translations to Rum and then destroyed the library of Istakhr; he buried whatever treasures he could not carry off.'[49] His death plunges the world into chaos and anarchy, until Ardashir (224–40 AD, the first of the Sassanians) declares himself king and reassembles the dispersed books of learning. A similar story appears in the fifteenth-century historian Mirkhond: after the crucifixion of Darius' murderers 'he married Roushang [Roxane] and installed the brother of Dara over Fars, appointing him to be the chief of the ninety-nine governors, who were surnamed the kings of the nations. By order of Eskandar, the books on medicine, astronomy and philosophy were translated from the language of Persia into that of Greece, and conveyed to that country. He burnt the religious books of the Magi, and destroyed their fire-temples, removing the priests of that blameworthy religion.'[50]

Mirkhond (like Nizami) writes from a Muslim perspective, in which the destruction of Zoroastrian sacred books is an admirable act. But it is not so presented by the other historians who refer to it. The earliest attestation of this tradition seems to be in the *Book of the Deeds of Ardashir*, a Middle Persian work of the sixth century AD, though based on earlier redactions.[51]

> Then the cursed spirit of evil, the Liar, with the aim of making men sceptical of religion, sent Alexander the Greek, the cursed one, who was in Egypt; he entered the kingdom of Iran with terrible violence, war and torture, and killed the king of Iran, and destroyed and razed to the ground the court and the kingdom. And this religion, to wit the whole *Avesta* and the *Zand*,[52] which were written on ox-hides carefully prepared and encrusted with gold, were kept in a depository at Stakhr and Papakan. This wicked, heretical, corrupt and criminal enemy, Alexander the Greek, who was in Egypt, attacked the fortress and burnt the texts and the fortress. Then he massacred many theologians and judges, and the *herbad* and the *mobad*,[53] the defenders of religion, the experts and wise men of the kingdom of Iran, and spread vengeance and strife among the great men and nobles of the kingdom of Iran, one

against the other. In the end he destroyed himself and was plunged into Hell.[54]

A similar account appears in the 'Letter of Tansar', a work composed probably in the reign of Chosrow I Anushirvan (AD 531–79) but purportedly written by one Tansar who was, it is said, charged under Ardashir (AD 226–42) with collecting the scattered teachings of the Zoroastrian religion.[55] It incorporates a purported letter of Aristotle to Alexander in which Aristotle advises the king to destroy the nobles and promote the base, to divide and rule, and to 'leave a sweet memory'.[56]

It has been generally supposed that this tradition went back to the days of the conquest and somehow developed in parallel with the favourable tradition, represented by Firdausi and the later writers, which derived from the Greek *Romance*. Mary Boyce writes:

> It is Alexander himself, and not his Seleucid successors, who is execrated in Zoroastrian tradition, in which he is remembered as 'accursed' (guzastag), an epithet which he shares with Ahriman alone. In a Sogdian fragment he is set among the worst sinners of history, the wickedness being that he 'killed magi', and in one Pahlavi text . . . it is said that he slew 'many teachers, lawyers, herbads and mobads', in another . . . that he 'quenched many fires'. These crimes were presumably committed when his soldiers plundered temples and sanctuaries, whose priests may well have perished in vain attempts to defend their holy places . . . . Another . . . temple at Ecbatana (Hamadan) is said to have been pillaged repeatedly by the Macedonians, who stripped away even its silver roof-tiles and the gold plating from its columns.[57]

Some scholars, however, have been sceptical of the story of the destruction of the sacred books: Ibn Khaldun in the fourteenth century was already unconvinced (III. 1044–5), and H.W. Bailey suggested that the story was a clerical myth invented to explain the absence of ancient manuscripts of a text which in fact was only fixed after the fifth century, in a specially devised alphabet.[58] Though Pausanias (5.27.6) refers to the Magi of his own day chanting from books, Saint Basil in the third century AD states that the Magi had no books.[59] It would be remarkable if these books, which were in prose, had survived in oral tradition to be recopied in the Sassanian period: so the *Deeds of Ardashir* and other texts suggest that one copy survived and was sent to Rome to be rescued later. The reference to Rome indicates that this story is unhistorical.

As for the fire temples, it is not clear that Alexander ever knew of their existence when he entered Persia: it seems that this important element of Persian religion was unknown to Aeschylus, and presumably to Greeks generally, in the fifth century BC.[60] Conversely, the Patriarch Eutychius of Alexandria (c. AD 876–937), writing under Arab rule, in his *Annals* (*PG* 111 col. 970) presents the dying Darius begging Alexander to preserve the noble clans, to refrain from destroying the fire temples, and to marry his daughter and avenge his murder. There is no mention of preserving the sacred books.

In an elegant demonstration, Claudia Ciancaglini (1997) has shown that the whole story must have been concocted in the Sassanian period. The Persian kingdom that succeeded the Seleucid Empire, carved out of Alexander's dominions, was that of the Parthians, and the Parthian kings based their territorial claims against the Romans on the regions ruled by Cyrus and by Alexander (Tacitus, *Annals* 6.31). The Sassanian dynasty that succeeded the Parthians, by contrast, traced its line back to the Achaemenids, of whom Darius III was the last. The reign of Alexander in Iran is, in this perspective, a historical anomaly.[61] The priests or mobeds were powerful in the Sassanian Empire, forming a kind of established church: the story of the texts' destruction by Alexander would support their claims to power stretching back into the distant past. It is no surprise that the story should have been written down, even as late as the sixth century when the Arabs were already at the gates, for the district of Fars retained considerable autonomy for some time, even centuries before Iran was fully converted to Islam.

The upshot is that the story of Alexander's destruction of the sacred books is probably not true. He may have shown as much respect for them as he did for any other religion he encountered. If he extinguished the sacred fires (as we are told he did later on the death of Hephaestion: Diodorus Siculus 17.115) that is because it was the proper thing to do following the death of a king; they would have been reignited after the accession of the new king. Just as in Egypt, Alexander, after his smooth acceptance in Babylon, probably followed all the proper procedures to make himself King of Kings,[62] and there was no shame for Firdausi in following the quasi-hagiographical account given in the *Romance*. It is notable that the *Romance*, alone of the Greek sources, puts in the mouth of Alexander a proclamation to the peoples of the Empire (*AR* II. 21). If such a speech was not made, it would have had to be invented. And there is a similar speech in the *Shahnameh*.[63]

It is also notable that history attests no revolts against Macedonian rule until that of Bagadates at the end of the reign of Seleucus, around 280 BC

(Polyaenus, 7.39–40): as Mørkholm writes, 'That the first oriental reaction against Macedonian rule should come from Persis, the homeland of the Achaemenids, is hardly surprising. It is only difficult to understand why it came so late.'[64]

The later Persian authors, as Muslims, were less inclined to blame Alexander for the destruction of these sacred treasures. In fact Nizami has Alexander put to death the wicked Zoroastrian priests – quite an exercise in revisionist history. All the classical Persian authors, from Firdausi onwards, welcome Alexander's conquest, not only because he is in some sense a legitimate member of the royal house, but because Darius was a bad, weak king and *de facto* because he lost the war.[65] For Nizami, he was hated by his subjects; and his violence and terror are also features of his behaviour in the Arab authors on whom Firdausi and Nizami drew, namely Tha'alibi and Tabari. In Nizami Alexander in fact agrees, reluctantly, to the assassination of Darius, to which he is made privy beforehand by the traitors themselves. So in Nizami, Alexander is not only legitimate by virtue of his descent, he is a liberator of the Persians from tyranny, and furthermore he is a champion of Islam against false religion. This was just the kind of portrayal to flatter Nizami's own royal patron.

So much for the Persian version. What of the legends that Alexander knew of Persia?

Land of Gold

The Persian Empire was a land of legend and mystery to the Greeks. Alexander, who was a well-read person, would have known the detailed account of Herodotus of Halicarnassus (fifth century BC) in his history, as well as the *Persica* of Ctesias of Cnidus (*c.* AD 450–post-393 BC), a Greek physician who had been employed at the court of Artaxerxes II – a work which may have drawn on epic and romance narratives about Persia. Ctesias had also written an *Indica*, which will have whetted Alexander's appetite for the wonders of that remoter region, where his own historians duly recorded many of the improbable sights that Ctesias 'saw' and invented some of their own (see Chapter 4). Herodotus had set out to give a detailed account of the origins and course of the Persian wars and the two invasions of Greece. In the second of these, the temples on the Athenian acropolis had been sacked; and it was this impiety that gave the ideological motive for Alexander's invasion of Persia and enabled him to carry Greek opinion with him (part of the time, anyway).

Herodotus presented Persia as, among other things, a land of fabulous wealth and exotic luxury. Aeschylus' evocation of the court in his *Persians* repeatedly refers to the gold that adorns their walls and furniture: in fact they are in legend born of gold, since Perseus (the eponym of Persia in Greek ideas) was conceived by Danae when Zeus visited her in a shower of gold.

That these descriptions were not idle ones is borne out by the Old Persian record that Darius I composed about his palace at Susa: 'This palace which I built at Susa – its materials were brought from afar . . . Cedar of Lebanon, the Syrian peoples brought it to Babylon, and from Babylon Greeks and Carians brought it to Susa . . . Gold was brought from Lydia and Bactria; lapis from Sogdia; (another sort of) lapis from Chorasmia; silver from Egypt; the wall decorations from Greece; ebony from Ethiopia (?), India and Arachosia; the marble columns were worked by Greeks and Lydians; . . . the gold-workers were Medes and Egyptians . . . may Ahuramazda protect me and Hystaspes my father . . .'.[66]

Both wealth and luxury were epitomised by the décor of the king's bedchamber, with its golden plane tree and golden vine (Hdt. 7.27). Herodotus speaks of these things as if they were well known, but it is one of Alexander's historians, his chamberlain Chares, who gives us the first detailed description of them:

> The Persian kings had come to such a pitch of luxury, that at the head of the royal couch there was a supper-room laid with five couches, in which there were always kept five thousand talents of gold; and this was called the king's pillow. And at his feet was another supper-room, prepared with three couches, in which there were constantly kept three thousand talents of silver; and this was called the king's footstool. And in his bed-chamber there was also a golden vine, inlaid with precious stones, above the king's bed. (Chares in *FGrH* 125F4, quoted in Athenaeus 12.54ff.)

Another historian, Amyntas, adds that 'this vine had bunches of grapes, composed of most valuable precious stones; and not far from it there was placed a golden bowl, the work of Theodorus of Samos'. And another, Agathocles, in his *History of Cyzicus*, says that 'there is also among the Persians a water called the golden water, and that it rises in seventy springs; and that no one ever drinks of it but the king alone, and the eldest of his sons. And if anyone else drinks of it, the punishment is death' (*FGrH*).

The wonders might move from one Persian capital to another. Philostratus (*Life of Apollonius of Tyana* I. 25.2) refers to the golden palace of Babylon, where 'four golden wrynecks hang from the ceiling'; Diodorus has the golden vine in Susa. Some Arcadian ambassadors came back from

Persia in the middle of the fourth century and reported that 'the great wealth of the King was mere trickery; even the golden plane tree, about which there was such a song, was not big enough to give shade to a grasshopper' (Xenophon, *Hellenica* 7.1.38).

Linked with the story of the golden plane is another example of the arboricultural interests of King Xerxes: near Sardis, Xerxes 'found a plane tree so beautiful, that he presented it with golden ornaments, and put it under the care of one of his Immortals [the king's bodyguards]' (Hdt. 7.31). That plane tree captured the imagination of the anonymous seventeenth-century librettist of Handel's *Serse*, and it is celebrated in one of Handel's most famous arias, *Ombra mai fu*. The Greek writers did not go so far as to make the Persian king fall in love with his tree, but the details of the palace of Xerxes were so exotic that, when the author of the *Alexander Romance* came to describe them, he put them not in their proper place in the narrative, when Alexander arrives in the Persian capital after his defeat of Darius, but much later, in the account of his adventures in lands of wonder that Alexander writes of in a letter to his mother Olympias (*AR* III. 28). Plutarch says, in his *Fortune of Alexander* (2.11, 342B), that the young Alexander was such a wise student that, when learning about the Persian Empire, he was indifferent to such fables:

> Upon Alexander it was Virtue who laid the kingly and godlike Labour, the end and aim of which was not gold, carried about by countless camels, nor Persian luxury, banquets and women, nor the wine of Chalybon, nor the fish of Hyrcania, but to order all men by one law and to render them submissive to one rule and accustomed to one manner of life . . . . Once, when ambassadors came from the Persian king to Philip, who was not at home, Alexander, while he entertained them hospitably, asked no childish questions, as the others did, about the vine of gold, or the Hanging Gardens, or how the Great King was arrayed; but he was completely engrossed with the most vital concerns of the dominion, asking how large was the Persian army; where the king stationed himself in battle . . . and which roads were shortest for travellers going inland from the sea – so that the strangers were astounded and said, 'This boy is a "great king"; our king is only wealthy.'

The Alexander of the *Romance* need not be so single-minded. Conquest achieved, he recounts the marvels of three successive cities. The first is the City of the Sun, with its twelve towers of gold and emeralds. Next comes the Harbour of Lyssos, where a golden birdcage hung from the ceiling and in it was a bird somewhat like a dove,[67] which called to me in a human voice, in Greek, and said: 'Alexander, desist now from struggling against the gods; return to your own palace and do not strive to climb the paths of heaven'. . . . When I went out into the temple precinct I saw two engraved golden mixing bowls, each holding sixty measures.

The mountain on which the city stands now begins to smoke, and the army departs in haste and arrives at the palace of Cyrus, which seems in some respects a duplicate of the Harbour of Lyssus.

They told me that a bird was there that spoke with a human voice. When we entered the building we saw a great many things worth seeing. It was built entirely of gold. In the middle of the ceiling hung a golden birdcage, like the previous one, and in it was a bird like a golden dove. They said that this bird could speak to the kings in tongues. There I also saw, inside the palace of Cyrus, a large engraved golden mixing bowl, which held 160 measures. The craftsmanship was amazing: on the rim it had statues, and on the upper band of decoration a relief of a sea battle . . . . There was also a throne of gold and precious stones, and a lyre which played of its own accord. Around the throne was a sideboard 24 feet long, and standing at the top of a flight of eight steps. Above it was an eagle of gold which spanned the entire circuit with its wings. There was also a golden vine with seven branches, all made of gold. But why should I tell you so much about all the other sights of the palace? They are such that their very quantity prevents us from describing their astonishing excellence. (*AR* III. 28)

Here we see legend in the making, in the hand of a writer who knows how to expand on the famous lore of Persia and add to it the mystical dimension of the admonitions from the speaking bird. Such was the influence of these legends that in the Middle Ages no palace was complete without such golden plants and automata. When Liudprand of Cremona visited the court of the Emperor in Constantinople in the early tenth century, he observed:

Before the emperor's seat stood a tree, made of bronze gilded over, whose branches were filled with birds, also made of gilded bronze, which uttered different cries, each according to its varying species. The throne itself was so marvellously fashioned that at one moment it seemed a low structure, and at another it rose high into the air. It was of immense size and was guarded by lions, made either of bronze or of wood covered over with gold, who beat the ground with their tails and gave a dreadful roar with open mouth and quivering tongue.[68]

Such Byzantine automata were clearly not just fictional. Based on Heron of Alexandria's engineering principles, they may have been derived from early Arab (Abbasid) prototypes, and became quite widespread in Byzantium.[69]

Sir John Mandeville[70] saw something similar at the court of the Mongol Khan:

> On festival days great tables of gold are brought before the Emperor on which stand peacocks and other birds, cleverly and intricately made. Those birds are so wonderfully made by man's craft that it seems as if they leapt, and danced, and flapped their wings, and disported themselves in other ways.[71]

Theses mechanical marvels remained part of the Alexander tradition in the Middle Ages, too. The earliest German translation of the *Romance*, by Pfaffe Lamprecht (*c.* AD 1150), elaborated on them considerably, to include a mechanical deer, and transferred them to Candace's palace (Lamprecht 5997–6029): *das tier was vil herlich/ eineme hirze gelich./ An sin houbit vorne/ hattiz dusint horne/ uf allir horne gelich/ stunt ein fugil herlich/. . . so si di belge drungen/ di fugele scone sungen,/. . . so blies ouh der man sin horn so galpeden ouh di hunde.* (The beast was a beautiful model of a deer. On its head it had a thousand horns, and on each horn stood a beautiful bird . . . . When they pumped the bellows the birds sang beautifully . . . and when the man blew his horn, the hounds started to run).

The *Alexander Romance* had many legacies in the western Middle Ages, and the transmutation of the Greek traditions on Persian splendour is one of the simplest to delineate. For Mandeville as for Herodotus, Persia could stand for the whole of the exotic and barbarian east.

CITIES OF ALEXANDER
Jews and Arabs Adopt the Hero

Jerusalem

When he learnt that Alexander was not far from the city, the high priest went out with the priests to meet him . . . . When Alexander . . . saw the multitude in white garments, the priests at their head clothed in linen, and the high priest in a robe of hyacinth-blue and gold, wearing on his head the mitre with the gold plate on it on which was inscribed the name of God, he approached alone and prostrated himself before the Name and first greeted the high priest.

(Josephus, *Antiquities of the Jews* 11.331)

This story of Alexander's visit to Jerusalem is almost certainly fiction, in its outline as well as its details. No other historian mentions it, and there would seem to have been little time for an excursion to Jerusalem while Alexander was preoccupied with the sieges of Tyre and Gaza in 332, though Pliny (*Natural History* 12.55.117) indicates that he (or his staff writers) had time to observe the local way of tapping the balsam trees for their resin.[1] However, the story of Alexander's visit to Jerusalem became well known later.

A slightly different version appears in the gamma recension of the *Alexander Romance* (II. 24). Here the inhabitants of Judaea are alarmed at the approach of Alexander's army: they send spies to discover more about them, and, after being captured and released, they report back to their leaders. 'The sons of Macedon surprised us in a ravine and poured arrows down like rain: no sooner had Alexander given the order than it was done. It was not their bravery in the face of death that astonished us, so much as their lack of expectation of any reward. They simply marched of their own free will towards death.'[2] The leaders determine to surrender in style. 'The priests

12 Alexander makes obeisance to the High Priest in Jerusalem. From Johann Hartlieb, *Alexander*. Bayerische Staatsbibliothek, Munich, Cgm 581. f. 13v.

dressed themselves in their priestly robes and went out to meet him, together with a multitude of followers . . . "Your appearance is like gods" [said Alexander]. "Tell me, what god do you worship? I have never seen priests of any of our gods dressed like this." "We serve one god," the priest replied, "who made heaven and earth and all that is visible and invisible. No mortal man can discover him." "You are worthy priests of the true god," responded Alexander. "Go in peace. Your god shall be my god and my peace shall be with you. I shall not treat you as I have done the other nations, because you are servants of the living God."'

This must be one of the fastest conversions in religious history. The passage contains numerous echoes of biblical language and sets Alexander firmly in the framework of Jewish history as a benefactor of the race. Later retellings of the story are in the *Chronicle* of George the Monk (I. 19), which was completed in AD 866–67; in the tenth-century account of Jewish history known as 'Yosippon', which draws heavily on Josephus;[3] and in the Armenian translation of Eusebius' *History of the Church* (2.223).

Yet the fictionality of the story can easily be shown: not simply by the fact that there is not the slightest evidence anywhere else in Alexander's career for a conversion to Judaism, but by the fact that the Book of Daniel, which the priests show to the king, was not written until about 165 BC, nearly two hundred years after Alexander passed through the region.

Even more surprising than the transparent fictionality of the story is the fact that its representation of Alexander as admirable, pious, and pro-Jewish conflicts radically with other accounts of Jewish history. The First Book of Maccabees begins (1.1):

Alexander of Macedon, the son of Philip, marched from the land of Kittim, defeated Darius, king of Persia and Media, and seized his throne, being already king of Greece. In the course of many campaigns he captured fortified towns, slaughtered kings, traversed the earth to its remotest bounds, and plundered innumerable nations. When at last the world lay quite under his rule, his pride knew no limits.

This passage was written about 103 BC, earlier than any of the surviving full-length histories of Alexander. Later Jewish writings make of Alexander a ravening monster. His Macedonians are 'the birds of heaven – eagles, vultures, kites and ravens' which attack a flock of sheep 'to dig out their eyes and to eat their flesh', according to I Enoch 90. The third book of the *Sibylline Oracles*, which was composed in the reign of the Emperor Nero, is more explicit:

Macedonia will bring forth a great affliction for Asia . . . . At a certain time there will come to the prosperous land of Asia a faithless man clad with a purple cloak on his shoulders, savage, stranger to justice, fiery. For a thunderbolt beforehand raised him up, a man. But all Asia will bear an evil yoke, and the earth, deluged, will imbibe much gore.[4]

It is not impossible that, whoever wrote Isaiah 23 – the prophecy of the destruction of Tyre – had Alexander's campaign in mind (see colour plate 2), though the passage nominally refers to an attack by the Babylonians also referred to in Ezekiel 26–28.

How, then, did it come about that a writer roughly contemporary with the third Sibylline Oracle such as Josephus could proffer such a rosy account of the conqueror? Various answers have been given to the question of who invented it, when and why. It has been associated with Agrippa's visit to Jerusalem in 52 BC and with Julius Caesar's guarantee of religious freedom to the Jews.[5] The clue seems to lie in the first and third sections of the story in Josephus (*AJ* 11. 321–5, 340–5: only the first is given by Yosippon and neither features in the other rewritings of the story such as the *Romance*). Here the Samaritans under the leadership of Sanballat offer their support to Alexander at the siege of Tyre; Alexander allows them to build a temple of their own, independent of that in Jerusalem. Later, the

Samaritans of Shechem, seeing the favour accorded to the Jews by Alexander, decide to profess themselves Jews. But Alexander puts them off on the ground that they may not really be counted as Jews, and takes Sanballat's soldiers to establish a garrison in the Thebaid. The two stories are inconsistent with one another, but both focus on disputes between Jews and Samaritans. Arnaldo Momigliano ingeniously argued that both stories should be associated with disputes that raged in Alexandria rather than in Palestine.[6] There was a very similar dispute between the Jews of Alexandria and the Samaritans of Mount Gerizim about the relative status of the two temples, in Jerusalem and on Mount Gerizim, which took place in the reign of Ptolemy VI Philometor (180–45 BC). Momigliano associates the disputes with the arguments over the legitimacy of the temple founded at Leontopolis by Jews who had left Palestine under the leadership of the Oniads. Jews and Samaritans in Egypt had been quarrelling about the relative legitimacy of their ways of life since the reign of Ptolemy I (Josephus, *AJ* 12.10), and the arrival of Jews of the Palestinian tradition, who nevertheless wanted to set up an alternative temple, would have intensified the conflict between the groups.[7]

The idea of an Alexandrian origin for all three tales is given support by the observation[8] that the phraseology of Alexander's confession of faith in the God of the Jews is couched in language closely paralleled in Hellenistic Alexandria, both in the works of the philosopher Philo and in the Septuagint, the Greek translation of the Hebrew Bible that was made under the auspices of Ptolemy II.

Many other pieces of evidence indicate Alexander's favour to the Jews of Alexandria. According to Josephus (*cAp* 2.33ff.) it was he who first gave them civic rights, though it is certain that their position was only established formally under Ptolemy I (Josephus *AJ* 12.8). Thus the answer to our question seems to lie in Alexandria. It was in the city founded by Alexander that the conqueror became a hero of Jewish legend and a bearer of meaning for Jewish civilisation. We shall encounter many legends in this book which can be traced to a Jewish origin. Mainly originating in the Talmud, and often transferred to an Arab tradition by the eighth-century writer Wahb ibn Munabbih, they achieve their fullest expression in the five Jewish *Alexander Romances*, which not only differ widely from one another but also diverge very considerably from the Greek *Romance*.[9] The earliest may date from the ninth century AD, but is more probably of the twelfth. In all of these Alexander is a model king, but in his style of kingship he bears only the most tenuous relation to the pious prophet of the Persian tradition. He is a Solomonic hero, not just a ruler but a problem-solver and a wise judge.[10]

Alexandria

'O King, thus Phoebus of the ram's horns says to you:
If you wish to bloom for ever in incorruptible youth,
Found the city rich in fame opposite the isle of Proteus,
Where Aion Ploutonios himself is enthroned as king,
He who from his five-peaked mountain rolls round the endless
world.' (*Alexander Romance* I. 30 and 33)

Then Alexander gave orders for the perimeter of the city to be marked
out . . . . The workmen marked out the limits with wheat flour, but the
birds flew down, ate up the meal and flew away. Alexander was very
disturbed at the possible meaning of this omen; he sent for interpreters
and told them what had happened. Their reply was: 'The city you have
ordered to be built, O king, will feed the whole inhabited world, and
those who are born in it will reach all parts of the world, just as the birds
fly over the whole earth' (*Alexander Romance* I. 32).

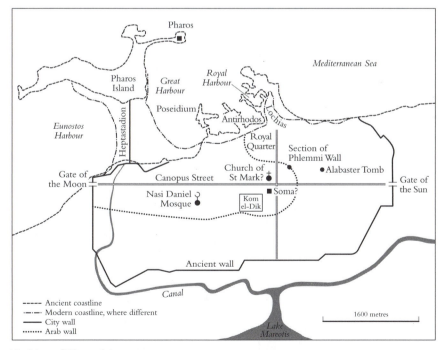

13 Map of Alexandria.

The foundation of Alexandria by Egypt was Alexander's most famous and successful act. Almost immediately, it became a large and flourishing city. Of the numerous other Alexandrias founded by Alexander, none achieved the rank of an imperial city, though several still stand today as something more than ruins: Alexandria in Areia (Herat), Alexandria in Arachosia (Kandahar), Alexandria on the Oxus (Ai Khanum), Alexandria the Furthest (Khojend). Other cities named Alexandria may not have been founded by the conqueror himself: P.M. Fraser has argued that many of them are subsequent foundations by the successors, and that the number of those actually established by Alexander should be reduced to six.[11]

But there has never been any doubt about Alexandria by Egypt. (Its official name indicates that it was not conceived as lying within the country of Egypt itself, but on its fringe.) Ancient writers praise its greatness, and even after political power had moved to Cairo Arab and Persian writers remembered its magnificence:

First on the shore of the sea (of Rum) a city (Sikandria)
He founded; – a city like the joyous spring.
In populousness and spaciousness like Paradise;
For it was both a market-place and a sowing-place.
When by Sikandar that city was completed,
They gave to it even the name of Iskandriya.

(Nizami, transl. Clarke 1881, pp. 224–5)

The historical record on the foundation of the city is quite full, and here too the *Romance* comes closest to being valuable as a historical source. There is no doubt that the portion of Book I relating to the foundation of Alexandria exhibits detailed local knowledge. Unfortunately the passages in question, full of unfamiliar names and details, became garbled in copying, and the single manuscript of the first recension (A) exhibits so many lacunae and cruces that the authors or scribes of the later recensions forbore to copy this section, and thus much of the detail is uncertain. Julius Valerius, who made the first Latin translation, was a native of Alexandria, as a reference to 'our . . .' makes clear, but by then it was too late to restore the garbled portions.

The story as it is told in the *Romance* places the foundation of Alexandria after the visit to the Oracle of Ammon at Siwa in the western desert in winter–spring 332–331 BC, and other ancient sources agree.[12] Two other historians, however, tell us that Alexander made his expedition to Siwa to consult the god after the foundation of the city.[13] The *Romance* is the only text that suggests the foundation of Alexandria was enjoined by the oracle (in the text quoted at the head of this section). It further tells us that after the city was founded Alexander spent time in Memphis, the capital of Pharaonic Egypt, and was crowned there as Pharaoh: the other sources make no mention of any coronation, and it has been assumed that he had no time to stop for ceremonies during his tour of conquest. On both these points, however, the *Romance* may actually be right.

C.B. Welles argued forcefully that the foundation of a city is commonly preceded by a visit to an oracle to obtain the god's approval and advice.[14] It would be strange to visit an oracle immediately after committing oneself to an important act such as the foundation of the city. The topography of the narrative also bears on the argument. Of the two main historical sources used by Arrian, Ptolemy states that the party returned from Siwa directly (i.e. across the waterless desert) to Memphis. Aristobulus, however, said that the party returned by the route by which they had gone, namely back to the coast and eastwards via Paraetonium and Taphosiris. This is precisely the route indicated by the *Romance* (I. 31):

> As he was walking [at a certain village], a very large hind ran by and disappeared into a cave. Alexander called to one of his archers to shoot the creature. But when the archer loosed his bow, he missed the hind. 'Fellow, your shot went wide', said Alexander. And therefore that place was called Paratone because of Alexander's remark. He founded a small city there, and settled some of the most distinguished of the natives in it . . . . Then he came to Taphosirion. He asked the local people why it had that name, and they replied that the sanctuary was the grave of Osiris. After sacrificing there also, he approached the goal of his journey and reached the site of our present city.

Ptolemy's route for the journey would have been a dangerous and irrational one to take if there was an alternative. Ptolemy was often inclined to exaggerate Alexander's daring. Suspicion is further aroused by his statement (unusual in this historian who, as Arrian said,[15] could not have lied since he was a king) that the party was led to the oasis at Siwa by two talking snakes. (The alternative story, that they were led by crows, is more credible, since birds would naturally indicate the way to water.)[16]

Maybe the foundation of Alexandria was a decision taken during the journey to Siwa, as Bosworth suggests.[17] Even in this case, the oracle would have been consulted before the foundation took place. The other sources are famously mysterious about what exactly Alexander asked the oracle (Plutarch says he received some secret answers which he would tell only to his mother when he returned), though they tend to suggest that it had to do with his paternity: a consultation about a city foundation would be a substantial reason for the journey.

When he reached the site of Alexandria, the *Romance* tells us, 'he saw a great open space, stretching into the infinite distance, and occupied by twelve villages. Their names were Steiramphes, Phanenti and Eudemos, Akames, Eupyros, Rhakotis, Hegiosa, Ypones, Krambeitai, Krapatheis and Lydias, Pases, Teresis or Nephelites, Menuia, Pelasos.' This list of twelve villages with sixteen names between them occurs only in the first recension of the *Romance* and is typical of the puzzles that led later copyists to despair. But it is undoubtedly the product of local knowledge, as are the passages that follow, identifying various localities in the great city.

The architects, it is said, advised Alexander to reduce the planned size of the city ('if you make this city as great as you have sketched, those who live here will always be at odds with each other, because the population will be so huge'). There follows the episode of marking out the perimeter with barley meal. When the foundations had been laid,

> Alexander inscribed [on what?, one asks] five letters, ΑΒΓΔΕ [the first five letters of the Greek alphabet]. A for 'Alexander', B for *Basileus*, 'king', Γ for *Genos*, 'descendant', Δ for *Dios*, 'of Zeus', E for *ektisen* . . . , 'founded an incomparable city' . . . . As the gate of the sanctuary was being put in place, a large and ancient tablet of stone, inscribed with many letters, fell out of it; and after it came a large number of snakes, which crept away into the doorways of the houses that had already been built. Nowadays the door-keepers reverence these snakes as friendly spirits when they come into their houses – for they are not venomous, and they place garlands on their working animals and give them a rest day. Alexander was still in the city when it and the sanctuary were being built, in the month of Tybi. For this reason the Alexandrians still even now keep the custom of celebrating a festival on the twenty-fifth day of Tybi. (*AR* I. 32)

The passage contains a number of points of interest. The snakes represent the Egyptian god of fate, Shai,[18] and a snake appears as supporter of images of Alexander the Founder.[19] The appearance of Shai here makes it very clear that this is a text by a local writer who was an enthusiast for the Macedonian rule inaugurated by Alexander. In *The Oracle of the Potter*,[20] by contrast, a document of the 'resistance' to Macedonian domination in Egypt, it is foretold that Shai will leave Alexandria and take up residence in Memphis, the ancient Egyptian capital.

The date given for the foundation, in both A and the beta recension, is also significant in a different way. In 332 BC 25 Tybi fell on 7 April.[21] (The Egyptian calendar was lunar and its months thus precessed through the year, like in the modern Muslim calendar.) The later recension of beta, L, interpolates the statement that Tybi was equivalent to January, which was only true after the harmonisation of the Egyptian calendar with the Julian (solar) calendar, in Roman times (after which 25 Tybi was always 20 January). The use of an Egyptian date in the A recension[22] thus indicates the early origin of this portion of the text.[23] Arrian (*Anabasis* 3.5.6) says that Alexander left Memphis 'when spring began to show itself', which could hardly be in January, even in the climate of Egypt.

The division of Alexandria into five regions known by Greek letters is well attested, and has begun to take on more substance as a result of the excavations undertaken both in the city and underwater in the harbours since 1990. In later times, and certainly by AD 38, the Delta was the home of the Jewish population: it lay close to the Royal Quarter. Josephus (*cAp* 2.33ff.) says that it was Alexander who gave the Jews civic rights in Alexandria. In fact it is certain that their position was only established formally under Ptolemy I (Josephus, *AJ* 12.8), though it may well be that the designation of a particular area for Jews to live in goes back to Alexander. Several stories about Alexandria survive in the Jewish tradition, and all of them seem to have the purpose of establishing the right of Jews to regard Alexandria as a home because of their close association with the founder.

One of these stories concerns the snakes. The third-century AD work, *The Lives of the Prophets*, which goes under the name of Pseudo-Epiphanius, tells us (in the second recension)[24] that the dangerous character of the snakes (and of the river-snakes 'which the Greeks call crocodiles') was neutralised by the prayers of the prophet Jeremiah (who had, as a matter of fact, taken refuge some centuries earlier in Tell Defenneh (Daphnae). Later, the same text tells us:

We hear from the old men descended from Antigonus and Ptolemy that Alexander the ruler of the Macedonians stood by the tomb of the prophet [Jeremiah] and recognised his rites, and transferred his remains to Alexandria, erecting a circle around them, and thus the race of snakes was banished from that country, and likewise from the river; and he threw in the snakes called *argolaoi*, that is, snake-fighters, which he brought from Argos in the Peloponnese, which is why they are called *argolaoi*, meaning 'clever ones of Argos'; and they have a very sweet and well-omened utterance.[25]

We learn further from the *Spiritual Meadow* of John Moschus (*c.* AD 600, Chapter 77, 'The Story of Three Blind Men') where exactly this tomb was: 'This place called the Tetrapylon is held in very high esteem by the citizens of Alexandria for they say that Alexander took the relics of the Prophet Jeremiah from Egypt and buried them there.'

The Tetrapylon is quite probably the site of another legendary action of Alexander's. Unfortunately its location has not been identified, but it may well be the highest gate of the city, described in the late gamma recension of the *Romance* as the eastern gate.

> The highest [tower] of all he built at the eastern gate, and placed on top of it a statue of himself, surrounded by Seleucus, Antiochus and Philip the doctor. The statue of Seleucus had horns, and the sculptor made it distinctive by its brave and ferocious expression: Philip's was distinguished by his military attire; and Antiochus was holding a spear. When all this was finished and the city had been made exceedingly beautiful in the eyes of all, Alexander ascended the tower, stood up and condemned all the gods of the country. He proclaimed the one true God, who cannot be known nor seen nor sought out, who is surrounded by the seraphim and glorified with the name of 'thrice holy'. Alexander made a prayer: 'O god of gods, creator of all that is visible and invisible, be my helper now in all that I intend to do'. Then he came down from the tower and went to his palace. (*AR* I. 28)

The two passages were used by Friedrich Pfister to argue that major elements of the gamma recension were the product of Jewish invention in Alexandria.[26] In his introduction to the reprinted version of this article in Pfister's *Kleine Schriften*, Reinhold Merkelbach points out that the discovery, subsequent to Pfister's original article, of the epsilon recension, which must be dated not earlier than AD 700 and which influenced the gamma recension, invalidates the suggestion that there was a Hellenistic Jewish *Alexander Romance* which formed the basis for the gamma recension; he avers that gamma must in fact be of Christian origin. Now it is certain that gamma contains a good deal of Christian material; but that does not invalidate the point that these two stories are likely to have originated in Hellenistic Jewish circles.

There were plenty of similar stories which did not make it into the *Romance*. Two of them concern King Solomon. The first, told in 2 Targum Esther 1.4,[27] relates how Alexander brought the Throne of Solomon to Egypt. When it had previously belonged to Nebuchadnezzar, the king had attempted to ascend it, but one of the golden lion's paws that formed its supports stretched out and broke his leg. Alexander wisely avoided trying to sit on the throne, though a succeeding Pharaoh, Shishak, did and was lamed. In the reign of Antiochus Epiphanes, the leg of the throne was broken; and, according to Esther Rabbah. 1.2.12, the fragments could still be seen at Rome in the second century AD.

The second story belongs to a common pattern.[28] It states that, when Alexander conquered Jerusalem, he found there Solomon's books of wisdom. He gave them to his teacher Aristotle, who translated them into Greek and then destroyed the originals; thus all the wisdom of the west is really derived from that of Solomon, but Aristotle passed it off as Greek. This is a story which puts Alexander in a hostile light, as a thief and a destroyer, yet at the same time firmly locates him in the development of Jewish civilisation. The same story is of course told of his appropriation of the Zoroastrian wisdom (see above, p. 41); and it is also said of the Arabic translations of Greek science that they were originally Persian.[29] The anecdote has even been recycled in modern times to suggest that all of Aristotle's work was stolen from African writings he discovered in the Library at Alexandria: he removed the names of the original authors and replaced them with his own.[30]

The last Jewish story to be considered in this section is not associated specifically with Alexandria, though it is set in Egypt. During Alexander's expedition to the Red Sea, the Jewish horsemen included an archer named Mosollamus. The army halted while the seer took the omens from a bird that was flying nearby. Mosollamus immediately raised his bow and brought down the bird. When the seer remonstrated with him, he replied, 'How could this bird, which did not provide for its own safety, say anything about our march? For had it been able to know the future, it would not have come to this place, fearing that Mosollamus would draw his bow and kill it.'[31]

Again, the anecdote belongs to a common story-pattern, along with the story about Alexander's murder of Nectanebo in *Romance* I. 14. Alexander apparently tests Nectanebo's knowledge of the future by killing him when he does not suspect it: but Nectanebo trumps Alexander by revealing that he had foreknown that he would be killed by his son – and thus the truth of Alexander's paternity is revealed. (See Chapter 1, p. 24 and n. 46.) In this story the seer is vindicated, but in the story of Mosollamus the point made is exactly the opposite: that divination by birds does not work. This is a natural enough position for a pious Jew to take, and once again we see an Alexander-related story serving as the vehicle for a demonstration of Jewish religious superiority.

Sarapis

Let us return to the *Romance*'s account of the foundation of Alexandria.

Alexander followed the instructions given to him by the Oracle of Ammon (see above): he 'searched for the all-seeing one and built a great altar opposite the hero-shrine, which is now called the Grand Altar of Alexander, and made a sacrifice there.' After he had prayed and placed gifts on the altar, 'Suddenly a huge eagle swooped down and seized the entrails of the sacrifice, carried them off into the air, and then dropped them on another altar' (*AR* I. 33). Alexander follows the eagle to the spot, which turns out to be an ancient sanctuary containing images clearly intended for Sarapis and Isis, accompanied by the three-headed dog Cerberus. On the

14 Sarapis. Marble statue of the Roman period in the Greco-Roman Museum, Alexandria.

perimeter wall is an inscription reading (in hieroglyphs: the Alexander of legend is probably the only Greek ever to be able to read hieroglyphics!)[32] 'King Sesonchosis of Egypt, the ruler of the world, erected this to Sarapis, the renowned god of the universe.' Alexander then receives an oracular dream vision of Sarapis, who foretells the greatness of Alexandria. Alexander takes the opportunity to ask him the question that will trouble him throughout the *Romance*: 'Lord, show me also, when and how I am going to die.' Sarapis politely refuses to answer, as do the other figures he consults later in the *Romance*, until the Talking Tree tells him the horrible truth (Chapter 10), but predicts: 'You shall live in [this city]/For all time, dead and yet not dead. /The city you have built shall be your tomb.'

This narrative raises several points of interest. First, the story about the eagle recurs in several other Hellenistic conquests. The sixth-century AD chronicler John Malalas tells the same story of the foundation of Seleuceia by Seleucus I (8.12, p.199), and also of the same king's foundation of Antioch (8.13, p.200). For good measure, Seleucus is said also to have sacrificed a virgin at the foundation ceremony, and Malalas duly says the same of Alexander at Alexandria (8.1, p.192). It is possible that the whole story grew up in a complex of legends about Seleucus: P.M. Fraser argues that there existed a Seleucus Romance in which many stories were told of Seleucus, some resembling those about Alexander.[33]

Secondly, if one were tempted to believe that there is a historical core to the legend, one should note that the cult of Sarapis was certainly established in Alexandria by Ptolemy I, not by Alexander. His aim was to create a god who could be a religious focus for the Greek population of Alexandria while preserving many Egyptian features.[34] He restyled an existing cult of Osiris-Apis at Memphis which was already popular with the Greeks of Egypt. The attribution of the foundation of the cult to Alexander is a natural way to give it weight and authority and to emphasise the legitimacy of Ptolemaic rule. The god Sarapis is fully anthropomorphic and in art normally resembles a blend of Zeus and Hades.

The *Romance* is unique in attributing this close interest in Sarapis to Alexander. It may nevertheless not be altogether wrong. It is possible that Alexander did take a particular interest in this god, and that the cult was already active in the fourth century BC. The curious story that his generals consulted the god in the 'Temple of Sarapis' at Babylon during Alexander's final illness[35] may bespeak a particular interest in the god among his companions, even if the temple itself cannot have been dedicated to Sarapis: it is likely that this was a syncretistic way of referring, in familiar Greek terms, to the Temple of Bel-Marduk. Stambaugh has suggested that Ptolemy's involvement was in introducing the cult statue, rather than in establishing the cult itself. This could be the burden of the account in Tacitus (*Histories* 4.83) and Plutarch (*Isis and Osiris* 28), which says that Ptolemy imported a statue of the god from Sinope in Pontus: it seems that they garbled a reference to the hill Sinopion at Memphis, which is probably the Egyptian se-n-h'api, 'seat of the Apis'.[36]

Whichever is the case, Sarapis went on to become an important and popular god for the Greek-speaking population of Egypt at least until the third century AD.[37] Rufinus, in his *Ecclesiastical History* (II. 23, in *PL* 21, 294c) tells us that the sanctuary at Alexandria contained a statue of the sun-god which was made to float in mid-air by the use of magnets:[38] as he was writing two hundred years after the destruction of the Serapeum by Christians in AD 389, his cannot be regarded as eyewitness testimony.

It would appear that the Jewish story about Alexander preaching the One God in Alexandria was devised as a counterblast to this pagan, Sarapis-worshipping Alexander. By making him a nominal Jew, the Jewish population attempted to strengthen their position in the city.

The Pharos

A monument which is attributed with even less justification to Alexander is the Pharos, the lighthouse built by Ptolemy II (308–246 BC) which came to be regarded as one of the Seven Wonders of the World. The concept of the Seven Wonders has its roots in Hellenistic writing, beginning after the completion of the Colossus of Rhodes in 292 BC,[39] but was first codified by the Roman writer Varro. Six of the wonders are fairly standard, but the seventh is variable.[40] Pliny the Elder was the first to include the Pharos (completed in 283 BC) in his list of the seven in his *Natural History* (Book 38); but several later writers, including Gregory of Nazianzus (Epigram 50), give lists that do not include the Pharos. Later lists had to stretch to eight, or even ten, to accommodate all the candidates.[41] In the sixth century Gregory of Tours (*De cursu stellarum* 1) added a new twist, writing that 'The seventh is the Alexandrian Pharos, which is said to have been erected, in miraculous fashion, on four crabs. These certainly cannot have been small ones, since they had to bear such a gigantic building in height and breadth; tradition says, that a man who lies down on the claw of one of the crabs will not cover it completely.' The same story reappears in a work attributed to the Venerable Bede, which specifies that the crabs were made of glass and that each was twenty double paces across (i.e. about 100 feet): 'How these enormous crabs were cast, how they were lowered into the water without breaking them, how it was possible to build cement foundations on top of them and to get the cement to harden under the water, why the crabs do not break or why the foundation does not slip off them – all that is a great marvel, and how it was done is hard to understand.'[42]

A great marvel indeed. The explanation seems to be that the writers confused the Pharos with an obelisk standing before the Temple of Caesar, which was supported on four crabs of metal. The companion obelisk which travelled to London, Cleopatra's Needle, may have stood on similar crabs carved from obsidian (which is volcanic glass).[43]

The plot thickens when we read in Eutychius (*PG* 111, col. 971) that the Pharos was the work of Alexander. Eutychius was a Christian Arab who became Patriarch of Alexandria and lived from AD 876 to 937. '[Alexander] also built the Pharos at Alexandria, which he placed there as a beacon for all those at sea, to direct them to Alexandria.' The slightly later Arab writer Mas'udi (d. AD 956), in his *Meadows of Gold*, a world chronicle, recounts:[44]

> According to most historians of Misr [Egypt] and Alexandria who have written about their country, it was Alexander, the son of Philip of Macedon, who built the lighthouse of Alexandria . . . . According to other authors, it was Daluka 'the old queen' who built it and made of it an observation post for enemy movements. Others attribute its origin to the tenth Pharaoh. Finally, some say that it is to the founder of Rome that Alexandria, the Pharos and the Pyramids owe their existence. According to this view, the name of Alexandria derives simply from the celebrity of Alexander who conquered most of the world. (837) . . . . The true creator of the Pharos built it on a foundation of glass in the form of a crab which rested on the bottom of the sea, at the extremity of that tongue of land which protrudes from the continent.[45] He crowned it with statues of bronze and other metals. One of these statues had its right index finger turned constantly towards the part of the sky where the sun was; if it was in the middle of its course, the finger indicated its position; if it descended towards the horizon, the hand of the statue sank with it. Another statue indicated with its hand the part of the sea from which an enemy was approaching, when it was still a night's sail away. When it arrived in view, a terrifying sound, audible over two or three miles, was emitted by the statue . . . . A third statue indicated all the hours of the day and night with a harmonious sound which varied for each hour.

In the reign of the Caliph al-Walid I, a secret envoy was sent by the Emperor of Byzantium to pretend to convert to Islam and to reveal to the Caliph where certain treasures were hidden, that he had learnt of from his books:

ANSICHT DES PHAROS VOM MEERE AUS

15 The Pharos. One of many hypothetical reconstructions, this one, by H. Thiersch (1909), is regarded as the most reliable.

The fact is, the treasures of the earth are buried under the Pharos of Alexandria. When Alexander took possession of the goods and precious stones of Shaddad son of Ad and of other Arab kings of Egypt and Syria, he had caves and subterranean chambers constructed, with vaults and arcades above them. There he deposited all the treasures of gold and silver and precious stones. On top of these chambers he built the Pharos, which was not less than 1000 cubits in height, and placed on the summit the mirror surrounded by criers. When, by means of this mirror, they saw the enemy nearby, they cried out to alert the neighbouring sentry posts and raised banners to alert the more distant ones.[46]

Al-Walid set off with soldiers and had the Pharos demolished to half its height, and destroyed the mirror; but they did not find the treasure. Now the inhabitants of Alexandria realised that it had all been a cunning ruse to destroy the mirror and facilitate an attack by sea; but the secret envoy made his escape by night.

The rigmarole continues with an account of the Maghribi king Ubayd Allah, who attacked Egypt in AD 913–15 and 919–21. In one of these invasions,

A group of horsemen penetrated the Pharos and became lost in the labyrinth of roads which ended at the precipice at the bottom of which lay the glass crab; there were also ravines leading down to the sea; the soldiers plunged into the void with their horses and, as was later discovered, the number of victims was considerable. According to another version, they fell from the height of a platform which extended in front of the Pharos. This space is now occupied by a mosque.

The source of this bizarre legend is quite obscure, though the talismanic statues belong to a recognisable type of story. Several similar ones were known in Constantinople of the same period.[47] The magic statues may thus be Greek rather than Arab legends; and the magic mirror might be a recollection of Archimedes' famous experiments with mirrors.

Another story involving the harbour at Alexandria concerns Alexander's diving bell. We shall return to this invention in Chapter 6, but it is Mas'udi who gives the best motivated account of its invention. When the city was founded, the harbour was full of sea-monsters which emerged every night and destroyed the building that had been done during the day. Alexander therefore constructed a glass diving bell and went down to have a closer look, accompanied by several artists (Mas'udi 1965, 830–1). When he re-emerged, he had bronze replicas made of all the monsters as the artists had portrayed them. These were erected along the sea wall, and scared the monsters off so that they troubled the builders no more.

The story of the diving bell is also found in the Talmud,[48] though it is used as a vehicle of exploration and covers many days' journey; it is not associated at all with Alexandria. When it eventually arrives in the Greek *Romance*, in the L recension (datable later than beta, *c.* 500, from which it derives, but possibly much later), it is just one of Alexander's many explorations and has nothing to do with Alexandria; instead, it is associated with his quest to go beyond the limits of mortals, which is a dominant theme of the *Romance*. Has a story about Alexandria been extended to a wider significance? Or has the Arab tradition adapted a Jewish story of more general application and attached it to the legend of Alexandria? And how did the Jewish story arise? The answers are imponderable, and we shall return to them in Chapter 6. Meanwhile, the stories surveyed in this chapter have been crucial in establishing the image of the conqueror that entered the Islamic and eastern traditions.

THE MARVELS OF INDIA

(329–326 BC)

Meanwhile Alexander had withdrawn to the uttermost regions of the north, almost beyond the border of the inhabited world.

Aeschines, *Against Ctesiphon* 165

If you defeat the whole human race, you will be ready to make war on woods, on snow, on rivers, on wild animals.

A Scythian addressing Alexander, Quintus Curtius 7.18.3.

Alexander will encounter unending night, monstrous beasts, the end of nature.

Quintus Curtius 9.4.18

All those who wrote about Alexander preferred the marvellous to the true.

Strabo, *Geography* 2.1.9

I set [the story] in India so that its improbability might be bearable.

Jorge Luis Borges, 'Afterword' (1952) in *The Aleph* (1998), 135

Once Darius was defeated and dead, it might have been thought that Alexander's task of conquest was done. In fact mopping-up operations consumed the next two and a half years, from summer 330 to winter 328/7; Darius' murderer and self-proclaimed successor, Bessus, had to be hunted down, and a revolt by Spitamenes in Sogdia had to be suppressed. It was this expedition, deep into central Asia, that prompted the comment of the orator Aeschines quoted above: this was already further east and north than any Greek had travelled before. But the suppression of Spitamenes did not mark the end of Alexander's wanderlust: instead, he continued to march his army onwards for another thousand miles, across the Hindu Kush and into the Indus Valley. Why? There was no strategic reason for this advance into regions that had never been more than loosely attached to the Persian Empire. The reason lies rather in Alexander's own psychology – his *pothos*, or longing, as the historian Arrian called it.[1]

Alexander was perhaps the first human being in recorded history to be seized by the romance of the east. In part this was due to his knowledge of mythology and of the legendary genealogy of the Macedonian kings. First, Heracles, the ancestor of the Macedonian royal line,[2] had travelled through these parts and, it became known, had failed to conquer a certain rock fortress. Alexander had to emulate and outdo his ancestor, though the story no doubt originated in Indian circles as a tale of Krishna. Secondly, the god Dionysus, the presiding deity of Macedon with its culture of heavy wine-drinking, had come from the east with his retinue of panthers and maenads, and Alexander wished to retrace his steps. Somewhere in the mountains west of the Choaspes a local chieftain named Acuphis came to Alexander and told him that the place where they stood, Nysa, had been founded by the god when 'he had subdued the nation of the Indians, and was returning to the Greek sea . . . to be a memorial to posterity of his wanderings'.[3] The Macedonians were the more ready to believe him as it was the only place they had encountered where ivy, the sacred plant of Dionysus, grew. When the army returned in triumph to Carmania (Kerman province in Iran) in autumn 325, after their sufferings in the Gedrosian desert (Baluchistan), the procession took on an explicitly Dionysiac character.[4] And thirdly, the Babylonian queen Semiramis had conducted an expedition of conquest to India,[5] returning through the desert of Gedrosia: Alexander had to do the same.

There was a scientific purpose, too, to Alexander's penetration of India. He travelled with a considerable scientific staff, including a historian (Callisthenes), a geographical writer (Onesicritus) and various botanists and zoologists, not to mention a philosopher (Anaxarchus) who described to the king the theory of a plurality of worlds – at which Alexander expressed regret that he had yet to conquer one completely.[6] It is often supposed that the scientific mission was prompted by Alexander's old teacher, Aristotle[7] – an idea delightfully dramatised in L. Sprague de Camp's novel, *An Elephant for Aristotle* (1958), which recounts the difficulties of sending the prized beast back from the Punjab to Macedon. Certainly Aristotle supposed that the eastern Ocean that bordered the world would be visible from the summit of the Hindu Kush,[8] so at that point Alexander could have imagined the conquest of the entire eastern world to be his grasp.

The impact of Alexander's *pothos* on later writers was immense; the main lines of European knowledge of India and the east were fixed for nearly 2,000 years by what he discovered and his historians recorded.

Earlier Writers

Alexander and his staff, if they had done their research, had some idea of what would await them in 'India'.[9] The first traveller to describe India was the fifth century writer Scylax of Caryanda, who mentions Sciapods, Big-Ears, One-Eyes and Enotokoitai.[10] The most extensive account of the region had been published nearly a century earlier by Ctesias of Cnidus, who had been employed as a physician at the Persian court from 405 to 397 BC. His *Indica* is one of the many lost works of antiquity of which we would like to have more; however, a long summary survives in the tenth-century writer Photius,[11] who kept a full notebook of his omnivorous reading, to which can be added many quotations and allusions in later writers such as the geographer Strabo and Aelian in his books on animals.

Ctesias[12] started his account modestly by describing the River Indus, 200 stades (furlongs) across at its widest, and the 'worm' [the crocodile] that lives in its waters. He speaks of elephants and monkeys, giant cockerels, and the parrot 'which speaks Indian like a human being, but if it learns Greek, then it speaks that as well'. He described the spitting cobra and the 'Indian reed', which seems to be the banyan tree. The dogs are big enough to fight lions. A creature that had a long subsequent history, though rarely seen by man, was the martikhora or manticore,[13] which is the size of a lion, has an 'almost human' face, human ears and three rows of teeth, while its tail is loaded with numerous stings which it can fire at its enemies.

Of human races Ctesias mentions the pygmies of central India, about one and a half cubits high, with long hair and beards down to the ground, who tend flocks and herds of similarly pygmy stature. In the mountains there are men with dogs' heads whose language consists of barking, though they can understand Indian; they dwell in caves and live by hunting, and live to 170 years, or even 200.[14] Beyond these people is another race that lives exclusively on milk: they have no anuses and their buttocks are joined together, so that instead of defecating they induce vomiting each evening to remove waste from their stomachs. In the Indian mountains where the reeds grow there is a race of men who up to the age of thirty have white hair all over their bodies, but then it begins to darken until at the age of sixty it is entirely black: their ears are long enough to cover their arms and backs. (Later writers refined this detail by noting that they could cover themselves with their ears when sleeping.)

The animals of India are generally of larger size than elsewhere, including wild asses the size of horses with purple heads and blue eyes, and worms like those that attack fig trees, but seven cubits long, so thick that a child of ten can scarcely put its arms around one (it is not clear why it should want to).

There are several springs with miraculous properties, including one which fills each year with liquid gold, and at the bottom of the spring there is iron: Ctesias says he possessed two swords made from it. Another spring repels anyone who jumps into it, though it is good to drink from and helpful for curing leprosy. Another has water which sets like cheese, and there are also rivers which flow with honey and amber. In one of the rivers is found the pantarbe stone (45a), which glows in the dark: it became a popular motif in later fiction.[15]

Ctesias also mentions one of the most famous pieces of Indian lore, familiar since Herodotus (4.13): the griffins that guard the gold. The griffins, he says (46b) are 'four-footed birds the size of a wolf with legs and claws like a lion; the feathers are red on the breast and black on the rest of the body'. Herodotus goes into more detail than Photius in his summary, though he locates the griffins among the Scythians in south Russia or central Asia. He tells how Aristeas of Proconnesos 'journeyed to the country of the Issedones, and that beyond the Issedones live the one-eyed Arimaspians, and beyond them the griffins which guard the gold, and beyond the griffins the Hyperboreans [the people beyond the North Wind], whose land comes down to the sea'. The passage famously inspired John Milton's simile for Satan –

> As when a gryphon through the wilderness
> With wingèd course o'er hill or moory dale,
> Pursues the Arimaspian, who by stealth
> Had from his wakeful custody purloined
> The guarded gold.[16]

A writer of the third century BC, Megasthenes, who acted as ambassador for the Seleucid king to the court of Chandragupta Maurya, described in detail how the gold was mined:

> Beneath the surface there are mines of gold, and here accordingly are found the ants which dig for that metal. They are not inferior in size to wild foxes. They run with amazing speed, and live by the produce of

the chase. The time when they dig is winter. They throw up heaps of earth, as moles do, at the mouth of the mines. The gold dust has to be subjected to a little boiling. The people of the neighbourhood, coming secretly with beasts of burden, carry this off. If they came openly the ants would attack them, and pursue them if they fled, and would destroy both them and their cattle. So, to effect the robbery without being observed, they lay down in several different places pieces of the flesh of wild beasts, and when the ants are by this device dispersed they carry off the gold dust.[17]

Megasthenes was the first of many writers who built on the account of Ctesias to make India a place of fable and enchantment.[18] He moved on from more or less plausible creatures such as the parrot, the pangolin, a giant horse, sea-snakes, whales and sea-hares to strange races of human beings: the pygmies, the people with reversed knees, the dog-heads, those who feed on smells,[19] those who cover themselves with their ears to sleep,[20] and the one-eyed people. Pliny the Elder in his *Natural History* (7. 9–32)[21] reprised many of these races, as did Pomponius Mela (3.61–6) around AD 44, and Solinus (third/fourth-century AD).[22] A strange work known as the *Letter of Pharasmanes* (of Hadrianic date) put an account of the beasts of India into the mouth (or pen) of the king of Chorasmia who, according to Arrian (*Anabasis* 4.15.4), had invited Alexander to visit him and told him that the land of the Amazons was, as it were, around the next corner. A little later, Philostratus (*Vit. Ap. Ty.* 3.45–9) discusses the traditional wonders as well as the pantarbe stone of Ctesias (3.46). In late antiquity the accounts were revisited by the authors of the *Physiologus* (c. AD 200, but expanded in the fourth and fifth centuries) and of the *Liber Monstrorum* (eighth to ninth century AD): these mainly contain genuine animals but with some admixture of wondrous ones such as the giant ants and the odontotyrannus (see below), as well as the 'Indian stone'.[23]

The fabulous races became the staple of medieval accounts and illustrations: a page of Hartmann Schedel's *Chronicle* usefully depicts them all together.

Mandeville's *Travels* (ch. 22) is the locus classicus and has been much discussed: he places them all beyond Ceylon, in an archipelago which seems to be the Andaman Islands.[24]

Certainly Alexander's staff could expect plenty of material for their specimen cases and their descriptive talents; one of them, Baeton (*FGrH* 119F5 = Pliny *NH* 7.2.11), mentioned the people with reversed feet, and perhaps the anthropophagi. One of Alexander's generals, Craterus, wrote a letter to his mother in which he claimed to have seen the Ganges (though in actual fact the army turned back before that point). But the fullest account was that by Onesicritus, whom Strabo called 'the master fabulist as well as the master pilot of Alexander'. The beasts which prompted Strabo's tart assessment were two serpents, respectively 80 and 140 cubits in length. But from what else we know of Onesicritus' writings it seems that he was particularly interested in social structures, not least in the long-lived inhabitants of the kingdom of Musicanus, whose polity was a kind of utopia, and in the naked philosophers of Taxila (see Chapter 5). The local rulers played up to the Macedonians' preconceptions, and brought them skins of the gold–guarding ants, larger than foxes, as Nearchus reports.[25]

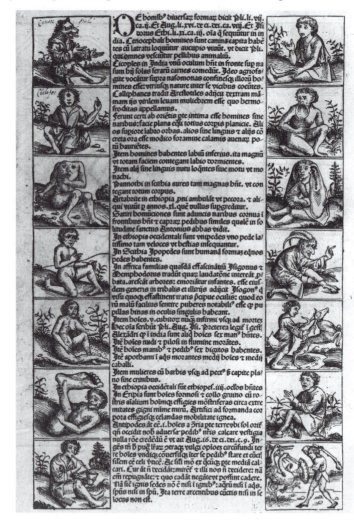

16 A page of 'monstrous races'. From Hartmann Schedel's *Liber chronicarum* (Nuremberg 1493).

India in the *Alexander Romance*

Many of these animals were not content to sit and be looked at: in the *Romance* they fight the invaders ferociously. The first episode of the *Romance* where Alexander faces a bevy of monsters occurs in Book II, 32–44, immediately after the death of Darius, when Alexander and his men 'go deep into the desert . . . in the direction of the constellation of the Plough'. Here they encounter giant fleas the size of frogs and numerous strange races including men with the faces of lions, giants with hands like saws and a creature that sounds like nothing so much as King Kong: when he is handed a naked woman, he grabs her and eats her. They are attacked by invisible whips when they try to collect the sap of the myrrh tree and encounter the fish-eaters. The geographical confusion here is as puzzling as the nature of the monsters, for the fish-eaters (and perhaps the myrrh trees) belong to the journey through the Gedrosian desert on the way back from India (in autumn 325). The fish-eaters, it is casually mentioned, had no heads and had their faces in their chests: they had a long and picturesque subsequent history in art, and these 'men whose heads Do grow beneath their shoulders' were mentioned by Shakespeare's Othello, among the wonders he describes to Desdemona.

A second set of adventures occurs in the gamma recension as an extension of this portion of the story (II. 29–34), when they encounter wild women covered with hair, ferocious man- (and horse-)eating ants, pygmies, wild men with hair like gristle, 'King Kong' (again), men with six hands and six feet, and finally the dog-headed men.

Alexander's *Letter to Aristotle about India*

The fullest account of Alexander's encounter with the wonders of India occurs in the work known as the *Letter of Alexander to Aristotle about India*.[26] Originally composed in Greek, this found its way in heavily mutilated form into the first recension of the *Alexander Romance*. (In the subsequent recensions it becomes a third-person account and part of the continuous narrative.) But it was translated into Latin by the seventh century AD, and again into an Italianate Latin in the tenth century. Immensely popular in the Middle Ages, it is preserved in a very large number of MSS,[27] and was the first work ever to be translated into English, for the Old English translation is one of the four texts in the unique codex which preserves *Beowulf*.[28] Its most recent re-emergence is in Umberto Eco's *Baudolino* (2002), which draws heavily on the *Letter* and other Alexander stories for its narrative.

The *Letter to Aristotle* resists summary, for it is long and colourful. It starts with the defeat of Porus in July 326 BC and a description of the palace of Porus. Alexander then advances to the Caspian Gates (see below for discussion of the geography) and proceeds through sandy wastes of extreme danger, led by unreliable guides. The river he and his men discover is bitter and undrinkable, but eventually they observe an island inhabited by Indians in a castle built of reeds. Alexander sends some of his soldiers to swim to the island, but hippopotamuses emerge from the water ('they are called hippopotamuses because they are half men and half horses') and devour the men. So Alexander has the guides thrown into the river, where they too are devoured by the beasts, which 'swarm like ants'.

Presently some Indians appear in a boat and guide them to a lake of sweet water. But when the army has pitched camp, they have to endure a 'Night of Terrors'.[29]

> When the moon began to rise, scorpions suddenly arrived to drink in the lake; then there came huge beasts and serpents, of various colours, some red, some black or white, some gold; the whole earth echoed with their hissing and filled us with considerable fear . . . . It was already the third hour of the night, and we were hoping that we should get some sleep, when more serpents arrived. These had crests on their heads and were thicker than columns . . . their breath too was poisonous. We spent more than an hour of the night fighting them, and they killed of our party thirty servants and twenty soldiers . . . . After the serpents had gone away, there arrived crabs with hard backs like those of crocodiles, and when we threw our spears at them they did not penetrate; still, we killed a good many of them with fire.
>
> (transl. Stoneman 1994a)

Next to arrive are white lions, bigger than bulls, followed by giant pigs and huge bats with human teeth. Biggest of the lot is 'a beast larger than an elephant, with three horns on its forehead. In the Indian language it was called Odontotyrannus or Tooth-tyrant. It looked a bit like a horse and its head was black.'[30] It kills several dozen Macedonians before they overcome it. Before dawn arrives they have to face shrews the size of foxes and bright red vultures with black beaks. It is a relief to be able to strike camp, tired as they are, and to march onwards.

The striking thing about the 'Night of Terrors' is the Monsters Who did not Bark in the Night. Almost none of the creatures Alexander encounters is familiar from Ctesias. The castle of giant reeds does indeed seem to recall the Indian reed of Ctesias, which can be used for boat-building: the Loeb

17 The Odontotyrannus. From the Armenian translation of the *Alexander Romance*. John Rylands Library, Manchester MS Arm. 3 f. 123.

translator identifies the plant confidently as the bamboo,[31] while other commentators make it the palmyra palm; the most exhaustive study of India in early Greek literature, that of Klaus Karttunen,[32] declines to make a commitment. The Odontotyrannus, too, might be derived from the giant fanged worm of the Indus which Ctesias calls the Monoceros; other candidates have included the mammoth, the kraken, the rhinoceros and the crocodile.[33] A good suggestion of Gunderson's is that it may be a description of a monster portrayed in Indian sculpture, of a type going back to at least the mid-fourth century BC.[34] Whatever it was, it was well established in Indian zoology. By the time of Cosmas Indicopleustes in the sixth century AD, the *monokeros* had taken the form of the modern image of a unicorn: he admitted that he had never seen one but adduced good scriptural authority for its characteristics.[35]

Why does the *Letter to Aristotle* not mention the griffins, gold-guarding ants, Sciapods, cannibals, people who live on smells, alligators and parrots? It has been suggested that Ctesias was concerned to vary his account from that of Herodotus and thus did not include many of the items that the latter had mentioned; perhaps the author of the *Letter* felt the same about Ctesias. Or perhaps he could not remember them. Or perhaps we should credit him with a delight in invention, for his creatures are indeed remarkable and they lived on for centuries after him through his work.

After his final defeat, Porus in the letter becomes an ally of the Macedonians and joins Alexander in his explorations. 'We marched on to the sea, to find out whether we could sail round the earth via Ocean, and since the men of that region said that that was a region of darkness, and that Hercules and Father Liber [Dionysus] had not dared to advance so far, I gave orders that we should circumnavigate the leftward part of India. I wanted there to be no place that remained unknown to me, and that Porus should hide none of his kingdom from me' (*Letter* 36).

The travels with Porus became a part of the legend. When Philostratus in the second century AD wrote his life of the wonder-worker Apollonius of Tyana, he included extensive travels in India, in the course of which Apollonius and his companion Damis visit Taxila in the Punjab: 'and they saw a temple . . . which was not far short of 100 feet in size, made of porphyry, and there was constructed within it a shrine . . . deserving of notice. For bronze tablets were nailed into each of its walls on which were engraved the exploits of Porus and Alexander' (*VA* 2.20). They also visited a Temple of the Sun (2.24) 'in which was kept loose a sacred elephant called Ajax, and there were images of Alexander made of gold, and others of Porus, though the latter were of black bronze'. The association continued in the Middle Ages. The *Roman d'Alexandre* gives a description of Porus' palace (III. 48), and after their second battle Porus surrenders (189ff., 123); the two kings then become friends and go travelling together, but after the visit to the oracular trees they engage in a single combat (III. 218ff.) and Porus is killed (236). In Ulrich von Etzenbach, who largely follows Walter of Châtillon, the two fight a duel, visit Porus' palace (20,788 – not in Walter), become friends and go travelling. And in the fourteenth-century

Perceforest Porus invites Alexander to his coronation at Glodofar (2400ff.). In one of the Persian accounts Alexander actually marries Porus' daughter.[36]

The journey with Porus leads to the next great set piece of the *Letter*, where by the banks of the River Buemar the Macedonians face a herd of elephants. Alexander, the cunning strategist, knows that elephants are terrified of pigs and cannot abide their squealing.[37] So he enlists a herd of pigs to frighten the elephants away. The story reappears in sober historians of the later Hellenistic age: Polyaenus (4.6.3) describes how the Megarians fought King Antigonus with pigs smeared with pitch and set on fire. In the Middle Ages the episode is combined with the use of red hot bronze soldiers to defeat elephants.

The climax of the *Letter* (16–19) occurs with the visit to the Sanctuary of the Sun and Moon. Here at last is a feature already familiar from Ctesias (46a): 'There is a sacred spot in the desert, which they venerate in the name of the sun and moon, to be reached after fifteen days' journey from Mount Sardo. The sun is cool in that locality for thirty-five days of the year in order that the Indians may perform rites there and return without getting scorched.' From this slight beginning the author of the *Letter* makes one of the most striking episodes of his narrative, which becomes the climactic moment of the whole *Alexander Romance* (see Chapter 10).

The final episode of the *Letter* (20) is the arrival in the Valley of Jordia, where there live serpents that have jewels (emeralds) in their necks, a prototype of the story of the Valley of Diamonds (see below, p. 85).

The Caspian Gates, the World Map and the Monstrous Races

So far I have been writing as if the location of these adventures in India were unproblematic. Though each of the three sets of adventures we have recounted belongs to India, they are described in the texts as beginning somewhere near the Caspian Sea, or the Caspian Gates. Where are the Caspian Gates?[38]

The Caspian Gates described by Arrian (*Anabasis* 3.19.2), through which Alexander passed on his way to the east, are to be identified with a defile in the Elburz Mountains south-west of Rey. In classical times, however, the name was applied to at least two other locations: the Pass of Derbend between the Caucasus and the western shore of the Caspian Sea, and the Dariel Pass which runs north–south through the Caucasus from Tbilisi to Ordzhonikidze (formerly Vladikavkaz). These erroneous locations were discounted by Pliny (*NH* 6.12.30), but both showed great staying power.[39] However, Nero's general Corbulo, during his campaigns in Armenia, fixed the location of the Caspian Gates at the Dariel Pass,[40] and this became standard in classical geography; this is the tradition followed by the *Alexander Romance*,[41] so that the events following the death of Darius become attached to the Caucasus region rather than the Hindu Kush.

This was more readily done because several of the Alexander historians attached the name of Caucasus to the Hindu Kush (in antiquity called Paropamisus), a habit which persisted even in Arrian (*Anabasis* 3.28.4f.). In his *Indica* (2.2ff., cf. 5.10), however, Arrian made clear that he knew the difference: 'the Macedonians who fought with Alexander called [Paropamisus] Caucasus, a different Caucasus from the Scythian; so that the story ran that Alexander penetrated beyond the Caucasus'. Eratosthenes had understood the error,[42] and suggested that 'the Alexander-historians misnamed Paropamisus in order to bring Alexander to the regions where Heracles had performed exploits' such as the freeing of Prometheus. This association is made clear in Curtius (7.3.19–23) who has Alexander cross the Caucasus (which he never did) near to where Prometheus had been bound.

The conflation of these two snowy and mountainous regions is further assisted by the need to bring Alexander in contact with the Amazons (see further, Chapter 7). The normal position for the Amazon realm in classical thought is near the River Thermodon in north-eastern Asia Minor, roughly where the Caucasus begins.[43] Strabo tells us (11.11.5–6) that some, however, placed the Amazons on the Jaxartes (Syr Darya): King Pharasmanes of Chorasmia (Arr. *Anab.* 4.15.4, above) told Alexander that he lived virtually next door to the Amazons. Plutarch explains that Alexander 'thought that the Jaxartes was the Tanais [Don]', i.e. that he was unaware of the existence of the Aral Sea at all, and that he (like most of the ancients) thought the Caspian Sea a branch of the Northern Ocean and that it was possible for a river of central Asia to flow directly into the Black Sea; in Brunt's words, 'that it was possible for a people to be not far from both Bactria and the Black Sea'.[44]

The confusion in these writers may be a little easier to understand if we try to envisage the world view held by the contemporaries of Alexander. The best known map surviving from antiquity is the *Tabula Peutingeriana*,[45] which, after allowance is made for its flattened and elongated shape and its function as an itinerary rather than a map in the strict sense, does seem to represent a view of the world similar to that which can be deduced from Eratosthenes.[46] In this map, a continuous west–east line is formed by the Taurus, Caucasus, Paropamisus and Himalayas. The Caspian Sea is a gulf of Ocean and the Caspian Gates lie due south of the Caspian Sea and just south of the mountain range. The *Tabula* does not actually mark the

Caspian Gates though it does have a region Caspiane in approximately the right place. (Curiously, this region is also the source of the Ganges on the map.) Far to the east, and north of the mountains, two altars are marked on the *Tabula usque quo Alexander* ('thus far Alexander') and *hic Alexander responsum accepit* ('here Alexander received the [oracular] response').

On a map of this kind, though Alexander's journeys take him both south and north of the mountains, he is constantly going in a general easterly direction. The *Tabula Peutingeriana* is a broadly scientific work, and it does not contain any monstrous peoples or races. Furthermore, its rectangular shape, though corresponding to the maps of Eratosthenes and Ptolemy, is a divergence from the maps of the period preceding Alexander which, like that of Hecataeus, were circular in shape. Unfortunately no such map survives, but their layout can be deduced from a much later map, the thirteenth-century *Mappa Mundi* in Hereford Cathedral.

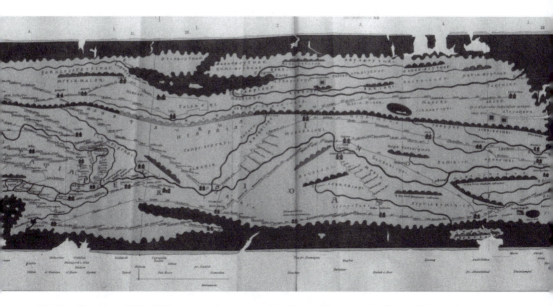

18 The Peutinger Table. This section depicts the Far East, with the twin altars of Alexander visible.

This is the most elaborate of a number of medieval maps based on the T/O format, in which the land enclosed by the circle of the surrounding Ocean is broken up by a T-shaped body of sea representing the Mediterranean, Black and Red Seas, which divide the world into Europe, Asia and Africa. Other such maps include the Psalter Map and the Ebstorf Map (destroyed by fire during the Second World War II).[47] (See colour plates 3 and 4.)

This family of maps, though they contain medieval material, is certainly based on a map commissioned by Julius Caesar, the detail of which seems then to have been used to illustrate the world history of the fifth-century writer Orosius. The tripartite division of the world goes back to Herodotus and Hecataeus, and was transmitted to the medieval world by Orosius and Isidore of Seville.[48]

In this map Jerusalem lies at the centre, the Earthly Paradise at the top, on an island in the encircling Ocean, under an illustration of Christ in majesty. North is to the left. The Mediterranean divides at the east into three prongs, the eastern Mediterranean to the right, the Propontis (north of Troy) in the centre and the Black Sea to the left. Directly above the Black Sea (i.e. to the east) are the Caspian Gates, and just to the right Noah's Ark,

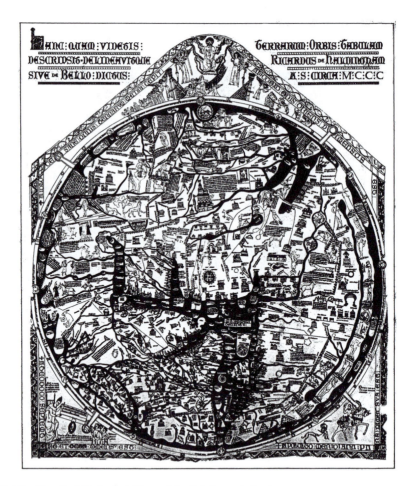

19 The Hereford Cathedral *Mappa Mundi* (schematic key).

resting on Mount Ararat. To the left of the Black Sea are griffins, cannibals, a minotaur and some dog-headed people; the island of Terraconta, inhabited by the Unclean Nations of Gog and Magog, is indicated above the dog-heads; just above Noah's Ark is a manticore. Above him the River Oxus (Amu Darya) flows into the Caspian Sea, which is an arm of the encircling Ocean. In the upper section of the map a Sciapod may be seen, and to the right of him the Ganges flows east (up), while four rivers flow out of the island of the terrestrial Paradise, below which is India, containing crocodiles, parrots and three altars of Alexander as well as the city of Bucephala. The Hereford Cathedral booklet on the map, by Meryl Jancey, remarks that 'the form of the map has caused much constriction here, so that the peoples of the far north are confusingly close to those of western and central Asia'.

To someone with a world view like this, a passage through the Caspian Gates would indeed bring Alexander beyond the known world directly into the world of fable. It could lead simultaneously to the north (the Caspian Gates corresponding to the Dariel Pass) and to the east (the Caucasus corresponding to the Hindu Kush). One could make an easy circuit through the land of fabulous beasts and, proceeding through India, find oneself at the Earthly Paradise. (We shall return to Alexander's visit to Paradise in Chapter 8, and to his encounter with the Unclean Nations in Chapter 9.)

A detailed verbal account corresponding to this portion of the map is given by Isidore of Seville (AD 602–36), *Etymologiae* 14.3.1–5:

Asia is so called from the name of a certain woman who in antiquity held the empire of the east. It is located in the third part of the world, with the sunrise on its east, the Ocean on its south, our western sea on its west, on the north the Maeotian Lake [Sea of Azov] and the River Tanais [Don]. It has moreover many provinces and regions, the names of which I shall briefly run through, beginning from Paradise. [Paradise is described in detail. Next comes India.] India is named after the River Indus, which bounds it on its western side. It extends from the southern sea as far as the rising of the sun, and on the north as far as Mt Caucasus; it contains many peoples and cities, and also the island of Taprobane [Sri Lanka], full of gems and elephants, Chrysa and Argyre which abound in gold and silver, and also Tile where the trees grow that never shed their leaves. It also has the rivers Ganges, Indus and Hypanis which bathe the Indians. The land of India, healthy with the breath of Favonius (zephyr), bears crops twice a year; instead of winter it has Etesian winds. It gives birth to men of dark colour, large elephants, the beast Monoceros, the bird Parrot, ebony wood, and cinnamon and pepper and the aromatic reed. It produces ivory and precious stones: beryl, chrysoprase and diamond, carbuncle, lychnite, pearls [of two kinds], for which noble women burn with desire. There are mountains of gold which it is impossible to approach because of dragons, gryphons and men of monstrous size.

Isidore's brief account of India was the basis for medieval knowledge. (It has been said that if Augustine had had his way, classical literature would have been obliterated, and all that subsequent generations would have known of antiquity is what Isidore saw fit to include in his book.) It can clearly be seen that it summarises the natural history of Ctesias and the later writers, and the geography that I have outlined. Isidore provides the armature on which Alexander's legends entered the Middle Ages.

The monstrous races were a particular problem for medieval writers. Should they be characterised as humans, and if not, what did that imply about God's plan for his creation?[49] Augustine (*City of God* 16.8–9) was worried by the legends of the existence of monstrous races which had been established by his time through the accounts of Mela, Pliny and Solinus. He was sceptical about the human nature of such creatures. 'What am I to say of the Cynocephali, whose dog's head and actual barking prove them to be animals rather than men?' Yet he acknowledges that such races may exist, just as monstrous births occur to certain human individuals. The problem is, 'if such peoples exist, then either they are not human; or, if human, they are descended from Adam', and thus capable of salvation. But some writers assert that such creatures live in fact in the Antipodes (literally, 'opposite our feet') and are thus technically speaking outside our world. Are they, or are they not, part of God's plan and capable of salvation?

The dispute rumbled on for centuries, and the map-makers followed different traditions. In the eighth century, St Boniface engaged in a long and bitter controversy with the cosmographer Aethicus Ister over the latter's belief that the monstrous races in the Antipodes were entirely separate from our world.[50] Aethicus is the pseudonym of an Irish cleric, Virgil (i.e. Fergal) of Salzburg, who attributed his work to a pseudonym in order to deflect criticism of his heretical ideas. His cosmographical ideas led him to fall foul of Pope Zacharias, as we know from the latter's letter to St Boniface (Boniface, *Letters*, LXIV (80), p. 125): 'as to the foolish and sinful doctrine which he teaches: if it should be made clear that he believes there is below this earth another world and other men, and also a sun and moon, then summon a council, depose him from the office of priest, and cast him out of the church'. Virgil/Aethicus' heresy consisted in believing that the world is a sphere and that there were Antipodes where the monstrous races dwelt, outside our world and thus outside God's plan of salvation. The Hereford *Mappa Mundi* places the monstrous races within the world, while the Psalter Map arranges them in a series of compartments (a bit like cages) on the far right (south), i.e. in the Antipodes and outside our world.

Alexander's expedition was the most important available piece of evidence on the matter, since according to the legend he had travelled in the east and actually encountered these creatures; ergo, they must be inhabitants of our world. If that was so, it was no surprise that he should also have reached the Earthly Paradise, which was similarly shown on the medieval maps as lying in the Far East. Christopher Columbus knew of these accounts, and on the far side of the Atlantic encountered (or thought he did) many of the freaks of this part of the world,[51] which he took for a sure sign that he was approaching Paradise. But a full account of that complex of legends must be deferred until Chapter 8.

The River of Sand, the Valley of Diamonds, and the Poison Maiden

Several legends that became familiar in later times can be traced back to the stories of Alexander, though not all are fully elaborated in the *Romance*. About fifty years before the creation of the Hereford *Mappa Mundi* (c. 1300), Alberic of Trois Fontaines wrote in his *Chronicle* (c. 1232–52) that in the year 1165 a letter arrived in Christendom from 'Prester John, King of the Indians'.[52] In this letter Prester John described his kingdom, with its rivers of milk and honey and its absence of venomous reptiles; the River Physon which flowed out of Paradise, brimming with precious stones of all kinds; and 'a sandy sea without water'. 'The sand moves and swells into waves and is never still. It is not possible to navigate this sea by any means and what sort of country lies beyond it is unknown . . . . Three days' journey from this sea there are mountains from which descends a waterless river of stones, which flows through our country to the sandy sea. Three days in the week it flows and casts up stones both great and small, and carries with it also wood to the sandy sea . . . On the other four days it can be crossed.'[53]

This story derives directly from an episode in the epsilon (25.4) and gamma (II. 29–30) recensions of the *Alexander Romance* (it is not in the earlier recensions), in which the army comes to a river 'so broad that it took three days to cross it'. The men start to build a 'rampart' (apparently a dam), but

the water suddenly dried up and became sand instead. Then
Alexander. . . ordered square containers to be constructed of wooden
planks. These were placed on the river-bed, and when the first one was
in place, it was filled with stones so that it would not move. Next he
ordered his men to bring very long planks, 15 to 20 cubits long, and to
place them on the first box, stretching over to the second . . . . And so
with the third and subsequent ones, until they had bridged the river. It
took the army thirty six days to cross the river. When they had crossed
it, Alexander named it the River of Sand; it flowed three days with water
and three days with sand.

The method of dealing with the hazard shows Alexander's inventiveness to
advantage, but our concern here is with the provenance of Prester John's
remarkable river. Located in the Far East (the next stop is with the pygmies)
it may yet be connected with the Serbonian bog, which divided Syria from
Egypt, where the sand floated on the surface of the water, giving the illusion of solid ground.[54] But the fact that it appears only in the epsilon and
gamma recensions, with their heavy admixture of Jewish material, is a clue
to its origin, as is the fact that it flows for three days with water and three
days with sand. The implication is that it rests on the seventh day, and is
therefore a Jewish river. It is in fact the Sambatyon, beyond which the ten
lost tribes were exiled, and which, as R. Akiva explains, 'flows so swiftly on
weekdays that it pulls up the stones from its bed, but does not pull them up
on the Sabbath, when it rests'.[55] It was from the utopian lands bordering
the Sambatyon that the traveller Eldad, of the tribe of Dan, emerged in AD
880 with stories of the wonders of the east.[56] Setting out from Somaliland,
he was captured by cannibals but eventually reached the tribes of Dan,
Naphtali, Gad and Asher in Hamilah on the Gulf of Suez. Beyond the
river a people dwelt in glorious castles, there were no wild beasts, the sheep
gave birth twice a year and the people lived to the age of 120. They
communicated with the four tribes on the hither side of the Sambatyon by
pigeon post.

Prester John's account also includes a neighbouring river: 'Between the
sandy sea and the mountains we have mentioned is a desert. Underground
there flows a rivulet, to which there appears to be no access; and this rivulet
falls into a river of greater size, wherein men of our dominions enter, and
take therefrom a great abundance of precious stones. Beyond this river are
ten tribes of Jews, who, although they pretend to have their own kings, are
nevertheless our servants and tributaries.' In another version of the letter
(Slessarev 1959, 72f.) the arrangement is a little different. 'The Sandy Sea
originates in our country . . . Nobody can cross it, no matter how one

tries, except us, for we let ourselves be carried by the griffins, as Alexander did when he was about to conquer the enchanted castle. Not far from this sea there flows a river in which one finds many precious stones and herbs that are good for many medicines. Between us and the Jews there runs a river full of precious stones and it descends so swiftly that nobody can cross it except on Saturday when it stands still.'

The legend of Alexander and the enchanted castle, fascinating as it sounds, does not appear elsewhere; but the river of precious stones recalls another of Alexander's adventures in the *Romance* (II. 22) when the army advances into the Land of Darkness. An old man advises them to pick up stones as they go. When they return to the light, it turns out that they have collected nuggets of gold and precious pearls. The episode took on a life of its own and became combined with a different legend first told by the fourth-century writer Epiphanius, Bishop of Salamis, in his book *De gemmis* (*On Gems*):[57] he describes a gorge in the mountains of 'Great Scythia' which is so deep and dark that one cannot see to the bottom; but the local people 'slaughter lambs, flay them and cast the carcasses into the depths. The gems adhere to the flesh and, so they say, the eagles which nest in the crags, uneasy because of the hunger of their fledglings, scent the odour of the carcass, descend into the blind darkness of the abysses and bring up the carcasses of the lambs onto the summits of the mountains. As the eagles devour the carcasses of the lambs the gems are left behind and men come to collect them' (see colour plate 5).

The story is first associated with Alexander by Qazvini. The valley is now in India,

> the bottom of which the sight reacheth not; and in it are venomous serpents which no one seeth but he dieth;[58] . . . Al-Iskandar commanded to take some mirrors and to throw them into the valley, that the serpents might see in them their forms, and die in consequence. It is also said that he watched for the time of their absenting themselves, and threw down pieces of meat, and diamonds stuck to these: then the birds came from the sky, and took pieces of that meat, and brought them up out of the valley; whereupon al-Iskandar ordered his companions to follow the birds, and to pick up what they easily could of the meat.[59]

The story is familiar from the Second Voyage of Sindbad the Sailor, and is repeated in the *Travels of Marco Polo* III. xix. Both Epiphanius and Sir John Mandeville (*Travels*, ch. 30) attribute various magical properties to these stones. For Epiphanius, they protect from the burning of fire and also during childbirth; for Mandeville, they protect him in war and against witchcraft and wild beasts, and heal the insane.

The serpents that can kill with a glance, and can only be defeated, like the Medusa, by the sight of their own countenance, are also creatures with a long antecedent history. *The locus classicus* is Pliny's *Natural History* 8.33.78, followed almost verbatim by Solinus 27.50, and summarised by Isidore 12.4.6–7. Pliny's basilisk lives in Cyrenaica and 'does not move its body forward in manifold coils like the other snakes but advances with its middle raised high. It kills bushes not only by its touch but by its breath, scorches up grass and bursts rocks . . . . Yet to a creature so marvellous as this . . . the venom of weasels is fatal.' This sounds like a confused reminiscence of the spitting cobra and of its vulnerability to the mongoose: so we are back in India. It was said that Aristotle had devised the trick of killing the basilisk by placing a mirror in front of it (and of course he taught it to Alexander: the story is in the *Book of Stones* of Pseudo-Aristotle, ch. 6). The *Gesta Romanorum* (139) tells how Alexander's army was besieging a city and the men were being killed without any visible wound. He consulted his philosophers, and they explained that a basilisk was perched on the walls of the city, killing his men. The remedy was to place a mirror between the army and the wall, 'and no sooner shall the basilisk behold it, than his own look, reflected in the mirror, will return upon himself, and kill him'. Alexander, according to Roger Bacon, also once catapulted a basilisk into a besieged city to infect its population.[60]

Even more dangerous might be the poison-maidens of India. These can kill with a look, or even a breath, and a kiss might be instantly fatal. A story in an ancient Indian collection, the *Katha Sarit Sagara* ('The Ocean of Story') by Somadeva, about a minister of King Brahmadatta named Yogakarandaka, is one of the earliest references to these secret weapons: 'He tainted, by means of poison and other deleterious substances, the trees, flowering creepers, water and grass all along the line of march. And he sent poison-damsels as dancing-girls among the enemy's host, and he also dispatched nocturnal assassins into their midst.'[61] Another example is the practical advice of Kautilya in his manual of statecraft, the *Arthashastra* (*c.* AD 100–150; 436): 'if the enemy king is avaricious or fond of women, secret agents shall tempt him using rich widows . . . or young beautiful women . . . When he falls into the trap [of making an assignation at night] the agents shall kill him with weapons or poison.' In the seventh century AD a play by Visakhadatta about King Chandragupta described how he was saved from a poison-damsel sent by his enemy Rakshasa by the advice of a clever minister. Chandragupta was king of eastern India at the time of

Alexander's invasion, and benefited from the havoc he created to establish the Maurya Empire shortly afterwards, in 313 BC.

Now it is well known that Sanskrit literature is unique among old world literatures in having no legends or narratives about Alexander.[62] But the classical sources hint at a familiarity of Chandragupta and Alexander with each other: Diodorus tells us that one Phegeus gave him information about the Kingdom on the Ganges, 'whose king was Xandrames' (DS 17.93.2), and Plutarch (*Life of Alexander* 62.9) tells us that 'Androcottus, when he was a stripling, saw Alexander himself'. So, though no actual contact can be shown between the two kings (wouldn't it be nice if the king who sent the poison-damsel to Chandragupta was Alexander?),[63] the stage was set for a connection between Alexander and poison-damsels.

Aristotle warns his pupil most seriously against these secret weapons of the Queen of India in a spurious work that was highly influential in the Middle Ages, the *Secret of Secrets (Secretum secretorum)*.[64] It took the form of a long letter which was supposed to have been written by Aristotle to Alexander to advise him on the duties of a ruler. In fact it was originally written in Arabic around the year 800 by Yahya ibn Batriq, though the latter claimed to have translated it from a Syriac translation of a Greek original. Parts were translated into Latin in the twelfth century, but the first complete translation into Latin appeared in 1232. Its influence on other works soon became apparent. The story of the poison-maiden, which is in chapter 25 of the *SS,* is told again in the *Gesta Romanorum*. Originally written in the thirteenth century, this became one of the most popular story-books of the Middle Ages. It circulated in numerous variant manuscripts and was first printed at Utrecht in 1473. In chapter 11 we read:

> The Queen of the North nourished her daughter from the cradle upon a certain kind of deadly poison; and when she grew up, she was considered so beautiful, that the sight of her alone affected many with madness. The queen sent her to Alexander to espouse. He had no sooner beheld her, than he became violently enamoured, and with much eagerness desired to possess her; but Aristotle, observing his weakness, said 'Do not touch her, for if you do you will certainly perish. She has been nurtured on the most deleterious food, which I will prove to you immediately. Here is a malefactor, who is already condemned to death. He shall be united to her, and you will soon see the truth of what I advance.' Accordingly the culprit was brought without delay to the girl; and scarcely had he touched her lips, before his whole frame was impregnated with poison, and he expired.[65]

Though this story mostly appears as a free-standing anecdote, it did get inserted into some of the continuous narratives of Alexander's adventures, notably the *Alexanders Geesten* (1256–1260) of Jacob van Maerlant, where it comes soon after his defeat of Nicolaus of Acarnania in the chariot race when he is still an adolescent. It also appears in the popular *Iskandarnameh* of the fourteenth century, where 'the son of the emperor of China contrived a plan to poison Alexander through his concubine, and how the king discovered that by sagacity'.[66]

Once again, in the *Gesta Romanorum* we see the confusion between India and the remote north. Though the legend arises later than Alexander (and if it had been known in Hellenistic times it would certainly have made an appearance in Nicander's *Alexipharmaka*), it seems to have started off in Herodotus' Scythia. The historian tells (4.9) how Heracles was returning from his theft of the cattle of Geryon near Cadiz, and arrived in Scythia (south Russia). As he slept, his mares vanished. 'On waking, he went in quest of them, and after wandering over the whole country came at last to the district called "the Woodland", where he found in a cave a strange being, between a maiden and a serpent, whose form from the waist upwards was like that of a woman, while all below was like a snake.' In order to get his mares back, Heracles agreed to make the girl his mistress, and she gave birth to three sons, one of whom, Scythes, became the ancestor of the kings of Scythia. Though Heracles suffered no ill-effects from the liaison, and the girl is not said to be poisonous like a snake though she has the lower body of one, the germ of the Indian idea may be transmitted here by Herodotus in a garbled form. Megasthenes' story (Arrian, *Indica* ix) that Heracles had many sons but only one daughter, Pandaia, with whom he had incestuous intercourse and from whom all the kings of India are descended, might also contain an echo of the legend: but one would expect that Megasthenes, who never missed a fabulous tale if he encountered one, would have told of the poison-maidens if he had known about them.

Alexander's Nineteenth-Century Descendants

India was for the Greeks a land of wonders and enchantment, and the things that Alexander did there became the basis of the wonder tales of subsequent ages. We have not said farewell to India, the background for most of the further adventures we shall trace in this book. But enough has been said to set the scene. His further adventures in India – the encounter with the Brahmans, the search for the Water of Life and for Paradise – take us to the heart of the Alexander story. But if Alexander made no impact on Sanskrit literature, his name continued to reverberate down the centuries in the legends of Afghanistan and of the Hindu Kush. When Marco Polo visited the city of Balkh (ancient Bactra), his hosts still spoke of the marriage that had taken place there between Alexander the Great and Roxane.[67] The kings of Bactria down to the nineteenth century claimed descent from Alexander, and the Mir of Nagir, Shah Sikander Khan, minted coins on which his profile bore a striking resemblance to that of his putative ancestor.[68] Even the horses of Badakhshan were, Marco Polo was told, descended in a direct line from Bucephalus: but 'this breed was entirely in the possession of one of the king's uncles, who, because he refused to let the king have any, was put to death by him. Thereupon his wife, to avenge her husband's death, destroyed the whole breed, and so it became extinct' (*Travels*, transl. R. Latham 1958, 77).

Alexander 'Bokhara' Burnes, travelling in the region in the 1830s, found the legend still alive nearly six hundred years after Marco Polo.[69]

From [the Tajiks] I heard a variety of particulars regarding the reputed descendants of Alexander the Great, who are yet said to exist in this neighbourhood, and the valley of the Oxus, as well as the countries near the head of the Indus . . . . A tea merchant of our small caravan had amused me on the road from Khooloom, with the received lineage of these Macedonians. He was a priest, and believed Alexander the Great to be a prophet, which, in his eyes, satisfactorily accounted for the uninterrupted progeny of Greeks, since no human being could injure so holy a race. [And later] Marco Polo . . . informs us that the Meer of Badakhshan laid claim to a Grecian origin. The emperor Baber corroborates the testimony. Elphinstone . . . confirms the statements of Marco Polo, by the information that the chief of Durnaz, in the valley of the Oxus, claimed a descent from Alexander, which was admitted by all his neighbours.

A generation later the traveller Eugene Schuyler unearthed some more curious lore.[70] A legend in Bukhara told:

That once the site of that city was a marsh overflowed by the River Zarafshan. Alexander, wishing to drain it, went to the source of the river, and shut it up with a golden dam, thus forming the lake called after him, and making the valley habitable. The water, however, rubs off particles of gold . . . . This golden dam, the Bukharans say, is inaccessible, for it is guarded by a race of centaurs; water-spirits also entice into the lake and drown all who come to it.

Schuyler also repeated the information that the local princes claimed descent from Alexander, and added that a building in Marghilan was reputed to be the tomb of the conqueror.[71]

So it was no idle fantasy on Rudyard Kipling's part when, in his resonant story, 'The Man who would be King', two adventurers set out to gain power in a small kingdom of the north-west frontier on the pretext that one of them is a reincarnation of Alexander the Great. The real 'man who would be king', whose antics may have been known to Kipling, Josiah Harlan of Pennsylvania,[72] certainly modelled himself on the great conqueror in order to gain credence among the mistrustful local rulers of nineteenth-century Afghanistan, and declared himself Prince of Ghor, the heir to Alexander, in 1838. One at least of those rulers, Dost Mohammed Khan, was quite familiar with his history: 'Your appearance in the midst of my camp at this moment of general excitement may be attended by personal danger. When Secunder visited this country, he sent a confidential agent to the Prince hereabout, and the mountaineers murdered Secunder's ambassador.'[73]

Thus a legend lived on in oral tradition in Afghanistan perhaps longer than in any other part of the world except Greece, where it has never died.

HOW MUCH LAND DOES A MAN NEED?

Alexander's Encounter with the Brahmans (326 BC)

The Indian sophists were found by Alexander in the open in a meadow, where they used to have their disputations; when they saw Alexander and his army, they did nothing more than beat with their feet on the ground they stood on. When Alexander enquired through interpreters what their action meant, they replied: 'King Alexander, each man possesses no more of this earth than the patch we stand on; yet you, though a man like other men, are roaming over so wide an area away from what is your own, giving no rest to yourself or others. And very soon you too will die, and will possess no more of the earth than suffices for the burial of your body.'

Arrian, *Anabasis* 7.1.5–6[1]

Alexander said to them all, 'Ask for whatever you want and I will give it to you.' At once they all burst out, 'Give us immortality.' But Alexander replied, 'That is a power I do not have. I too am a mortal.' Then they asked him, 'Since you are a mortal, why do you make so many wars? When you have seized everything, where will you take it? Surely you will only have to leave it behind for others?'

Alexander Romance III. 6

'Ye make wars and battles, and war outwardly against men, because ye have not overcome the enemy within; but we Brachmans have overcome the inward battles in our members, and rest secure, and have no battles outwardly; we behold the firmament of heaven, her birds singing; we be healed and fed with leaves and fruits of trees; we drink water, and sing songs in worship of God, and take heed, and think of the life coming.'

The Lives of the Upright Heathens Briefly Noted (1683)

Alexander's encounter with the naked philosophers of Taxila is the moral heart of the *Romance*.[2] Like an early Allegro and Penseroso, it poses the contrast between the insatiable conqueror and the quietist ascetic who is contented with no more than is necessary to preserve life. Versions of the conversation with the 'king' of the philosophers, Dandamis or Dindimus, and other forms of the interview, were already literary set pieces by the time the *Romance* was written, and their afterlife was unusually rich, being actively rewritten up until the seventeenth century (see epigraph to this chapter), while what purported to be a Tibetan translation of a related work by Dandamis was discovered by a Chinese scholar some time before 1750 and published in English by Robert Dodsley in 1750.[3] Like most of the legends of Alexander, it has its starting point in a historical moment.

20 Alexander meets Dandamis, the 'king' of the Brahmans. From John Hartlieb's *Alexander*. Bayerische Staatsbibliothek, Munich, Cgm 581, f. 98r.

In spring 326 BC Alexander and his army arrived in Taxila in the Punjab. He and his entourage were fascinated by the 'naked philosophers': Aristobulus (as reported by Strabo 15.1.61) 'says that he saw two of the sophists at Taxila, both Brachmanes; and that the elder had his head shaved but that the younger had long hair, and that both were followed by disciples'. These characters carried out feats of self-discipline such as standing on one leg while holding a heavy log, for several hours, or lying naked on sharp stones – or simply remaining in the sun for hours when everyone else found the ground too hot to place their feet on. Alexander sent one of his staff writers, Onesicritus, to converse with the philosophers. Onesicritus had some difficulty in conducting a conversation since he had to use a series of three interpreters, after which, as he said, to establish their doctrines was like expecting water to flow pure through mud.[4] It is thus perhaps not surprising that much of what he recounts of the philosophers' teaching bears a remarkable resemblance to the ideas of the Greek Cynic philosophers, of whose teachings he is known to have been an adherent.[5] The spokesman of the philosophers, Mandanis, praised the Greeks for their intellectual interests, and Alexander in particular for taking the time to interview philosophers, but he reprehended their preference for custom over nature. Nevertheless he added the interesting information that 'he who suspects disease in his own body commits suicide by means of fire, piling a funeral pyre; and that he anoints himself, sits down on the pyre, orders it to be lighted, and burns without a motion' (Strabo 15.1.65). One of the philosophers, Calanus, in fact joined Alexander's entourage (which put him in bad odour with his fellow ascetics) and later did exactly the same in Persia.[6]

Arrian refers to these men as '(naked) philosophers', and Strabo characterises them as Brahmans: both he and his source Megasthenes had some understanding of the caste system of India and of the fact that the Brahmans were the highest caste and acted as advisers to kings, while the Garmanes (Sramanas, ascetics) lived in the forests and were known in Greek as Hylobioi (forest-dwellers). Confusion began to creep in because Arrian also uses the name Brahmans to describe a people of the Lower Indus whose last stronghold against Alexander was Harmatelia, perhaps ancient Brahmanabad.[7] Pliny too (NH 6.21.64) thought that 'Bragmanae' was the name of several Indian tribes. The author of the Alexander Romance writes (III. 4) that, following the conquest of Porus, 'He took all the treasure from the royal palace, and marched on the Brahmans, or Oxydorkai. These were not for the most part warriors, but philosophers who lived in huts and caves.' Oxydorkai (or Oxydrakai) is the Greek form of Khshudrakas, a warrior people of the Indus region who are mentioned in the Mahabharata along with the Malavas (the Malloi, in attacking whose town Alexander was severely wounded). So the naked philosophers become a people in their own right, known as the Brahmans, and the stage is set for a pregnant encounter.

Alexander's visit to the philosophers in the Romance falls into two parts. In the first, the king puts a series of questions to the philosophers. Starting, rather oddly, with the question, 'Do you have no graves?' (answer, the ground we lie on), he proceeds to some familiar conundrums of a type loved by Greek philosophers: 'Who are greater in number, the living or the dead? Which is greater, the earth or the sea? Which came first, day or night? Which is better, the right or the left?' There is more bite in two of the questions: 'Which is the wickedest of all creatures ? – Man. Why? – Learn from yourself the answer to that. You are a wild beast, and see how many other wild beasts you have with you, to help you tear away the lives of other beasts.' And 'What is kingship? – Unjust power used to the disadvantage of others; insolence supported by opportunity; a golden burden.'

A version of this dialogue was circulating by 100 BC at the latest, when it appears on a papyrus now in Berlin (*Pap. Berol.* 13044). In this text the questions are slightly different, though several are the same. They include: 'What is the most cunning of living creatures? – That which no man has yet discovered.' 'What should a man do in order to become a god? – By doing what it is impossible for a man to do.' 'How long is it good for a man to live? – As long as he does not regard death as better than life.' Again, some of the questions seem to bear on Alexander's own situation, but the striking point about this text is that it takes the form of what the folklorists call a *Halsrätsel*, a riddle where the answerer's life depends on getting it right.[8] 'Whoever I command to judge, he shall be your moderator; if I decide that he has judged well, he alone shall be let off alive.' When the questions are complete, Alexander asks the last speaker which one has given the worst answer. 'The Indian did not want anyone to perish as a result of his answer, so he replied that each had answered worse than the other. "Well then", said Alexander, "you shall all die, and you first of all because it was your judgment".' But this interlocutor argues (part of his reply is lost) that it is unjust for the king to kill them, and so he spares their lives.

Plutarch included a version of this dialogue in his *Life* (64–5) of Alexander, with slightly different questions again, but a better structured dénouement: when Alexander announces that he is going to kill them all, the philosopher replies, 'That cannot be, O king, unless you falsely said that you would put to death first him who answered worst.'[9] The quibbling answer is a form of the Liar Paradox, and such paradoxes were popular with Cynic philosophers and with their close congeners, the Megarians. They had the effect, which the Cynics liked, of annoying people; but sometimes the Cynics themselves condemned the Megarians for time-wasting in frigid paradoxes.[10]

Does the dialogue have anything to do with Indian philosophy? When I wrote about this passage in 1995 I thought probably not. I argued that the questions are of the kind that interested Greek thinkers, and that the episode 'tells us nothing new about Greek knowledge of India'. I am no longer so sure. Some of the arguments for Indian influence on Onesicritus' account of the meeting have not changed, not least the fact that the dialogue form is also popular in Indian philosophy. A notable example is *The Questions of King Milinda*, a Buddhist text put into the mouth of the Greek king Menander.[11] The idea that a sage who answers incorrectly will be punished appears in *Milindapanha* 2.1.3, though the actual questions and answers in *Milindapanha* are ethical and discursive, rather than riddles.

21   King Menander. Two coin portraits. Author's collection.

However, one may not need to think of Onesicritus wasting his and his interpreters' time putting irritating riddles and paradoxes to the philosophers of Taxila. It is much more likely that he laid hands on some text of Indian thought and worked it up as the philosophical content of his narrative of the encounter. A model is recognisably to hand in the Indian national epic, the *Mahabharata*. (The present form of this text is of course much later than the *Alexander Romance*, but its content surely goes back a long way.) In Book III, 'The Forest', 311–15, 'The Drilling Sticks',[12] Yudhisthira, parched with thirst, watches his brothers Nakula, Sahadeva, Arjuna and Bhima die from drinking the water of a beautiful spring. Approaching carefully, he hears the voice of a *yaksha* (demi-god) who forbids him to drink before answering a series of questions, more than a hundred in all. They range from 'What makes the sun rise?' (Brahma), 'What is weightier than the earth?' (mother), and 'What sleeps with its eyes open?' (a fish), to 'What is man's highest duty?' (to refrain from impurity) and 'Abandoning what does one become friendly, abandoning what does one not give, abandoning what does one become rich, abandoning what does one become happy?' (Pride, anger, desire, greed).

In an extraordinary literary development, the presentation of this episode about Yudhisthira in Jean-Claude Carrière's *Mahabharata* (completed in 1984: *Mahabharata* 1987), which is the basis of Peter Brook's epic theatrical version, includes, among some of the hundred questions from the original, several of those from the *Alexander Romance* which were quoted above.

Clearly the author has felt the affinity between the two texts, and it seems likely that Onesicritus, on discovering some important Vedic text of this kind, recognised its susceptibility to the sort of questions he was familiar with from discussions at home, and created a composite.

Questions of this kind also formed the staple of the Pythagorean *akousmata* or sayings attributed to Pythagoras (who wished to visit India but never got there). Mostly much later in date than the sixth-century philosopher, they include a category of questions in the form 'What is the most just?' (to sacrifice), 'What is the wisest?' (number), 'What is the loveliest?' (harmony), 'What is the most truly said?' (human beings are bad).[13]

There is a continuum here, of philosophers with an ascetic and contemplative bent, from Brahmans to Cynics to Pythagoreans, which permits this kind of material to move freely from one group's set of precepts to another. All these groups devote themselves to a life of simplicity with the minimum of ties to the earth and society, as a way of approaching to the divine. In Greek terms, the Brahmans are undoubtedly Cynics of a kind,[14] for Cynics cut themselves off from society and convention to live a life 'according to nature', like dogs (*kynes*). The interview has features in common with the famous encounter of Alexander and Diogenes when the king, impressed by the philosopher, offers him a gift, and Diogenes asks him to 'stand out of the sunshine'.[15] The interview of a king with a philosopher – as one might say, 'a dog may look at a king' – became a popular vehicle for later Cynic writers including Dio Chrysostom (*Or.* 2 and 4), Maximus of Tyre (*Or.* 29) and Musonius Rufus (8):[16] the contrast is between the world ruler (*kosmokrator*) and the 'citizen of the world' (*kosmopolites*), which was how the original Cynic, Diogenes, characterised himself.

The main themes of the first part of the encounter are repeated in some later writers who describe the Brahmans' quietist existence. The historian of philosophy Diogenes Laertius (third century AD: 9.35) tells us that Democritus was supposed to have visited the Brahmans. As one of his authorities, Antisthenes, was closely associated with Cynicism, it is likely that this tale, like that about Alexander, originated in Cynic circles. Much later, Philostratus (second/third century AD), in his *Life of Apollonius of Tyana*, tells how his hero visited the Brahmans in India:[17] 'I beheld men dwelling upon the earth, and yet not on it. I beheld them fortified without fortifications, I beheld them possessed of nothing, and yet possessed of all things.' He defends the Brahmans against the dismissive attitude of the naked philosophers of Egypt, whom he is visiting at the time, arguing that the Indian philosophers are the true ones. But it was the African location that remained fixed in fiction, for the gymnosophists are discovered again, in Ethiopia according to Heliodorus' *Aethiopica*,[18] where they function as advisers to the king.

There is much more substance in the second part of the encounter, when Dandamis briefly describes the ascetic, fruitarian way of life of the philosophers. 'Our possessions are the earth, the fruit trees, the daylight, the sun, the moon, the chorus of the stars, and water.' The philosophers also describe how 'at every new moon each goes to mate with his wife, until she has borne two children'. Alexander is clearly impressed and offers to give them whatever they want, which leads to their surprising demand for immortality. This, it appears, is simply a ruse to make the point that, if Alexander is not immortal, there is no point in his accumulating all this treasure through conquest. Informed that he will, in the end, have to leave it all behind, Alexander utters what seems to be a credo on mutability:

> It is ordained by Providence above that we shall all be slaves and servants of the divine will. The sea does not move unless the wind blows it, and the trees do not tremble unless the breezes disturb them; and likewise Man does nothing except by the motions of divine Providence. For my part I would like to stop making war, but the master of my soul does not allow me. If we were all of like mind, the world would be devoid of activity: the sea would not be filled, the land would not be farmed, marriages would not be consummated, there would be no begetting of children. How many have become miserable and lost all their possessions as a result of my wars? But others have profited from the property of others. Everyone takes from everyone, and leaves what he has taken to others: no possession is permanent. (*AR* III. 6)

This remarkable passage, in which for a moment it looks as if Alexander would like to become a pupil of the philosophers, provided the starting-point for the most extensive development of the episode, in a work known as *The Life of the Brahmans*.

The Life of the Brahmans and Utopian Tradition

This is a work with a complicated textual history. The first version is partially preserved on a papyrus of the mid-second century AD,[19] in which it forms one of a collection of Cynic diatribes, a form with some similarities to the Christian sermon.[20] It was however taken up and rewritten, with a new introductory section, in the fifth century AD. In this form it is ascribed to Palladius, the Bishop of Helenopolis (who died in AD 341 and was the author of the *Lausiac History*, about monasticism), and this attribution may be correct. It is a Christian protreptic designed to recommend the monastic life; but Palladius (if he is the author) states that the second, major part of the work is by Arrian. This is not impossible, and if so the papyrus would be almost contemporary with its composition. Arrian was an adherent of Stoicism, and his historical principles seem averse to such rhetorical elaborations; but he does at one point in the *Indica* promise a detailed account of the Brahmans, which is not otherwise preserved. It may be that the rhetorical work is an early work, written, like Tacitus' *Dialogus,* before the historian's craft was fully formed. However that may be, the form in which the work became known to later ages was that of Palladius.

Palladius' *On the Life of the Brahmans* is preserved in two Greek recensions and three Latin translations, one of which is falsely ascribed to St Ambrose.[21] Part I is addressed to an unnamed person and describes how 'I have learnt what I know about the Brahmans from a certain Theban scholar, who made the journey of his own free will, but against his will was taken into captivity . . . . He sailed with an older man first to Adule and then to Axum, where the petty king of the Indians had his seat.[22] He spent some time there and became well acquainted with the king; then he wanted to go to the island of Taprobane [Sri Lanka] where the so-called Long-livers dwell.' There he was arrested, put on trial, then held for six years and put to work in a bakery. He describes the long-livers' naturist way of life. 'Their men live on the far side of the Ganges in the quarter towards Ocean . . . . Their women however live on this side of the Ganges. The men cross over to the women in the months of July and August, which are the cold months among them. After forty days' intercourse with the women they cross back again . . . . The river is supposed to be very hard to cross, because of the so-called Odontotyrannus' (Pall. I. 4 and 13).

After this introduction the author goes on to reproduce what purports to be the work of Arrian. Already this preamble introduces a number of significant features. Not only do the people of Taprobane live to the age of 150, but the Brahmans' own polity exhibits several features characteristic of Hellenistic utopias.[23] Their character as utopians must derive from Onesicritus' association of them with Musicanus, whose land in his description is a political utopia with natural abundance, longevity and good health, and no slavery.[24] Longevity is a common feature of the peoples of the east, starting with the Macrobioi, the 'long-lived Ethiopians' of Libya in Herodotus 3.17. They reappear in the same general area in Pomponius Pomponius Mela (3.9.85) and Pliny (*NH* 6. 35.190), while Pliny also refers (*NH* 7.2.30) to the people of Taprobane as being exceptionally long-lived. The sixth-century AD author Theophanes (Photius 26b) refers to the 'Ethiopians; formerly called the Makrobioi, they are now known as

Homeritai'. (This splendidly positions the Ethiopian long-livers in Yemen – the Homeritai are the Himyarites.) Long life is also one of the fundamental characteristics of the peoples of more fully developed utopias, such as that of Iambulus (Diodorus Siculus 2. 55–60). Iambulus' account of the Island of the Sun, probably written in the third century BC, takes the form of a traveller's tale.[25] It is located in the Indian Ocean and is probably to be identified with Taprobane.[26] Iambulus discovers the island as a result of being set adrift in a boat after a period of captivity in Ethiopia. The people of the island live to an advanced age (150 years) and wives and children are held in common as a means of achieving harmony. They have many remarkable characteristics, being tall with hairless bodies and forked tongues. The days are all of equal length and fruit is in season all year round, in such abundance that there is no need for agriculture. If any of them becomes infirm by reason of disease or old age, he takes his own life by lying down upon a certain plant, and drifts peacefully away.

Similar tales were told of the legendary Hyperboreans, the people who live beyond the North Wind, famous in Greek literature from the earliest times. Much of their lore was collected by the Hellenistic writer Hecataeus of Abdera. Pliny (*NH* 4.12.89–91) and Pomponius Mela (3.30) mention their habit of concluding their happy lives with suicide. When Pliny (*NH* 6.20. 55) mentions the Attacorae as a people resembling the Hyperboreans, he is unwittingly talking about the same thing: for the Attacorae are certainly the inhabitants of the land the Indians called Uttarakuru, which means 'beyond the north wind'.[27] It was a land of milk and honey, a paradise of the north, also known to Megasthenes (F 27b, 29).

All these features fit well for a Land of Cockaigne, in which there is always plenty, no need of hard labour, and suffering is eliminated. To use Winston's (1976) distinction, we are concerned with a new natural order, not a new social order.[28] It is easy to parody, as Lucian's example in *True History* shows.[29] This is an account of a voyage to the moon, where the people eat roast frogs and make cheese from their own milky sweat (I. 24); the narrator later visits the fantastic Island of the Blest, where the vines bear fruit every month and the apples even more often, while corn puts forth not grain but finished loaves, saving the trouble of baking (II. 13).

Other utopias have a more political element, like that of Theopompus' City of Pious on the continent that surrounds the outer Ocean. Its inhabitants live twice as long as we do, they 'obtain the fruits of the earth without the plough and oxen, and they have no need to farm and cultivate. They remain healthy and free of disease . . . . They are indisputably just, so that even the gods frequently deign to visit them.'[30] Nearby are the Meropes, through whose land run two rivers, Grief and Pleasure. By each grows a large plane tree, and the fruit of the Tree of Pleasure causes a man to be rejuvenated: his life goes into reverse and he 'becomes a child and then an infant, after which he dies'.

Theopompus, like his contemporary Onesicritus, may have been an adherent of the Cynic philosophy,[31] and writings such as these demonstrate the interest of Cynics in imagining a better social order, one closer to 'nature'. In fact, Crates playfully described the city of 'Knapsack', the object in which he carried around his own personal utopia of peace and plenty.[32]

Euhemerus (fl. 311–298 BC) wrote about the land of Panchaia (Eusebius, *Praepáratio Evangelica* 2.2.29), which he reached by travelling southwards from Yemen towards Ocean. Again, Taprobane seems to be more or less in the right place. The land is a rural paradise like Homer's Phaeacia, with the usual abundance of fruits as well as mineral wealth. But, interestingly, society is also divided into three castes: priests and magistrates, farmers and soldiers. The caste system of India was known from the writings of Megasthenes and the characteristics of the sun-drenched Paradise are associated with India. Like Iambulus', Euhemerus' utopia is associated with a City of the Sun (Pliny, *NH* 10.2), and the sacred river is called the Water of the Sun. Private property is abolished, but our source makes no mention of community of women (such as Plato had commended in the *Republic*) or any other sexual arrangement.

Euhemerus' narrator undertakes his journey at the instance of Cassander, the king of Macedon; and as a matter of historical fact Cassander's younger brother, Alexarchus, established a communist utopia at the city of Ouranoupolis on the Athos peninsula (Athenaeus III.98d; Strabo 7 frg.). He represented himself as King Sun and the citizens were citizens of heaven. We know frustratingly little about its programme, though the description of his invented language is entertaining. It does seem to have been a real attempt to establish a new kind of society, and it attracted some real political adventurers; but its life was short.

Dandamis' Teaching

One striking feature of the utopias of Euhemerus, Iambulus and Palladius is that they are all set on an island. In fact, they are all on one particular island, Taprobane. Even Theopompus' utopias are on a continent lying beyond the River of Ocean, which is pretty much the same location. So it is no surprise to find the land of the Brahmans sharing many of the environmental characteristics of these other utopias. However, the physical pleasures of the land are quickly left behind as Palladius and his original

Cynic model develop an essentially ethical discourse contrasting Alexander's way of life with that of the Brahmans.[33] Dandamis begins by rejecting the example of Calanus, who was seduced by wealth, which the Brahmans reject (Palladius 4–5, 8–9), as they also reject warfare (6): their warfare is all against internal desires. They live simply on what the earth affords (10). At 12 Onesicratus (*sic*) is introduced again to Dandamis, and the sermon begins afresh. Dandamis now points out (14) that 'Alexander is no god, for he knows that he must die'. Gifts are useless, and 'if Alexander takes away my head he will not destroy my soul' (17). In the next section Dandamis asserts that the Brahmans do not love gold or fear death – the implication being that Alexander does both. In fact, his desire for wealth is a defence against the fear of death, fragments shored against his ruin. The idea occurs frequently in ancient philosophy, notably at Lucretius 3. 873, 878.[34] Alexander goes in person to sit at the feet of Dandamis (19) and listens to a sermon about his insatiable desires. 'You were created small of stature and naked, and came into the world alone: what is it that makes you great enough to slaughter all these people? To seize all their possessions? When you have conquered everybody, and taken possession of all the world, you will possess no more land than I have as I lie down . . . . Learn this piece of wisdom from me, Alexander: desire nothing, and everything will be yours, and you will lack nothing. Desire is the mother of penury; penury is the result of indiscipline treated with bad medicines' (22–3). Dandamis invites Alexander to come and live with him in the forest and be his disciple. Alexander is chagrined and tempted.

> I know that all you say is true. God created you and sent you to this place where you are able to live a blessed life, at peace with all nature, rich, lacking for nothing, enjoying great tranquillity. What shall I do, seeing that I live with incessant fears, and drowning in continuous disturbance? How far must I fear those who protect me even more than the enemy? The friends who advise me by day are worse for me than my enemies: I cannot live without them, but I am never cheerful when I am with them. By day I torment the nations, but when night comes on I am tormented by my own reflections, my fear that someone may come at me with a sword . . . . How can I begin to repudiate my actions? If I wanted to live in the wilderness, my troops would not allow me. (32–4)

The way of life Dandamis commends is very much in tune with Cynic philosophy, rejecting society and living in a state of nature. But the teaching on desire has a very Buddhist ring to it. This observation brings us back to the possible Indian sources of Cynic thought,[35] but it adds verisimilitude to the Indian setting of the dialogue.[36]

Thus far the text of Palladius sticks fairly closely to the papyrus, as far as we can tell from its fragmentary state. But after this point (45) it develops a discourse which is not found in the Cynic text, in praise of vegetarianism and inveighing against the killing of wild animals, notably in the wild beast shows of the Roman Empire.[37] For good measure the speaker throws in an attack on wine and on the castration of males for sexual purposes.

Christian and Jewish Echoes

Palladius' work has been described as a Christian protreptic[38] and I have myself expressed adherence to this view. I am no longer so confident. The level of Christianisation in the work is really very light, consisting mainly in the insertion of allusions to 'God' where the older text had 'the gods'. References to Providence are left to stand, and the discourse on the wild beast shows of the Roman Empire, which have been regarded as a topic particularly near the heart of Christian thinkers (who stood a good chance of being eaten by the beasts), does not show any sign of Christian concerns. In particular, there is no trace of the sexual renunciation which is a hallmark of most Christian writing on the ascetic life. Instead, I would prefer to think that Palladius (if he is the author) came across an old text which appealed to him because of its high moral tone, and made what is little more than a fair copy with stylistic updating, changing the most blatantly non-Christian references to a more appropriate form but otherwise not interfering with its message. The Brahmans' utopia, and Dandamis' message to Alexander, are left to speak for themselves.

The description of the Brahmans' way of life is closely reproduced, though without the involvement of Alexander, in a Christian work known as the *Narrative of Zosimus* edited by M.R. James (1893, 96–108). The Greek text is hard to date: it may be as late as the seventh century, though already in 250 the apocalyptic poet Commodian (Carmen, 936) knows of the Jewish tribes 'closed in beyond the Persian river'. 'Zosimus' in turn is based on a Jewish work, the *History of the Rechabites*, which is inserted into the Christian story of Zosimus.[39] Besides Greek, the *Narrative of Zosimus* is preserved in Slavonic, Syriac, Ethiopic and Arabic texts; in the Slavonic version the Blessed Ones are in fact named as Brahmans.[40] It also entered the medieval Jewish rewriting of Josephus' *Antiquities of the Jews* known as Yosippon:[41] now the Blessed are called the 'sons of Yonadab'.

The story concerns a hermit, Zosimus, who travels on a camel to the Land of the Blessed. These latter turn out to be the descendants of Rechab, one of the Lost Tribes of Israel, and their home is the Earthly Paradise. One of their number describes their way of life:

> Hear, ye sons of men, hear the way of life of the blessed. For God placed us in this land, for we are holy but not immortal. For the earth produces most fragrant fruit, and out of the trunks of the trees comes water sweeter than honey, and these are our food and drink. We also pray all night and day . . . with us there is no vine, nor ploughed field, nor works of wood or iron, nor have we any house or building, nor fire nor sword, nor iron wrought or unwrought, nor silver nor gold, nor air too heavy or too keen. Neither do any of us take to themselves wives, except for so long as to beget two children, and after they have produced two children they withdraw from each other and continue in chastity, not knowing that they were ever in the intercourse of marriage, but being in virginity as from the beginning. And the one child remains for marriage, and the other for virginity.
>
> And . . . all our day is one day. In our caves lie the leaves of trees, and this is our couch under the trees. But we are not naked of body as ye wrongly imagine, for we have the garment of immortality and are not ashamed of each other . . . . We know also the time of our end, for we have no torment nor disease nor pain in our bodies, nor exhaustion nor weakness, but peace and great patience and love . . . . If one quits the body in his youth, the days of his life here are 360 years, and he that quits the body in old age, the days of his life here are 688 years. (10–12)

In this remarkable narrative the chief traits of the Hellenistic utopia are entirely adapted to the Jewish–Christian vision of the Earthly Paradise. It will thus be no surprise when, in a later chapter, we find Alexander himself visiting this Paradise. The tale may have reached Jewish ears directly, from the *Alexander Romance* or Palladius, but the earlier part of the encounter, the ten questions, is already in the Talmud, *Tamid* 31b–32a, where 'Alexander of Macedon put ten questions to the Elders of the South'.[42] The Brahmans appeared in a great many later writings as one of the fixtures of the east,[43] not least in the Hebrew romance *Toldoth Alexander*.[44]

The Middle Ages and Beyond

Entering English literature through the metrical *Romance of Alexander* and the *Travels* of Sir John Mandeville (ch. 32) – where there are two islands, one of Brahmans and one of gymnosophists – the Brahmans appear again

22   A Brahman ascetic depicted in an eighth-century sculpture from the Silk Road.
Museum für Asiatische Kunst, Berlin: Bildarchiv preussischer Kulturbesitz 47. 620–1.

with a remarkable new function in Henry Nevile's fantastical *The Isle of Pines* (1668; so called because all the inhabitants in this utopia are descended from a man called Pine): 'here is a great many of those persons whom they call Brachmans, being their priests or teachers whom they much reverence'. In this island royal succession is through the sisters of the king; 'and these sisters of his choose what gentleman they please on whom to bestow their virginities; and if they prove not in a certain time to be with child, they betake themselves to these Brachman stallions, who never fail of doing their work'. This is, I suppose, the soft-porn version of the philosophical encounter.

The theme of Alexander's encounter with Dandamis was taken up in another work, *The Correspondence of Alexander and Dindimus*, which survives in a Latin version though it is to be presumed that there was a Greek original.[45] It was known in the eighth century, when Alcuin sent a copy to Charlemagne. It became popular in later literature: there is an alliterative verse translation into English from about 1340, and the section on the Greek gods and their vices was adapted by John Gower. The latest adaptation is a chapbook version of 1683.[46] The distinctive feature of this thoughtful exchange is that Dindimus does not altogether win the argument. Two ways of life are placed side by side and the merits of both are developed. Dindimus makes the same points as he usually does, with the addition of a long attack on the pagan gods, threatening his listener that he will get the afterlife he deserves and believes in; but Alexander in the final section fights back with an argument that 'the goods that you say you have are like the tortures of those in prison, and you endure of your own free will that which our law prescribes for condemned criminals . . . . There is nothing to admire in a man's living in poverty and want, but rather in living temperately in the midst of riches.' This very cogent point hits the nail on the head: is it more virtuous to eliminate desire or to master it?[47] Alexander attacks the Brahmans as living the life of beasts and says, amusingly, that the only reason they refrain from fornication is that their women are so unattractive because of their lack of adornment. 'Given that we have all the good fruits of the earth, and the abundance of the fish of the sea, and the delicacies of the birds that fly, your wish that we should abstain from all things will lead to your being judged either over-proud, for despising all these gifts, or envious, because you think I have been endowed with better gifts than you.'

The last fictional appearance of the Brahmans is in Klaus Mann's novel of 1929, *Alexander: Roman der Utopie*.[48]

They sat in out of the way groves, doing penance. They squatted, haggard and naked, their scaly skin was the colour of mud . . . . Macedonian soldiers who came across such men regarded them with a mixture of nausea and admiration. They had seen plenty of such sages sitting in the dung like this; at home they were called Cynics, because they acted like dogs. Here they were called Gymnosophists, because they were naked and discoursed on wisdom.

Alexander barks orders at them, demanding instruction and consolation, which they deny him because the state of his soul is unready. After a bit they condescend to utter: 'Who sees in the deed the non-doing and in the non-doing the deed, he does every deed with attention.' And then one of them goes on, 'For him Doing comes altogether to an end.' Having established their obscurantist credentials, they proceed to fill the mind of the dozing Alexander with their chants: 'Prana, the Breath, is Brahman; kham, Joy, is Brahman; kham, the Ether is Brahman. Breath of Life, Space, Heaven, Lightning – that am I, reveals Brahman.' These then are real Indian philosophers as the twentieth century knows them. They have adapted themselves successfully to another literary incarnation, and fill Alexander's dreams with longing for a utopia that he will never attain:

> Their voices had no seductive power any longer, they were just warning and weak. Alexander plunged away from them, in the process bending over great branches, trampling flowers and small animals. With sorrowfully glittering eyes the three aged ones gazed at him through the rainy night, as he mutilated the Creation and distanced himself from the path of Understanding, of Blessedness and of Redemption.

In all these episodes, the Brahmans – whether Indian, Jewish or Christian, whether ancient, medieval or modern – offer Alexander his chance of moral salvation; and he rejects it. The proud conqueror refuses to learn his place in the world.

FROM THE HEIGHTS OF THE AIR TO THE DEPTHS OF THE SEA
Alexander as Inventor and Sage

Rabbi Yonah said: 'Alexander of Macedon, when he wished to ascend into the air, used to rise higher and higher until he saw the world look like a ball and the sea like a dish. On account of this they depict him with an orb in his hand. . .'

Avodah Zarah III.1.42c[1]

Howe Aristotylle declarith to kyng Alisaundre of þe stonys.
Towching þe stone of philosofris olde,
Of weche they make most soverayn mencyon,
But there is oon, as aristotylle tolde,
Which alle excellith in comparison,
Stone of stones, most soverayne of renowne;
Towching þe vertu of this ryche thing
Thus he wrote to þe most soverayne kyng.

O alisaundre, grettist of dignities
And of þe worlde monarke and regent
. . . Alle worldeley tresoure breeflie schete in oon,
Is declared in virtue of this stone.

BM Add. MS 14408, st. 140–1, in John Lydgate and Benedict Burgh, *Secrees of old Philisoffres*, ed. Robert Steele (1894), xxxiii

Wise Saws and Modern Instances

One of the most notable features of the Alexander of the *Romance* is his cleverness. He has an answer for every adversary, a way out of every impasse. Like Jesus, he speaks in proverbs or little parables. When he encourages the troops before the battle with Darius (III. 16), he urges them, 'Let none of you be afraid: there may be ten thousand flies swarming a field, but when the wasps arrive, they frighten the flies away simply by the buzzing of their wings. Numbers are nothing against intelligence; and the flies are nothing against the wasps.' His strategic originality is apparent in many of his pronouncements, such as his speech urging the older Macedonians to march with him to war (I. 25): 'Fathers, join us on the campaign, not so much in order to fight the enemy, as to inspire the younger ones with courage. Both of you have a part to play. Yours is to strengthen the army with discretion; for even in war brains are necessary.' Or when he urges the soldiers, who are starving, to eat their horses (I. 44): 'We can easily get other horses, but where shall I get other Macedonians?'[2]

Several of his actions became textbook examples of good strategy, like his dismantling of the bridge over the Euphrates (II. 9) to make retreat impossible and thus to encourage bolder fighting. Even the most fabulous instances have an afterlife. On a night march, Alexander wishes to make his army appear to be bigger, and so he fixes torches to the heads of a flock of goats (II. 13); in the daytime, branches of brushwood are fixed to their tails to stir up the dust. (This scene is depicted on a coin of Aigeai [= 'goats'] in Cilicia of AD 217/18: a remarkable piece of evidence for the currency of the *Romance* at this time.)[3] The strategic writers Polyaenus and Frontinus tell this story in connection with more than one other Hellenistic general,[4] so it was regarded as a reliable trick. More improbable is Alexander's use of red hot statues to combat Porus' elephants (*AR* III. 3: see above, Chapter 4).[5]

23 Alexander's stratagem of fixing torches to the horns of a flock of goats is depicted on this coin of Aigeai (the name means 'goats') of AD 217/8. Ashmolean Museum, Oxford, Heberden Coin Room.

Alexander's talent for answering back becomes most apparent in his first exchange of letters with Darius (*AR* I. 36–8), when the king sends him a whip, a ball and a chest of gold – 'the whip, to show you that you ought still to be at play; the ball, so that you may play with your contemporaries instead of inducing such numbers of arrogant young men to come with you like bandits . . . . And a chest full of gold so that if you are unable to feed your fellow-bandits you can now give them what they need to return each to his own country.' Alexander of course reinterprets the 'gifts' (Darius really dropped himself in this one): 'I regard these as favourable omens. I accepted the whip, so as to flay the barbarians, and bring them to submission. I accepted the ball, as a sign that I shall be ruler of the world – for the world is spherical like a ball. The chest of gold you sent me is a great sign: you will be conquered by me and pay me tribute.'

The Syriac version of the *Romance* (Budge 1889, xxxvi–xxxix) adds a further exchange of symbols. Darius sends Alexander in addition 'ten measures of sesame seeds, that thou mayest know that I have myriads of troops even as these grains of sesame'. Alexander caps this offering by writing in his reply that he has tasted the sesame seeds, and they are 'numerous but insipid; in exchange he sends a handful of mustard seeds, which are 'small but pungent', like the Macedonian army.

It must be said however that the Alexander of the *Romance* misses some of the best opportunities taken by the historical Alexander, such as the reply to Parmenio when he advises Alexander to accept Darius' terms: 'I would accept that, if I were Alexander', to which Alexander replies, 'So would I, if I were Parmenio.'[6] In the *Romance*, Alexander simply says 'No' (II. 17). And his encounter with the Pythia at Delphi – when in the historians' accounts he throws her to the floor and demands an oracle, prompting her outburst, 'No one can resist you' – is flattened in the *Romance* to a straightforward greeting and prophecy of triumph.

The talent for twisting symbols comes out in his skill with omens and inscriptions.[7] He dreams a prophetic dream at Tyre (*AR* I. 35), which foretells his capture of the city; for he sees a Satyr holding a cheese out to him, which puns twice on the Greek 'Sa Tyros', 'Tyre is yours'. ('Tyros' in Greek means 'cheese'.) Even more striking is his working out of the riddle of Sarapis (I. 33) through the numerical equivalence of Greek letters. So it is no surprise that, perhaps uniquely among ancient Greeks,[8] Alexander has no difficulty in understanding inscriptions in Egyptian hieroglyphics. When he arrives in Memphis (I. 34) he sees a black statue of Nectanebo bearing the inscription, 'The king who has fled will return to Egypt, no longer an old man but a young man, and will subject our enemies the Persians to us', which tells him just what he needs to know.

(A historical parallel is his cutting of the Gordian knot, not mentioned in the *Romance*.)

Alexander is also a master of disguise. In II. 14 he goes in disguise as his own messenger to the Persian court, and gets away with it until he is recognised by a Persian who had been one of the ambassadors to Pella years before. The dénouement is a dramatic horseback ride in which he eludes the Persian army, who plunge through the breaking ice of the Stranga river while he escapes to shore. Again he disguises himself in order to visit Queen Candace (III. 18 ff.); here the plot is complicated by his having Antigonus disguise himself as Alexander, too. The point of the disguise is not altogether clear but it gives an opportunity for some fine dramatic irony and a display of wit by Candace, who has had his portrait painted (just as the Persian ambassadors had, in some versions of the story). Again, there are historical parallels for this subterfuge,[9] and the military writers discuss disguise as one of the accomplishments of the good general.[10]

Aesop

However, the character Alexander most resembles in such moments is not the textbook generals but another famous trickster of Greek tradition, Aesop. At the foundation of Alexandria, Alexander devises a riddle of his own in the acrostic inscription ΑΒΓΔΕ, which stands for '*Alexandros Basileus Genos Dios Ektisen*', 'Alexander the King, son of Zeus, built it.'[11] In the anonymous *Life of Aesop* (78–80)[12] the hero sees a monument inscribed with a series of letters, ΑΒΔΟΕΘΧ, which his master Xanthus asks him to interpret. Aesop has no hesitation in explaining that the inscription signifies '*apobas bemata tessara*[13] *oryxon heureseis thesauron chrysiou*', 'Go four paces, dig, and you will find a hoard of gold'. Aesop realises that Xanthus will try to take the treasure from him, so he gives a second interpretation of the inscription: '*apodos basilei Dionysioi hon heures thesauron chrysiou*', 'Offer to King Dionysius the hoard of gold you found here'. 'Why don't we share it?' proposes Xanthus hastily. Aesop duly interprets the insription again: '*anesthe badisate dielesthe hon heurate thesauron chrysiou*', 'Dig it up, go and divide the hoard of gold you have found here'. Xanthus is duly impressed, and both parties get the benefit of the slave's discovery.[14]

Aesop and Alexander converge in a story told in a Coptic *Romance of Alexander*, partially preserved on papyrus.[15] Aesop in the *Life* (103) has become fable-writer to King Lycurgus of Babylon. He adopts a son, who however accuses him of treason. The king orders Aesop to be killed, but Aesop's friend Hermippus hides him away in his house until the king finds himself wishing for the cunning slave's help again; all is then forgiven. A similar story is told of Alexander in the Coptic *Romance*, where he has already shown himself an expert at disguises. Here he is condemned to death by the king of Gedrosia. To protect him, his companion Antilochus hides him in a hole in his house until the king repents and wishes for his restoration. Antilochus is then able to restore a living Alexander to the grateful king.[16] Both stories seem to go back to that of Ahiqar, the hero of the Assyrian *Book of Ahiqar*, which has been characterised by M.L. West as 'the first international bestseller'.[17] Ahiqar was vizier to King Sennacherib of Assyria and to his son Esarhaddon (d. 669 BC). Ahiqar had a nephew Nadan, who betrayed him to the king. The man sent to execute Ahiqar, however, saved him and hid him in his house. In due course Esarhaddon began to regret his death, as he needed a magician to help him satisfy the challenges of the king of Egypt. Hey presto, Ahiqar is produced safe and well and regains his status. In due course he returns to Assyria, imprisons Nadan and lectures him interminably about animal fables until Nadan, unable to stand it any longer, explodes into tiny pieces.

Though there is no exploding nephew in Alexander's story, there are some further parallels, to which we shall return below. The convergence with Aesop tells us something both about Alexander and about the nature of the *Romance*. The picaresque story of a clever trickster is one of the many strands that go to make up the *Romance*, and the Egyptian affiliations of the story (both the Coptic version and the Ahiqar story) show how rooted the Alexander of legend is in Egyptian lore.

The Diving Bell

Alexander's exploration of the Ocean in a glass diving bell may be the most iconic of all his adventures. (See colour plate 6). Along with his construction of a flying machine (see below), it seems to typify the Alexander who pushes the boundaries of human knowledge and capability by the application of his ingenuity. The story is introduced in quite a matter of fact way in the *Romance* (II. 38), when the soldiers are walking on the beach in the land of wonders and come upon a giant crab, six feet across, with huge pearls inside it. Alexander supposes that they must originate in the depths of the sea. 'So I then made a large iron cage, and inside the cage I placed a large glass jar, two feet wide, and I ordered a hole to be made in the bottom of the jar, big enough for a man's hand to go through. My idea was to descend and find out what was on the floor of this sea . . . . I had a chain made, one thousand cubits long, and ordered the men not to pull me up until they felt the chain shake.' The dive is not a complete success, for, after several attempts, the vessel is seized in the jaws of a huge fish and dragged for a mile, along with the ships on the surface. 'When it reached land, it crushed the cage with its teeth and cast it up on the beach. I was gasping and half-dead from fright. I fell on my knees and thanked Providence above which had saved me from this frightful beast. Then I said to myself, "Alexander, now you must give up attempting the impossible; or you may lose your life in attempting to explore the deeps!"'

The story contains several of the leitmotifs of the *Romance*, not least the concluding moral against overreaching human limits. But it is in fact a late arrival in the *Romance*, and its origins are obscure. It first appears in one MS (C) of the gamma recension, and later in the expanded version of the beta recension in the MS L. It is not part of the original narrative of A and beta, nor is it in the derivatives of A such as the Syriac translation and Julius Valerius, nor yet in epsilon, which was a source for much that is in gamma. Nor is it in the accounts of the later antique historians who do include some fabulous material, such as Fulgentius and Eutychius, and it first appears in Latin literature in the eighth-century author Aethicus Ister. The earliest traceable appearance of the story is in fact in the Talmud,[18] where it follows the story of the flying machine. Alexander descends into the sea in the glass bell, taking with him a luminous stone and a live hen. He asks his companions to come and look for him if he does not reappear within a year. After three months Alexander feels he has seen all he needs to see, and so he slaughters the hen: the sea, which will not abide blood, immediately spews out the bell and its occupant, who emerges in a strange land where the people have enormous faces and feet but only one eye, and speak an unknown language. It is not stated how he is reunited with his companions.[19]

A Jewish origin for the tale is consonant with its appearing first in the gamma recension, which contains so much Jewish material. One wonders, too, whether the story was inspired by the experiments of Alexandrian scientists with air pressure. Already in the reign of Ptolemy II (285–247 BC), Ctesibius was experimenting with pneumatic machines and, a little later, Philo of Byzantium (*fl.* 200 BC) with siphons. Later, Hero of Alexandria (*fl.* AD 62), who invented a hydraulic organ, a windmill and a steam engine, describes in his introduction to the *Pneumatics* how a covered bell, when submerged and opened under water, will not fill with water; he also experimented with siphons and syringes. But it should be noted that the diving bell is not strictly a bell, but a closed chamber with just a small aperture for Alexander's hand to emerge from. It is more like a diver's hood, which is otherwise first described in an eleventh century MS of al-Biruni.[20] One has to wait for Leonardo da Vinci for another design for a diving bell, though not even he ever built one; that was, apparently, first done by Edmund Halley (*Encyclopaedia Britannica*, s.v. 'diving'). Already Aethicus had expressed scepticism about its possibility, but Roger Bacon (1210/15 – after 1292) was happy to quote Aethicus as an authority for the adventure, and insisted that such things had been made both in antiquity and in his own time.[21]

The Arab authors alter the focus of the story (see Chapter 3 above). In his account of Alexandria, Mas'udi (AD 943) tells how Alexander constructed the diving bell in the harbour at Alexandria, and used it to make images of the monsters of the deep; these images were then positioned on the shore to protect the city against their real life counterparts.

The Middle Ages developed the theme again. Alexander's motive for his descent is now to gain ichthyological knowledge. The earliest vernacular account of his descent is in a poem written about 1080–1120 about the life of Archbishop Anno II of Cologne, the *Annolied*.[22] After this it reappears several times in German literature, in Alexander Neckam (1157–1217),[23] and then in the Old French Prose *Alexander*, where it is accompanied in the numerous extant MSS by coloured illustrations of the adventure. In the *Annolied* the story is briefly told:

> He had himself lowered into the sea in a glass vessel. Then his faithless men threw the chains away into the sea. They said: 'If you want to see marvels, wallow for ever on the sea-bed.' There he saw many great fish float before him, half fish and half man, so that it seemed to him most terribly alarming. Then the cunning man thought how he might escape. The water carried him to the bottom. He saw many wonders through the glass until he addressed the dreadful sea with blood. When the water felt the blood it cast the lord ashore.

Following the French and German versions, the story then reappears in the thirteenth century in Latin in one MS of the second interpolated version of the *Historia de Proeliis* (see Chapter 1, 12). Here Alexander is abandoned on the seabed by his men, who think that he is dead; but he has taken the precaution of having with him a cat, a dog and a cock. The Latin author explains that the cock is there to tell him when each new day arrives; the cat functions as an air-purifier (a mysterious and inexplicable piece of lore), while the function of the dog is to be killed and to provide the blood which will automatically eject the diving bell from the sea.

In large part this version agrees with that depicted in the MS illustrations, with the exception that there is no mention of the lady preparing to cut the chain. Her presence is first explained in the world chronicle of a prolix Austrian author, Jansen Enikel (d. *c.* 1250). She is Alexander's mistress, but, while he is out of sight, out of mind at the bottom of the sea, a 'young heathen' comes and pays court to the lady; she is so smitten that she flings her arms around him, in the process dropping the chain into the sea. This account became the standard one in later medieval texts, notably that of Ulrich von Etzenbach (1280–87), where the woman is in fact Alexander's wife Roxana (here, Roxa). After Alexander's escape there is a touching reconciliation between the two.

The way in which this Talmudic story made its way into medieval literature is altogether obscure, for the French and German writers did not get it from any of the Greek or Latin versions of the *Alexander Romance* and, as we have seen, it only re-entered the Latin tradition subsequent to its first German appearance. It receives the briefest of mentions in a half-sentence in the rewriting of Josephus known as Yosippon (completed 953: see Appendix), 'he explored the depths of the Ocean' – not enough to explain the fuller versions of the later authors.[24] One can only suppose that the author of the *Annolied*, or an informant, was acquainted with the relevant passages of the Talmud and that the story made sufficient impression on him to induce him to add it to the rather settled standard story of Alexander. By the middle of the twelfth century the story was quite widespread and appears in several Hebrew MSS giving closely related accounts of the Alexander story.[25] These derive from the second interpolated version of the *Historia de Proeliis*.

The Flying Machine

As iconic as the diving bell, and perhaps even more widespread iconographically, is the story of Alexander's construction of a flying machine (see colour plate 7). Literally hundreds of representations of this adventure are known in the art of the Middle Ages from AD 1000 to 1600, in manuscript, in architecture and sculpture, and even on tapestries. Victor Schmidt's exhaustive book on the theme catalogues and illustrates almost one hundred examples.[26] Besides its appearance in MSS of the *Alexander Romance* and other versions of the Alexander story, the motif is an important one in church architecture, for reasons that have never been fully explained. A Byzantine relief on the north façade of St Mark's in Venice shows the scene (see Plate 35). It is found on misericords at Gloucester (see Plate 37) and Lincoln cathedrals, at St Cuthbert's in Darlington, Tewkesbury Abbey and Wells Cathedral; on a relief at Narni in Italy; on the tympanum of the church door at Oloron in France, and on a tympanum built into the chancel of the little Norman church at Charney Bassett in

Oxfordshire. It is particularly popular in the mosaic and sculptural decoration of the churches of southern Italy, including the damaged mosaic floor of Trani Cathedral and the column capitals at both Trani and Bitonto, as well as a tympanum at S Maria della Strada, Matrice, Campobasso. Its latest appearance is on the tapestries of the Palazzo Doria in Rome (1459).

The most striking example of all is its prominent appearance on the mosaic floor of the twelfth-century Otranto Cathedral. The cathedral was begun in 1088 and the mosaic floor, constructed between 1163 and 1195, in the reign of King William I of Sicily, was the work of Presbyter Pantaleon, under commission from Jonathan the Archbishop of Otranto. The depiction of Alexander appears at the bottom right-hand (south-west)

24 Alexander's flight, depicted on the twelfth-century mosaic floor of the cathedral at Trani.

end of a mosaic that covers the entire floor of the nave. Two elephants support a Tree of Life that rises through the whole mosaic, which depicts scenes from the Old Testament (Noah's Ark and the Tower of Babel) and from the Arthurian legend, the signs of the zodiac and the labours of associated months, a variety of wondrous and mythical beasts, from giraffes to a quadruped with two human heads, two-tailed mermaids and griffins. The left (north) aisle is devoted to a scene of the Last Judgment, Hell and Paradise, anticipating the imagery of Dante a century later. The right (south) aisle contains a variety of fabulous beasts and monsters. In the apse are assembled scenes of Jonah, the king of Nineveh, Samson, Abraham and Satan. The figure of Alexander is large in scale compared with many of the others; he is shown seated on a kind of stool anchored on the backs of two addorsed griffins. In either hand Alexander holds a stick with a lump of meat on the end: the griffins reach upwards to snatch it, and as it recedes they ascend into the air. The pose resembles that of a master of animals as much as that of an aviator; and the expression of anxiety on the king's face suggests that this is the first time he has tried the experiment.

Why is Alexander such a prominent part of the mosaic, and why is this scene so popular in southern Italy? It must always have been famous in the locality; perhaps it was its prominence that led a later Bishop of Otranto to acquire an elegantly written manuscript of the beta recension of the *Alexander Romance*, copied in 1468 by Nectarius, a monk of St Nicholas of Otranto (now Paris, BN Gr 1685).

The story, like that of the diving bell, first appears in western tradition in the eighth-century L MS of the Greek *Romance*, whence it derives from the Talmud (fourth century AD) by routes obscure, as discussed above.[27] The Talmudic passage (see epigraph to chapter) is laconic; we have to turn to the Greek *Romance* for a full explanation of how Alexander achieved his remarkable ascent (II. 41). As he explores the Land of Darkness, Alexander explains (the text is written in the first person at this point):

> Then I began to ask myself again if this place was really the end of the world, where the sky touched the earth. I wanted to discover the truth, and so I gave orders to capture two of the birds that lived there. They were very large birds, very strong but tame; they did not fly away when they saw us. Some of the soldiers climbed on their backs, hung on tightly, and flew off. The birds fed on carrion, with the result that a great many of them came to our camp, attracted by the dead horses. I captured two of them and ordered them to be given no food for three days. On the third day I had something like a yoke constructed from wood, and had this tied to their throats. Then I had an ox-skin made into a large bag, <fixed it to the yoke> and climbed in, holding two spears, each about ten feet long and with a horse's liver fixed to the point. At once the birds soared up to seize the livers, and I rose up with them into the air.

As he rises higher and the air becomes colder, a 'flying creature in the form of a man' approaches Alexander (colour plate 8), admonishes him for his temerity, and tells him to look down: he sees 'a great snake curled up, and in the middle of the snake a tiny circle like a threshing-floor'. These are the surrounding ocean and the inhabited earth. Satisfied with his view, Alexander returns to earth.

No very clear moral is drawn from the story in the *Romance*. In this there is a notable contrast with the later re-use of the motif in the Latin 'Dream of Scipio', which constituted the last part of Cicero's *On the Republic*. This popular story was familiar in the Middle Ages and was versified by Chaucer in his *Parlement of Foules*. In his dream, Scipio is taken into the air and shown the earth from above. His spirit guide 'showed how small the earth appears In view of heaven's own immensity', and draws the moral: 'Earth being shown so small, So full of pain, deception, and so base, That he no joy of it should take at all.' It is a lesson in contemning the earth's goods and keeping one's eyes on spiritual things – a lesson that Dandamis would have approved, but not one that is drawn by the author of the *Romance* here. One wonders if the vanity of the whole enterprise is the interpretation that lies behind the appearance of the Alexander scene in church contexts. But in the *Romance* Alexander is, once again, pushing the limits of human capability, and the angel gives him the usual message about not pushing his luck. His fault is *hybris*, not over-valuation of worldly things. He seems also to have obtained a view of the whole world which suggests that it is all under his dominion, and that is the message that the Talmudic author seems to draw from it.

The story's dissemination in medieval Europe, culminating in the Otranto mosaic, was a result of the increasing familiarity of the *Romance* in its Latin version, the *Historia de Proeliis* (see appendix). So it was the first recension of this eleventh-century text, still a recent work, that had come to the knowledge of the artist of the cathedral floor at Otranto.[28]

Appearing in a context, in the *Romance*, of his other adventures 'beyond the world', it seems to belong to Alexander's search for immortality (see Chapter 8), and as a result it has often been compared with the Babylonian story of the Flight of Etana on an eagle's back, as the story of the Water of Life (Chapter 8, below) has been compared with that of Gilgamesh.[29] The questions of the eagle and Etana's replies are the closest parallel: '"My friend, look at the country! How does it seem?" "The country has turned into a garden . . . . And the wide sea is no bigger than a bucket"' (Dalley, 1989, 198). But in truth the dream of flight goes back a long way and is not always a metaphor for transcending human limits. Several Greek stories play on the idea that a man might fly, including the flight of Trygaeus on the back of a dung beetle in Aristophanes' *Peace* and that of the ascent of the human heroes to the city of the birds, Cloud-Cuckoo-Land, in the same author's *Birds*, as well as the parodies of travellers' tales in Lucian's *True History* and *Icaromenippus*. But by far the closest parallel for the Alexander story is in another Greek text, the *Life of Aesop*, which we have already encountered (see p. 110, above). Aesop's return from disgrace is motivated

by the king's desire to win a contest with the king of Egypt (Nectanebo!)
to build a tower in the air. Aesop does so by harnessing four eagles to four
boys, to carry them up with their bricklayer's equipment; they then proceed
to build a wall in the middle of the air.

This part of the Aesop story is, like the earlier one, directly borrowed
from the *Tale of Ahiqar*, which goes back to Babylonian times;[30] but its
setting is an Egyptian one and the story seems rather to anchor the flight
in an Egyptian context. Bearing in mind that the Ahiqar story was also
known to the Jews of Elephantine in the fifth century BC,[31] one might
surmise that the familiar tale was applied by Jewish storytellers to the
Macedonian king in an Alexandrian context.

The same story is told by Tabari (d. 923) of Kai Kaus, whom the *devs*
(beneficent spirits) assist in building a castle in the air; and it reappears in
Firdausi's *Shahnameh*, often with beautiful illustrations.[32] The method is the
same except that the basket becomes a throne of aloe-wood and the livers

aber das rych Licuri gegen dem mynen · Esopus
schmollet vnd sprach: Es ist nit dar vnder: sonder
in vil dingen fast dar über · Wañ ze glycher wyß /
wie die sunn den mon betunkelt: Also betunckelt
das rych licuri dyn rych mit synem schyn·

25 Aesop's flying builders. This woodcut from Heinrich Steinhöwel's translation of Aesop's
Fables (Ulm 1476–77) depicts Aesop responding to King Nectanebo's request to build a wall
in the air, by sending up four boys in baskets held by eagles.

are replaced by legs of mutton (colour plate 10). The story seems also to have
influenced that of Sindbad in the *Thousand and One Nights*.[33] The imagery
of Alexander's flight became widespread in the Arab world, appearing for
example on a *cloisonné* plate of the eighth century AD (colour plate 9).

As with the diving bell, one can trace an interest in the technology involved in the sciences of Hellenistic Alexandria. True, no Greek text actually recommends harnessing birds to a basket and tempting them upwards as one persuades a donkey to go by dangling a carrot in front of it; but the use of magnets for flight is a recurrent motif. According to the sixth-century author Rufinus in his *Historia Ecclesiastica*, the statue of Sarapis in his temple in Alexandria was made to hover in mid-air by the use of magnets placed at an equal distance above and below. The story recurs apropos a statue of Arsinoe,[34] and a later Arab legend mentions the sarcophagus of Aristotle in Palermo, which similarly floated in mid-air.[35]

The Meaning of the Otranto Mosaic

Victor Schmidt (1995, 65) interprets the wonderful pavement as follows:

> The scenes in the nave refer to the constant hardships man faces here on earth. Life is a struggle; exemplary figures and instructive events are presented as an encouragement in this struggle . . . . It is in this thematic context that Alexander's flight should be seen. Given the fact that neither the iconography of the image nor the composition of the Otranto mosaic suggest a negative conception of the Flight, it is possible to interpret the Flight thus: the image of the airborne Alexander served as an indication of the salvation awaiting people in the afterlife.

While possible, it is difficult to find this wholly convincing. Other interpretations have been proposed. Chiara Settis-Frugoni (1973) suggests that the flight represents at one and the same time a type of Christ's ascension and an allegory of man's overweening pride.[36] H.P. L'Orange (1953) regards it as an image of cosmic kingship. Roger Loomis (1918) makes it a parallel to Lucifer's attempt on heaven. Father Grazio Gianfreda, in his book on the mosaic (1995),[37] sets the image in a wider context. He suggests regarding the floor as a kind of encyclopaedia; it reaches from the Tree of Life to revelation and includes material that is allegorical, biblical, patristic, literary, historical and mythological. It covers the whole history of the human race, not only the events of Old Testament but the daily life of man in the monthly labours illustrating the zodiac; geography and zoology in the animals, both real and fabulous, that are depicted. There are stories deriving from Ovid and Lucan; the tale of Barlaam and Yosafat; the Arthurian cycle (Arthur is killed by the cat of Lausanne); Gianfreda even finds an allusion to the triple female deities of Scandinavian mythology and a reference to Omar Khayyam. While some of this may be excessive, it is tempting to consider this mosaic as a pictorial equivalent to the contemporary world chronicles that gave an important place to Alexander.

Three such chronicles were composed in the course of the twelfth century. The first was that of Peter Comestor (Dean of Troyes 1147–64, d. 1179).[38] Peter draws on a wide range of learning to provide a retelling of the biblical narrative in a fuller framework of consecutive history: his account of Alexander summarises $HP J^2$ (the one without the flight and the diving bell), and begins the re-acculturation of Alexander as a player in sacred history (his enclosure of the Unclean Nations, now reinterpreted as the Ten Lost Tribes of Israel, is a central myth). Secondly, Godfrey of Viterbo (*c.* 1125–96), a cleric who was employed at the court of Frederick Barbarossa (1152–90) and, later, Henry VI (1190–98),[39] wrote a work entitled *Pantheon,* a world chronicle in Latin verse with some passages of prose. It covers the same ground as Comestor but continues the story to his own time. Thirdly, Vincent of Beauvais (1190–1264) composed his *Speculum Historiale* (*Mirror of History*) in the reign of Louis the Pious. This book, which is three times as long as the Bible, was composed more for reference than for reading. Book IV covers the story of Alexander as told in the *Romance*, with an admixture of some other sources. This work was in turn translated more than once, into French by Jean de Vigny (1322) and into Dutch by Jacob van Maerlant (d. *c.* 1292–1300), himself also the author of a book of Alexander legends, *Alexanders Geesten.* All three of these works contributed to making Alexander a central figure in Christian story as well as in history, even when the versions they told were different from those the artists depicted in the cathedrals.[40]

The process continued well into the fifteenth century. Besides the *Polychronicon* of Ranulph Higden (5.1364), the apogee of this development is represented by the northern European History Bibles of the fifteenth century,[41] which filled the gap between the end of the Old Testament and the Book of Maccabees by inserting the *Alexander Romance.*

The flight is placed at Otranto, then, as that was simply the most famous and recognisable of the Alexander stories: meaning may be secondary. Nevertheless the choice of this place must depend on its having meaning of its own, which made it so popular a feature of ecclesiastical décor; so that we do perhaps have to decide whether it is an allegory of the vanity of worldly power; of the possible ascent to heaven through virtue; or a story about knowing one's own limitations. The fact that we can easily draw three such diverse morals from the image is a mark of its potency.

Alexander's Horn

A less well known tradition is that according to which Alexander was the inventor of a wonderful horn, which could summon an army over a distance of 60 miles.[42] Aristotle tells Alexander, in the course of his instructions to him in the *Secret of Secrets* (see below, pp. 255–6), to take with him on campaign the pneumatic 'horn of Yayastayus' (probably Themistius, as in Roger Bacon's translation). This seems to have been a form of hydraulic organ, though the illustrations in the Arabic MSS resemble something by Heath Robinson more than an instrument of war.

Esoteric Wisdom

Alexander's cleverness lies at the root of another development of his character in, particularly, eastern thought. His status as a pupil of Aristotle, the greatest of all philosophers, made him a suitable vehicle for all kinds of wisdom. Sometimes he is a recipient of wise instruction in letters from Aristotle; at other times he is himself the author of wise sayings and books of wisdom and knowledge. None of this appears in the *Romance* but it begins to develop in Jewish tales, such as the ones where Alexander, like Solomon, solves problems that are put before him by those he encounters in his travels. A telling example is the dispute between two men, one of whom has just bought from the other a piece of land including a dunghill. Under the dunghill has been discovered buried treasure. Which of the two men does it belong to? Alexander's solution is Solomon-like. By good fortune one of the men has a son, the other a daughter, both of marriageable age. The two are wed and the property reunited, so there is no further need for dispute.[43] Alexander here fulfils the function that in ancient Greece might have been carried out by an oracle; a very similar case in Plato (*Laws* 913d4–914a5) about a buried treasure has to be solved in this way.[44] Sub-philosophical conundrums, if one might call them this, of this kind, were grist to the mill of ancient thinkers, as we saw in relation to the question-and-answer session with the Brahmans. There are several such in the Talmud and in the earliest Hebrew *Alexander Romances*.

   The idea of Alexander as a wise man goes much further in Arabic and Persian literature. His relation to Aristotle is central here. It was well known that he had been educated by Aristotle, and several Arabic texts build on this to make Alexander himself a source of wisdom.[45] Not only was Alexander the recipient of the supposed Aristotelian manual of statecraft, the *Secret of Secrets*, but Aristotle is supposed to have dedicated a number of other works, such as one on divination and another on astrology.[46]

Alexander becomes a notable figure in the Arabic wisdom tradition,[47] in which he is a scholar and a lover of music.[48] He is said by the tenth-century scholar Ibn al-Nadim to have been the first to enjoy recitations of tales at an evening.[49] He also appears very often in collections of proverbs and wise sayings; as a correspondent (usually with Aristotle) on matters of politics, science and philosophy; and as an author or instigator of scientific–philosophical works (in the broadest sense). Besides the works on divination mentioned above there was the *Thesaurus Alexandri*, 'translated from the Greek and Roman' on the order of the Caliph al-Mu'tasim (833–42),[50] which was a work on elixirs and amulets. It was supposed to have been composed by Hermes and to have incorporated a prologue and an epilogue by Aristotle.[51] The Persian writers continue to emphasise this aspect of Alexander in presenting him as a model king: in Nizami's *Iskandarnameh* he is a patron of philosophers and sages (a motley band who frequently include Plato, Thales, Diogenes, Hippocrates and Apollonius of Tyana).

Alexander and the Philosopher's Stones

Alexander features prominently in another work attributed to Aristotle, *De lapidibus* (*On Stones*). This strange and fascinating work is known in Arabic, Hebrew and Latin versions.[52] Its editor, Julius Ruska, proposed that it was a translation of a Byzantine book of the seventh century transmitted via a Syriac translation; but later scholarship has determined that it probably originated in the ninth century in the medical school at Jundishapur in Persia.[53] The earlier of the two surviving MSS (the Leodensis in Liège) is of the fourteenth century, and the second (Montpellier) a century later, but long before that it had been translated into Hebrew and into Latin. A Latin translation was made by Gerard of Cremona (d. 1187), but the work had already been quoted by Marbod, Bishop of Rennes (1035–1123), in his *De lapidum naturis*. The transmission is a neat example of the routes by which ancient wisdom and Arabic texts made their way into western tradition. The Latin text is a list of numerous types of stone with their fantastical and magical properties. In the first paragraph the writer tells us: 'This book was made by Aristotle the son of Nichomachus, the master of Alexander the Great the son of King Philip of Macedon. I translated it from Greek into the language of the Syrians.' Some parts of it made their way into the *Secret of Secrets*, but Marbod was by this time deemed a 'better' source.[54]

There were indeed many Greek books about stones,[55] starting with Theophrastus, the successor and heir of Aristotle, whose *De lapidibus* is a sober geological treatise. Later works are more preoccupied with amazing facts, and one work that has features in common with *De lapidibus* is *De mirabilibus auscultibus* (On Wonderful Things Heard) attributed to Aristotle, which contains many bizarre pieces of information about stones that behave in a remarkable way.[56] Poets were interested in gems for their exoticism and delighted to describe both them and the way they were engraved to make precious jewels.[57] In the Hellenistic period, Egyptian and Mesopotamian lore was incorporated into Greek thinking and various magical properties, especially of a medical kind, were attributed to specific stones. There is an echo of this interest in the description of Nectanebo's astrological tablet in Book I of the *Alexander Romance*, but writers such as Bolos of Mendes (*c.* 100 BC), and even Pseudo-Plutarch, *On Rivers*, developed this much further. The material appealed to the Hellenistic taste for 'wonders' of all kinds: the genre of paradoxography (tales of the improbable) seems to have been invented by Callimachus.[58] Jewish ideas also attached importance to stones, such as the twelve gems of the High Priest's pectoral and the oracular Urim and Thummim (which are referred to in George the Monk's account of Alexander's visit to Jerusalem).[59] The genre developed in a work by one Damigeron, who incorporated in it two letters allegedly written by King Evax of Arabia (unknown) to the Emperor Tiberius.[60] The zodiacal stones he describes have some correspondence with those of Nectanebo's tablet; and both Damigeron and Nectanebo are cited as authorities by Tertullian in his demolition of the superstition.[61]

But it is only the Pseudo-Aristotelian *De lapidibus* that contains the numerous allusions to Alexander, indicating how central the latter became to Arabic thinking about such matters.[62]

The first appearance of Alexander in Pseudo-Aristotle is in the story of the Valley of Diamonds, already known from Epiphanius' *De gemmis* in the fourth century and later to reappear in *The Arabian Nights*;[63] Alexander's cleverness makes use of the local birds to carry up the diamonds from the valley adhering to lumps of meat that he has hurled into the depths. A little later, Alexander is the discoverer of the gold-magnet, another useful item: 'This stone attracts and heaps up gold as other stones attract silver, lead, meat, water and fish [the text is a little garbled]. . . . My pupil Alexander who was in the east and reached also the west tested its qualities. The gold magnet is yellow with ashy markings; it is light and soft to the touch.' Later comes 'the stone called elbarchi, which some call lampus. The Indians make many spells from this stone. One of its properties is that it makes women wanton . . . . My pupil Alexander prevented his army from carrying it in case the women of the army should become too luxurious.' Next comes the Malcbs (*sic*) or Indian Stone, which can be used for water-divining and for driving away demons. 'My pupil Alexander saw sorcerers and sorceresses far off, and saw the men of his army wounded and infected in wondrous ways by the power of devils.' But when he and the kings who were with him used this stone 'the demons could no longer harm them'. Another stone is visible only at night: we shall meet this stone again in the journey into the land of darkness.[64] Another stone can be hung around a horse's neck, to prevent it from whinnying (a useful trick in an ambush), and it silences other animals too.[65] The stone called Polophos, which changes its colour at will (the name, unlike those of most of these stones, is Greek and not Arabic in appearance), can be used to repel demons, serpents and lions, and was used by Alexander for this purpose. The best of all comes at the end: the stone Elbehecte, which is only found in the depths of the waters where the sun never shines. It is small and golden in colour. 'When Alexander's army came upon these stones, all who looked at them became stupid and gazed with their mouths open as if they had lost their wits; they could not take their minds off them but remained gaping at the stones . . . . Alexander ordered his men to cover their faces, or close their eyes, and to throw cloths over the stones in order to carry back as many as possible to their tents without looking at them.'[66] Then he instructed his army to carry the stones to a place a month's journey away and to build a city with them; but in time wind and storms demolished the walls of that city and hid the stones beneath dust. Later, the Arabic translator adds, 'one of the kings of Nineveh read about this stone, gathered an army and sent it off to discover this city. When they arrived they made ladders to climb the walls in order to see inside . . . But the first who ascended, as soon as he saw the stones inside, opened his mouth and jumped into the city, never to return.' The same thing happened several times, until the king gave up trying to discover what was inside the city, and went away.

These remarkable pieces of lore might seem entirely aberrant. Nonetheless, the theme of the city, which swallows up its attackers as they gape in amazement, reappears in a story from the Maghreb that was well known in Muslim Spain.[67] Musa ibn Nusayr, the conqueror of Spain, takes on the role of the two-horned conqueror in the tale of the City of Brass, already made famous by Ibn al-Faqih (d. 903) in his *Kitab al-Buldan*. Anyone who climbs its walls is overcome by laughter and hurls himself to death within. He follows in the footsteps of 'Darius the Greek, King of Alexandria, and Dhu'l-qarnain'.[68]

Entering upon a fair land 'wide and level and smooth as if it were the sea when calm', they beheld a black castle on the horizon which was one of the landmarks to the City of Brass. Another three days brought them to a horseman of brass who revolved and indicated the direction of the fabulous city. Beyond him was another marker, a pillar of black stone which proved to be an *'ifrit*, or ogre, multi-armed and with a third eye, who – sunk up to his armpits – told them that the city was near at hand. On the horizon appeared a great blackness, a city, the walls of which were of black stone and which had twin towers of Andalusian brass which appeared like fires at a distance . . . . It was a city of death without an entrance. The army made a ladder of wood and iron, but the assailants jumped to their death from a kind of madness, and it was only by the piety of Shaykh 'Abd al-Samad that the wiles of Satan and his sirens . . . were defeated. The keys were found, and the sinister city of death, with its treasure, was entered. Within its palaces lay a dead damsel, beautified and adorned upon a couch. A golden tablet disclosed that she was none other than Tadmur, daughter of the king of the Amalekites, and that her subjects had died from famine and drought. Heavily laden with treasure, and reflecting the sorry fate of 'mortal man', Musa ibn Nusayr returned to the Caliph who had sent him.

This strange story echoes both the episode of Alexander's encounter with the dead Cyrus in the City of the Sun (*AR* III. 28) and the mood of Alexander's constant preoccupation with mortality.

The sinister city reappears in another legend of Alexander, this time as an obstacle to him rather than his own creation. This is the 'Christian Romance of Alexander', an Ethiopic tale, probably of 'comparatively recent times' (Budge), no doubt composed for recitation in monasteries.[69] In this story Alexander and his army come, in an unidentifiable region called the Land of Japhet, to a city enclosing a cylindrical citadel without gates: 'the dwellers in the city used to close its gates and then they danced day and night to the sounds of the organ, and reeds, and flutes, and horns, and trumpets, and drums, and various other instruments which were worked by cords, and pulleys, and levers, and wheels. The people were addicted to fornication. And when they ceased to dance, mechanical figures of men and women took their places and danced.' Alexander sends his soldiers to scale the inner citadel with ladders; but when the soldiers reached the tops of the ladders and looked in, 'they were so pleased with what they saw that they leaped off the ladders into the citadel and returned not. Whether they leaped off the ladders of their own free will, or were dragged down by magical means is not clear.' Alexander himself climbs up to have a look and sees the mechanical musicians and dancers, 'but God opened his eyes and made him to know that all these figures were cunning contrivances made of brass, and that they were without life and breath'. He sends up another team of soldiers, blindfolded, to enter the citadel and open its gates (though there were none a few lines back). Now Alexander discovers an inscription which God enables him to interpret, describing the booby traps for invaders and ending with the sad statement, 'When the wrath of God came upon us, our wealth and riches availed us nought, and they brought us no salvation; for the judgment of God is righteous.'

Alexander sends his men in to bring out the treasures of the city. He does not destroy the mechanical musician, which is regarded as an idol, but sets serpents to prevent anyone from entering the city again. Then he fills the space between two neighbouring mountains with the brass musical figure and all the other instruments, and sets up over them a gate of brass plastered with bitumen. If the serpents attack the gate, the instruments play and frighten them away. 'Therefore the things which Alexander buried under the gate remain there until this day, and there they will remain until God permits the filthy peoples of Gog and Magog to burst open the gate.'

The conclusion of this story about a false paradise borrows from the episode of the enclosure of the Unclean Nations, which will be discussed in Chapter 9. Though Christian in colour, the Ethiopic legends of Alexander derive from Arab sources, not least the history of al-Makin (d. 1273–74), and a story like this shows how intertwined in Arab tradition are the figure of the adventurer and of the sage. Not only is Alexander skilled in riddles, but he employs a stratagem like that of Odysseus with the Sirens to prevent his men from being overcome by the enchantments of the city to which he alone is resistant.[70]

Even the ordinary magnet had its part to play in the development of the Alexander story. We saw above how magnets might be employed for flight, or at least for aerial suspension.[71] The ancients were fascinated by magnets. Ptolemy the geographer (VII.2.30–31) tells of the Magnetic Mountain in the Far East, not far from the three islands of satyrs. 'Next along, it is said, there are ten islands called maniolai, in which they say ships built with iron nails are held fast, perhaps because the "Heraclean stone" is generated there, and for this reason the ships *are built on tracks* [the text is corrupt but may have referred to the use of wooden pegs]. These islands are home to cannibals called Maniolai.' The Magnetic Mountain is mentioned in *The Thousand and One Nights*,[72] where it is said that it will draw out all the nails from a ship and cause it to split apart.[73] For this reason, as Marco Polo knew, the ships of those parts were stitched together,[74] and the dangers are mentioned in the *Letter of Prester John*, whence they enter the *Travels* of Sir John Mandeville.[75]

There may be an echo of the legend in the account given by Aethicus Ister (*Cosmographia*, pp. 126–30) of the boats of the Meopari. The name of this imaginary people is a misunderstanding of that given, according to Isidore (*Etymologiae*, 19.1.21) to the reed boats of Germanic pirates.

Alexander is said to have attacked them for the purpose of discovering the secret of building ships without nails and with indissoluble caulking. He used this caulking (the Latin word is *bitumen*) not only for constructing his diving bell, but for sealing the gate that shuts out the Unclean Nations.

The Magnetic Mountain of Arab lore seems to be the basis of a related danger that faces Amir Hamza, the hero of a popular Persian tale, originating in the eleventh century and known also in Urdu.[76] But instead of a magnetic mountain, Hamza's ship is drawn inexorably into a hazard known as the Whirlpool of Alexander. Luckily the Amir spies in the middle of the whirlpool an inscription in Arabic instructing his deputy to climb the adjoining pillar and beat the Drum of Alexander. The Amir's brother Amar does so, and the ship escapes from the whirlpool. (Unfortunately Amar is left stranded on top of the pillar in the middle of the Ocean, but presently the prophet Khidr appears and rescues him.)

What this whirlpool has to do with Alexander is nowhere explained, but it seems that, rather than devising the hazard, Alexander was the one who found the solution and thoughtfully left his drum there for future use. The benefits of the sage continue throughout the centuries.

7

AMAZONS, MERMAIDS AND WILTING MAIDENS

The Amazons

Long ago the Amazon kingdom was begun through the arrangement and enterprise of several ladies of great courage who despised servitude, just as history books have testified. For a long time afterward they maintained it under the rule of several queens, very noble ladies whom they elected themselves, who governed them well and maintained their dominion with great strength . . . And thus . . . this kingdom lasted more than eight hundred years, and you yourself can see from the various epochs given in charts in different history books how much time elapsed from their founding until after the conquest of Alexander the Great, who conquered the world, during which the kingdom and dominion of the Amazons apparently still existed. For the historical accounts about him tell how he went to this kingdom and was received there by the queen and the ladies.

Christine de Pizan, *The Book of the City of Ladies*
(transl. E.J. Richards 1982, 11 and 51)

A perhaps surprising feature of the *Alexander Romance* is the absence of sex. The Greek romances in general revolve around erotic themes, and that is no less true of those on historical themes than of the five 'canonical' romances: *Ninus*, for example, contains a substantial erotic element. Ninus returns from campaign to the embraces of the glamorous Semiramis, and to beg for an early marriage. ('I had tried her virtue and stolen my enjoyment undercover . . . I am not shameless in discussing with her mother a daughter's longed-for marriage'.) Even *Sesonchosis* seems to have involved the engagement of the hero to a young woman, though its main focus is on the campaigns of adventure and conquest of the legendary Pharaoh.[1] The Alexander of the *Romance*, by contrast, has no erotic element. His story is a string of missed opportunities. Little attention is paid by the author of the *Romance* to the marriage to Roxane; and no mention is made of his long-time mistress Barsine, or of his amour with the eunuch Bagoas (which provided Mary Renault with the underpinning for a whole novel).[2] On the other hand, his relations with his mother are a central feature of the *Romance*. That at least is historical material, and his susceptibility (if that is the right word) to motherly queens is a constant feature in the histories. He hits it off with the exiled queen Ada of Caria, whom he addresses as 'mother' and who sends him daily presents of savouries and pastries until he persuades her to desist, on the grounds that 'he already had better cooks given him by his tutor Leonidas – a night's marching to get him ready for the morning meal, and short rations to prepare him for the evening meal'.[3] Ada's willingness to accept his rule is indicated by her adoption of him as her son (Arr. *Anab.* 1.23.7–8), and it is certainly significant that Arrian mentions here Semiramis as the model for female rulership in Asia, for Semiramis was another of Alexander's role models in his campaign of conquest.

Queen Cleophis, whom he encounters in Swat, is another young mother-figure, being the mother of a deceased king: Assacanus, and rumour had it that she bore Alexander a son. 'The queen herself placed her little son at Alexander's knees, and from him gained not only a pardon but also the restitution of her former status . . . . Some have it that it was the queen's beauty rather than Alexander's compassionate nature that won her this, and it is a fact that she subsequently bore a son who was named Alexander, whoever his father was' (Curtius Rufus. 8.10.35–6).

The most notable of these missed opportunities in the *Romance* is the meeting with the Amazons. In Greek legend the Amazons were a race of female warriors, who lived in a society without men, beyond the River Thermodon in north-eastern Anatolia.[4] In the fifth and fourth centuries BC the Amazons were known primarily for having been conquered by Heracles, and were adopted in Athenian iconography (and later elsewhere) as emblems of the barbarians whom Hellenism had perpetually to repel.[5] Achilles, too, had killed the Amazon Penthesilea, being smitten by her beauty at the moment she fell in death. The tomb of Mausolus at Halicarnassus, which Alexander would have seen, depicted that endless battle on one of its several encircling friezes. The essence of Amazons is that they are other in every way, an inversion of Greek society: they are barbarians and therefore they have a queen (though the separate society of Libyan Amazons described by Diodorus is a democracy); they are anti-male, 'the female sex at war', and represent the otherness of women as much as that of non-Greeks.

Any hero setting out to emulate the exploits of Heracles could expect an encounter with Amazons. Sure enough, Alexander found them. Atropates, the Satrap of Media, was said to have sent him a hundred women warriors of the Amazon nation (Arr. *Anab.* 7.13.2), and, even more importantly, Pharasmanes, king of the Chorasmians, informed him that the Amazons lived just next door to his kingdom (equivalent to modern northern Turkmenistan and Uzbekistan, south of the Aral Sea), beyond the Oxus (Amu Darya), and promised to lead Alexander to them.[6] The location is an example of the now familiar geographical confusion described in Chapter 4. Because the mountain ranges of the Taurus, the Caucasus and the Hindu Kush were regarded as lying in a continuous east–west line, it was easy to truncate the length of that line and to regard the crossing of the Thermodon into the region of the Caucasus as bringing a traveller into central Asia. The Don and the Oxus could become confused. So, sure enough, an even more famous story said that Queen Thalestris of the Amazons had visited Alexander while he was camped near the River Tanais (Don), and had stayed thirteen days, just long enough to be sure of conceiving a child, which would thus be the first Amazon ever to have an identifiable father. (Normally they kept their menfolk on an island and arranged periodic mating sessions, in a set-up which was precisely the corollary of the arrangements used by the Brahmans to maintain their society.) Despite the large number of author- ities for this visit,[7] it is certainly fictitious. When the account was read out at court, one of Alexander's companions, Lysimachus, responded, 'And where was I at the time?' (Plu. *Alex.* 46). The story seems to echo that of Heracles' marriage with a local goddess (Hdt. 4.8–9), which was also connected with the Country of Women in India (Arr. *Ind.* ix).[8]

The story in the *Romance* (III. 25) differs from the other historians' accounts. No queen is mentioned, and Alexander deals with the Amazons as a collective through the medium of letters. He writes to request a meeting, 'for we have come not to harm you, but to see your country and to do you good'. The Amazons' reply is a short account of their polity:

We live in the hinterland across the river Amazon. Our country is completely encircled by a river, and it takes a year to travel around it. There is only one entrance. We, the virgins who dwell in it, number 270,000, and we are armed. There is no male creature in our land. The men live on the other side of the river and farm the land. We hold an annual festival at which we sacrifice a horse to Zeus, Poseidon, Hephaestus, and Ares; the festival lasts six days. Any of us who have

26 The Amazons. From the MS Venetus (D), Hellenic Institute, Venice, Codex gr. 5.

decided to be deflowered move to the men's territory. Any female children are returned to us at the age of seven. When enemies attack our
country, 120,000 of us ride out on horseback; the rest remain to defend
the island . . . . If any of us is wounded in battle, she receives great
honours in our revels; she receives a garland and her memory is
preserved for ever. If any of us is killed in battle, her nearest relative
receives a considerable amount of money. If any of us brings the body of
an enemy onto the island, she is rewarded with gold and silver and dines
at public expense for the rest of her life . . . . If we conquer the enemy or
put them to flight, that is regarded as a humiliation for them for the rest
of time; but if they conquer us, it is only women that they have defeated.

Now beware, Alexander, that the same thing does not happen to you.

Alexander responds gently to this forceful letter, offering to take some of
the women warriors into his employ; and the Amazons respond by agreeing
to treat him as their lord, even though they dwell 'beyond the edges of the
world' (III. 26). In the gamma recension, the Amazons ask Alexander to
send them his portrait to revere. He sends them his spear, a remarkable
symbol of phallic domination.

The description of the Amazons' state recalls the situation of other Greek
utopias, not least that of the Brahmans in Palladius, who live on an island
in a river and keep their womenfolk the other side of the water. The details

of the horse sacrifice and of the magnificent burials of the fallen warriors have found echoes in archaeological discoveries of burials of women warriors with armour and horses in south Russia,[9] suggesting that the persistent legend of the Amazons may have arisen from real knowledge of this remote region in antiquity. Alexander may even have met one of these women when he was offered a Scythian bride at Maracanda in 328.[10]

Historical or not, the Amazons lived on through the Middle Ages, both Latin and Greek, in accounts of the mysterious east.[11] Sir John Mandeville (*Travels,* ch. 17) describes the Land of Amazonia or Feminia, 'next to Chaldaea' but between the Caspian and the Don (ch. 16), and often at war with Scythia. When all the country's women had been widowed in a war with Scythia, they determined to become a kingdom of women.

> And from that time hitherwards they never would suffer man to dwell among them longer than seven days and seven nights, nor that no child that were male should dwell amongst them longer than he were nourished and then sent to his father . . . . This land of Amazonia is an isle all environed with the sea save in two places where be two entries. And beyond that water dwell the men that be their paramours and their loves, where they go to solace them when they will. Beside Amazonia is the land of terra Margine, that is a great country and a full delectable. And for the goodness of the country King Alexander let first make there the city of Alexandria (and yet he made twelve cities of the same name), but that city is now cleped Seleucia.

Mandeville also provided the familiar etymology of the name Amazon, which said that they removed one breast by cauterisation – the left for those of great lineage who bore shields, the right for foot soldiers, 'for to shoot with bow Turkish, for they shoot well with bows'. This etymology, like the other information in his account, derived from classical sources, though the Amazons are never shown in art as single-breasted.[12]

The country of the Amazons is often depicted in the art of the Middle Ages as 'the island of women'. The detail of the two entries seems to be derived from the single entry of the *Romance* account, for this is not elsewhere a feature of their land. Mandeville's awareness of the *Romance* and associated texts is clear from the immediately following reference to Alexander, though he does not describe the encounter of the two. In fact, the medieval sources do not generally associate the Amazons with Alexander. Even the fictional author 'Pharasmanes' does not mention them, though it was his historical counterpart who introduced them into the Alexander story; but he does refer to the hairy women of *AR* III. 29

(gamma). In the eighth century, Aethicus' long account (179) places their polity by the Thermodon but does not mention Alexander, and the fourth-century historian Orosius places them in the category of geographical information rather than history. Though the *Letter of Prester John* speaks of the Land of Great Feminie, it makes no connection with Alexander;[13] nor does Marco Polo mention Alexander when he describes the Amazon lands. In fact, throughout the Middle Ages the context in which Amazons are mentioned is normally the Trojan War, as in Benoît de Sainte-Maure's *Roman de Troie*.[14] They do not appear on the Hereford or other *Mappae Mundi*. So it is a mark of deep reading that Christine de Pizan (epigraph to this chapter) in 1405 brings the Amazons once again into conversation with Alexander.

A full picture of the medieval view of Amazons, though unusual in its location, is given, three hundred years before Mandeville, by the chronicler Adam of Bremen (*History*, completed *c.* 1076–81). He described how the son of the king of Sweden, 'sent by his father to expand his dominions, came into the land of the women, who we think were Amazons, and he as well as his army perished there of poison which the women mingled in the springs'.[15] He expands in a later passage (IV. xix (19), 1959, p. 200):

> Round about the shores of the Baltic Sea, it is said, live the Amazons in what is now called the Land of Women. Some deduce that these women conceive by sipping water. Some, too, assert that they are made pregnant by the merchants who pass that way, or by the men whom they hold captive in their midst, or by various monsters, which are not rare there. And when these women come to give birth, if the offspring be of the male sex, they become Cynocephali; if of the feminine kind, they become the most beautiful women . . . . The Cynocephali are men who have their heads in their breasts. They are often seen in Russia as captives and they voice their words in barks.

Adam goes on, citing Solinus (who actually put them in Ethiopia, 27.58, 30.4) to mention the grey-haired Alani, the Husi, 'pale-faced, green and macrobiotic', and the anthropophagi.

When Christopher Columbus discovered the American continent and took it for the Far East, he was not in the least surprised to find a nation of women there.[16] The River Amazon itself was named in 1542 by Gonzalo Pizarro's captain Francisco de Orellana, as a result of meeting with women warriors.[17] A few decades later, Sir Walter Ralegh, who had described the Amazon land in his *History of the World*,[18] included in his *Discovery of Guiana* (1596) a conversation with a native chieftain who told him about the neighbouring race of Amazons.

They do accompany with men but once in a year, and for the time of one month, which I gather to be in April. At that time all the kings of the borders assemble, and the Queens of the Amazons, and after the queens have chosen, the rest cast lots for their Valentines. This one month, they feast, dance and drink of their wines in abundance, and the moon being done, they all depart to their own provinces. If they conceive, and be delivered of a son, they return him to the father, if a daughter, they nourish it and retain it; and so many as have daughters send unto the begetters a present, all being desirous to increase their own sex and kind; but that they cut off the right dug of the breast I did not find to be true.[19]

This remarkable vindication of Mandeville shows that the anxieties that engendered the Amazon legend were still persistent in the Renaissance, though one wonders if Ralegh speaks from personal amorous experience in his assertion that the women of Guiana were possessed of a full set of breasts. It took a female author such as Christine de Pizan (c. 1364–1430) to turn the legend of the Amazons, and even their encounter with Alexander, into an allegory of the rarely realised potential of women to maintain a state and a world of learning and achievement. Alexander himself is almost forgotten; here, in fact, is one world he never did conquer. The other stories of Alexander's encounter with women bear the same moral.

Candace

The novella-like story of Alexander's encounter with Queen Candace of Meroe immediately precedes the Amazon episode in the *Romance* (III. 18–23). Like the Amazon story, it seems to be a story of a missed opportunity for sexual conquest.

In the *Romance* it is made clear that she is a woman of middle age who, though still beautiful, is old enough to be Alexander's mother; and in fact she expresses a wish to adopt him in some ancient Greek recensions and their derivatives (see colour plate 11).[20] However, this conclusion was plainly unsatisfactory to many of the Byzantine chroniclers who reworked the romance material into their universal histories. John Malalas in the sixth century AD (8.195) has her say to him, 'Emperor Alexander, you have captured the whole world but one woman has captured you.' To which he replies: 'Because of the excellence and the quickness of your mind, I shall preserve from harm you, your land and your sons, and I shall take you to wife.' Marriage follows. The same denouement occurs in the ninth-century chronicle of George the Monk, and in a number of other works even up to the *Chronicle* of John Stanos, published in Venice in 1767.[21]

Given that the Candace episode in the *Romance* is not an erotic novella, what is it? The question involves an analysis of the narrative of the episode and its unusually protean later developments.

The episode begins (*AR* III. 18) with Alexander's desire to see 'the world-renowned palace of Semiramis' (the legendary queen of Assyria). Her country is now ruled by Candace of Meroe, 'a woman of remarkable beauty in her early middle age'. Alexander writes her a letter, to which she replies with a letter promising numerous exotic gifts such as '100 solid gold ingots, 200 young Ethiopians, 200 sphinxes, an emerald crown . . . 300 elephant tusks, 300 panther skins, 3000 ebony wands'. At the same time she secretly has his portrait painted and hides the portrait.

Now her son Candaules suffers an attack from a local people, the Bebryces, who carry off his wife. Candaules appeals to Ptolemy, Alexander's second-in-command, for help. Alexander and Ptolemy devise a plan: Ptolemy will disguise himself as Alexander, Alexander as Antigonus. (The episode recalls one in Quintus Curtius (8.13.21) where Alexander and Attalus exchange clothes to deceive the Indian king Porus). They make war on the Bebryces and recover Candaules' wife. The grateful Candaules then takes Alexander (disguised as Antigonus) to Candace's court as a supposed envoy from Alexander. They travel to Candace's palace via the Crystal Country, where Candaules points out the cave known as the Dwelling of the Gods. Here Candace gives him a tour of its splendours, including a kind of war-caravan. She has no trouble recognising Alexander from the portrait she has in hiding and soon lets him know she has broken his cover.[22]

One unusual variant is found only in recension lambda.[23]

> I saw the floor of the palace like waves of water. I stood and gazed at such brightness. I went in with the eunuchs to the queen – and I lifted up my robes, thinking that I was walking over water. As I later realised, water was running below the paving and dripping down from above: for the paving was of alabaster. When Candace saw me lifting my robes she smiled. She recognised me from my appearance.

This is borrowed directly from a familiar story of the Queen of Sheba, whom Solomon compelled to walk over a glass floor when he visited her, thus revealing that she had hairy legs – or, in some versions, a donkey's hoof.[24] The motif, which in the Qur'ān gives Solomon the chance to understand the nature of the queen, is transformed here into a practical joke, as the recognition element of the scene is achieved by the use of the portrait – though it does emerge that Alexander can speak Candace's language (59.11ff.) as Solomon can speak that of the beasts and birds (Qur'ān 27.16).[25]

Alexander now has cause for anxiety, because it turns out that Candace's younger son, Thoas, is married to the daughter of Porus, the king of India, whom Alexander has recently slain. Thoas and Candaules prepare to fight a duel, prompted by their respective attitudes to Alexander, but the latter (still in disguise) manages to reconcile them by promising to return and bring Alexander to them for vengeance. He then leaves with gifts from Candace (including a crown, cloak and breastplate) and the story moves into a new episode, the visit to the Dwelling of the Gods (Chapter 12). Thence he continues to the palace at Meroe.

Meroe[26]

The land of Meroe was situated in a bend of the Nile, close to the sixth cataract, in present-day Sudan, a little distance north-east of Khartoum. Pre-Hellenistic information about Meroe in classical authors is scant, except for the long description in Herodotus (Book 3), who at least in some points confuses its inhabitants with Homer's 'blameless Ethiopians' who live at the ends of the earth.[27]

But from the third century information becomes more plentiful. A fragment of Bion of Soli's *Aithiopika* (*FGrH* 668 = scholium to Acts 8.27) gives the crucial piece of information that the kings of Meroe were regarded as sons of the Sun, and that their mothers were all called Candace. A curious scrap from the unfortunately undatable author, Timocrates of Adramyttium (*FGrH* 672F1) refers to 'Berex – a people between India and Ethiopia', which looks very much as if it has something to do with the Bebryces of the *Alexander Romance*. Another author, Markellos (*FGrH* 671F2), refers to the high mountains of Meroe, which seems to be a confusion with Ethiopia proper. A general growth of interest in Meroe in the third century is indicated by the mention of visitors to the region by Pliny (*NH* 6.35.183–8), and by the expedition sent by Ptolemy II, some time after 274, to obtain elephants: the beginning of an important trade.[28] Pliny mentions not only the elephants, but also the 'sphingia' apes, which seem to be what Candace offered to Alexander in her letter. Further, Pliny locates the monstrous races known to us from the *Romance*'s description of the Far East in the country adjoining Meroe.

But the most important source on ancient Meroe is the account by Diodorus Siculus (3.2ff.), which derives from a monograph by

Agatharchides of Cnidus (*c.* 200–130 BC). This account reflects a period – the third century BC – which the leading authority on ancient Meroe, Laszlo Török, has characterised as the Meroitic miracle. It includes the eclipse of Napata by Meroe as the spiritual centre of the kingdom, the building of the first lion temple, the rise of gods with non-Egyptian names in the pantheon, and the development of the Meroitic alphabet. Diodorus (3.5) also informs us of an important change in the political arrangements of Meroe. It had been the custom that the priests would, at the due time, issue orders to the king that he must die; 'but during the reign of the second Ptolemy (285–246) the king of the Ethiopians, Ergamenes, who had had a Greek education and had studied philosophy, was the first to have the courage to disdain the command'. Instead, he 'put the priests to the sword, and after abolishing this custom thereafter ordered affairs after his own will'. This is probably King Arakakamani, the first ruler known to have been buried at Meroe.

The story is evidence for a much greater interplay of Meroe and Greek culture in the early Ptolemaic period, and suggests a likely context for the emergence of a story connecting Alexander with Meroe. Knowledge, however, clearly remained limited. Like the Egyptians, the Meroites practised sibling marriage and thus, as Nicolaus of Damascus informs us,[29] the kings of Meroe handed the succession to the children of their sisters. However, for centuries yet, Greek writers believed that the Candaces were in fact the queens of 'Ethiopia'; for example the author of Acts (8.27) refers to the eunuch servant of Queen Candace converted by the Apostle Philip, and in late antiquity both Heliodorus and Eusebius regarded queens as a characteristic feature of the Ethiopian polity.[30] And I cannot resist mentioning the apocryphal work, the Apostolic History of Abdias (probably sixth/seventh century) which, through the fog of the author's brain, transmits a story about an Ethiopian eunuch called Candacis, who had been converted by Philip and who plays host to St Matthew on his visit to his city of Naddaver, during which the apostle enters into a contest with two magicians, Zaroes and Afraxat, to drive away a couple of dragons.[31]

Quintus Curtius (4.8.3) mentions Alexander's interest in visiting Ethiopia, 'beyond the boundaries of the Sun', and the historian Callisthenes claimed to have explored the upper regions of the Nile in Ethiopia during Alexander's expedition.[32] Pseudo-Callisthenes, as so often, takes the hints of Alexander's desires as expressed in the historical sources, and turns them into reality. Another episode in Quintus Curtius impacts on the Middle Greek version of the story, where the queen's name becomes Cleophila: here she is assimilated to Queen Cleophis of Massaga, modern Swat

(Curtius 8.10.34; Justin 12.7.9), by whom Alexander is said to have had a child. Apart from this there is little connection between the *Romance* narrative and any historical realities; though it is possible that the visit to the City of the Sun in Ethiopia, which follows this episode in the *Romance* (3.28), has some connection with the 'Table of the Sun' which Herodotus describes as an important religious site for the people of Meroe.[33]

The positioning of the story in the *Romance* is significant. It follows after the encounter with the Brahmans and the visit to the Temple of the Sun and Moon; and it is followed by Alexander's encounter with the Amazons and then by the visit to the City of the Sun. The dominant theme of all five of these episodes is Alexander's concern with his own mortality and his desire to know the date and circumstances of his own death. The Brahman episode expresses the central paradox of his career: his unlimited conquest face to face with his inevitable death. The search for information about his death occurs in the episode of the Oracular Trees of the sun and moon, and the episode at the City of the Sun concludes with a warning to him not to overreach. It must then be significant that the central episode of all these, the Candace story, incorporates (and in the medieval versions contains at its centre) the *katabasis* to the cave of the gods and the refusal of Sesonchosis to tell him what he wants to know.

The *katabasis* is clearly modelled, and even more plainly in the later versions, on Odysseus' descent to the Underworld. It is interesting to recall other *Romance* texts which contain a similar *katabasis*, not least the story of Cupid and Psyche (Apul. 6.20: cf. 11.23.7); the latter's descent is integral to the love story. Lucian's *Kataplous* is another example of a novelistic encounter with the gods: but I have not found other examples where such a *katabasis* encapsulates a theme of the larger work.[34] The change in the medieval versions – see Chapter 12 below – to a vision of the doomed gods fits the new Christian context, in which Alexander is not so much an overreacher as a servant of God.[35]

The second function of the episode in the *Romance* as a whole is to be the first of two emblematic conquests by Alexander of female opponents. The Amazons, who came next, offer submission to his rule without demur to his rule; Candace seems equally complaisant, despite the trick she plays on him. But it has to be said that the symbolic elements of these episodes are not drawn out; they are presented, as it were, paratactically, and the reader or listener is left to divine their import from their cumulative effect. And the conquests are scarcely conquests at all, as Alexander just goes on his way.

Greek Folk-Tales

The figure of Alexander in Greek folk culture has been exhaustively studied by Georg Veloudis, and it is to his works that I owe the following folk-tales.[36] Several such tales are clearly inspired by one or other of the medieval Greek literary texts, or the *Phyllada*; of those relating to this episode, the first concerns Alexander's rescue of an abducted woman, which seems to parallel the rescue of Eurymithres' wife in the Candace episode. The second (*Veloudis* 1969, 55) is the story of a princess of Sparta, who finds a black lamb in the road and brings it to her room. Once inside, it changes into Alexander the Great. The king now institutes a contest for the hand of his daughter, which involves jumping over a high wall. Only Alexander is successful, but, once over, he runs off and disappears. The princess searches for him; when she finds him, he gives her three magic cigarettes and disappears again. When she finds herself in danger, she lights one of the cigarettes; Alexander appears with his ships, rescues her and vanishes again. Eventually a snake shows her where to find him, and they marry. (This story may seem to have little to do with Candace, apart from the idea that Alexander is winning a bride; but the way in which he wins the bride will shortly become relevant to my argument.)

A second strand of Alexander lore in the medieval Greek tradition concerns the much disputed question of the indebtedness of the legend and the poem of Digenis Akritas to the figure of Alexander.[37] Digenis, the 'twice-born' (i.e. Greek and Arab) border-lord, is a character from the marches of Byzantine and Arab lands: his legend and songs about him, as well as an epic poem, all originating in the tenth century, remained popular for several centuries. The folk-song about the abduction of Digenis' wife and her recovery may owe something to the Candace episode; and it is certain that the figure of Alexander was often present in the mind of the composer of the heroic poem about Digenis. Not only does Digenis have a liaison with the Amazon Maximo, like Alexander with Thalestris in the vulgate tradition – and Digenis also frees a girl who has been abducted by Musur[38] – but the walls of Digenis' palace on the Euphrates are decorated with scenes of 'triumphs of the ancients' which include the Candace episode.

The first was Samson's battle with the gentiles . . . .
And in the middle David quite unarmed,
Holding in his hand his sling and stone;
Next was Goliath, who was great in stature,
Fearful to look at, mighty in his strength.
        (G–vii 63, 71–4)

The decorations continue with scenes of Achilles, Odysseus and the Cyclops, and Bellerophon.

> Alexander's triumph, Darius' defeat,
> The reign of Candace, and her wisdom too,
> Reaching the Brahmans, then the Amazons,
> And other feats of the wise Alexander . . .
>   (G-vii 90–94)

The presence of Candace in the medieval Greek tradition, then, has two main elements: the chroniclers regard her as an erotic conquest of Alexander's, and the form of the story lies behind some folk-tales and aspects of the Digenis cycle; while, again in *Digenis*, she is regarded as one of the central episodes of Alexander's career, along with the Brahmans and Amazons. Both these elements have their impact on a further development of the medieval Alexander, which concerns another female hero: Semiramis.

From Semiramis to the Sirens

Candace, as is made clear at the outset of the story, lives in the palace of Semiramis, and is in fact regarded as her descendant. Alexander's interest in making her acquaintance seems thus to be inspired by his interest in that Assyrian queen, which is well documented as a trait of the historical Alexander. She was held to be the most successful conqueror before Alexander, and his admiration for her is frequently mentioned by Curtius and other sources (Curt. 7.6.20, 9.6.23, Strabo 15.2.5, 15.1.6). In particular she was seen as the only predecessor to have conquered India (Curt. 9.6.23), and her crossing of the Gedrosian desert was the main reason for Alexander's disastrous expedition across the same region (Arr. *Anab.* 20.1–2). The Middle Greek prose tale (75)[39] also dwells on Alexander's relative failure in comparison with the conquests of 'Seramido', an attitude which goes back to Arrian's remarks (*Anab.* 7.15.4) on how Semiramis had conquered Ethiopia, while Alexander only received envoys from there. Once again the *Romance* acts as wish-fulfilment, and Alexander achieves in its pages what he longed for in reality.

The legend of Semiramis had developed in Mesopotamia and had become known to the Greeks through the writings of Ctesias in the fifth century.[40] Probably in fact a princess from Armenia or north-eastern Iran,[41] she had come to be regarded as the daughter of the mermaid goddess Derceto or Atargatis and had acquired semi-divine status. However, it was her human achievements that interested the Greeks. It appears that the Greek legend of Semiramis underwent some transformations in the period following Alexander, probably as a result of what Cleitarchus wrote about her in his Alexander history.[42] We find her now achieving conquests which anticipate those of Alexander. In addition to the ones Alexander himself was aware of – most notably the conquest of India[43] – her use of elephant dummies (DS 2.16) recalls Alexander's similar stratagem of using red-hot dummies to *fight* elephants.

The figure of Semiramis gained wide resonance in Hellenistic literature: she became the heroine of a largely lost romantic novel,[44] and also appeared in an uncertain legendary context on a relief of the Augustan period at Aphrodisias. Continuing interest in her from the inhabitants of Mesopotamia is reflected in the prominence she receives in Syriac writings,[45] and it would be consonant with the intense interplay of Syriac and Byzantine culture in the sixth and seventh centuries for her to acquire a presence in medieval Greek writing too. (One wayward example may be the statement in the Romanian *Alexander Romance*, which almost certainly derives from a Greek text of its Balkan neighbour, that the Brahmans of India had been the pupils of Semiramis and the Byzantine emperor Heraclius.)[46] It is therefore not altogether surprising – though from another perspective it is breathtaking – to find Semiramis, in place of Candace, becoming the heroine of an erotic encounter with Alexander in a medieval Greek text of uncertain date.

This tale is told in a recently published poem preserved in Codex 197 (f.81r–102v) at the Monastery of Varlaam at Meteora in northern Greece, and in Codex Sinaiticus gr. 2122, at St Catherine's Monastery in Sinai.[47] The first manuscript also includes the *Life of Aesop* and three homilies by Maximus the Peloponnesian. It is dated to the year 1529, though the text probably belongs to the fourteenth or early fifteenth century. It would appear that the monks of Varlaam had some interest in the figure of Alexander, since one of the very rare representations of Saint Sisoes contemplating the bones of Alexander appears among the frescoes of this monastery (colour plate 12).[48] The poem about Alexander and Semiramis is of exceptional interest, as it corresponds in close detail to the story perhaps better known to us from Puccini's opera *Turandot*.[49] Alexander comes to Princess Semiramis as a suitor. All her suitors are threatened with execution unless they can answer a series of riddles. Some of these are simple conundrums, such as 'What tree has twelve branches with sixty leaves, half of them black and half of them white?' – 'The year'. But most have an answer of a moral or religious character: for example, 'What do angels feed on?' – 'The good deeds of men'; 'What sin brings man to

Paradise?' – 'The one that is repented.' The religious character of these questions, as Dimitroulopoulos points out, is entirely appropriate to the location of the codex in a monastery and in fact suggests possible clerical authorship.

I should like to consider a little further the implications of these riddles. Riddle contests go back a long way in the Middle East (at least to the visit of the Queen of Sheba to Solomon, an episode with other resemblances to ours as well), and the particular form of the story which Puccini and his librettist adopted comes from the *Thousand and One Days*, a French compilation of oriental tales modelled on the *Thousand and One Nights*.[50] But whence, exactly, did a precisely similar riddle contest involving Alexander make its way into the modern Karagiozis shadow play about Alexander, *Alexander the Great and the Dreadful Dragon*? Alexander is making his way to the cave where the dragon lurks, and is stopped by a beautiful young woman, Sireine, who asks him three riddles:[51]

Alexander:	I have come from Mesopotamia for love of you, Sireine. Aren't you going to love me?
Sireine:	If I did not love you, Alexander, I would not have denied father and mother and country for you . . . . [she asks him the riddles].
Sireine:	What are the two things which stand still, the two things which run and the two which resemble each other and do not resemble each other?
Karagiozis answers:	Barba, the two which stand still are tarama [cod's roe] and kephalotyri [a hard cheese], the two which run are you and I.
Alexander:	Sireine, the two which stand still are the earth and the heaven. The two which run are the Sun and the Moon. And the two which resemble each other and do not resemble each other are the Sky and the Sea.
Sireine:	The second riddle is a four-syllable word which means 'beautiful winged creature'. If you cut it in half you get a holy city and a strong fortress.
Alexander:	The answer is 'Kanarion'. [The Judaean city of Cana, the fortress of Rhion on the Gulf of Corinth].
Sireine:	The third riddle: Robbers came to a city, and the city fled through the windows but the citizens were captured.

1 The death of Darius. Alexander holds the dying king in his arms. On the left, the murderers stand bound, awaiting punishment. From Firdausi, *Shahnameh* (Book of Kings). Oxford, Bodleian Library MS Elliott 325 f. 379r

2 The siege of Tyre. From Thomas of Kent's Anglo–Norman *Alexander*. Cambridge, Trinity College MS O. 9. 34, f. 4v

3 The Ebstorf Mappa Mundi. Kloster Ebstorf, Germany

4 The Psalter Map. British Library

5 Alexander in the Diamond Valley. Dublin, Chester Beatty Library per. 195 f. 382v

6 Alexander's Diving Bell. From Johann Hartlieb, *Alexander*. Munich, Bayerische Staatsbibliothek. Cgm 581 f. 134r

7 Alexander's Flying Machine. Johann Hartlieb, *Alexander*. Munich, Bayerische Staatsbibliothek. Cgm 581 f. 133r

8 Alexander is admonished by 'a flying creature in the form of a man' to turn back from his quest. From the Armenian translation of the Alexander Romance. Manchester, John Rylands Library, Arm 3 f. 108v

9 Alexander's flying machine. Copper gilt with cloisonné and champlevé. Artuqid plate, first half of 12th century. Tiroler Landesmuseum Ferdinandeum, Innsbruck, Austria

10 The flight of Kai Kavus. Dublin, Chester Beatty Library per. 157 f. 81v

11 Queen Candace in her palace. Johann Hartlieb, Alexander. Munich, Bayerische Staatsbibliothek Cgm 581 f. 80v

12 Saint Sisoes and the Bones of Alexander. Fresco: Meteora (Greece), Varlaam Monastery

13 Sirens emerge from the lake and dance around the camp while Alexander and his men sleep. From the MS Venetus (D) f. 131r

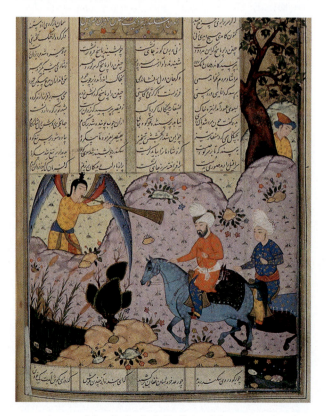

14 Alexander encounters the angel Israfil. Oxford, Bodleian Library MS Ouseley 344 f. 392v

15 Alexander, at the Gate of Paradise, is shown the Wonderstone by an old man. Solothurn, Zentralbibliothek MS 217 f. 290r

ſouden en tiſſen Deſe paep en deſe
lude van dien lande ſi plagen wel. et
?ar te leuen oſſte mier

Boe alexander ſim eerſte antwoerd
ontfinc vander ſonnen bome. en
Je paep ſeide tot alexander he
?n hert en u eename naer n

16 Alexander visits the Oracular Trees, which are attended by a dog-headed priest. From Den
Haag, Koninklijke Bibliotheek, 78 D 39, f. 374v

17 An Islamic interpretation of the oracular tree: the tree of heads is a version of the waq-waq tree of Arab tradition. From Firdausi, *Shahnameh* (Book of Kings). Oxford, Bodleian Library, MS Ouseley Add. 176, f. 311v

18 Albrecht Altdorfer (*c.* 1480–1538), 'The Battle of Alexander' (detail). Munich, Alte Pinakothek PA 63

19 The Cave of the Gods. From Johann Hartlieb's Alexander. Munich, Bayerische Staatsbibliothek, Cgm 581 f. 83r

20 Alexander the Great as a puppet for the Karagiozis shadow play

Alexander: The robbers are fishermen, the windows are the
         holes in the net, the sea is the city and the fish are
         its inhabitants.
Alexander now enters the cave of the dragon.

My interest here is in the name Sireine, which seems at first blush to denote
one of the mermaids known in folklore as sisters of Alexander. However,
another interpretation is possible; and it brings us back to Semiramis.

The interesting study of the figure of Semiramis in oriental legend by
Eilers (1971) has demonstrated the remarkably plastic character of this
heroine, such that she shares a number of traits with the Persian Shirin, the
heroine of Nizami's *Chosrou and Shirin*. Not only are both Semiramis and
Shirin lovers of kings, but legend knows Shirin as a descendant of
Semiramis (in Nizami, her niece). She is known as a great builder (Qasr-i-
Shirin), she is a Christian from Armenia; she has the hero Farhad penetrate
Mount Bisutun with a tunnel to bring her a river of milk, just as Armenian
aqueducts are attributed to Semiramis; and her name in Byzantine Greek
sources is Seirem or Sire. Persian illuminated manuscripts, furthermore,
sometimes confuse the two similar scenes of Shirin gazing on a portrait of
Chosrou with that of Candace (Nushaba in Persian texts) recognising
Alexander from his portrait. In fact the latter scene has been inserted in a
MS of Nizami in the British Library (image 480407), where the former is
required.

The story of Alexander and Candace is among the most protean of any
in the *Romance*. Its female protagonist acquires characteristics that make
her a kind of oriental Everywoman, as she takes on in turn the roles of
the widowed dowager queen Cleophis, the Jewish and Muslim heroine
the Queen of Sheba, the legendary Babylonian conqueror Semiramis
(who herself becomes a Persian heroine, originally a princess of China),
and at the last merges into the Persian Shirin, beloved of Chosrou. If the
skein is found to be continuous, then it is perhaps only appropriate that,
as Eilers suggests, Shirin is the basis for another renowned and resourceful
princess: the teller of the tales of *The Thousand and One Nights*,
Scheherazade herself.

The Mermaids

'Who are you, Sea Lady,
And where in the seas are we? . . .
How should I know your lover,

Lady of the Sea?'
'Alexander, Alexander,
The King of the World was he . . . .
His mother was the foam-foot
Star-sparkling Aphrodite;
His father was Adonis
Who lives away in Lebanon . . .
But where is Alexander,
The soldier Alexander,
My golden love of olden days
The King of the world and me?'

James Elroy Flecker, 'Santorin'

A famous passage of Patrick Leigh Fermor's classic book, *Mani*, recounts the legend of the two-tailed mermaids, or 'gorgons', who inhabit the eastern Aegean and the Black Sea.

> In these waters, beautiful solitary gorgons suddenly surface in the hurly-burly of a Cycladic or Euxine storm – especially, for some reason, on Saturday nights; they grasp the bowsprit of a pitching caique and ask the captain in ringing tones: 'Where is Alexander the Great?' He must answer at the top of his voice 'Alexander the Great lives and reigns!' perhaps adding, 'and keeps the world at peace!' At this the Gorgon vanishes and the waves subside to a flat calm. If the wrong answer is given, the tempest boils up to a deafening roar, the Gorgon tilts the bowsprit towards the sea's bottom and the caique plunges to destruction with all hands.[52]

This legend, so familiar to generations of Greeks that it appears in the fiction of Myrivilis and Venezis,[53] and in the poetry of Seferis, and even in the works of James Elroy Flecker, whose wife was a Greek, marks one of many appearances of Alexander in the folklore of the Levant. As far east as Baghdad, mothers would scare their naughty children into obedience by threatening that 'the two-horned Alexander will get you!' R.M. Dawkins thinks his power over the spirits is borrowed from Solomon's control of the djinns.[54] But can one determine how Alexander acquired this connection with the mermaids?

The answer seems to be the *Alexander Romance*, though Leigh Fermor is sceptical of this argument, which was put forward by J.C. Lawson.[55] Three stories in the *Romance* concern encounters with aquatic women. The first, in the *Letter to Aristotle* (22), tells how women with hair that covers their whole body emerge from the river and drag his men into it. The second

27 A Greek mermaid.

(epsilon 33.3 and gamma II. 41 only) relates how 'sirens' emerged from a lake and danced around it at night before disappearing again. The scene is beautifully illustrated in the MS D (Venetus) of the *Romance* (colour plate 13), and again in many of the MSS of Nizami's *Iskandarnameh*, where the encounter takes place on the borders of Ocean, beyond China. However, the women simply appear and then disappear, without interacting with Alexander and his men in any way.

A more important encounter with the eternal feminine (again involving questions of immortality) is the story that appears in II. 39–41 of the *Romance*, where Alexander undertakes an expedition to discover the Water of Life.[56] Advancing through the Land of Darkness,[57] Alexander (the narrative here is in the first person) describes how:

> We came to a place where there was a clear spring, whose water flashed like lightning, and some other streams besides. The air in this place was very fragrant and less dark than before. I was hungry and wanted some bread, so I called the cook Andreas by name and said 'Prepare some food for us'. He took a dried fish and waded into the clear water of the spring to wash it. As soon as it was dipped in the water, it came to life and leapt out of the cook's hands. He was frightened, and did not tell me what had happened; instead, he drank some of the water himself, and scooped some up in a silver vessel and kept it . . . . Alas for my misfortune, that it was not fated for me to drink of the spring of immortality, which gives life to what is dead, as my cook was fortunate enough to do. (II. 39)

It is not until the party has emerged into the light again that the cook explains what has happened. But still he does not tell Alexander that he has drunk the water himself.

> But then the cook went to my daughter Kale, whom one of my concubines, Unna, had borne to me, and promised to give her some of the water of immortality; which he did. When I heard of this, I will admit, I envied them their immortality. I called my daughter to me and said, 'Take your luggage and leave my sight. You have become an immortal spirit, and you shall be called Neraida because you have obtained immortality from the water . . . . She left my presence weeping and wailing, and went to live with the spirits in the desert places. As for the cook, I ordered that he have a millstone tied around his neck and be thrown into the sea. He thereupon became a spirit himself and went away to live in a corner of the sea which is called Andreas [Adriatic] after him (III. 36 and 41 gamma, in MS C only, and L, and epsilon 33.1).

Many features of this passage betray its late origin in the Christian period
– the names Unna (Hun) and Adriatic, the story of the miracle of the fish,
which is also attributed to St Peter,[58] the interpretation of the name
Neraida as coming from the modern Greek word *nero*, water. Kale, or St
Kale, was once Artemis Kalliste, and became 'the beautiful one of the
mountains' of Greek folklore.[59] An even more colourful version of the
story was collected in Crete by I. Kondylakis in 1887.

In this version, three wise men tell Alexander of the existence of the
Water of Life, which is guarded by a dragon beyond two mountains that
beat unceasingly together. (The echo of the Symplegades of the Argonaut
story is unmistakable.) Alexander departs on his flying horse, Bucephalus
(who has evidently become a congener of Pegasus):

> He slew the drakos and took the glass that held the water of life. But
> once the misguided one had returned to the palace he failed to take
> good care of the water. His sister looked it over and, without a
> thought as to what it might be, poured it all away. It chanced to fall
> upon a wild onion plant and that is why the wild onion will never
> wither away.[60]
>
> Some hours later, Alexander went to drink of the water of life, but
> what had become of it? He asked his sister, who told him that as she had
> had no idea of what it was, she had poured it away. The King nearly went
> mad with grief and frenzy, and he laid a curse upon her that she should
> become fish from the waist down and suffer torture until the world
> should come to stand in the middle of the ocean.[61]

The story continues with the familiar tale of the appearances of the
mermaid at sea in storms, protecting his reputation.

But its origin can be taken back well before its appearance in L by its
occurrence in the Qur'ān, where Andreas becomes the prophet Khidr (see
Chapter 8). The story is one of the clearest soundings of the leitmotif of
Alexander's desire for immortality in the *Romance*. The bitter irony of the
fact that his daughter receives the gift while he is fated to forgo it explains
the anger that is expressed in the Aegean storms that he, apparently,
controls. The mermaid who is his daughter in the *Romance* is usually his
sister in modern folklore; in either case, it is a woman in his life who is
beyond the pale of sexual relations.[62] Is there some connection between
this renunciation of sex by Alexander and his universal power, that
continues even after he is dead? One thinks of Mime's bargain with the
Rhinemaidens in Wagner's *Ring*, that he will forswear love for ever in order
to obtain the absolute power that the ring can give. The teasing nixies of

the *Ring* are no doubt distant cousins of the gorgons or Nereids of the Aegean.

A l'ombre des jeunes filles en fleurs

How different is the medieval European take on the theme of Alexander's relations with women. Even Candace becomes a medieval beauty, '*bele et blanche*', in the work of Thomas of Kent.[63] One of the most notable additions of the Middle Ages to the Alexander legend is the encounter with the Flower Maidens, another theme echoed in Wagner.[64]

This episode is a memorable part of the French *Roman d'Alexandre*, III. 189–200. It was presumably already in Alberic of Besançon's lost poem, since it appears in the Middle High German *Alexander* of Pfaffe Lamprecht.[65]

> *Vil manich scone magetin/ wir al da funden/ di da in den stunden/ spilten uf den grunen cle. Hundert tusint unde me/ di spileten und sprungen . . . . owe wi si mih ruwen/ do ih sa si sterben / und di blumen verterben/ do schiet ih trurich dannen/ mit allen minen mannen.* (Many beautiful maidens we found there, who played all day on the green sward. Hundreds of thousands and more played and jumped around . . . . Alas, how sad I was when I saw them die, and the flowers wilt: I became very sorrowful, along with all my men.) (Lamprecht 5210–6, 5354–8).

Ruttmann (269) calls it an 'oriental fairy tale', but its inspiration seems to be the trees that grow and die in a day, described in the *Historia de proeliis* J[1], 105.[66] These beautiful young women, insatiable for the love of men, dwell in a forest guarded by two automata armed with mallets. The girls spend their nights with Alexander's men but cannot leave the forest. Alexander remains chaste, as always. He enquires of his elders the explanation for these creatures: 'By what marvellous chance do these women live in the forest? Is it law? A judgment? Where do they come from? And their clothes? And who gives them food sufficient to feed all my army? Have they committed a crime against the gods? Where have they found their eternal youth? I have not seen any graves in the forest.' The explanation is that every winter the girls sink back into the earth, to be born again each spring, ever fair and young. The fantasy has as much to do with immortality and eternal youth as with endless pleasure and love. Indeed, it is an episode in a steady progress towards Paradise,[67] which in the *Roman* occupies the position of the Land of the Blessed in the ancient versions. The girls appear again in the myth of Parsifal, tempting the hero to dalliance which the

Christian, unlike Alexander's men, must fiercely resist. But this variation on the theme of sex only shows how absent it is from the Greek core of the *Alexander Romance*, and how Alexander changes to fit the demands of a new genre. Yet again, the women remain remote and unconquered.

8

THE SEARCH FOR IMMORTALITY

No one is satisfied with their current situation, but desires and strives for just those things that they lack and are in want of . . . as, for example, to be a ruler, or a king, or like Alexander, to be immortal. And even if he achieves this, he'll want, I think, to become Zeus himself.

Teles (*c.* 295 BC), ed. O. Hense, pp. 42–3 ed.

And where we are progressing to, we have, if we are honest, known all our lives, to death, except that most of the time we are careful not to admit it. And because we have the certainty of doing nothing other than progressing towards death and because we realize what that means, we try to employ all kinds of aids to divert us from that realization, and thus, if only we look closely, we see in this world nothing except people continually and all their lives engaged in such a diversion. This process, which is the principal process in most people, naturally weakens or accelerates the whole development towards death . . . Everything about everybody is nothing but diversion from death.

Thomas Bernhard, *Yes* (1991), 70–1.

[Alexander speaks] 'The kingdom of happiness and eventual blessedness is only to be realized on earth when we have conquered even the heavenly hosts, our fiercest opponents, the angels . . . . What have we achieved, if we have *not* built the kingdom of happiness and eventual blessedness, on earth?'

Klaus Mann, *Alexander: Roman der Utopie*, 176

I am not certain whether I ever believed in the City of the Immortals; I think the task of finding it was enough for me.

Jorge Luis Borges, 'The Immortal', in *The Aleph*

Almost from the beginning of his expedition, Alexander's campaign of conquest became a campaign in search of something more: all knowledge, all wisdom, universal rule. Arrian described this urge of Alexander's as his *pothos*, an almost religious longing that determined his actions and drove him on, to further adventures and more distant lands.[1] Alexander seems to have felt, ever since his accession, that he had a special relationship with the gods as a result of the rumours that circulated about his divine birth. Immediately after the conquest of Egypt in late 332 BC, he made for the Oracle of Ammon at Siwa in the western desert. What question he put to the Oracle we shall never know, though Plutarch tells us that 'he received the answer he wanted', and that this involved assurance that he was indeed the son of Ammon. (The historian Callisthenes duly made the traditional identification of Zeus with Ammon and asserted that Alexander was hailed as son of Zeus.) But it was not only the Oracle's utterance that gave Alexander immortal longings: as legitimate Pharaoh of Egypt, Alexander was indeed son of Ammon, and he must have wondered what this meant for him. Later in his career he required worship as a god from the Greeks, prompting sarcastic responses from several Greek statesmen, among them Damis the Spartan, with his laconic 'Let him be a god if he wants to.'[2]

The Alexander of the *Romance* is also interested in his relationship with the gods, but his interest takes a very different form. For one thing, the Greek gods scarcely figure in the *Romance*, and Zeus and Ammon are nowhere to be found in this context. Instead, the episode of the encounter with Ammon is completely reworked as a vision of the god Sarapis (*AR* I. 33). After the foundation of Alexandria, he establishes an altar opposite a hero-shrine; but an eagle swoops down, removes the sacrifice and places it on a different altar, which is revealed as that of Sarapis. Here for the first time is sounded the theme of Alexander's preoccupation with death. 'Lord,' he addresses the god, 'show me also, when and how I am going to die.' Sarapis' wise reply is in verse:

> It is better for a mortal man, and more honourable
> And less painful, not to know in advance
> The time appointed for his life to end.
> Men, being mortal, do not understand
> That this rich, varied life is endless, as long
> As they have no knowledge of its misfortunes.

Nevertheless the god relents and informs Alexander

Many people from many lands will worship you
Even in your lifetime, as a god.
After death you shall be deified and worshipped
And will receive the gifts of kings. You shall live in it [the city of
Alexandria]
For all time, dead and yet not dead.
The city you have built shall be your tomb.

The desire to know and have more than mortal men can have is a leitmotif
of later adventures: when Alexander goes up in his flying machine, he is
reprimanded by 'a flying creature in the form of a man' who tells him to
remain on earth. One of the themes of his encounter with the Brahmans
(Chapter 5) is the possibility of immortality. The reprimand of Dandamis in
Palladius concerns Alexander's insatiable desire for conquest, which in the
end cannot protect him against death. The story of the Water of Life
(Chapter 7) revolves around the offered glimpse of the possibility of
immortality, which is snatched from him by the actions of his cook and his
daughter. And towards the end of his adventures in India he is led by local
guides to the oracular trees of the sun and moon. The question he asks
them is not recounted, but their answers focus on the inevitability of his
mortal end. (See further, Chapter 10.)

The Water of Life

It was hardly a new thing in human history that Alexander should be
distressed at the inevitability of death and should seek some props to shore
against his ruin, whether universal conquest or eternal survival. At the dawn
of literature, the first story ever told is that of Gilgamesh, who was overcome with horror at the death of his friend Enkidu; who mourned by his
body 'until a worm came out of his nose'; and who set off to seek the secret
of immortality. Gilgamesh's search for the Plant of Immortality occupies
tablets 9–11 of the fullest recension.[3] He goes to visit Utnapishtim, the
Babylonian Noah, who knows its whereabouts. Gilgamesh has to pass
through high mountains, whose gate is guarded by Scorpion-men; they
warn him that the way is impassable because of the darkness in the mountains. When, however, Gilgamesh has passed safely through this Land of
Darkness, he finds himself in a bright place full of plants blossoming with
gemstones (sometimes identified by commentators with Bahrain). Here
Sidur the alewife advises him to approach the ferryman Urshanabi to gain
passage across the lethal waters to the home of Utnapishtim. After a fight,
Urshanabi conveys the hero across the waters, but when he reaches

Utnapishtim he is told there is no remedy for mortality. Utnapishtim explains how he himself escaped death when the Flood came, and at last tells Gilgamesh of the plant which gives immortality and gives it to him. Gilgamesh then returns across the water with Urshanabi, carrying the plant. But when they stop for the night, Gilgamesh goes into a pool to bathe, and a snake carries off the plant, at once sloughing off its skin and leaving this as the only evidence of its visit. Gilgamesh weeps at the loss of his chance of immortality.

The similarities between this tale and that of Alexander are obvious. In 1894 Bruno Meissner published his book, *Alexander und Gilgamos*,[4] in which he argued for a close dependence of the *Romance* on the Babylonian epic. Yet that can hardly be sustained, for the differences are also very great. Immortality in the Gilgamesh story comes from a plant, not from water. Alexander's quest is not prompted by the death of a friend; in fact, it is not a quest at all, since he comes upon the water by accident. And the snake does not occur in the Alexander story, or the cook in the Babylonian one.

The similarities of the two tales are as general as those between Alexander's flight (which has a similar moral) and another Babylonian tale, that of Etana, who flew to heaven on an eagle's back.[5] Here the common denominator is little more than that of flight, another universal dream. Much closer parallels for Alexander's flight can be found, as was indicated in Chapter 6. There is no need to assume a direct dependence of the *Alexander Romance* on Mesopotamian literature. As was suggested earlier, its links are rather with Egyptian literature, which does not seem to tell such a story.

The idea of a fountain of life seems to go back to Greek lore about India, which was full of magical springs and rivers.[6] The spring Silles,[7] in which nothing would float, constituted the border of Uttarakuru, the wondrous land of milk and honey, scattered with jewels, in which people lived for several millennia.[8] Longevity was, as we saw in Chapter 5, a common feature of the utopias of the east, and especially of Indians.[9] The idea of a magic rejuvenating liquid also occurs in Greek myth in the story of Medea's (failed) attempt to rejuvenate Jason's father after she has successfully experimented on a sheep. The idea of a Fountain of Youth became popular in the Middle Ages through the legend of Prester John,[10] where it is said that anyone who bathes in it regains the age of thirty-two, and that this can be done an indefinite number of times. It is one of the most persistent themes of folk literature,[11] and became a theme for painters in the Middle Ages (e.g. Cranach's *Fountain of Youth* in Dresden). It is brought into connection with Alexander in one of the MSS of the *Histoire du roi Alexandre* from the library of the Dukes of Burgundy, where an illustration

28 The Fountain of Youth. *Histoire du roi Alexandre*. Bibliothèque Nationale, Paris, FR 9342 F 161.

of the magic fountain, guarded by lions and griffins, is captioned 'How Alexander discovered the fountain of youth.'

But youth is not immortal, and the water of immortality is a different thing from a fountain of youth. The key features of the story of Alexander and of the Water of Life look forward to eternity rather than backward to youth. This is the mainspring of Alexander's ambition in the *Romance*, and it is likewise the focal point of his adventures in the most extensive development of this episode, which occurs in Arabic literature. How did this come about?

Arabic Traditions on Alexander[12]

Sura 18 of the Qur'ān is much preoccupied with Alexander, and one of the two episodes with which it is concerned is the search for the Water of Life. (The other is the enclosure of the Unclean Nations, on which see Chapter 9.) The dried fish is the clue to the transmission. The fish that returns to life when dropped into the spring in *AR* II. 39 (see Chapter 7) first appears in recension L of the Greek *Romance*.[13] It is not in the Syriac version, but it does appear in the poem (or 'Discourse') of the sixth-century Syrian author

29 Alexander and Khidr in the Land of Darkness. From a Turkish MS, 'Treatises on Astrology and Divination'. Pierpont Morgan Library, New York, MS M 788 f. 75v.

Jacob of Serugh about Alexander.[14] This is fairly certainly the direct source of the story in Sura 18 (59–60) of the Qur'ān, which tells how Moses and his servant (or 'an old man') travelled to the confluence of 'the two seas' (Arabic *bahrain*) with a dried fish, but carelessly let it escape. The Old Man is generally identified by commentators with the Islamic hero or saint Chadhir or Khidr. So it is no surprise that, in the very extensive Arabic Romances that treat of Alexander and his search for the Water of Life, he is accompanied by Khidr.[15]

The Qur'ān refers to Alexander by the name of Dhu'l-qarnain, the two-horned one. Persian authors were confident of the identity of the two figures, and related the stories of Dhu'l-qarnain as actions of Iskandar; but some Qur'ānic scholars, both in the past and recently, have doubted that Dhu'l-qarnain of the Qur'ān has anything to do with Alexander.[16] However, there is so much convergence of the extant Arabic romances of Dhu'l-qarnain with Alexander stories that there can be little doubt that their authors saw them as one, and used stories from the *Alexander Romance* to elaborate their accounts of Dhu'l-qarnain.

The second part of Qur'ān, Sura 18, is an answer to a problem raised thus: 'They will ask you concerning Dhu'l-qarnain.' The name must derive from the iconography of Alexander, in which the hero is portrayed wearing the horns of Ammon on coins of the successors.[17] However, the question being asked in Sura 18 of the Qur'ān concerns the ram with two horns in the prophecy of Daniel 8, who is generally agreed to be Cyrus, while the goat with one horn represents Alexander. So it seems that the author of the Qur'ān has confused the two figures, under the influence of the prevailing iconography of Alexander with two horns, and has attached the designation to the wrong king.[18]

Though Alexander's entry into the Qur'ān is thus explained, the transmission of the romance as a whole from Greek to Arabic has been obscure. The fact that the story of the *Romance* forms the basis of two long narratives of the eighth and ninth centuries (see below) has encouraged scholars to search for an actual translation of the Greek or Syriac *Romance* into Arabic. Furthermore, the Ethiopic translation of the fourteenth century was plainly derived from an Arabic original, because of the arabisms in its language, especially in the proper names.[19] A notable feature of the Ethiopic translation is that, unlike in all other known Arabic texts (which follow the Persian model here), Alexander is the son of Nectanebo and not of the Persian king Dara.[20] There are two reasons for this: first, the national pride inherent in the Persian version, which makes the conqueror a legitimate Persian king; secondly, the polytheism implied by the Greek story of the birth of Alexander, which was particularly objectionable to Muslim authors.[21]

But no such missing link could ever be found.[22] It was to be expected that the activity of the translation school or House of Wisdom in Abbasid Baghdad in the ninth century AD would have produced such a translation, even though most of its other products were works of medicine, science and philosophy; very little literature.[23] The *Romance* seems to have been known to two of the main translators of the period, Hunayn ibn Ishaq (809–73) and Yahya ibn Batriq (the latter's name indicates that he was a Christian), both of whom worked on Alexander material.[24] Could one of them have made a full translation?

There have been many hopeful suggestions or claims of the discovery of this missing link or will o' the wisp, an Arabic *Alexander Romance*. A.R. Anderson thought that a Spanish–Arabic version of the *Romance*[25] was a witness for a ninth-century Arabic translation, for it contains much of the structure of the Syriac *Romance* – the monsters, the visit to China, the encounter with Candace, the Water of Life, his letter to his mother, his burial in Alexandria – with additional material such as the 'sayings of the philosophers'. But this, like the *aljamiad*[26] *Rrekontamiento del Rrey Ališandre* of the sixteenth century,[27] which it resembles, is too late to act as evidence for a ninth century version: though Islamic in conception (like the two early *Romances* to be considered below), its sources could be many and various.[28] Anderson, after proposing that the Spanish text might be a witness for the Arabic, went on to conclude that the Arabic romance was 'lost and likely to remain lost' (1932, 30).

But hope springs eternal, and several scholars have thought they found evidence or fragments of this text.[29] In 1901 Karl Weymann drew attention to Berlin cod. Arab 9118,[30] which constitutes an abbreviated version of Alexander's letter to his mother and an account of his last days, deriving from the alpha tradition and the Syriac, and argued that this was part of a full translation, probably made in the ninth century, which might one day be found, and which was the direct source of the Ethiopic version.[31]

More compelling was the existence of the *Ahbar al-Iskandar* of Mubaššir ibn Fatik (c. 1020–1100), a brief summary of the story of the text as recounted in the Greek *Romance*.[32] This incorporates other details from various sources, including the tribute of golden eggs (Syriac and Persian), Alexander's monotheism (first in the gamma recension), his visit to the king of China (Syriac), a reference to the Turks, the story of the man who found a treasure in a house he had bought (Jewish), a variant version of the Brahmans story concerning people who have graves in their house-courtyards, as well as the usual Brahman story, the prophecy that Alexander will lie after death between an iron earth and a golden sky (from Eutychius, the Arab Patriarch of Alexandria), and the sayings of the philosophers at his

death (Syriac, and already familiar as a discrete Arabic text). The existence
of this short text (less than 17 pages) leads one to suppose that it is a
summary of a longer Arabic text, written probably in the ninth century: but
nothing could be proved.

However, just a few years ago a Dutch scholar, Faustina Doufikar-Aerts,
discovered a seventeenth-century MS which appears to contain large
portions of this putative 'missing link', a discovery which will cause accounts
of the Arabic *Alexander* to be rewritten.[33] Now for the first time it is possible
for Arabists to read a text that essentially tells the story as it is given in the
Syriac recension and provides the transition to the Ethiopic version.

The Arabic Romances

The process of composition of the first Arabic romances thus becomes
clearer. The key to the narrative in all of them is the search for the Water
of Life and Immortality, which is also important in their Persian successors;[34] to this are added numerous episodes from the Greek/Syriac
Romance, perhaps from this Arabic intermediary; and finally a good deal of
free invention, to turn Alexander into a hero of Islam and prophet of God.
The first full-scale narrative is that of 'Umara ibn Zayd (767–815).[35] In this
account Alexander's mother is a descendant of Noah and the Romans (*sic*)
and a practising astrologer. Learning from her books about the Water of
Life, Alexander sets off, after his father's death and after he has converted
his people to Islam, to find it. He travels to the far west and east, to the
magic cities of Jabarsa and Jabalqa, to the South and the North Poles, and
to Egypt, where he builds Alexandria. It is in Jabalqa that he is told of the
River of Sand. Accompanied by the prophet Khidr, he sets off into the Land
of Darkness.

This land is already familiar from the Greek *Romance*, where Alexander
has to take special precautions not to get lost for ever in the darkness. He
seeks the advice of an old man, who advises: 'It must be clear to you that
you will never see the light of day again if you advance without horses.
Select, then, mares with foals. Leave the foals here, and advance with the
mares; they will without fail bring you back to their foals' (II. 39).[36]
Alexander takes the advice and the narrative proceeds immediately to the
episode of the cook and the Water of Life. Things do not go so quickly in
'Umara's account.

In the Land of Darkness large numbers of bright stones were visible on
the ground. Some of Alexander's men picked them up, others preferred to
keep their burdens light. When they emerged into the light, the stones
turned out to be precious gems, so that 'both those who collected them,

and those who did not, were full of regret — the first that they did not collect more, the second that they did not collect any at all'. These stones seem to be remotely related to the emeralds of the Valley of Jordia in the *Letter to Aristotle* (20). In due course Khidr uses one of these gems, which glows in the dark (we met it before in the Pseudo-Aristotle *De lapidibus*) as a lantern to discover the Water of Life.[37] Khidr bathes in the water and becomes immortal. Alexander arrives too late, sees Khidr taking his bath (and scrubbing down his horse in the fountain, in one delightful Persian miniature), but is denied his chance of immortality.

Nothing daunted, he sets off again for Mount Qaf, the legendary holy mountain of the Islamic cosmos. Here he encounters Israfil, the angel of death, with his trumpet poised ready to sound. The latter admonishes him, as winged creatures usually do, to desist from seeking what is impossible for a man (cf. *AR* II. 40). The encounter is beautifully described by Firdausi, who adapted the whole narrative a century after 'Umara:

Seeing Sekandar on the mountain Esrafil roared with a voice like thunder,

'Stop struggling, slave of greed, one day, at last
Your ears will hear the mighty trumpet's blast —
Don't worry about crowns and thrones! Prepare
To pack your bags and journey on elsewhere!'
Sekandar said, 'I see that I'm to be
Hurried about the world perpetually,
And that I'll never know another fate
Than this incessant, wandering, restless state!'[38]

(See colour plate 14.) Once again Alexander sadly acknowledges his lot: that journeying is his métier and that his desire will never be satisfied — what he seeks will never be found.

'Umara's narrative now becomes rather repetitive. In addition to a visit to Mecca, and a pause to give judgment over the treasure buried in a dunghill,[39] the hero makes a visit to the Brahmans, who describe the way to Adam's tomb. It is to be reached through valleys of jewels and giant ants, and Alexander's route takes him to a valley of sand, a land of darkness, and a mountain which he tries to climb to reach the tomb, but he is warned to desist, for this is the location of Paradise. Another disconnected section describes yet another journey to the Land of Darkness, and a journey with Khidr to a castle where a bird on a pillar asks Alexander, 'Did you not have

30 Khidr at the Fountain of Life. Nizami, *Iskandarnameh*. Chester Beatty Library Persian
Coll. MS 196 f. 349.

enough behind you, that you have to come here too?' The same message is repeated in virtually every one of the hero's encounters.

The same warnings are sounded in the second major narrative about Alexander (Dhu'l-qarnain) in Arabic, that of Wahb ibn Munabbih, an eighth-century Yemenite author. His work is known through the presentation by Ibn Hisham in the latter's *Book of Crowns concerning the Chronicles of the Kings of Himyar*.[40] In this text, Dhu'l-qarnain is identified with the Tubba' king of Yemen, as-Sa'ab,[41] and the story begins with as-Sa'ab's vision of hell. Travelling to Jerusalem, the hero consults the prophet Khidr, who is here identified with Moses (Musa), and the latter interprets his dream to mean that he will be a world-conqueror, but must beware of his final end. His travels include the usual visit to the Land of Darkness and the failure to obtain the Water of Life (while Musa succeeds), as well as the appearance of Israfil to tell him to go no further. He visits a people called the Tarjmaniyun, who could be the Turkmens, but are more likely to be the Brahmans (with incorrect pointing of the Arabic letters برحمانتون), since their habits are exactly those of the Brahmans. A new element in this romance is the very extensive campaign of conquest and slaughter, which extends to Andalusia among other places. Many are the nations to whom he gives the choice: convert to Islam or be killed. The narrative thus serves the purpose of justifying the Islamic conquests in the west and of glorifying the South Arabian dynasty and its conquests in Egypt. A notable feature is the appearance of Turks in the ethnographic mix.

A similar narrative to 'Umara's appears in an eleventh-century account by al-Tha'alabi (d. 1036), in his *Stories of the Prophets*:[42]

Dhu'l-qarnain said: 'I wish that I might live to worship God as He deserves.' . . . Then Raphael said: 'Somewhere on earth God has made a spring, which is called the Spring of Life; of His goodness, whoever drinks a single draught from it shall never die until he himself asks his Lord for death'. . . . Then Dhu'l-qarnain summoned all the learned men of the earth, and those who had studied the scriptures and traditions of the prophets . . . until one of them said: 'I have read the testament of Adam; and in it I read that God made on earth a Darkness in which neither men nor *jinn* have set foot, and there He set the Well of Immortality.' . . . So Dhu'l-qarnain . . . set out in search of the place where the sun sets. He travelled for twelve years before reaching the edge of the Darkness; and when he found it, it was like vapour, not the darkness of night.

The story continues as in the *Romance*: they take mares with them into the darkness, leaving foals behind as a guarantee that the beasts will find their way back. Khidr carries a luminous gem and by its aid he finds the spring, though not in quite the same way.

> He came to a valley and threw the gemstone into the middle of it, and stood at the valley's edge. After a long while, the stone called out to him, and he made towards it; and when he found it, it was lying beside the spring. Khidr took off his clothes and entered the spring; and lo! Its water was whiter than milk and sweeter than honey . . . . But when Dhu'l-qarnayn passed that way, he missed the valley.

Alexander is, as ever, denied the immortality he seeks.

The constant leitmotif of these Arabic romances is the warning given to Alexander by the angels against overreaching. Conqueror of the world he may be, and a hero and prophet of God; but immortality is not to be his lot.

Alexander Visits Iram of the Columns

The same message is pressed home by his visit in Nizami's *Iskandarnameh* to the Tomb of Shaddad, son of 'Ad, in the city of Iram of the Columns. Shaddad's story is one of the anecdotes inserted in later versions of *The Thousand and One Nights*.[43] The city of Iram was discovered in the reign of Mu'awiya by a man searching for his camel in the Yemeni desert. The story was that Shaddad had read in books about the Paradise beyond, and had determined to construct an earthly version in his own kingdom. It was a city of gold and silver, rubies and pearls, with columns of chrysolite and avenues of fruit trees; and it was twenty years in the building. When it was complete, Shaddad set out to visit it; but when he was one day's journey distant from it, 'God sent down upon him and upon the obstinate infidels who accompanied him a loud cry from the heaven of his power, and it destroyed them all by the vehemence of its sound. Neither Shaddad nor any of those who were with him arrived at the city or came in sight of it, and God obliterated the traces of the road that led to it; but the city remaineth as it was in its place until the hour of the judgment.'[44] Shaddad was buried by his son in a cave in the Hadramaut (not apparently in Iram), and the corpse was laid on a golden couch and covered in robes of gold, with a golden tablet at his head bearing these words:

Be admonished, O thou who art deceived by a prolonged life!
I am Shaddad the son of 'Ad, the lord of the strong fortress;
The lord of power and might and of excessive valour.
The inhabitants of the earth obeyed me, fearing my severity and threats;
And I held the east and west under a strong dominion.
A preacher of the true religion invited us to the right way;
But we opposed him, and said, Is there no refuge from it?
And a loud cry assaulted us from a tract of the distant horizon;
Whereupon we fell down like corn in the midst of a plain at harvest;
And now, beneath the earth, we await the threatened day.

The lost paradise of Iram is sometimes seen as the forerunner of an actual Muslim city. Mas'udi[45] relocates the wondrous city and its inscription in duplicate to the site of the future Alexandria, where Alexander comes upon them. 'You who see these ruins, you who know my history, my long life, the certainty of my views, my prudence and watchfulness, do not be led astray, for fortune is treacherous, takes away what it has given and recovers what it has provided.' After pondering the sombre words, Alexander immediately sets about building the city more wondrous than before.

The tomb that Alexander visits in Nizami[46] is in Iram itself, still pristine with its trees of gold bearing golden oranges, silver lemons and apples and pomegranates of jewels, its pools of crystal surrounded by plants of emerald and roses of ruby. The inscription on Shaddad's tomb differs from that in the Arab story and sounds the usual warning to the visitor, who is of course tempted to help himself to the treasure:

He who erects columns for his Iwan [palace] is erecting his own tomb. But consider what happens in the end: the wind bears him in all directions like dust. Who knows whose horse will one day shatter the bones of Shaddad with his hooves? Leave my dust in peace in its crypt: dust to dust. No sign shall you see of my body, whose dust the wind has scattered, except for the golden mountain. You who penetrate this secret, be fearful of the same end and acquit yourself well towards us. Do not consider your self secure because you are free, because in the end you too are of mortal stock. The whole treasure can be yours, and our crown and throne are at your disposal . . . . Take as much as you like, but do not concern yourself with us!

Alexander weeps and, sobered by the message, decides to take nothing from the treasure but goes on his way. Persuaded of the vanity of worldly goods and power, he sets off again into the desert in search of home. Alexander is

the epitome of the man who has everything, yet it profiteth him nothing
for he is doomed to die.

Alexander Visits Paradise

The visits to the Brahmans described by 'Umara and Wahb both chime
with this theme. In Wahb the Brahmans preach to him the now familiar
truth that even a rich man can only eat and drink so much as will fill him,
and can only wear so much clothing as will protect him from the elements;
all else is vanity (Nagel 1978, 25).[47] In 'Umara the philosophers are a stage
on the way to the Land of the Blessed or the Earthly Paradise, to which
they can direct him, though when he reaches it he is forbidden to go near.
The conception here of the Earthly Paradise, location of the tomb of
Adam, is that familiar from Jewish apocalyptic and other literature, for
example I Enoch, the Third *Sibylline Oracle*, and the Similitudes of Enoch.
In the latter, datable to about 50 BC to AD 50, the Paradise in Eden is a land
of milk and honey (as well as oil and wine), where the elect already dwell
and enjoy regular good meals.[48] In Chapter 5 we encountered the
Rechabites, whose home is the Earthly Paradise and who replicate many
features of the Brahmans' way of life. Yosippon even has Alexander visit the
sons of Yonadab (i.e. the Rechabites) himself.[49] The Arab texts thus bring
Alexander within striking distance of Paradise.

By the fourth century thinkers in both east and west were sure that
Paradise could be reached if one travelled far enough to the east.[50] Jerome
(*Epistolae*, 125.3) stated with confidence that Paradise could be reached by
sailing beyond India,[51] while a pilgrim handbook of uncertain date, written
in Greek, is entitled *Itinerary from Eden, the Earthly Paradise*, and charts the
way from Eden to Rome (not the other way about). Isidore of Seville
enshrined this view of the east in his encyclopaedia, which was so influential on the Middle Ages: 'Asia . . . has many provinces and regions, whose
names and locations I shall briefly expound, beginning from Paradise.
Paradise is a place in the eastern regions, whose name is Greek and may be
translated into Latin as "garden" (hortus)' (*Etym.* 14.3.1–5). The conception
was strengthened by the great *Mappae Mundi* of the thirteenth century.[52]
East is at the top and Jerusalem at the centre. The Earthly Paradise is shown
in the far east (top), just inside the River of Ocean. Just to the south-west
of Paradise the Hereford Map shows the twin Altars of Alexander. These
appear even on the very pragmatic late antique *Tabula Peutingeriana*, with
the inscription '*usque quo Alexander*' ('this is as far as Alexander got') and '*hic
Alexander responsum accepit*' ('here Alexander received his response', namely
from the flying creatures).[53]

Not all believed in this location of Paradise. Thinkers in the Greek east, such as Ephraim the Syrian, did not believe in an earthly location of Paradise.[54] The eccentric sixth-century cosmographer, Cosmas Indicopleustes,[55] who believed that the shape of the world was that of a long box, just like the Ark of the Covenant, insisted that:

> If Paradise did exist in this earth of ours, many a man among those who are keen to know and enquire into all kinds of subjects, would think he could not be too quick in getting there: for if there be some who, to procure silk for the miserable gains of commerce, hesitate not to travel to the uttermost ends of the earth, how should they hesitate to go where they would gain a sight of Paradise itself?[56]

Aethicus Ister, on the other hand, wrote (235):

> We have learned from those who have returned to us from the bold and shameless neighbours of those who inhabit the truly happy regions of India, that in those parts is situated Eden, the sacred grove of the god of heaven and a garden inaccessible to carnal creatures.

As geographical knowledge increased, it became more difficult to find a slot for Paradise anywhere in the known globe. Albertus Magnus believed that it was separated from the earth by the Bitter Sea, and that Enoch and Elijah had been enabled to cross it only by a miracle, while Duns Scotus averred that Paradise was indeed on earth, but it was beyond human power to discover where.[57] Nonetheless, even in the age of exploration, maps continued to follow the *Mappa Mundi* tradition, to show the places associated with Alexander, and to find a spot for Paradise, whether in the east or in the south.[58] It remained a matter of faith and doctrine that the Earthly Paradise was out there somewhere, even if one could never reach it. Ulysses in Dante's *Inferno* (xxvi. 133–5) caught sight in his voyaging of the mountain on which it stands, but a storm drove his ship away. So it was a mark of divine favour equal to that shown to Enoch and Elijah that Alexander should have been able to reach the Earthly Paradise.

That he did so was assured by a story first told in the Talmud,[59] recounted in Wahb and Nizami, and first presented to western readers in the twelfth-century Latin work, *Alexander the Great's Journey to Paradise*.[60] (It became the climactic episode of Pfaffe Lamprecht's *Alexanderlied*, 6667–7302, and was therefore in his source, Alberic's lost poem of the twelfth century.) In this work Alexander advances, after his conquest of India is completed, by ship up the River Ganges. After sailing for about a month, the sailors catch sight of a distant city. As they approach, they discover that it has extremely smooth walls, entirely covered with moss.[61] After sailing around it for three days, they espy a very small window (see colour plate 15). Alexander sends messengers who knock and, when the window is opened, they say:

> We are messengers of no ordinary king, but of the king of kings, Alexander the unconquered, to whom all the world pays homage, before whom every power trembles. This is the message his majesty sends you . . . . 'If you wish to continue to enjoy your hope of life, your bodily safety, and quiet times, do not puff yourselves up with insolence but pay me tribute according to the custom of all other peoples of the world.'

The man at the window disappears, and presently

> He opened it again and showed himself to the waiting sailors. He held out a jewel of unusual colour and remarkable brilliance, which in size and shape much resembled a human eye. He handed it to the men and said, 'The inhabitants of this place send this message to your king: "Call it whatever you like, a gift or a tribute owed, but accept a memento in the gift of this remarkable stone, which we send to you as a kind of charitable alms. It has the power to take away all your longings. When you have learnt its nature and virtue, you will cease from all ambition."'

When Alexander receives this gift, he is duly puzzled. The fleet sails away to Susa, and there Alexander summons all the wisest men from among the Jews and gentiles to explain the mystery. At length an aged Jew named Papas comes forward. He calls for a pair of scales, and places the stone in one pan and a huge pile of gold coins in the other; the pan with the stone sinks right down, no matter how much wealth is piled into the other pan. Then Papas

> Took again the smaller pair of scales, in which they had piled so much weight, and on the one side he placed the stone, this time covering it with a thin film of dust, while on the other side he placed one gold coin. Immediately the coin sank and pulled the stone upwards with no trouble at all. The Jew took out the coin and replaced it with a feather; but it still exceeded the stone in weight.

31 The Weighing of the Wonderstone. Pierpont Morgan Library MS M. 268 f. 21v (lower register).

The Jew goes on to explain:

> As far as its shape and colour are concerned, the stone is indeed a human eye, which, for as long as it has access to the light of life, is constantly agitated with the heat of desire; it grazes on the multiplicity of novelties and, even as gold ministers to its ever-renewing hunger, it never reaches any kind of satiety . . . .[62] But as soon as the vital motion is removed, and it is committed to the keeping of the earth from which it was born, it is beyond the use of any useful thing, it enjoys nothing, it desires nothing, it is unmoved by any external stimulus, because it is without feeling. Thus even a light feather, be it never so small . . . is able to outweigh the stone once it is covered with dust.
>
>   This stone is you, your majesty, you – the master of all wisdom, the conqueror of kings, the possessor of kingdoms, the lord of the world; the stone is your counsellor, your castigator; its little substance shall keep you from the yearnings of shoddy ambition.

Alexander, it seems, has finally learnt the lesson that the Brahmans, the angels he met in his flying machine, the oracles of Sarapis and the admonitions of Sesonchosis and the ancient kings in the Cave of the Gods,[63] and all the rest, could not teach him. He is a mortal man and his power is all vanity. This message is conveyed by the pagan authors. In this text it is pronounced by a Jew; it was among the Jews that this particular story originated; the Muslim authors also recount it; and it is also a Christian message.

Perhaps here is one of the secrets of the universal appeal of Alexander, the lord of the world who is doomed to die.

The story is told in a slightly different way by the Arab and Persian authors: for Wahb and in Tha'alabi it is a continuation of the story of the march through the Land of Darkness (where it is told for the second time). Alexander reaches a place where a trumpeter announces that he has reached the Land of the Angels and explains how Israfil will begin the Last Judgment. The angel-trumpeter gives him the mysterious stone, and it is his companion Musa (Khidr, in Tha'alabi) who explains its meaning. According to Nizami the stone is again given to him by an angel, and directly after the episode where the soldiers gather stones that glitter on the ground, Alexander looks again at the stone, and Khidr explains its meaning.

The story became familiar in the west,[64] and reappears in Gilbert Hay's *Buik of Alexander*. Though the delights of Paradise are described in detail, the culmination is slightly different. Instead of a messenger with a stone, it is an angel who comes to the wall and hands Alexander an apple:

> For thy tribute an apple here I give;
> And think that thou hast short time for to live.
> And keep it well, when thou comest home to weigh;
> It shall turn hue what time that thou be fey.[65]

Though the profundity of the story is lost here, the link of Alexander with the story of the Fall puts him on a par with the heroes of scripture. This is neatly expressed in the *Parlement of the Thre Ages* (332–6);

> After this sir Alysaunder alle þe worlde wanne,
> Bothe the see and the sonde and the sadde erthe,
> þe iles of the oryent to Ercules boundes,
> There Ely and Ennoke ever hafe bene sythen,
> And to the come of Antecriste unclosed be þay never . . .

The Voyage to Paradise became quite a popular medieval genre, and most of the texts make extensive use of Alexander-motifs. One of the most notable is the *Life of St Macarius*,[66] whose protagonist lived in the fourth century AD: the text is probably pre-Carolingian, though the earliest MSS are of the eleventh century. Macarius' adventure includes his reaching the Pillars of Alexander, an encounter with the Talking Birds, his being sent back by an angel, and the Water of Life. The Voyage of St Brendan[67] also borrows some motifs including the Land of Darkness, St Brendan's birds and the finding of precious stones in the path of the travellers. Around 1389

John de Hese composed a chapbook on his journey to Paradise and the land of Prester John.[68] So despite the difficulties of access, and the fact that neither Mandeville nor Marco Polo claimed to have got there, it was not really surprising when Christopher Columbus wrote at the mouth of the Orinoco:

> I believe that this water may originate from [Paradise], though it be far away . . . . These are great indications of the earthly paradise, for the situation agrees with those holy and wise theologians . . . and the very mild climate supports this view.[69]

This secularisation of what had hitherto been a mystical voyage is a textual parallel to the turn from the *Mappa Mundi* to the post-exploration maps of the world, which still had to find a place for Paradise somehow. Alexander's aims were no doubt as secular as those of Columbus, but his co-option by Muslim and Christian writers turned him into a scriptural figure in his own right. As we shall see in Chapter 10, Alexander plays a part in some medieval texts that makes him almost as central as Christ. To set the scene for that partial fusion, let us consider first his dealings with Antichrist.

9

THE UNCLEAN NATIONS AND
THE END OF TIME

Mount Caspius, which gives the Caspian Sea its name, is in India. Gog and
Magog are said to have been confined between this mountain and the sea by
Alexander the Great. They are extremely savage tribes, mentioned in Ezekiel
[38.1–3], who feed on the raw flesh of humans and animals.

> Gervase of Tilbury (*fl. c.* 1200), *Otia imperialia* II.3, pp. 184–5
> Banks and Binns

In the same land are the hills of Caspian which are called Uber[a Aquilonis]. The
Jews of the Ten Lost Tribes are shut up in these hills; they are called Gog and
Magog, and they can get out on no side. King Alexander drove them here, for
he intended to shut them up with the work of his men. When he saw he could
not, he prayed to God that he would finish what he himself had begun. And
although he was a heathen, God of his special grace heard his prayer and closed
the hills together, and they are so big and high that they cannot be passed.

> Sir John Mandeville, *Travels* (*c.* 1356), ch. 29
> (following Higden, *Polychronicon* III.451)

For þan xall gogmangog nere cum	shall
Owte of þ. Mowntes of calpye.	
That god closyd all & sum.	
At Alexandyrs prayre suyrly.	
þey xall dystroy all crystendome.	
þey xall cum owt so hydowysly.	
Men all most wax defe & dum.	must
So xall þey drede here felony.	their

All þe worlde þey xall over-runne.
And work howge & grett.
þey xall devowre men.
& women with schyld ete.
Edders and snakys þat brede in fen.
Hem xall þink deynty mete.
Regnes þey xall dystroy & bren.
& fowly mankynde þey xall threte.

þan xall come an emprore
Of greys & rome lord xall he be
To Ierusalem with gret honoure
& regne vii yere in þat cuntre
In þat place þat owre saueyowre   saviour
Cryst was waylyd on rode tre
& he xall myldly yelde þat cure
Hys croune & hys dygnyte

Hys crowne he xall set full ryte
On þe cross þat cryst on deyde
& be-toke hys gost to godds myte
þat for hym sufferyd wownds wyde
Than xall he loke upward on hyte
& hold hys hands to heuyn þat tyde
And þan xall be sen a syte
þe sygne of a cros in heuyn abyde

But þan xall cum werst of all
Antecryst þe develys bryde. . .

Pseudo-Methodius, the Middle English translation 770ff.,
in D'Evelyn 1918

Dragon-Slayer

The Alexander of the *Romance*, besides his abilities as a warrior and strategist against human enemies, is also a fighter of monsters. Like Jason, the
hero of the *Argonautica* of Apollonius, a poem probably contemporary with
the earliest versions of the *Romance*,[1] Alexander defines the limits of the
Greek world in a new way by putting paid to the strange beasts that
threaten it, and threaten also to upset its conceptual order. The *Letter to*

Aristotle about India is the first appearance of the assorted monsters that plague Alexander: first a huge tusked river beast and then giant scorpions and lions with teeth two feet long, elephants, ox-rams, bull-stags, men with six hands, strap-footed men, dog-partridges and others (see Chapter 4). Alexander and his men drive them off with weapons. Worst of all was the odontotyrannus. 'I ran back and forth and beseeched my brave companions to make fires and protect themselves lest they meet a horrible death. The beast in its eagerness to hurt the men ran and fell into the flames. From there it charged into the army, killing twenty-six men at once. Thirteen hundred men were hardly able to drag him away' (*AR* III. 16, cf. *Letter to Aristotle* 8).[2] The list continues with giant bats, night-foxes and crocodiles. The Latin *Letter* also describes crested serpents, thicker than columns, that moved with their breasts erect and spat venom from their eyes (clearly cobras). Later, a cross between a hippopotamus and a crocodile can only be dispatched with iron hammers (*Letter* 11).

Further monsters turn up at other stages of the eastern travels in the gamma recension. Centaurs (not named as such) threaten the army at II. 41, and are undeterred by arrows: 'as men they despised the arrows because of their harmlessness, but as beasts they were incapable of understanding the devilment of men'. So the Macedonians eventually dispatch them with sharp swords. Even more alarming are the wild men, 'naked and hairy, terrifying, enormous, black . . . [with] hair like stretched gristle' of II. 33 (gamma).[3]

> Alexander had an attractive young woman brought to him and told her, 'Go up to that man, so that you can observe the wild man's nature and see if he is human in all respects.' The woman went up to him, but when he turned round and saw her, he leapt up, seized her and straightaway began to eat her. Alexander at once ordered some soldiers to go and rescue her from the beast. The soldiers ran up to him; he took no notice of them at all, but had his mouth clamped on her leg and was chewing her like a dog. One of the soldiers struck him with his spear, at which the beast ran off barking like a dog, leaving the girl half-dead. (III. 33 gamma)

As soon as the poor girl is rescued, the wild men attack. The battle lasts some time as the wild men seem to have infinite reinforcements available, but eventually the Macedonians drive them away with burning brands – another trick of 'clever Alexander' (see Chapter 6 above).

This battle with the monsters may be seen as the counterpart to the search for immortality: it is a *katabasis* of the hero into a world of otherness

before the ascent to the interview with the gods that follows in the
Romance. In another context it could be seen as a harrowing of hell.
Alexandru Cizek has gone so far as to interpret this battle at the sweet lake
as an apocalyptic scenario, in which the culture hero battles with forces of
evil, like the last battle of mankind in Revelation 9.3–13, where scorpions
swarm like locusts.[4] However that may be, Alexander's status as a monster-
slayer and culture hero certainly fitted him for an apocalyptic role.

The battles with monsters continue in later retellings. The Persian
romances make much of the strap-legged men, who also provide a number
of curious illustrations in the manuscripts of Qazvini, showing how these
dangerous creatures entwine their legs around the necks of their opponents
and cannot be dislodged. (Though mentioned in the gamma recension in
the 'obituary' [III. 35], they play no role there.)

The Syriac version (Budge 1889, 107–9) tells the story of a dragon that
terrorises the inhabitants of a country east of Prasiake.[5] They describe the
creature as a 'great god in the form of a dragon'. Alexander asks if the god
has a temple, to which they reply, 'Who can go near him that can swallow
an elephant by drawing in his breath? . . . We know that a number of people
are swallowed up by him every year, besides two oxen which they give to
him regularly every day for food.' Alexander goes down with the day's
offering of oxen to the river bank: 'and when I saw the beast, I thought that
it was a black cloud which was standing upon the bank of the river, and the
smoke which went forth from its mouth was like unto the thick darkness
which comes in a fog'. Alexander's stratagem is to make the beast very
hungry by giving it only two calves on the next day; and on the following
day he brings two huge oxen which have been slaughtered and their skins
stuffed with gypsum, pitch, lead and sulphur.[6] 'As soon as the gypsum
entered its belly, we saw that its head fell upon the ground, and it opened
wide its mouth, and uprooted a number of trees with its tail . . . . I ordered
a smith's bellows to be brought and balls of brass to be heated in the fire
and to be thrown into the beast's mouth; and when they had thrown five
balls into its mouth, the beast shut its mouth, and died.' The story is told in
very similar terms by Firdausi,[7] but does not appear in Nizami, who has
instead a series of seven campaigns against the Rus, a (more or less) human
enemy. And, though the dragon story does not appear in any of the ancient
or medieval texts of the *Romance*, it does emerge in one of the popular
stories of the Karagiozis shadow-puppet theatre in modern Greece,
'Alexander the Great and the Dreadful Dragon'.[8]

The Unclean Nations

Such resourcefulness in the face of monsters stands Alexander in good stead in the face of his greatest challenge, the Unclean Nations. These make their first appearance in epsilon (ch. 39), whence they enter the gamma recension from which the following quotation is taken.[9] Alexander finds himself at war with a people called the Belsyrians, under their king, Eurymithres.[10] He pursues them beyond two mountains in the unknown called 'The Breasts of the North'.[11] Here he makes a prayer to God and:

> Immediately the mountains came together, though they had previously been eighteen feet apart. When Alexander saw what had happened, he praised God. Then he built bronze gates, fixed them in the narrows between the two mountains and oiled them. The nature of the oil was such that it could not be burned by fire nor dislodged by iron.[12] Within the gates, stretching back to the open country he planted brambles, which he watered well so that they formed a dense mane over the mountains.
>
> So Alexander shut in twenty-two kings with their subject nations behind the northern boundaries – behind the gates that he called the Caspian and the mountains known as the Breasts. These are the names of those nations: Goth, Magoth, Anougeis, Aigeis, Exenach, Diphar, Photinaioi, Pharizaioi, Zarmatianoi, Chachonioi, Agrimardoi, Anouphagoi, Tharbaioi, Alans, Physiolonikaioi, Saltarioi and the rest . . . . They used to eat worms and foul things that were not real food at all – dogs, flies, snakes, aborted foetuses, dead bodies and unformed human embryos; and they ate not only animals but the corpses of humans as well. Alexander, seeing all this, was afraid that they would come out and pollute the inhabited world; so he shut them in and went on his way.[13]

The importance of the story is that it is the main vehicle for the insertion of Alexander into the sacred history of the Christian world. The Dutch and German History Bibles of the late Middle Ages, which provide lavishly illustrated texts of the sacred book, include between the end of the Old Testament and the beginning of Maccabees – otherwise something of a gap in the sacred record – none other than the *Alexander Romance*, in an abridged version.[14] Of the few episodes which the illustrators of the History Bibles concentrate on, the most prominent is this, the enclosure of the Unclean Nations. To understand why this episode acquired the standing of holy scripture, we have to look at the origins of the story.[15]

32 Gog and Magog eating people. From Thomas of Kent's Anglo-Norman *Alexander.* Trinity College Cambridge, MS O.9.34, f. 23v.

33 The Enclosed Nations. From a History Bible. Koninklijke Bibliotheek, The Hague, 78D 38 II f. 76r.

The central element is the enclosing of the Unclean Nations, called Goth and Magoth in the *Romance*. Now these are none other than those old enemies from the Hebrew Bible, Gog and Magog, who first feature in Genesis 10.2 (cf. Josephus *AJ* 1.123) and Ezekiel 38.1–3, and are then adopted into the New Testament by the author of Revelation (20.7–8): 'and when the thousand years are expired, Satan shall be loosed out of his prison, and shall go out to deceive the nations which are in the four quarters of the earth, Gog and Magog, to gather them together to battle: the number of whom is as the sand of the sea'. As Augustine explained in his discussion of this passage in *City of God* XX. 11–13, at the end of the Millennium (the period for which Christ will hold Satan bound), Satan will emerge and gather the enemies of mankind for the last battle that precedes the coming of Christ's kingdom.[16]

The location of the place where Gog and Magog were imprisoned was quite well-known by the end of antiquity. Jerome (*Epistulae* 77.8) knew that they had been enclosed behind a wall in the Caucasus by Alexander the Great, and furthermore was confident that they were to be identified with the Huns, even now breaking loose on the classical world, like harbingers of the last days.[17] A little later, the prophetic poet Commodian[18] was equally confident that they were the Goths (even the name fitted). As the centuries went by, and the end of the world failed to arrive, Gog and Magog came to be identified successively with the Arabs, the Turks (Aethicus), the Rus, the Tartars, and even the Lost Tribes of Israel (Peter Comestor).[19] In Godfrey of Viterbo, too, by a curious piece of syncretism (and hence in Mandeville), they are the Lost Tribes of Israel. In the fourteenth-century Dutch *Book of the Vengeance of God*[20] it is the Jews who have been enclosed by Alexander (a son of Chuseth, as in Methodius), and who will break out and ravage the world at the end of time.

But the means by which Gog and Magog became so well known to those with an eye to the coming end was not their mention in Revelation; nor did the average apocalypticist spend much time reading the letters of Jerome. There were two channels of information: the *Alexander Romance* and, even more importantly, the source from which the tale entered the *Romance*, namely the *Revelation* of Pseudo-Methodius.

Pseudo-Methodius

The real Methodius was Bishop of Patara in 311. The work attributed to him was written more than three centuries later, originally in Syriac, and was quickly followed by a translation into Greek. The author of the Pseudo-Methodius drew on two earlier Syriac works, the first known as the

'Christian legend concerning Alexander', and the second, a poem attributed to Jacob of Serugh.[21] Rather similar in content, these works tell of Alexander's construction of a gate of bronze designed to keep out the Unclean Nations, in the Christian legend still identified with the Huns, though Jacob just calls them Gog and Magog. These works can be dated with some confidence to the early seventh century AD: the poem, the earlier work, refers to the Khazar invasion of Armenia in 628 but not to the Arab conquest of Jerusalem in 636. Both works reflect the period in which the Emperor Heraclius was engaged in defensive wars on his eastern frontiers, the members of the Syrian church looked with apprehension to the east, and the cataclysm of the Arab conquest had not yet taken place.[22]

The Pseudo-Methodius was written some decades later: the date that seems to be gaining consensus is 692. The author adapts the Syriac tale but Gog and Magog, inevitably, now come to stand for the Arabs, or Saracens. The work belongs to a time when Arab rule in Syria was already well established but could still be seen as liable to coming to a dramatic end.[23] The prophecy encapsulates the hopes of its writer and his co-religionists for a return to a Christian world, while justifying the Arab conquests as part of God's plan for the end time. A number of contemporary texts, including that of the Armenian historian Sebeos, the Syriac *Gospel of the XII Apostles* and the *Chronicle* of Michael the Syrian,[24] express anxiety that the Christian God is letting down his people after the battle of the Yarmuk (AD 636). Sebeos, quoting Isaiah 19.20, claimed that it was the Christians' own fault: 'I shall describe the calamity which beset our time, the rupture of the veil of the old south and the blowing on us of the mortal hot wind which burned the great, leafy, beautiful, newly planted trees of the orchards. This happened rightly because we sinned against the Lord and we angered the Holy One of Israel.'[25] Pseudo-Methodius is a more extensive theodicy of the defeats.

Pseudo-Methodius presents a history of the world from Adam and Eve to the end of time, based on the presupposition that the end of the world is imminent: the sixth millennium has reached its close and the seventh and last is just beginning.[26] The conclusion of the work introduces another central figure of Byzantine apocalyptic, the Last Emperor.[27] After the reign of Antichrist, the Last Emperor of Rome will present his crown to God, and it will be taken up into heaven atop the Cross – as described, for example, in the Middle English translation at the head of this chapter.

Pseudo-Methodius became an enormously influential work, if influence is to be judged by the number of translations into the vernacular. It was translated first into Latin, by about 700, and into Greek a decade later. The Latin translation was an influence on the *Cosmography* of Pseudo-Aethicus by the ninth century.[28] It was further translated into most western European languages before 1500, and there are some 220 separate manuscripts (Marco Polo only made it into about 150 copies).[29] It had an impact on a recently unearthed work of Byzantine apocalyptic, Pseudo-Hippolytus *De consummatione mundi*.[30] It directly informed the Armenian *Sermo de Antichristo* of Pseudo-Epiphanius (*c.* 1150), which reflects the hostilities of the Emperor Manuel Comnenus.[31] It was even known, it seems, to Christopher Columbus, because when he reached the vicinity (as he supposed) of the Earthly Paradise he discovered in his path, as was to be expected, people with a similarly revolting diet, who 'eat all the snakes and lizards and spiders and all the worms which are found in the ground. So it seems to me that their degradation is greater than that of any beast in the world.'[32]

Islam and the Unclean Nations

Even more remarkable than this influence in the west is the fact that the story of Alexander's enclosure of the Unclean Nations was adopted from the Syriac sources directly into the Qur'ān, Sura 18. 83–100.[33] Here Alexander bears his usual Arabic name of Dhu'l-qarnain, The Two-Horned One:

> . . . between the two mountains, he found on that side of them a people who could hardly understand a word. They said: O Dhu'l-qarnain, Gog and Magog do mischief in the land. May we then pay thee tribute on condition that thou raise a barrier betweeen us and them? He said: That wherein my lord has established me is better, so if only you help me with strength, I will make a fortified barrier between you and them. Bring me blocks of iron. At length, when he had filled up the space between the two mountain sides, he said, Blow. Till, when he had made it [as] fire, he said: Bring me molten brass to pour over it. So they were not able to scale it, nor could they make a hole in it. He said, This is a mercy from my Lord, but when the promise of my Lord comes to you he will crumble it, and the promise of my Lord is ever true. And on that day We shall let some of them surge against others and the trumpet will be blown, then We shall gather them all together, and We shall bring forth hell, exposed to view, on that day before the disbelievers.[34]

The version of the story in the Qur'ān is very close to that in Pseudo-Methodius. The main difference, in fact, is that the Unclean Nations are not identified with any specific race – and, of course, certainly not with the Arabs, as in the Pseudo-Methodius text! The story became enshrined in Arabic literature, and is referred to by, for example, al-Tha'alabi; it also features in the tenth-century Persian translation of al-Tabari, who speaks of the reign of Antichrist, when Gog and Magog will break through Alexander's wall.[35] Mas'udi[36] refers to them in a location to the north of Europe. Nizami identifies them with a people known as the Elephant-Ears.

'Umara enhances the story with an account of a further defence built by Alexander, a series of mechanical trumpets which warn of the approach of Gog and Magog. The story seems to have become widespread in the west. It is told by Ricold of Monte Croce, who explains how the trumpets gradually get blocked up by owls' nests, thus releasing the forces of Antichrist. The tale is repeated in Fazio degli Uberti (II. 26) and the trumpets are shown on the Catalan map of 1375 as well as Mercator's of 1569, though he did not understand their connection with Alexander.[37]

Apocalypse Later: The Last Emperor

What then of the Last Emperor, who will usher in the end of the world?[38] This again is a figure who has his origins in classical historiography: in the late fourth century the *Historia Augusta* (*Life of Tacitus*, 152–4) recounts:

On this occasion the soothsayers foretold that at some future time there would be a Roman emperor from their family, descended through either the male or the female line, who would give judges to the Parthians and the Persians, subject the Franks and the Alamanni to the laws of Rome, drive out every barbarian from the whole of Africa, establish a governor at Taprobane [Sri Lanka], send a proconsul to the island of Iuverna [Ireland], act as judge to all the Sarmatians, make all the land which borders on the Ocean his own territory by conquering all the tribes, but thereafter restore the power to the senate and conduct himself in accordance with the ancient laws, being destined to live for 120 years and to die without an heir. They declared, moreover, that he would come one thousand years from the day when the lightning struck and shattered the statues. It showed no great skill, indeed, on the soothsayers' part to declare that such a prince would come after an interval of one thousand years, for their promise applied to a time when such a story will scarce be remembered, whereas, if they had said one hundred years, their falsehood could perhaps be detected.

(Does one detect in the last sentence one of those quiet anti-Christian side-swipes which characterise the traditional pagan attitudes of the anonymous author of the *Historia Augusta*?)

The Last Emperor was a figure as protean as Gog and Magog and could take on the identity of almost any Byzantine emperor; he appears not only in Pseudo-Methodius but also in later Byzantine apocalypses and also in western ones like that of Adso. Indeed, Frederick Barbarossa sometimes seems to don his mantle.[39] One of the few fixed identities in this tale of preparation for the end is Alexander. Though he never takes on the character of the Last Emperor himself, he does sometimes explicitly relinquish his power to the Last Emperor (for instance in Godfrey of Viterbo).[40]

An interesting sideline on this protean power of Alexander occurs in a Jewish legend about the sacred history of the world.[41] The *Book of Exempla* begins: 'Ten kings ruled over the whole world: – God, Nimrod, Joseph, Solomon, Ahab, Nebuchadnezzar, Koresh [Cyrus] (Ahasuerus [Xerxes] ruled over half). Alexander of Macedonia not only ruled over the whole world, but went also to the end of the desert and intended ascending to Heaven. And the Lord divided his kingdom into four parts, to the ends of the world. The ninth will be the Messiah and then the kingdom will return to the first ruler, i.e. God himself, who will be the tenth.'

Whence comes this anxious desire to periodise the history of the world and to divide it into neatly parcelled sections of a sacred plan? Various views have been proposed as explanations for the appeal of apocalyptic literature. The most influential, Norman Cohn's,[42] sees such works as arising from, and representing, the concerns of periods of great social unrest. This fits in very well with a situation like that of seventh-century Syria, where, as we have seen, this legend of Alexander took shape. The infinite adaptability of the Unclean Nations to the guise of any enemy that is bothering people at a particular time helps people to come to terms with their suffering and to believe that it is part of some greater plan. However, it is not easy to find precise social and historical correlatives for every recopying of what was in effect a best-selling text between 1050 and 1500.

Bernard McGinn in his book on Antichrist[43] takes a more theological perspective in defining the motive force as 'the human fascination with evil'. There is no need for particular historical enemies; what is to be explained is the propensity of others to behave in a way you find objec-tionable, for example by eating flies and foetuses. Such a reading carries a hint of Jewish purity laws, which were certainly not entirely absent from the thoughts of the author of the gamma recension of the *Alexander*

Romance. The story of the Unclean Nations becomes an exercise in defining 'them and us', with Alexander as the culture-hero.

The apocalyptic strain needs to be distinguished from the 'classical' tradition of prophecy. The works of classical antiquity that most resemble the genre are the *Sibylline Oracles* and some demotic works such as the *Oracle of the Potter*. However, both contain largely *ex post facto* prophecies. Their function is to enable their authors – and their complicit listeners – to say 'I told you so'. They validate the outlook of a particular class or group, though the identity of that group or class may itself be shifting. It is usually an oppressed class, but not always: as David Potter writes of some of them, 'These texts do not reflect sentiments that can be regarded as anti-Roman; rather they reflect sentiments that may be regarded as typically Roman.'[44] The prophecies are making a claim that this is the way the world is.

Something like this can be argued also of Pseudo-Methodius. Though the work consists of a combination of (selective) history and fantastic visions of the future, it represents a similar attempt at making sense of the processes of history, of offering an organised conception of the world. Averil Cameron writes of the stories told by early Christians: 'these texts have something important to tell us, in terms of the sociology of knowledge, about how the Christian system was articulated in the early period, and thus about how it got itself established in the Roman Empire'.[45] The text, that is, becomes a performative utterance.

I would suggest that the mentality that produces these prophecies can be in some way illuminated by the parallel efforts at geographical organisation known from late antiquity and the Middle Ages. A major text of late antique geography, the *Cosmographia* of Aethicus Ister,[46] pays considerable attention to the peoples of Gog and Magog. They occur several times in his narrative, a reflection of their importance in his mental landscape. Here they inhabit the edges of the world. The Breasts of the North are neighbours of the islands in the River of Ocean. The visual counterpart of this work are the great *Mappae Mundi* of the medieval world, which depict Gog and Magog as being enclosed behind Alexander's rampart.[47]

If one may pursue a little further Averil Cameron's insight that intellectual discourse is performative, then one may see such literary creations as a way, not just of organising the world, but of stating how the world ought to be. A treatise, or a map, becomes the equivalent of a prayer: keep these creatures far from me! Apotropaic activity and intellectual analysis merge in their intentions, and the hero of history becomes a spiritual hero as well.

The Wall of Alexander

Given the intense interest in this world-saving action of Alexander's, it is not surprising that many people in later times were interested in finding the wall that he had built. The search had to begin from the Caspian Gates, which by the end of antiquity were located at the Pass of Derbend in the Caucasus.[48] It became the canonical location of the Iron Gate from about the sixth century AD, and fortifications there (actually built by Khosrow Anushirvan, 531–79) came to be known as the Wall of Alexander.[49]

Later rulers of Persia searched frequently for the wall, hoping to strengthen their defences against the central Asian threat, but usually to no avail.[50] Yazdigird, the son of Bahram-Gur, is said to have found and repaired the wall but left the work incomplete. Chosrow Anushirvan built the iron gates in the wall, which 'enabled a hundred men to defend it against 100,000'.[51]

The wall remained an important defence in the Byzantine period, as Edward Gibbon recounts in *The Decline and Fall of the Roman Empire*:[52]

> A fortress, designed by Alexander, perhaps, or one of his successors, to command that important pass, had descended by right of conquest to a prince of the Huns, who offered it for a moderate price to the emperor; but, while Anastasius paused, while he timorously computed the cost and the distance, a more vigilant rival interposed, and Cabades forcibly occupied the straits of Caucasus. The Albanian and Iberian gates [two other passes] excluded the horsemen of Scythia from the shortest and most practicable roads, and the whole front of the mountains was covered by the rampart of Gog and Magog, the long wall which has excited the curiosity of an Arabian caliph and a Russian conqueror.

Gibbon adds a note, 'The imaginary rampart of Gog and Magog, which was seriously explored and believed by a caliph of the sixth century, appears to be derived from the gates of Mount Caucasus, and a vague report of the wall of China.'

The caliph to whom Gibbon refers is Wathiq (Vathek); but before him, as soon as the Arabs arrived in the region, they also took an interest in the wall.[53] Before the year 740 Abd el-Malik made a point of visiting it.[54] Wathiq sent an expedition to repair it in 842–44. The wall was a real one, but the narrative is fantastical.[55]

The story is in Ibn Khordadbeh:

Sallam the Interpreter related to me that when Al-Wathiq bi-'llah dreamt that the wall built by Dhu'l-qarnain between us and Gog and Magog was cracked, and he sought a man to send to the place in order to gain news of it, Ashnas [a Turkish leader] said, 'There is no one here except Sallam the Interpreter who is fitted (for the business). And Sallam spoke thirty languages. 'So', says Sallam, 'Wathiq summoned me and said, "I wish you to go out to the Rampart, that you may actually see it, and bring me news of it". And he gave me a company of fifty men, young and strong, and bestowed on me 50,000 dinars, and 10,000 dirhams in addition as compensation for the danger incurred. He ordered every one of the fifty men to be given 1000 dirhams and food for a year.

'. . .We stayed for a day and a night with the king of the Khazars. Then he sent us with five guides, and we departed from him. Twenty-six days' marching brought us to a black, stinking land;[56] but we had provided ourselves before entering it with vinegar to smell as a precaution against the evil odour. Then we travelled through it for ten days, and afterwards reached some ruined cities, through which we journeyed for twenty days. On our asking about those cities we were informed that they were cities which Gog and Magog had invaded and destroyed.'

There follows a long description of the gate, with its foundations of iron and copper, thirty cubits deep, and the pillars of iron bricks covered with copper, each 50 cubits high, and topped by 37 pinnacles. The bolt of the gate alone was seven cubits long and located 25 cubits from the ground. Every day a guard would ascend and bang on the bolt to let the Enclosed Nations know that the watch was still being kept. In this elaborate narrative, the story which had originally related to the threat of Muslim invasion in a Christian land has been adapted to represent the external threat to the now powerful Muslim Empire.

The Russian ruler mentioned by Gibbon is Peter the Great, whose involvement is described at the end of a long passage excerpted by Gobdelas (1822) from the *Genealogical History of the Tatars* by Abu'l-Gazi Balkander, Khan of Khwarezm (I translate from Gobdelas' Greek):

The people of China built a great wall to protect their country. This wall has two iron gates, used by travellers and merchants, which are called Sat, the Arabic for 'fortress'. . . . Alexander the Great built a similar wall to protect the borders of his empire, but this was built from all kinds of metal. His aim in building it was to prevent the nation of Yajuj-Majuj [Gog-Magog] from making incursions into his land, which they had already devastated. It is a common tradition among the Tartars that the people just referred to consists of men with dogs' heads; and these people (if we can call them such) made fruitless attempts until the present to break through the wall; but while they will be unsuccessful until the Day of Judgment, at that time they will undertake savage raids through the world . . . . The remains of the wall which the Persians affirm was built on the orders of King Anushirvan, from the Caspian Sea to the Black Sea, are three feet thick throughout, but the height of the wall varies greatly, from seven feet in some parts to two in others, and in others it is level with the ground. At first sight you would say it is built of stone, but if you examine it more closely you will see that it is just petrified earth, strengthened with sand and pottery fragments . . . . The last emperor of Russia, when he was planning his expedition against Persia, took the trouble to go and visit these ruins . . . . He was impressed by the toughness of the mixture, which he found so hard that he could not break off any pieces of it . . . . He would have repaired the whole wall, if he had not had enemies to contend with other than time; but the hands of men had thrown down what they had built; and the houses of numerous cities, villages and dwellings in the vicinity had been built from the ruins of that wall.

The author of this passage seems unsure whether he is describing the wall of Derbend or the Great Wall of China, and the confusion between the two became entrenched.[57] Sallam may in fact have visited the Great Wall of China,[58] or at least the Tien Shan mountains, in the process of investigating the effects of the collapse of the Uighur civilisation.[59] Idrisi (1154) puts the wall somewhere in the Altai mountains. Rashid ed-Din, who described the defences built by the Chin dynasty (1115–1234), repeatedly talks of them as the Sedd-Iskender (the Wall of Alexander). In 1347 the Arab traveller Ibn Battutah, asking in China about 'the rampart of Gog and Magog', was told that it was about sixty days' journey away, in a region occupied by wandering tribes who 'ate such people as they could catch'.[60]

It is notable that the peoples of Gog and Magog are confounded or identified with the cannibals in some of these passages, and even with the dog-heads (known since Scylax and Ctesias: see Chapter 4).[61] This too goes back to the *Alexander Romance*, or at least to that version of it that became the Ethiopian *Alexander-Book*, where Alexander interviews the neighbours of the Unclean Nations and asks them who lives beyond them. They reply, 'There are nations living beyond them. They are the Taftas, that is to say, the Nagashawiyan whose faces are like those of dogs. The number of them is unknown, and no man can tell their names; no man hath ever been able to enter their country, wherein there is nothing except lofty mountains. Above the tops of these high mountains is Paradise . . .'.

And with that view of Paradise, perceptible even from the benighted lands of Gog and Magog, we may leave the Unclean Nations, enclosed until the end of time, and enshrined on all the maps of the Middle Ages on a peninsula to the north-east whose encircling walls are always clearly marked – until, as Anderson notes, they were abolished by the cartography of Mercator.[62]

10

DEATH IN BABYLON

(323 BC)

The 24th, clouds . . . / Clouds crossed the sky. The 27th . . . / . . . stood to the east. The 29th, the king died; clouds . . . . / . . . cress, 1 sut 4 qa; sesame 31/2 qa [B Obv]

Year 1 of King Philip, Month IX [= December] . . . the 4th, the first part of the night, a meteor which was like a torch . . . a ewe gave birth and (the newborn had) three heads and necks, three buttocks, . . . 6 . . . ., 3 . . . . [D Obv]

Babylonian oracles for year 14 of Alexander III = year 1 of Philip III (323 BC); from Sachs and Hunger 1988, no. 322; see also van der Spek 2003

When he had crossed the Tigris with his army on his march towards Babylon, Alexander was met by the Chaldaean seers, who drew him aside from his Companions and begged him to stop the march to Babylon; it is said that they had an oracle from their god Belus that his entry into Babylon at that time would do him harm.

Arrian, *Anabasis* 7.16.5

It is said that the gods have great powers of foresight. One of the women here bore a child whose upper body was human as far as the flanks, but from the hips downward it had the legs and paws of a wild beast . . . the upper body of the baby was lifeless . . . . [Alexander asked one of the Chaldaeans to explain the omen] 'King', came the reply, 'you may be no longer numbered among the living . . . you yourself are the human part, and the animal elements are those around you. If the upper part were alive and moved like the animal parts below, so would you, O king; but just as the animal parts are, so are those around you: they have no understanding and are savage towards men.'

Alexander Romance III. 30

The astrologers had foretold to his mother at his birth that he would die in a place where the sky was of gold and the earth of iron . . . . As his sickness got worse, two tables were placed beneath him, with an iron breastplate on top of them, on which he reclined, while he was covered with a gilded shield. When he saw this, he remembered what his mother had told him, summoned his secretary, dictated a letter to his mother, and died.

Eutychius, Patriarch of Alexandria (876–939), *Annals* (*PG* 111), 285–7

Oracles and Portents

Oracles were always important to the historical Alexander. He regularly consulted his seer Aristander before major engagements and other events,[1] and his visit to the Oracle of Ammon at Siwa may have been the defining moment of his career. An eclipse of the moon before the Battle of Gaugamela (Arr. *Anab.* 3.7.6) was favourably interpreted by Aristander as a sign of imminent victory; and it was taken by Babylonian seers as a premonition of Darius' defeat.[2] On his return to Babylon in 323 BC Alexander paid attention to what the portents foretold but, because he did not altogether trust the Chaldaeans, he elected to take them with a pinch of salt. One of the characteristics of the clever Alexander is his ability to deal with omens and riddling texts and to draw interpretations of them (see Chapter 6). So the Alexander of the *Romance* seeks oracles where he may find them. His anxious consultation of Sarapis in Book I is paralleled by his visit to the Cave of the Gods in Book III. 24, where he returns to the question of when he is to die. He meets both Sesonchosis, the former world-conqueror, and Sarapis, the god who warned him in Alexandria not to seek to know his end, seated on a throne in a mist glowing with fire. Sarapis repeats his earlier advice, that 'it is best for a living man not to know when his end will come. As soon as he learns the hour of his death, from that moment he is as good as dead.' The Psalmist would have understood, for when he asks (Ps. 39.4) 'Lord, make me to know mine end, and the measure of my days, what it is; that I may know how frail I am', it is not a privilege that he seeks, but a humbling.[3]

The most extended encounter with an oracle occurs in III. 17, in the course of the adventures in India. The wise men of Prasiake (Porus' kingdom) invite Alexander to visit the trees that speak with a human voice.[4]

So they brought Alexander to a place where there was a sanctuary of the Sun and Moon.[5] There was a guardpost here, and two trees closely resembling cypresses . . . The two trees in the middle of the garden spoke, the one with a man's voice, the other with a woman's. The name of the male one was Sun and of the female one Moon.

(See colour plate 16.)

The fuller account in the *Letter to Aristotle* (17) describes the attendant of the shrine:

We entered the sacred precinct and saw the high priest, who was over ten feet tall, with black skin, pointed teeth like a dog's, and pierced ears with jewels suspended from them.

The priest explains: 'In the morning, when the sun rises, a voice issues from the tree of the sun, and again when the sun is in the middle of the sky, and a third time when it is about to set. And the same applies to the tree of the moon.' Furthermore, the sun tree speaks in 'Indian', while the moon tree gives its oracles in Greek. Just then the sun sets, and the sun tree makes a pronouncement which his guides reluctantly translate: 'King Alexander, soon you must die by the hand of one of your companions.' At moonrise, the moon tree amplifies the message in Greek: 'King Alexander, you are to die in Babylon, by the hand of one of your companions, and you will not be able to return to your mother Olympias.' At dawn Alexander returns and asks the trees if the full span of his years will be completed.

As the sun rose and the first rays fell on the top of the tree, a resonant voice came forth: 'The span of your life is completed now, you will not be able to return to your mother, Olympias, but must die in Babylon. A short time afterwards, your mother and your wife will be horribly murdered by your own people.[6] Ask no more about these matters, for you will be told no more.'

In a masterpiece of (for once) understatement, the author tells us that Alexander was 'very unhappy' when he heard this, and departed at once for Persia (meaning Babylon).

This episode is told in very similar form to that of the Greek *Romance* in most of the later versions, including the Syriac and Ethiopic. Firdausi also tells it in the same way (including the historical prophecies at the end), but the tree in the illustrations to the *Shahnameh* is regularly depicted as a tree with human heads for fruit. (Colour plate 17). The source of this image is not the *Alexander Romance* but Arabic tradition about the waq-waq tree, found in the islands of Waq-Waq, whose fruit is human heads (or, sometimes, tiny people).[7] The medieval European tradition also varies the detail in the illustrations, which often take their inspiration from the depiction of the priest in the French *Roman d'Alexandre:*

> The priest rose on their arrival; he was hairy, shaggy like a bear, and wore no clothes. From his ears hung onyxes, topazes and precious stones from the Euphrates. Black as coal, he had dog's teeth and measured a good fifteen feet in height. (*Rd'A* 212, Harf-Lancner 1994, pp. 532–3)

34 The monstrous birth that predicts Alexander's death. John Rylands Library MS Arm. 3 f. 140v.

Not merely fanged, this priest is shown as a dog-headed man. Once again the dog-heads make their way from the edges of the world into the Alexander story. By this time they have behind them a rich tradition of dog-headed saints in Christian iconography,[8] so that there is nothing (perhaps) surprising in his appearance in this form. (The description of the priest is not in the first recension of the *Historia de proeliis* 1, so the source of the *Roman d'Alexandre* must be the *Letter*.)

None of these prophecies deters Alexander from entering Babylon. (No more did the quite different omens that are described by the historians.) Once in Babylon, a further portent occurs in the *Romance,* when a woman gives birth to a monstrous child. (See epigraph to this chapter.) A first interpretation, according to which Alexander is the human part of the child, ruling over the savage beasts represented by its lower part, is set aside by a second Chaldaean interpreter, who explains it as an omen of the king's death. After which 'Alexander began to put his affairs in order' (*AR* III. 30). Babylonian seers did indeed note such monstrous births, and the one quoted in the epigraph, which took place about six months later, may well have been the inspiration for the *Romance*'s story (if, indeed, there was not another such birth that is not preserved in the oracular tablets).

In Babylon, as in the historical accounts, the *Romance* describes how Alexander met his death after being suddenly taken ill at a banquet hosted by Medius. The rumours of poisoning that were already known to Plutarch (*Life,* 77) take centre stage in the *Romance*, as the story is told that Alexander was poisoned by a draught sent by Antipater in Macedon and served by Antipater's son, Alexander's cupbearer Iollas (or Iolaus). The poison 'could not be carried in any vessel of bronze, glass or clay', so Antipater placed it in a jar of lead enclosed in a jar of iron. (In other versions the poison is water from the River Styx and has to be carried in a horse's hoof.)

Knowing that his end is near, Alexander, after a failed attempt at drowning himself in the Tigris, which is thwarted by Roxane, makes his will, writes a letter of consolation to his mother, and receives a march-past of the army. In the gamma version his horse Bucephalus distinguishes himself in one of the most extravagant passages of the whole *Romance*. (In history Bucephalus was of course dead by now, having died in the battle on the Hydaspes in 326 BC.) Alexander addresses his horse lovingly, and

When Alexander spoke like this to Bucephalus, the whole army howled, making a tremendous noise. The treacherous slave who had prepared the poison and who had plotted against their lives thought that Alexander was dead, and came running to see. When Bucephalus saw him, he cast off his morose and dejected look, and, just as if he were a rational, even a clever man – I suppose it was done through Providence above – he avenged his master. He ran into the midst of the crowd, seized the slave in his teeth and dragged him to Alexander; he shook him violently and gave a loud whinny to show that he was going to have his revenge. Then he took a great leap into the air, dragging the treacherous and deceitful slave with him, and smashed him against the ground. The slave was torn apart; bits of him flew all over everyone like snow falling off a roof in a wind. The horse got up, neighed a little, and then fell down before Alexander and breathed his last. Alexander smiled at him. (*AR* III. 33)

Alexander dies immediately afterwards.

Consolation and Moralisation

Needless to say, that is not the end of the story. But before passing to the events following Alexander's death, let us look at the very different complex of stories that grew up about Alexander's death in the Syriac and Arabic traditions. They take their starting-point from the final letter of Alexander to his mother, prompted by the fulfilment of the prophecy that he would die in a place where the sky was gold and the earth of iron. This prophecy is first mentioned in the *Annals* of Eutychius, Patriarch of Alexandria at the end of the ninth century (see epigraph). Eutychius, who was an Arab and wrote in Arabic, drew on the same Alexandrian sources of information that were also available to Mas'udi (see Chapter 3), and this anecdote resonates through the Arabic texts on Alexander. Its next appearance is in tenth-century Mubaššir ibn Fatik's summary account of Alexander's life, *Ahbar al-Iskandar*.[9]

The story leads in to Alexander's dictation of a letter of consolation to his mother. This is found also in the Greek versions, though its earliest appearance is in the eighth-century L (which also features the diving bell and the Water of Life for the first time), so it is possible that it entered the Greek tradition from Arabic and not vice versa.[10]

'King Alexander greets his sweet mother. When you have received this, my last letter, prepare a fine banquet in honour of Providence above which gave you such a fine son. But if you wish to honour me, go out by yourself and invite all, both great and small, both rich and poor, to the banquet, and tell them, "See, the banquet is prepared; come in and enjoy yourselves. But let no one come who knows of past or present sorrow; for I did not make this banquet for sorrow but for joy." Mother, farewell.'

Olympias did as she was bidden; but no one could be found, great or small, rich or poor, who had known no sorrow, and so no one came. Then Olympias perceived Alexander's wisdom, and realized that Alexander had written this as a consolation to those whom he was leaving, so that they should realize that what had happened was nothing unusual, but something that had happened and would happen to everybody. (*AR* III. 33)

The central conceit of this story is a common folk-tale motif, and one frequently used in Greek literature: the Emperor Julian in his letter 69 to Himerius quotes a story from Democritus (68A20 DK). King Darius was sunk in grief over the death of a beautiful wife, and Democritus 'promised him that he would bring back the departed to life, if Darius were willing to supply him with everything necessary for the purpose'. Darius of course agrees, but the one thing needful turns out to be that 'if he would inscribe on his wife's tomb the names of three persons who had never mourned for anyone, she would straightway come to life again'. Darius of course fails, and Democritus unkindly bursts out laughing, as was his wont: 'Why then, O most absurd of men, do you mourn without ceasing, as though you were the only man who had ever been involved in so great a grief?'[11] There is also a story of the Buddha persuading a woman that he will restore her son to life if she will bring him a mustard seed from the house of one who has never known sorrow.[12] Democritus, who had travelled in the east, may have introduced the motif to Greek literature.

The letter of consolation occurs in Eutychius as the sequel to the prophecy mentioned above, and it is similarly positioned in Mubašhšir and in five other MSS of the episode of the Last Days.[13] In Kai Ka'us' *Qabus Nama*[14] it is accompanied by the information that Alexander, in his will, demanded that he be placed in his coffin with his hands protruding, so that it could be seen that he left the world empty-handed. This motif occurred also in Jami's *Iskandarnameh*, where the instruction reads: 'Leave one of my hands outside my coffin, and say, "Iskandar conquered the whole world and made it his realm from one extremity to the other, but when death came upon him he was vanquished by dust, and, relinquishing his dominion over the face of the earth, he took away with him only this piece of rough cloth."' Earlier (in Jami) Iskandar has summoned his sages and given them a short sermon: 'If death could be repulsed with arms and soldiers, here are the armies of the whole world; and if it could be repulsed with prayers and rosaries, here are the sages and sheikhs of the whole world . . . and if it could be bought off with riches and treasures, here are all the treasures of the face of the earth.'[15] Alexander's self-knowledge is greater in the Islamic texts than it had been in the Greek ones, where he was disinclined to listen to Dandamis making a similar, but more strident, point about the vanity of conquest. But perhaps the career of conquest was not vain, for the Persian writers. It was a worthy pursuit for a great king who is nonetheless realistic about his mortal end. (The moral implicit in the account of the modern Greek *Phyllada* is similar.) The traditional Persian view of life, that the world is evil because it condemns all living things to die, is here overlaid with an Islamic acceptance of God's will.

The ultimate source of the letter, and of the moralising discussion that follows, seems to be the *Sayings of the Philosophers* of Hunayn ibn Ishaq (d. 873).[16] The letter is one of the most persistent elements of the Arabic tradition and its existence in several MSS is an important pointer to the possible existence of a complete Arabic *Alexander Romance* at an early date.[17]

After the letter of consolation this text continues with a series of sayings uttered by the great philosophers gathered around Alexander's tomb. The *Sayings of the philosophers* was very influential in its Arabic form, influencing Petrus Alfonsi's *Disciplina clericalis* and thence the third recension of the *Historia de proeliis*. Mubaššir's work was also translated twice into European languages as the *Bocados de Oro* and the *Libro de los buenos proverbios*.[18] The episode does not appear in the Ethiopic *Romance*, but it is in another Ethiopic text, the *History of Alexander* by al-Makin.[19] Aristotle speaks first: 'Inasmuch as there must be an end to this world, it was better for Alexander to leave it before it came to pass.' Antigonus, Philemon and Plato, Diogenes, Taros and Nilos follow, plus a number of others to a total of twenty. Nilos says, 'Thou, O Alexander, dost rebuke others for heaping up riches, for yesterday thou wast the treasure house for gold, and today thou art thyself treasured up in gold.' Another recapitulates a familiar theme: 'Since formerly the surface of the whole earth was deemed insufficient for thee, how canst thou now contain thyself within this narrow box?'

But there is a parallel development in a Syriac version which derives from Eutychius, or Eutychius' source, so that the Christian versions are distinctly different from the Muslim ones. In Eutychius the speakers of wise aphorisms on death are Plato, Aristotle, Naren (?), Nilon (?), Lotas (?), Metron (?), Sis (?), Demetrius, Philokaton (?) and a number of others who remain unnamed – twenty-nine in all. The same names appear in the Syriac, except that Naren appears as Theon (the former being perhaps a misreading of the Arabic letters).

It is perhaps difficult to understand the enduring appeal of these mostly banal little paradoxes, of which the best may be 'Alexander did not instruct us by his speech as he now instructs us by his silence' (Syriac 9).[20]

'This City shall be your tomb'

The disposition of Alexander's body is the theme of the last paragraphs of the *Romance*. The body is embalmed (III. 34): Eutychius says in the *Annals* that it was covered in honey in its coffin, and Firdausi expands this in Alexander's last letter to his mother: 'First, see that my coffin is of gold and that my body's shroud is worthy of me; let it be of Chinese silk impregnated with sweet scents, and see that no one neglects the offices due to me. The joints of my coffin should be sealed with pitch, as well as camphor, musk and ambergris. Honey should be poured into the coffin, then a layer of brocade placed there, on which my body is to be laid; when my face has been covered there is no more to be said' (Firdausi, transl. Davis 2004, 113). But the preparation of the body for burial is just the beginning of another story.

In the *Romance* after Alexander's death, an oracle in Babylon pronounces that his body is to be brought to Memphis for embalming and burial.

> When the people of Memphis heard that he was coming, they came out to meet the body of Alexander and escort it to Memphis. But the chief priest at the temple in Memphis said, 'Do not bury him here, but in the city that he founded in Rhacotis. Wherever his body rests, that city will be constantly troubled and shaken with wars and battles'. So Ptolemy at once brought the body to Alexandria and built a tomb in the temple, which is now called Alexander's Monument; and there he deposited Alexander's mortal remains.

To the best of our historical knowledge, Alexander's body was buried in Memphis in 321 BC[21] and remained there for some time before being moved to Alexandria, possibly as early as 320 BC. It would appear that Ptolemy made use of the sarcophagus which Nectanebo II had prepared for himself, which was lying vacant at Memphis: the tomb at Memphis was very probably associated with the Temple of Nectanebo II fronted by an exedra of classical statues, now in very poor condition, near the vaults of the Apis Bulls at Saqqara.[22] This fact may have given rise to the association between Alexander and Nectanebo and to the idea, encouraged by the historian Manetho, that the old Pharaoh had returned in Alexander.[23]

The idea that Alexander was the Pharaoh Nectanebo reincarnate is at the root of a story told only in the gamma recension of the *Romance* about Alexander's triumphal entry into Memphis on his conquest of Egypt (I. 27):

> When Alexander entered the palace, there was a statue of Nectanebo standing before the door, with an inscription on it, and a crown in its right

hand and a sphere in its left . . . . On the statue's breast was inscribed 'Whoever enters my house, and I place this crown on his head, you shall all recognize this man as my son. He will travel over the whole earth. His name shall be given to this city.' And just as Alexander entered the gate, the statue placed the crown on Alexander's head. Alexander swivelled around in amazement, and stretched out his hand to the crown that had just been placed on his head. And then the statue placed in Alexander's hand the globe that was in its left hand. Everyone who was there was astonished. Alexander embraced the statue and recognized the features of Nectanebo; then he looked down at the inscription on the statue's chest and rubbed it out with his own hand. He honoured the statue that had thus prophesied his rule by gilding it all over. Alexander did not want to be considered the son of Nectanebo, but of Philip and the gods.

The story as it stands betrays its Jewish origins. First, the entry into Memphis seems to be relocated to Alexandria, which had not been built at the time ('this city'). Secondly, Alexander happily accepts the omen of his rule while rejecting and obliterating the suggestion that he is the son of Nectanebo and thus a Pharaoh rather than a conqueror. Both features would fit well with the Jewish origin that is apparent for much of the gamma recension. The Jews inhabited Alexandria and that, not Memphis, was the city that gave them their place in Egypt, which they owed to Alexander. Secondly, just as Alexander is made to be a worshipper, not of the Egyptian god Sarapis, but of the One God (I. 28 gamma), so here his Egyptian ancestry is discounted; the Jews were better off with a Macedonian than with a Pharaoh.

From Ptolemy's point of view, the Nectanebo connection was to be cultivated, and the removal of the body from Memphis to Alexandria[24] was a natural part of his establishment of Alexandria as the capital: it needed a heroic cult of the founder, and so the body of the founder was imported and placed in the enclosure known as the Soma (Body): 'The Soma also, as it is called, is a part of the royal district. This was the walled enclosure which contained the burial places of the kings and that of Alexander' (Strabo 17.1.8).

It may be that there is a flicker of anti-Ptolemaic propaganda in the story of its removal in the *Romance*. John Dillery (2004) has found an echo of the phraseology of the *Oracle of the Potter*, composed probably in the 120s BC, though with a fictional date in the reign of Amenophis (which one?). This *Oracle*, probably associated with the revolt of Harsiesis in 129 BC, looks forward to the expulsion of the 'girdle-wearers' (i.e. the Macedonians) and the return of the Agathos Daimon (the 'beneficent god') from Alexandria to Memphis. 'The girdle-wearers, sons of Typhon [Seth] as they are, will destroy each other. And then the Agathos Daimon will leave the city that has been founded and will enter into Memphis and the city of the foreigners will become a desert. This will be the end of the evils, when greening of the fields shall return to Egypt. And the city of the girdle-wearers will become a desert in the same way as my kiln has done because of the iniquities they have done to Egypt.' (Koenen 1968, p. 3 Col 111, 49–53) (The *Oracle* also refers to the Cult of Sarapis as an *idion plasma*, a 'personal invention' of Ptolemy.) Now it is certainly true that some of the same terms are in operation here, and that the reference in the *Romance* to Alexandria by the name of Rhacotis (*Raked*, 'building site') is not especially complimentary. And the priest's prophecy that Alexandria will be tormented by war and strife is in stark contrast to the pronouncement of Sarapis in I. 33. But I incline to think that the name Raked is simply a realistic description of the condition of Alexandria in 321 BC, and that the *Romance* should be read straight: Ptolemy is creating a new founder cult for his new city, and the *Romance* reflects the milieu of the Macedonians and Greeks in Egypt who have supplanted the old order based on Memphis. The body came to rest, as Sarapis had prophesied (*AR* I. 33), in the city Alexander had founded: 'You shall live in it for all time, dead and yet not dead. The city you have built shall be your tomb.'

The body may have been removed to Alexandria as early as 320 BC,[25] or as late as 275/4 (by Ptolemy II).[26] The first High Priest of Alexander is attested in 290–5.[27] The story is complicated by the fact that there were several shrines of Alexander in the city: a certain Jason wrote a book 'On the sanctuaries of Alexander in Alexandria' (Athenaeus 14.12, 620d). Furthermore, the body was apparently moved by Ptolemy IV to a new location, known as the Sema or Monument, which was part of the Royal Palaces (Strabo 17.1.8). The Soma (Body) thus became a kind of cenotaph.[28] There was also both a dynastic cult of Alexander and a chthonic founder cult of Alexander, though which was located where is uncertain: Fraser (1972, 215) places the dynastic cult at the tomb, along with that of the Agathos Daimon, while Stewart (1993, 193, 247) places it at the Sema. It was apparently the Sema that later visitors saw, including the Roman Emperors Julius Caesar and Augustus (the latter of whom broke off the mummy's nose while placing a garland upon it).[29]

The later fortunes of the tomb are another story. It apparently survived the tsunami of AD 365 (Ammianus Marcellinus 26.10.15–19, Sozomen 6.2) for it was still visible in 390 according to Libanius (*Orationes*, 14.11–12). Ibn Abd al-Hakim (who died in 871) saw what he called the 'Mosque of Dhu'l-qarnain situated near the gate of the city and its exit', while Mas'udi also saw something that he referred to as the tomb of the 'King and Prophet

Iskandar'. These observations belie the rant of John Chrysostom in the fourth century: 'Where, tell me, is Alexander's tomb? Show it to me, and tell me the day on which he died'.[30] Establishing the location of Alexander's tomb became an obsessive pursuit for later generations. The best clue was the description in Achilles Tatius (5.1): 'From the Sun Gate to the Moon Gate led a straight double row of columns, about the middle of which lies the open part of the town, and in it so many streets that walking in them you would fancy youself abroad while still at home. Going a few stades (furlongs) further, I came to the place called after Alexander, where I saw a second town; the splendour of this was cut into squares, for there was a row of columns intersected by another as long at right angles.' E.M. Forster commented,

> he tells us that the crossways bore the name of Alexander, and that the Mausoleum close to them was Alexander's tomb . . . . The passage gleams like a jewel amid the amorous rubbish that surrounds it. The vanished glory leaps up again, not in architectural detail but as a city of the soul. There (beneath the mosque of Nebi Daniel) is the body of Alexander the Great. There he lies, lapped in gold and laid in a coffin of glass. When Clitophon made his visit he had already lain there for eight hundred years, and according to legend he lies there still, walled into a forgotten cellar.[31]

The mosque of the prophet Daniel has been a persistent location for the lost tomb, but not the only one. In the 1950s and 1960s a Greek waiter, Stelios Coumoutsos, conducted several trial excavations in various parts of the city, punctuated by periods of work in a café to earn the money for his next dig. One of these was in the precinct of the Church of St Mark, close to Nabi Daniel Street, where in the sixteenth century Leo the African said that he had seen the tomb.[32] None of these excavations produced any result, and some had to be halted by the authorities when he desecrated churchyards without permission.[33] This was the more frustrating as, in 1850, a dragoman at the Russian Consulate named Ambroise Schilizzi claimed to have entered the vault beneath the mosque. Schilizzi came at last upon a worm-eaten wooden door and, peering through the cracks, perceived a body, seated as if on a throne and encased in a sarcophagus of crystal or glass. A golden diadem surmounted the figure's head. But before Schilizzi could investigate further, he was dragged away by the keeper of the mosque.[34]

Such tales kept hope and fantasy alive, though, to be sure, it is of little moment which bunghole Alexander's dust is now stopping. But the topographical co-ordinates, such as they are, suggest, now that the topography of Alexandria is better understood following recent excavations, that the tomb lay further to the east, at the crossroads of the ancient Canopic Way (later Rosetta Street, now Horreya Street) and of the north-south road running to the Lochias peninsula and lying directly east of the Royal Quarter: thus a visitor entering the city would come upon it just as he reached the 'second city' of the palaces. Attention has been directed recently to an imposing tomb (the Alabaster Tomb) in the Latin Cemetery, 600 metres north-east of the crossroads and outside the Arab walls. A section of Ptolemaic wall nearby might be part of the enclosure of the Soma.[35] A speculative argument by Andrew Chugg has proposed that the tomb was declared a church of St Mark precisely to protect the pagan founder's remains from the invading Arabs, who would show more respect to a Christian shrine. Further, the removal of the bones of St Mark to Venice, later in the Middle Ages, concealed in a barrel of pork, may have been a case of mistaken identity. If this latest twist to the knotted skein is true, it is not St Mark but Alexander the Great who lies under Venice's cathedral, whose exterior is adorned by a Byzantine relief of the great king and conqueror in his flying chariot, borne by griffins. Of such stuff are legends made.

35 Alexander the Great in his flying machine. Eleventh-century Byzantine relief on the north façade of St Mark's Basilica, Venice. Photo: Alinari.

UNIVERSAL EMPEROR
The Christian Hero

The storie of Alexander is so commune
That every wight that hath discrecioun
Hath herd somewhat or al of his fortune

Geoffrey Chaucer, 'The Monk's Tale', 641–3

'I tell you, captain, if you look in the maps of the 'orld, I warrant you sall find,
in the comparisons between Macedon and Monmouth, that the situation,
look you, is both alike, There is a river in Macedon, and there is also moreover a river at Monmouth .... If you mark Alexander's life well, Harry of
Monmouth's life is come after it indifferent well ... Alexander, God knows,
and you know, in his rages, and his furies, and his cholers, and his moods, and
his displeasures, and his indignations, and also being a little intoxicate in his
prains, did, in his ales and his angers, look you, kill his best friend, Cleitus.'

William Shakespeare, *King Henry V*, IV.vii

The Twelfth Century: Creation of a Tradition

In about 1147 the Bavarian chronicler Otto of Freising included a few
pages on Alexander in his world chronicle entitled *The Two Cities* (ii.
24–6).[1] Otto was one of the first intellectuals of the twelfth century,
and the first to give evidence of a knowledge of the works of Aristotle in
medieval Germany. In writing his pages on Alexander his aim was to
produce credible sober history, but he was hampered by the limited sources
available. Apart from a couple of allusions in Cicero and the brief account
of Orosius (which he follows closely in some portions of his history),[2] the
main lines of his account follow the narrative given in the *Alexander
Romance*.[3] He tells several stories known from the gamma recension of

the Greek *Romance*: the visit to Jerusalem, the preaching in Alexandria, the single combat with Porus, as well as the visit to the Oracular Trees and the poisoning (common to all recensions). He also knew the *Letter to Aristotle*, as the following passage makes clear.

> If anyone desires to know about Porus' golden house and the silver-and-gold vine with clusters of grapes made of precious stones, let him read the letter of Alexander to his teacher, Aristotle the philosopher. Therein the careful student of events will find the perils he endured, and the images[4] of the sun and moon that foretold his death, and many matters so strange that they seem actually beyond belief.

Such scepticism befits one of the founders of modern historiography, but it shows vividly what kind of material a writer in the twelfth century had to work with.

This chapter steps back from the analysis of stories to show how the figure of Alexander endured in the west after the establishment of Christianity, and to draw out some of the meanings that readers found in his career. The subject was the theme of George Cary's indispensable *The Medieval Alexander* (1956), which was never completed owing to his early death: my chapter does not set out to repeat his survey and analysis but to set the changing image of the conqueror in a historical and literary context.[5]

The new Christian culture of late antiquity and early Middle Ages had swept away much of the knowledge of the classical past. Writers of the Roman Empire had shown little interest in the legends of the conqueror, but used the historical Alexander as a 'tool for thinking' and as an example of luxury, pride, drunkenness and tyranny.[6] But, as antiquity came to an end, this negative view was forgotten, and Alexander became instead a kind of symbol for the 'pagan revival' of the fourth century. Some of the mysterious medallions known as contorniates carry images of Alexander with the legend *Alexander filius dei*, in an obvious riposte to the Christian designation for Jesus,[7] and were probably used as magical talismans to bring good fortune.[8]

The *Historia Augusta* (14. 3–6: not necessarily a reliable source) tells us that the members of the family of the Macriani adorned their tableware and jewellery with images of Alexander. The mosaic at Soueidié-Baalbeck in the Lebanon (Plate 3),[9] which depicts the birth of Alexander, is perhaps another token of the mystical importance of Alexander at this date.

Such a view of Alexander was bound to make him an object of little interest in an age dominated by the need to establish Christian orthodoxy.

36 A contorniate depicting Olympias and the serpent, and the Abukir-Medallion of
Alexander. Staatliche Museen zu Berlin, Münzkabinett. Objekt-nr. 18200664 and 18200016.

The last writer of antiquity to write at any length about Alexander, and the
first to use the *Romance*,[10] is Fulgentius, in his *De aetatibus mundi et hominis*
of the late fifth century. Fulgentius drew most of his information from some
version of the *Romance*, and tells the Nectanebo story as well as that of
Candace and the wonderstone – but not the episodes of the diving bell, the
flying machine and the Unclean Nations, which must have entered the
Romance tradition after this date.[11] Fulgentius' other works were quite
well known in the Middle Ages, with numerous MSS existing from the
ninth century onwards; but the *De aetatibus* (which is possibly by a different
Fulgentius) is known in only two MSS from the twelfth and thirteenth
centuries. By contrast, Orosius, Otto's main source, survives in about 250
MSS, indicating a much wider distribution in the Dark Ages of the sixth to
tenth centuries.[12]

Otto's second source of information, the Latin *Letter to Aristotle,* was
already widely current, having been copied many times from the ninth
century onwards,[13] as well as being translated into Old English and incorporated in the *Beowulf* MS around the year 1000. It flourished as a source
of geographical information, regardless of its connection with Alexander.

The *Collatio*, the dialogue between Alexander and Dindimus, remained
quite well known, as it was a Latin text: in the eighth century Alcuin sent
a copy of it to Charlemagne.[14] Whether there was a Greek original cannot
be established, though it seems likely. The Latin version may be as early as
the fourth century.

But the *Romance* itself had sunk into obscurity after the Latin translation
made by Julius Valerius in the fourth century, and the historical accounts of

Arrian and Quintus Curtius were also unknown. The brief historical account known as the *Itinerarium Alexandri*, possibly also written by Julius Valerius and certainly of about the same date, must have been unknown: it survives in a single MS in Milan;[15] while the breviary known as the *Epitoma rerum gestarum Alexandri Magni* similarly survived in a single codex in Metz, which was destroyed by fire in the Second World War.[16] The only version of Julius that could have been known to Otto was the *Epitome* of his work made in the ninth century, known as the *Zacher Epitome* (there are some 66 MSS).[17] Otto's case is a typical example of the state of knowledge and learning in the early twelfth century, and makes all the more remarkable the transformation of knowledge that came about in the course of that century and the next.[18]

The turning point in the story of Alexander in the Middle Ages was the rediscovery of the Greek original of the *Alexander Romance* by Leo the Archpriest of Naples during a diplomatic mission to Constantinople in the tenth century (951–69) (see Chapter 1, and Appendix).

Leo translated the *Romance* into Latin, and one complete and one partial MS of his translation survive. The complete version, which can be dated at latest around the year 1000, was made in south Italy, and entered the cathedral library in Bamberg (MS E III. 14) in 1022, presumably as a consequence of the Emperor Henry II's creation of the episcopal city of Bamberg in the year 1007 and his assembling of an extensive library there.[19] This was just one element in a growing interchange between the courts of Byzantium and the Holy Roman Empire, which also led to the marriage of German princesses to Byzantine rulers and vice versa, and to the strong influence of Byzantine style on the art of the Ottonian era.

The MS that contains Leo also contains four other short works on Alexander, the *Commonitorium Palladii*, with the text attributed to Arrian that introduces it, the *Letter to Aristotle*, and the *Correspondence of Alexander and Dindimus*.[20] The scribe had clearly made a compilation of Alexander works for the Bamberg library. Leo's version of the *Romance* does not correspond exactly to any of the known Greek recensions, though it is close to the alpha recension as known from the Syriac.[21] It is evident that the Greek work was still being copied and adapted in Byzantium when Leo went there, though in Byzantium it was the epsilon recension that was to become the dominant influence (see Chapter 12).

Somehow Leo's work became well known, and three expanded versions of it were made in the course of the twelfth century and became known under the title of 'The History of Alexander's Battles', the *Historia de proeliis* (*HP*). (See Chapter 6, and for details of the editions the Appendix.) The three recensions are known as the Interpolated Versions 1, 2, and 3 (I, or

J[1,2,3]). The first, though closest to Leo, also incorporates elements from other works, including Josephus, Jerome, Orosius, Solinus, Isidore, the *Letter of Pharasmanes* and the Indian treatises. There are only two MSS, but the existence of this version is an indication of the range of (Latin) texts that a scholar could draw on to improve his predecessor's work. The second recension is sometimes known as the 'Orosius recension' because of its heavy use of that author: in addition it draws on Valerius Maximus (for anecdotal material), Pseudo-Methodius (the Unclean Nations), Josephus (the visit to Jerusalem), Pseudo-Epiphanius and the Indian treatises: it directly influenced the Old French *Alexander* and two Middle English poems. But the third recension was the one that became best known, and was the source of an enormous number of translations into the vernacular languages of Europe, not least the verse reworking by Quilichinus of Spoleto, whose date of 1236 provides a *terminus ante quem* for its creation. Not only are there numerous MSS, but it was printed several times from 1471 onwards. (It should be noted that all of these recensions draw on Latin sources for their elaborations of the original: there was no further use of Greek after Leo's initial, one might say epochal, act of translation.) The result was that, while the image of Alexander in the Islamic world had become more or less established and static by the twelfth century, in western Europe its development was only just beginning.

During the next three centuries the *Romance* would be translated more frequently than any other work except the Gospels; the figure of Alexander would be incorporated into Arthurian legend and into sacred scripture; he would become an example for moralists and theologians and a vehicle of the scientific knowledge of the age; a model for kings and emperors and an emblem of the life of man equal, sometimes, even to Christ.[22]

By the end of the twelfth century the history of Quintus Curtius was becoming known[23] and became the source of a parallel tradition of accounts of Alexander. Its widespread distribution was due to Walter of Châtillon's (1178–82) *Alexandreis*, which in turn became the source for Alberic of Besançon around 1100.[24]

The most important derivative of Walter was the Spanish *Libro de Alejandro*, composed a little later in the thirteenth century.

The Spanish *Libro de Alejandro* is one of the classics of Spanish literature. The bulk of the narrative covers the events of the conquest of Persia, with some excursions on Greek mythology. In the latter part it includes some of the fabulous adventures from the *Historia de proeliis*: the headless men, the diving bell and the flying machine, the trees of the sun and moon. It also shows signs of influence from the Arabic tradition, notably the letter of consolation to Olympias. As befits its model in the classical

tradition, it is a secular and heroic work, and the sacred role of Alexander
is not part of the author's scheme. Perhaps the most striking addition to
the usual story, in both Walter and the Spanish text, is the episode (Walter,
X. 93 ff., *Libro*, 2325ff.) where Nature, alarmed at Alexander's penetration
of her uttermost regions, descends into hell to seek the assistance of the
infernal powers in stopping his advance. Satan is ready to assist, for he fears
that Alexander will reach as far as Paradise and thus precipitate the Second
Coming and the destruction of his realm (Walter, X. 140–2, *Libro*, 2440).
At X. 191–204 Walter addresses Alexander directly: 'To what lengths does
your hunger go, Alexander? What end will there be to your possessions,
what limit to your requirements, what goal to your labours? Madman, you
are accomplishing nothing! You may have confined all kingdoms under
one rule and subdued the entire world, yet you will always be in need.'
Walter rather neatly unifies the moral tradition (from the Dindimus
episode) about Alexander as overreacher with the story of his reaching
Paradise. 'The devil has a sin for everyone,' the Spanish author declares
(*Libro*, 2398), and pride is Alexander's. He is brought down by one of
Satan's minions, Treachery, in the form of Antipater's poison plot. From
this it is clear that Walter is well aware of the Romance tradition, but
chooses to enfold its lessons into a classically styled epic based otherwise
on a real historical source.[25] Despite its importance, Walter's poem had
nothing like the impact of the *Historia de proeliis* over the next three
centuries.

The Growth of Learning

The twelfth century was an age of enormous intellectual advance in
western Europe,[26] and of heroic rediscovery of the lost learning of the
classical world. If, in the eleventh century, Boethius had been the master of
those who wanted to know, in the twelfth century Aristotle became the
master of those who did know.[27] As was apparent in Otto's account of
Alexander, a critical spirit had entered the writing about the past, not least
as a result of the availability of more evidence. One of the most notable
spurs was the increasing knowledge of foreign lands. To quote Southern
again (1953, 52): 'the civilization of the twelfth century owes a great deal
to the tears which were shed in the eleventh': that is, the pious motive of
pilgrimage led willy-nilly to a familiarity with the lands of the east, and in
the Crusades that exposure to wider knowledge reached thousands. Fulcher
of Chartres (1059–1130), in his chronicle of the Crusades, drew on the
Alexander stories as providing useful and genuine knowledge about the
lands of the east, and in this he was not alone.

There were several points of focus for the growth of learning in twelfth-century Europe. As early as the tenth century, Arab scholars in Cordoba had been recovering and translating Greek works which were still unknown to Latin-speaking contemporaries; in the eleventh and twelfth centuries translators working in Toledo translated numerous works from Arabic into Latin.[28] Gerard of Cremona alone translated 87 different works; Peter the Venerable translated the Qur'ān. Hermann of Carinthia and John of Seville were also key figures in this translation movement, the latter being the first translator of another 'Alexander' text, the *Secretum secretorum* (see Appendix I). The fall of Toledo in 1085 improved access for westerners to the wisdom of the Arabs, much of which was mediated through the sizeable Jewish population in Spain, and thence to the wider world when the Jews were driven out in 1140.

Contemporary with the heyday of Toledo, the recently established Norman kingdom of Sicily, with its cosmopolitan mix of Arabs, Greeks and Latins, became a centre of learning, with a free interchange of cultural baggage and a vigorous programme of translation. Roger II (1095–1154)[29] and Frederick II (1194–1250)[30] both fostered scholarship at their courts and maintained links with the rulers of Byzantium and the Sultans of Egypt. Roger was the patron of the great Arab geographer Idrisi, and also encouraged Greek scholarship: Henricus Aristippus was active in the 1150s, as was Eugene of Palermo. There were links with the Byzantine court (when the two kingdoms were not at war over Apulia), and embassies regarding dynastic marriages in 1143.[31] Both the Byzantine Emperor Manuel II Comnenos and his niece Theodora married Franks (Bertha in the first case, and Henry, brother of Conrad of Austria, in the second).[32] Manuel may have liked to be compared to Alexander, since Bishop Eustathius uttered praises of the latter in an address to the Emperor in 1174.[33] He presented a copy of Ptolemy's *Almagest* to William the Bad of Sicily in 1158 – presumably in Greek, though Gerard of Cremona was busy translating it from Arabic in 1175.

Frederick continued Roger's patronage of learning, and even took his logic tutor on crusade with him.[34] Kantorowicz's great study of Frederick II (1931) showed how the figure of Alexander reverberated through the minds of those at his court: his deeds were compared with those of Alexander (Kantorowicz 1931, 61), his meeting with St Francis in 1222 invited comparisons with that of Alexander with Diogenes (160), in 1235 he was hailed by minstrels as a 'new Alexander' (409, and see 494), and he was even supposed to have horns, like Moses and Alexander (609)! Frederick's court astrologer, Master Theodore of Antioch, was a man of wide learning, sent to Frederick some time before 1236 by the Sultan of

Egypt. He worked on the *Secretum secretorum* and was the recipient of a mythical account of Alexander's conquests as well as of other Romance material.[35] This was perhaps the source of the third recension of the Latin *Historia de proeliis*, which formed the basis of the poem in Latin hexameters by Quilichinus of Spoleto. Quilichinus, who was connected with the court of Frederick II, may have been inspired to compose his poem by the Emperor's known interest in Alexander's career.[36]

In northern Europe, learning grew rapidly as a result of several factors. People and ideas moved freely between the Norman courts of England and of Sicily. William II of Sicily took an English bride, Joanna, in 1177. Gervase of Tilbury (1150–1220), too, moved between Canterbury and the Sicilian court of William II: perhaps this was where he picked up the assorted Alexander stories that adorn his *Otia imperialia* (*c.* 1200). The traffic went the other way too, as Simon of Apulia became Dean of York and then Bishop of Exeter.

The cathedrals of France became centres of active scholarship and provided a focus for the work of John of Salisbury and Peter Comestor. The former, as perhaps the foremost scholar in Europe, was associated with Canterbury Cathedral for thirty years and visited Italy no fewer than six times. Walter of Châtillon dedicated his *Alexandreis* to William of the White Hands (1176–1202) at Rheims. The decline of the Benedictine monasteries with their tradition of poverty was counterbalanced by the rise of the Cistercian order founded by the formidable Bernard of Clairvaux, in whose monasteries a vigorous tradition of copying classical manuscripts developed.

Other courts went some way towards emulating the glittering culture of the Courts of Roger II and, later, Frederick II in Sicily: Henry II of England, as Walter Map tells us, provided a focus for scholars and poets,[37] as did even more his queen, Eleanor of Aquitaine, with her intimate connections to the troubadour movement in France: the rise of the Arthurian Romance in England is certainly to be associated with her influence. Henry may have encouraged Arthurian literature as a basis for a new British identity, as he strove to create a kingdom from the lands he ruled.[38]

The scandal of the sack of Constantinople by the fourth Crusade in 1204 led to the destruction of much priceless knowledge, but many Greeks escaped to the west, bearing manuscripts that would enrich the learning and would employ the copyists' labour in the monasteries of Europe.

Universal History and Universal Emperor: Dissemination and Elaboration in the Thirteenth Century

A further aspect of the twelfth century which is relevant here is the enthusiasm for Universal Histories. Scholarly confidence had grown as a result of the expansion of learning, and it seemed possible to compose histories of the world that did not simply repeat what was in the Bible but incorporated the knowledge obtainable from classical sources as well. (By the thirteenth century a university curriculum was established, and Roger Bacon thought it would be possible to compose a compendium of all knowledge for teaching purposes.)[39] In the Universal Histories the main source for Alexander was the *Historia de proeliis*. The Alexander story of the *Historia de proeliis* provides the source for the Universal Histories of Peter Comestor, Dean of Troyes 1147–64 (d. *c.* 1179) and Godfrey of Viterbo (1125–96). Both these writers offer an account of world history which is structured on the narrative of the Bible but which makes an impressive synchronism with what was known of Greek and Roman history too. For Alexander, the main source is the *Historia de proeliis* (J^2), which incorporates his visit to Jerusalem, the *Letter to Aristotle*,[40] the correspondence with Dindimus and the Oracular Trees. In Godfrey, as in Comestor, the nations of Gog and Magog are identified with the Lost Tribes of Israel: as a result, Alexander becomes a type of the 'Last Emperor' who will usher in the end of the world and the reign of Christ.[41] Alexander, the instantiation of the problematic nature of the role of world ruler, stands between the evil of Gog and Magog and the ineffectuality of the Brahmans as an emblem of active virtue, an ideal king.[42] As with the Muslim Alexander of the Qur'ān, it is Alexander's role as the conqueror of the Unclean Nations that makes him fit to be regarded as a part of history in a Christian world.

In the thirteenth century the main Universal Histories were those of Vincent of Beauvais (1190–1264) and Ranulph Higden (d. 1364). Vincent's *Speculum historiale*, more than three times as long as the Bible itself, covers biblical history, the classical world, and more recent times up to the Crusades. It was translated into French (1322) and into Dutch by the important Dutch author, Jakob van Maerlant.[43] Maerlant's *Spiegel Historiael* is briefer and more readable than the original. Maerlant, as has been mentioned, also wrote an earlier work, *Alexanders Geesten*, a free translation of Walter of Châtillon's *Alexandreis*. Since the latter followed the Curtian tradition (see below), the elements of the narrative differ widely. Maerlant considers the *Spiegel* as more reliable (being sacred history), and regards Walter's version as 'fables'.

Ranulph Higden's *Polychronicon* made heavy use of Vincent of Beauvais, but also cites Comestor as well as ancient authors including Justin, Josephus, Trogus and Eutropius – but not Curtius. Higden also incorporates the 'Sayings of the Philosophers' at Alexander's tomb, from the third recension of the *Historia de proeliis*. Higden's work was translated into English by John Trevisa in the 1380s, and was thus contemporary with Mandeville's *Travels*, in which geography is the dominant mode.

Sacred history and geography are combined again in the great *Mappae Mundi* that depict the world as being centred on Jerusalem and arrange the sites of history in relation to God's plan. The Hereford Map of the 1280s shows the great world 'felloed with death', as the poet David Constantine puts it:[44] the outermost circle of the map contains the letters M O R S. The creation of such *Mappae Mundi* begins in the tenth century, but the first to include sites relating to Alexander is the Ebstorf Map of 1235–40; later maps, such as the Hereford Map, generally include them as well. The Psalter Map of *c.* 1265 is a copy of a large one that hung in Henry III's chamber, and this too shows such features as the trees of the sun and moon, and the enclosure that contains Gog and Magog. Several of these maps had religious settings, like that in the monastery at Ebstorf; the Hereford Map was perhaps originally an altarpiece. The moral judgments that circulated on Alexander the man took second place to his important role in sacred history and geography. Some words of Pierre Mabille, quoted by Jacques le Goff, are apposite here: 'Beyond entertainment, beyond curiosity, beyond all the emotions such narratives and legends afford, beyond the need to divert, to forget, or to achieve delightful or terrifying sensations, the real goal of the marvelous journey is the total exploration of universal reality.'[45] These words are as applicable to universal histories as to world maps.

Also in the thirteenth century the *Secretum secretorum* began to circulate widely (see Appendix I for details). This text purported to be by Aristotle and was composed in the form of a letter addressed to Alexander on statecraft and associated topics.[46] It added Alexander the Wise King to his parallel roles as universal ruler and as player in the drama of man's salvation. Partially translated in 1125 by Johannes Hispalensis (there were also translations into Spanish and Hebrew), it received its first complete Latin translation in 1232, by Philip of Tripoli, who may have been working at the court of Frederick II.[47] Its popularity was enormous and the text continued to be influential up to about 1550. After that time, increased critical awareness raised doubts about its authenticity, and its content had been largely superseded by more reliable works on the same topics.[48] It lost its usefulness as a university textbook.

The French and German Traditions of the Thirteenth and Fourteenth Centuries

An increase of classical learning in the schools led to the rise of romances on classical themes as well as in the Arthurian and the chivalric tradition that went back to the *Song of Roland*.[49] This was the age of the Arch-Poet, of the *Carmina Burana* and of Adelard of Bath, as well as of the troubadours in the vernacular: literature, both Latin and vernacular, had broken away from religious necessities, to reflect the activities and aspirations of daily life and the desire for amusement as well as for improvement. Heroic poetry gave way to chivalric tales. The first French romances took on classical themes in the *Roman de Thèbes* (1150, based on Statius), the *Roman d'Enéas* (1160, from Virgil, soon to be translated into German by Heinrich von Veldeke) and the *Roman de Troie* by Benoît de Sainte-Maure (1165, using Dares Phrygius and Dictys Cretensis). In the same years, Geoffrey of Monmouth (writing about 1135) created the beginnings of the Arthurian legend, and the Tristan story emerged around 1150, while Chrétien de Troyes invented the legend of the Grail in the 1160s. There was no book market as such and literature required aristocratic patrons. It was the emergence of a knightly class that made the development of this literature possible, and its manifestations are always intimately interwoven with the chivalric values of that class. We cannot identify the patrons who took an interest in the *Historia de proeliis* and caused its being recopied in Latin and translated into vernacular languages, but the fact that Alexander cycles were

37 Misericord, Gloucester Cathedral.

providing the wall decorations in residences such as Clarendon (by 1237) and the Queen's Chamber at Nottingham under Henry III (1252)[50] is suggestive of the currency of his tale in the British Isles.[51]

It is a little later that his flight becomes a popular theme for misericords and other elements of cathedral architecture in England, but that, as we have seen, was already a standard subject for the Norman cathedrals of Apulia, with their deep Greek influence. (Despite the Norman Conquest, the impress of Apulia's Byzantine centuries remained strong, and the region even returned to Byzantine rule for a few years in the late twelfth century.)

The process of bringing the Alexander story into the vernacular began in France and was closely paralleled in Germany.[52] In the first third of the twelfth century Alberic of Besançon wrote a poem on Alexander.[53] Only 105 verses survive, covering Alexander's childhood (without the Nectanebo story, though the latter features there as a magic teacher), but it was adapted by 1155 into German by Pfaffe Lamprecht, whose work survives. There are two MSS: the Vorau version stops at the death of Darius, but the Strasburg one is fuller and includes the later adventures such as the visit to Candace. It emphasises geographical details and the associations of the places Alexander visits. In the visit to the Cave of the Gods (6425ff.), it is Ammon whom Alexander meets, not the Sarapis and Sesonchosis of the *Romance*. Lamprecht also adds the journey to Paradise (6800ff.). As in the Universal Histories, it is Alexander's role in Christian salvation that is stressed, though Alexander the man is criticised for his guilt and vanity.[54] We cannot of course be sure how much of the moral tone comes from Alberic and how much is added by the German priest.

The slightly later Anglo-Norman Alexander poem of Thomas of Kent, *Roman de toute chevalerie* (c. 1175–1200), draws mainly on Julius Valerius and the *Epitome*, and uses the Nectanebo story and also the *Letter to Aristotle*.[55] It cites Aethicus and Solinus (4606); at 5470 Alexander goes to Taprobane; the story of the wonderstone is told, and that of the trees (7097); Gog and Magog are identified with 'the dog-eating Turks' (6012); and even Noah's ark gets a mention at 6620.

Several further French poems of the 1170s elaborated the story: Eustache's *Fuerre de Gadres*, Lambert li Tort's *Alexander* and probably a third poem as well, all of which were combined in a work now known from two Paris MSS (in the Arsenal and Bibliothèque Nationale 789). In the years following 1180 a master-poet, Alexandre de Paris, welded all these works into a long romance of 16,000 verses, each of the source works constituting a separate 'branch' of the poem.[56] This famous and distinguished poem provided one of the dominant images of Alexander for the Middle Ages: the chivalric hero of a feudal society who swears by Jupiter but also prays to God and intro-

duces cults of saints; the Persian enemy becomes the Saracens, and his visit
to Jerusalem, inevitably, becomes a crusade. Alexander is an example of the
good king, exhibiting clemency, wisdom, caution and a willingness to listen
to the advice of Aristotle. The virtue of largesse is also central to the idea of
the chivalric hero, and was always prominent in the depiction of Alexander
(see colour plate 18).[57] He is a hero more than he is a king (unlike, for
example, Charlemagne, who is always a king first and a hero second). As
Maurice Keen incisively observes, Alexander was suitable for adoption as a
chivalric hero because of his possession of a famous horse, and because he
fights orientals.[58] By 1313 he is enshrined as one of the Nine Worthies: the
others are Hector and Caesar (from the classical world); Joshua, David and
Judas Maccabeus (from the Old Testament); and Arthur, Charlemagne and
Godfrey of Bouillon (from the world of chivalry).

In the thirteenth century the *Historia de proeliis* provided the source for
the French *Roman d'Alexandre en prose*.[59] This retold the story for a new
readership in the age of Thomas Malory: one of the most beautiful of all
Alexander MSS is the illuminated version made for Margaret of Anjou on
the occasion of her marriage to Henry VI in 1445.[60]

In Germany, Lamprecht's first successor was Rudolf von Ems (*fl.*
1220–50). Rudolf, a nobleman in the service of the Count of Montfort,
wrote his work as a portrait of an ideal ruler. It reverberates with themes
recalling the figure of Frederick II (d. 1250). Like Lamprecht's, it emphasises Alexander's role in sacred history and as the Last Emperor. (The details
of the succession of empires are taken from Peter Comestor.) But in the
main Alexander is characterised as a humble knight of the Cross: his vices
are played down, and the knight's courtly side is almost non-existent, even
in the episode with Thalestris (almost the only opportunity for a love
interest), who presides over a group of ladies of the court.[61] Like many of
Rudolf's works, his *Alexander* is unfinished, but probably reached its present
form in the lifetime of Frederick II, and thus before his similarly unfinished
Weltchronik, which refers to Frederick's death.[62]

By the end of the fourteenth century the story of Alexander had been
absorbed into general literary awareness and appears in many contexts,
often under the barest of allusions, as in Chaucer's 'Monk's Tale' (see
epigraph to this chapter).[63] Thus, for example, the story of his birth is
familiar material for John Gower (1325–1408: see Chapter 1). Alexander's
career is a subject for Ranulph Higden, and sufficiently familiar to receive
allusions in passing from Sir John Mandeville. The enclosure of the Unclean
Nations is mentioned briefly in Fazio degli Uberti's (1305–67) poem *Il
Dittamondo*, an account of the human world almost as comprehensive as
Dante's of the world to come.[64] Christine de Pizan mentioned Alexander's

attempt to drown himself after his poisoning in her *City of Ladies* (1405: II. 29.3), and knew of his encounter with the Amazons.

The fourteenth century also saw the composition of several vernacular works based on the *Historia de proeliis* tradition: Domenico Scolari's *Istoria Alexandri regis,* the first Alexander book produced in Italy, was in Latin but was quickly followed by several vernacular ones;[65] the Swedish *Romance* is also of this date.[66] Seifrit's translation of *Historia de proeliis* J[2] (1352) makes its hero into a bourgeois.[67] In England, Thomas of Kent's *Roman de toute chevalerie* was translated into Middle English as *Kynge Alisaundre*, while *The Wars of Alexander* (MS of 1450) may be as early as the 1360s (its style and language resemble those of the Gawain poet). Several more English and Scots versions followed in the fifteenth century.[68]

Among the most intriguing indications of knowledge of the Alexander story is the denomination of the Grail in Wolfram von Eschenbach's *Parzival* (thirteenth century) as *lapsit exillis*. There is little doubt that this puzzling phrase is a derivation from the description of the wonderstone in *Alexander's Journey to Paradise*, 'lapis exilis', 'a little stone'. The learned Wolfram seems to have taken this symbol of humility and adapted it to the great symbol of Arthurian legend.[69]

The Fifteenth Century: The Compendious Approach

Perhaps the most interesting and enjoyable rewriting of the Alexander story from the fifteenth century is Johann Hartlieb's Middle High German *Alexander*. This deserves attention not least for the beautiful cycle of illustrations that adorns most of the MSS. Hartlieb's work, however, is based on a much earlier composition, the Latin *Liber Alexandri Magni* preserved in a unique MS in Paris, BN n.a.l. 310. This dates from the second half of the twelfth century, the age when the outlines of the Alexander tradition were still being forged. Its author set out to create a compendious account of all the available versions of the story, using Leo, the *Epitome* of Julius Valerius, Orosius, Comestor, both the *Commonitorium* and the *Correspondence* for the Brahmans episode, and the *Letter*. One result of this is some repetition: the episode with the Brahmans occurs twice, introducing them first as gymnosophists (1147ff.) and then as Brahmans (1349ff.). Some other MSS of the twelfth and thirteenth centuries similarly contain compendia of Alexander texts,[70] but none attempts to weld them into a single narrative as this author does. This was the text that Hartlieb translated into German prose in about 1444. Besides the nineteen MSS, there were eighteen printings between 1472 and 1670; the *Liber* was used as a source by Hans Sachs and was translated into Danish in 1584.

There were several other retellings of the Alexander story in the fifteenth century, not least the Italian accounts which include *I nobili fatti di Alessandro Magno* (prose) and the *Alessandreida in Rima* (1444) in verse.[71] This was also the age of the major translations into eastern European languages.[72] Even more remarkably, Alexander took a further step into centre stage with the incorporation of the entire *Romance* into the Dutch and German History Bibles, to fill the gap between the end of the Old Testament and the beginning of the Book of Maccabees.[73]

At the same time there was a movement to incorporate the hero in the now dominant Arthurian cycles. A successor of Wolfram von Eschenbach continued his unfinished *Titurel* in *Der Jüngere Titurel*, of which a long episode is devoted to battles in the region of Paradise, with explicit allusions to Alexander's earlier visit there. But the acme of this syncretism, if one may call it that, is the long French romance *Perceforest* (mid–fifteenth century, printed 1528 and 1531), which begins with an account of Alexander's arrival on the shores of Britain, where his lieutenants Betis and Gadifer are crowned as, respectively, kings of England and Scotland.[74] Alexander becomes a chivalric lover (of Sebille), a humble and gentle knight, and he dictates his history to Perceforest's scribe, Cresus.

38 Alexander's lieutenant Betis is crowned king of England. From *Les Voeux du Paon.* Rijksmuseum, Amsterdam, MS 3042, f. 50v.

In the latest of the great Latin-language compilations of the Middle Ages, the *Gesta romanorum* (datable from 1362 to 1473), Alexander appears several times, often in unfamiliar tales. One of the most striking is number xcvi (p. 168ff.), which contains both an echo of his letter of consolation to Olympias and a whiff of the atmosphere of Malory:

> King Alexander placed a burning candle in his hall, and sent heralds through the whole kingdom, who made the following proclamation: 'If there be any under forfeiture to the king, and he will come boldly into his presence, where the candle burns, the king will forgive the forfeiture. And whosoever is in this predicament, and comes not before the expiration of the candle, he shall perish by an ignominious death.' Many of the populace, hearing the proclamation, came to the king and besought his mercy. The king received them kindly; but there were many who neglected to come; and the very moment in which the candle expired, they were apprehended and put to death.
>
> Application. My beloved, Alexander is Christ, the burning candle is the life present, and the heralds are the preachers.

Yet as the Middle Ages drew to a close the figure of Alexander seemed to lose its centrality. The reasons may be sought partly in social development, partly in the growth of learning. In the first place, the strong link between Alexander and the chivalric tradition meant that, with the rise of bourgeois society and the waning of chivalric ideals, this God-fearing courtly crusader seemed less relevant. The *Romances* too, made in many cases in fine unique illustrated manuscripts for an aristocratic readership, inevitably did not reach the newer reading public.[75] As a corollary, there were not enough aristocrats to sustain a printing industry, so printers produced what the middle classes would buy. H.S. Bennett's survey of what was printed in England between 1475 and 1557 shows a predominance of religious and scientific literature.[76] There are, however, several romances, including the classical ones of Aesop and Apollonius of Tyre, as well as Eglamoure and Huon of Bordeaux. Mandeville, the *Gesta romanorum* and the *Golden Legend* are prominent. Among translations there are the *Morte D'Arthur* (1485), *Apollonius* (1510), the *Alexander Romance* (1550) and Quintus Curtius (1553), as well as the *Histories of Troy*. The first book printed in England was the *Dictes and Sayings of the Philosophers*, soon followed by Higden and Chaucer.[77] In Germany, *Parzival* and *Titurel* were printed but do not seem to have been successful.[78] The fact that the *Historia de proeliis* was printed a number of times from 1486 onwards, as was Hartlieb, is thus an indication of Alexander's staying power.

But the *Romance* view of Alexander was no longer the dominant view; for, in the second place, the continuing recovery of classical works during the Renaissance made much of the medieval lore on Alexander seem old-fashioned. The *Secretum secretorum* fell from favour as newer sources of knowledge superseded it.[79] Curtius' history became more widely known and was translated into Italian as early as 1438; Arrian's history was translated into Latin by 1460, and into Latin and Italian in 1544.[80] And as the classical authors came to be more widely read, the view of Alexander that had been conveyed by Seneca began to establish itself.[81] Already Walter Map (191) had been aware of the philosopher's criticisms of Alexander's pride, vanity and violence. When Walter Ralegh came to write his *History of the World*, a new critical spirit led him to doubt Alexander's encounter with the Amazons (IV. 309), though he admitted that they may have existed (after all, he had met some himself, in Guiana).[82] The interpretation he offered of Alexander's career (IV. 343–5) was a thoroughly Senecan one: that of a violent and arrogant conqueror, no trace of the messenger of God about him.

> Alexander's former cruelties cannot be excused, no more than his vanity to be esteemed the son of Jupiter, with his excessive delight in drink and drunkenness . . . . If we compare this great conqueror with other troublers of the world, who have bought their glory with so great destruction and effusion of blood, I think him far inferior to Caesar and many others that lived after him . . . . For conclusion, we will agree with Seneca, who, speaking of Philip the father and Alexander the son, gives this judgment of them . . . . 'They were no less plagues to mankind, than an overflow of waters drowning all the level; or some burning drought, whereby a great part of living creatures is scorched up.'

The last appearance of the noble Alexander of the *Romance* is in a chapbook of 1683, which is another rewriting of the correspondence between Alexander and Dindimus, *The Upright Lives of the Heathen Briefly Noted*.[83] In this little text, as Dindimus concludes his defence of the abstinent life of the Brahmans,

> These things Alexander heard (as it's said of Herod concerning John Baptist) not only without wroth, but with a placid countenance, and replied, O Dindimus! Thou true teacher of Brahmans, thou comest of God, I have found thee the most excellent of men, by reason of the spirit that is in thee . . . . But what shall I do, who inhabit with continual

slaughter? I live in great dread, and am afraid of my own warders . . . how shall I defend myself before God, who hath assigned me this lot?

Thus the Alexander of the *Romance* ends as he began in the third century BC, comparing his life of conquest with the quietism of the Indian philosophers, and showing himself a seeker, but an eternally frustrated seeker, after the grace of God.

12

KING OF THE WORLD
Alexander the Greek

Next day, Alexander entertained all the kings and lords who were with him, and all his army. They came from the east, from the west, from the regions of the north, from the south, and from the islands of the sea, bringing tribute (*harac*) for many years, and many gifts. His teacher Aristotle also came from his mother Olympias . . . . Aristotle said: 'All the world rejoices, and is at peace, because of you.'

Phyllada tou Megalexandrou (1680), ch. 202 (ed. Pallis 1935, p. 203)

Around the time that the Great Alexander was returning from war at Troy, an Assyrian king established himself at a site just south of Assiros called Aghia Anna, and the village [of Assiros] is named after this Assyrian.

Story collected in Assiros: see Karakasidou 1997, 36

The Byzantine Alexander

If at the close of the Middle Ages the Alexander of Romance and legend was being displaced for good by a colder-eyed view of the Alexander of history, in Greece his career was only just beginning. Alexander remains today a living figure in Greek lore. His trajectory in Greek literature of the Middle Ages and modern times has been very different from that in the west; yet still the *Alexander Romance* is at its core. The subject of Alexander in Greek tradition has been exhaustively studied by a number of scholars,[1] and this concluding chapter aims to do no more than point to some of the constants and their lines of transmission.

As in the west, so in Byzantium a serious loss of contact with the classical past took place as the result of the establishment of Christianity. Before the resurgence of classical learning from the twelfth century onwards, legends and scraps of half-digested knowledge were the main access to the past. So in eighth-century Constantinople, one thing that everybody knew was that 'Alexander had built the Strategion'. The information was in the strange handbook of local lore, the *Patria Constantinopoleos*.[2] It was derived from the sixth-century chronicle of John Malalas (1192), where it appears as almost the first piece of information in the two brief pages he devotes to Alexander's career, in which he also mentions the visit to Candace. Though there is no historical basis whatever for this piece of information (Alexander never went near Byzantium), it stuck, and reappears in the fourteenth-century verse rewriting of the beta version of the *Romance* (ll. 1179ff.). The Strategion is no more, and we are not even quite sure what it was; but it is the first of many buildings in Greek lands that were to be attached to Alexander's name in the centuries that followed. These include the Pharos at Alexandria (see Chapter 3), the Wall at Derbend (see Chapter 9) and the Temple at Sounion; Alexander also gave the city of Kavalla its name and cut the Bosphorus and the Euripus through solid land.[3]

Alexander's name had magic properties, as it did in the west: John Chrysostom[4] refers to the wearing of bronze coins with his image as talismans around the neck and ankles, of the same kind as the medallions known from the western empire (see beginning of Chapter 11). According to Procopius,[5] Alexander was even worshipped, along with Ammon, at a shrine called Augila in Egypt's western desert; but the Emperor Justinian replaced the building with a church of the Mother of God. While Alexander could not be allowed to displace the Christian saints, his image retained talismanic power.[6] The Senecan hostility known from the Latin tradition is completely absent from the Greek.[7] As K. Mitsakis put it (1967, 18), Alexander 'died an antique pagan and was born again as a Byzantine Christian'.

In the seventh century the main appearance of Alexander in Greek literature is in the apocalyptic writings of Pseudo-Methodius that we looked at in Chapter 9, and in related texts. In the *Apocalypse* of Pseudo-Daniel[8] he makes a lightly disguised appearance as 'the Great Philip', who 'will rise up and gather his troops in the Seven-Hilled City [i.e. Constantinople] and make war such as there has never been, and rivers of blood will run in the streets of the Seven-Hilled City . . . . Four angels will bear him to Agia Sophia and crown him king . . . and he, accepting the orb from the angels, will trample the Ishmaelites, Ethiopians, Franks, Tartars and every nation . . . . Then his four sons will rule, one in Rome, one in Alexandria, one in the Seven-Hilled City and the fourth in Thessalonike.' In this text as in Pseudo-Methodius, Alexander's triumph announces the beginning of the End Time, and his reign is localised in Constantinople. A similar prophecy, which does not name Alexander, is contained in the text of the *Apocalypse of Daniel* included in Charlesworth's collection.[9] It belongs to the context of the iconoclast controversy of the late eighth century, and the restoration of the icons is seen as tantamount to the end of the world.

Soon after this Alexander begins to reappear in the historical record, and the influence of the *Romance* is evident in the choice of material. The earliest example is the *Chronicon Paschale*, completed soon after AD 628, which mentions Nectanebo's flight to Pella in disguise, Alexander's visit to Jerusalem and foundation of Alexandria, and his poisoning in Babylon. (It also mentions that he built the Strategion).[10] In the eighth century George Syncellus gives a long account of the visit to Jerusalem but is clearly using, in addition, a historical source on the military campaigns.[11] The more extensive account in the *Chronicle* of George the Sinner (George the Monk), of the ninth century, concentrates on the visit to Jerusalem, which reads like a fashion report on priestly clothing, and the Brahmans episode.[12] In the eleventh century George Cedrenus derives material from Syncellus but also adds the Nectanebo story and the Brahmans episode. The twelfth century sees a change in approach as the historian Zonaras, in his history of the world from the creation to AD 1118, offers an account that looks much more like real history, using Plutarch for example, as well as retailing the familiar story of the foundation of Alexandria and of the transference there of the bones of Jeremiah.[13]

From these scraps it is difficult to derive a coherent picture, except for the assurance that the story of Alexander, and a form or forms of the *Romance*, were continuously available before the resurgence of learning and literature in the twelfth century, the century of the Comnenoi.[14] Another scrap of evidence is the contents of the library of a Cappadocian landowner named Eustathios Boilas (d. *c.* 1059).[15] Among his eighty volumes, which included religious and liturgical texts and even two copies of the *Ladder* of John Climacos, were Achilles Tatius' romance, *Clitophon and Leucippe*, and also the *Alexander Romance*. One wonders if his MS was better than the almost contemporary MS we have, Parisinus gr. 1711 (datable 1013–1124), which is the sole witness for the alpha tradition.[16]

The *Alexander Romance* lived on in the artistic tradition too, as is shown by the appearance of several motifs in Byzantine art. Nectanebo divining with his bowl appears on an ivory diptych of the tenth century alongside a scene which is probably the reconciliation of Philip and Olympias (*AR* I. 22), while the taming of Bucephalus, as well as the dog-headed men, appear on manuscripts of the eleventh century.[17] The flight is depicted on an eleven-century coffer, now in the cathedral at Sens,[18] and on a twelfth-century relief at the Peribleptos church in Mistra.

Another sign of the currency of the *Romance* in the middle Byzantine period is the emergence of several motifs from it in the heroic poem, *Digenis Akritas* ('the twice-born border lord'), which dates from the thirteenth century but was certainly in process of formation from the tenth century onwards: it reflects the conditions when the marches of the Byzantine Empire on the Euphrates were tensely disputed between Byzantium and its Saracen neighbours. Elements of the Alexander story

39 A twelfth-century relief of the ascent of Alexander. Mistra, Church of the Peribleptos. Mus. Inv. N. 10813.

that have influenced Digenis include his supernatural birth, his precocity and early deeds, his taming of beasts and his fights with wild beasts, including a dragon.[19] A song from the extensive *Cycle of Digenis* (early modern if not older) even has him fighting a giant crab like Alexander.[20] Furthermore, Digenis has an encounter with an Amazon named Maximo. Maximo, according to *Digenis* (6. 386–7) 'was descended from some Amazons taken by Alexander from the Brahmans'. Digenis' palace on the Euphrates is decorated with reliefs depicting the adventures of Alexander with Candace, the Brahmans and the Amazons.[21]

The twelfth century, as in the west, is the age in which the *Alexander Romance* begins to extend its influence. The Comnenian dynasty oversaw an explosion of literary activity, not least Princess Anna Comnena's own *Alexiad* and the scholarly activity of John Tzetzes, as well as the popular poetry of Theodore Prodromos, who is the first writer to refer to the songs about the Akritai. A two-way traffic between east and west, such as a

Byzantine embassy to Henry II in 1170 regarding the marriage of a Byzantine princess to Prince John, and the settlement of Latin Franks in Constantinople,[22] led to a burst of romance composition as well as to the translation of western romances into Greek. Besides the four novels,[23] there were texts on classical topics such as the Trojan War, the *Achilleis* (notably influenced by western romance) and the *History of Belisarius*.[24] The French *Flore et Blancheflore* took on new life as *Florios kai Platziaflora*. In this ferment the *Alexander Romance* undoubtedly also took its place.[25]

Besides alpha, the beta text was also well known by this date, forming the basis of the Bulgarian translation of the tenth/eleventh century.[26] The rewriting of the *Romance* known as epsilon probably dates from the eighth century, and the gamma version which combines this with the earlier recensions is probably not much later. In epsilon the treatment of Alexander is more heroic and he becomes more like a Byzantine emperor: he receives acclamations like an emperor at the Olympic Games, for example, and takes on features of the 'ideal king'. The growing popularity of the image of Alexander's flight is probably due to perception of him as *kosmokrator*, 'ruler of the world'.[27]

The later Byzantine centuries saw the composition of several new Alexander texts, the first being the *Byzantine Poem* of 1388, in *politikos stichos* (the metre of Greek folk poetry).[28] Its narrative is based on beta but with some additional material from alpha, and the presentation of the hero again assimilates him to the imperial style. A later verse account, also in *politikos stichos*, and also based on beta, is known as the *Rimada*.[29] It was published in Venice in 1529 and went through fourteen editions, which are illustrated with a number of woodcuts.[30]

However, it was epsilon that provided the basis for all the prose rewritings of the Alexander story. There are several variant versions of the late Byzantine *Prose Romance*, which dates from about 1450–53.[31] These in turn provided the model for the immensely popular folk-book known as the *Phyllada tou Megalexandrou*, first published in 1680. There have been forty-three subsequent editions, and several are in print at the present time.[32]

The *Phyllada tou Megalexandrou*

The *Phyllada* may be the most compelling of all the retellings of the Alexander legend. It is a work of much higher quality than its ancient predecessors. Following epsilon in rearranging the material in a more logical way, it also adds a great deal that is new and constructs a well-ordered, well-motivated narrative. The episodes familiar from the *Romance* are all present: Alexander's birth by Nectanebo and his childhood; his wars with Darius and Porus; his visits to Jerusalem and the Land of the Blessed (standing in for the Brahmans); the Amazons, the Unclean Nations and Candace; his death in Babylon. The diving bell is present, though not, surprisingly, the flight. But the atmosphere of the narrative is changed considerably. The terminology is firmly of the Middle Ages: the soldiers wear plate armour and chain mail, Alexander's ministers are called *voyvodes* and the king is indignant that Darius describes him as a 'klepht'.

Alexander is a Byzantine Christian Greek and has nothing but bad words for the old pagan gods: when he conquers Athens (a long episode), he laughs at the Athenians' flight to the Temple of Apollo: 'if the Greek gods were real gods, perhaps they would help you'. An awareness of the Old Testament means that Darius is described as preparing his final battle at the Tower of Babel (i.e. Babylon). The visit to Jerusalem is correspondingly important, though it is surprising to find that his reception by the Jews, a gift of the Robe of Solomon and the interpretation of the Book of Daniel all take place on his earlier visit to Rome. When he really comes to Judaea (which is under the rule of the Persian king Darius, as if he were Cyrus), he writes to the leaders of the Jews offering, with the help of the God of Sabaoth, to free them from the idolaters. They reply that in fact they worship Sabaoth already! But Jeremiah assures his fellow-countrymen that Alexander will be their liberator. (Jeremiah later plays an important role by appearing to Alexander in dreams at crucial moments of decision.)

The Jews are among the first to welcome Alexander as 'King of the World' (*kosmokrator, kosmou basileus*), a motif which becomes more insistent as the book proceeds. When he enters Babylon, he is given the crown of Sosonchos (i.e. Sesonchosis: the text offers various spellings), the erstwhile ruler of the world. When he reaches the country of the Wild Men, he finds a pillar set up by Sosonchos, with the doleful warning: 'The Wild Men killed me and all my army. Go no further.' Alexander quickly hides the inscription and assures his men that it describes a beautiful country that lies ahead. Thus he persuades the army to carry on, and reaches the Land of the Blessed, which even Sesonchosis had failed to do.

This visit to the Blessed is the longest and perhaps the climactic episode of the book. These characters, who replace the Brahmans of the *Romance*, are naked and live on an island; but they are descendants of the Old Testament patriarch Seth, and they have acquired many of the characteristics of the Blessed in the *Narrative of Zosimus* (Chapter 5). The Blessed are curious to know why Alexander has come 'from the sinful world', and tell him that Eden lies beyond but that he cannot visit it. He tries of course, but is sent back from the Land of Darkness by human-headed birds who tell him that his job is to go back and conquer Porus.

Having done so (it takes a long time), he visits the Amazons, encloses the Unclean Nations and then proceeds to Candace's court, where her son shows him the Cave of the Gods (see colour plate 19 and pp. 135–6). This episode has been quite transformed since antiquity. The first major change comes in the epsilon recension (eighth century), and thereafter both in the lost medieval Greek version (*zeta), which is reconstructed by Moennig from the Old Serbian version,[33] and in the Middle Greek prose *Tale of Alexander*.[34] In these texts the visit to the Dwelling of the Gods takes places at the point where Candaules points out the cave, on the way to Candace's palace. The latter two are explicitly Christian texts, and in *zeta Alexander sings a hymn to the God of Sabaoth before encountering a number of rulers who thought themselves gods and have been imprisoned for that reason; after seven thousand years have passed, they will go to hell. These rulers include Sesonchosis, Porus and Darius. The tenor of the story is thus quite different from that in the Pseudo-Callisthenes and in epsilon, where Alexander consults Sesonchosis about his future and the day of his death (without, however, getting a satisfactory answer). In the *Phyllada* this *katabasis* episode is expanded still further: Alexander sees in the cave the ancient Greek gods – Herakles, Apollo, Kronos and Hermes – and others, bound in chains. One of the prisoners addresses him: 'King Alexander, those whom you see were kings like you, rulers of all the world, but because of their overweening pride and their arrogance which made them equal to God, he was angry at them and sent them to this cave to be punished together, so that he can throw them into Tartarus and punish them forever.' The speaker then reveals himself as Sosonchos, the former King of the World: 'after my uprising, I set off for the edge of the world, but when I wished to go to Paradise, the Wild Men came upon me and killed me and all my army, and the demons carried me off here in chains to be punished for my ignorance. Mark my words, Alexander, do not be puffed up, or they will imprison you too.'[35]

This stirring admonition means that there is no need for the episode of the Oracular Trees. Alexander returns to Babylon and rules for many years as a great king, 'brave, handsome, wise, merciful, just and gentle', forwarding the 'four virtues' of happiness, truth, fidelity and justice. His contentment is only marred by a dream of Jeremiah, who tells him that his days are numbered; but his courtiers console him: 'why should you be gloomy, when you are ruler of the whole world?'

The end comes when the devil prompt two evil men to poison the king. When he realises he is dying, Alexander calls on Earth, Sun and Mountains to mourn him; he makes his will, which includes not only the disposition of his empire but the admonition to his people to be just and to help the poor. When he dies, Roxane commits suicide, and the pair are buried in two gold coffins in Alexandria. The book concludes with a moral: Life is like a flower that fades. 'Death makes no distinction of king and subject, of rich and poor, of young and old, but takes them all alike and spares none . . . . So there is only one thing we need to know, to accoutre ourselves with good and Christian works, with fear of God, with mercy and kindness to our brothers . . . as Solomon said, "vanity of vanities, all is vanity".'

Thus the ancient pagan dies a Byzantine Christian, a man reconciled to his lot, whereas the Alexander of the *Romance* was forever fighting his destiny. As his reward, he has lived a life of peace, 'keeping the world at peace'; he has avoided the fate of Sesonchosis imprisoned in his cave of punishment, and he has some hope of the Paradise to which the Blessed themselves will return after 5,500 years. An Alexander like this is, like Christ, never truly dead, and here is the basis for his role in Greek folklore as the king of the storms, who 'lives and reigns and keeps the world at peace'.

Modern Folklore

Some of Alexander's appearances in folklore were mentioned in Chapter 7, and there are many others. He is a character in the Karagiozis shadow play, where his chief exploit is the killing of a terrible dragon (colour plate 20). He features in spells for everything, from love magic to driving away mice.[36] In one locality the hoofprints of Bucephalus are pointed out; at Philippi a stone is used by women to concoct a potion which will make them bear children as strong as Alexander.[37] Local foundation legends, as at Assiros, relate the village's history to the reign of Alexander.[38] The story of the Water of Life appears in many variants and regions as a folk-tale, as does the story of the march through the Land of Darkness (often redescribed as the Underworld), collecting stones. The story of the diving bell is in one version relocated to the crater of Santorini.[39] Stories of Alexander some-times combine with those of other heroes: in Epirus and Crete he becomes the hero of the story we know from Greek mythology about King Midas who had ass's ears; again in Crete, he is one of the suitors of Helen before the Trojan War.[40] In 1776, in his *Voyage littéraire de la Grèce*, Pierre Augustin Guys published a letter from Mme Chénier (the mother of the poet), in which she described a visit to a dance performed in Constantinople, the Arnaout.[41] The song to which the dance is performed begins

Που ιν ο Αλέξανδρος ο Μακεδονίς, που ορισεν τιν οικουμένην
ολην –

'Where is Alexander the Macedonian, who ruled the whole world?' Mme Chénier may have been indulging her imagination in supposing that the fifteen dancers each represented one of the companions of Alexander, and that the dance depicted the events of the Battle of the Granicus; but there can be no doubt that this was a rare example of a popular song telling of the ancient conqueror, in words that echo those of the mermaids.

Perhaps curiously, Alexander's vivacity as a folk hero has not led to his appearance like, say, Faust, in works of high literature. One exception, G.P. Gikas' 'legendary biography of Alexander' (1973), does not achieve the lustre of Marlowe or Goethe. In Nikos Kazantzakis' book about Alexander, he becomes another instance of the Greek 'Superman', like Zorba. Theo Angelopoulos' film *Alexander the Great* (1980) concerns a bandit chief who set himself up as a leader of a local utopian community under the name of the hero. Welcomed as a dragon-slayer, like the wind, like the sun, he fails to live up to his promise and is eventually murdered: the pattern seems a reprise of Kipling's story, *The Man Who Would Be King*, conveying the lesson that modern people cannot carry off the role of Superman.

40 A series of Greek stamps in the 1980s portrayed the legendary adventures of Alexander. This one depicts the British Library illustration of the diving bell.

But if he is no longer a figure of literature, he is certainly a name to conjure with in politics. The liberators of the War of Independence invoked him as their watchword,[42] and in the 1870s a book called *The Prophecies of Alexander* was circulating in Greek schools in Macedonia, in which the hero foretold that Macedonia would eventually be liberated from the Ottoman Empire by the Greeks.[43] In 1913 Bulgaria claimed him for its own,[44] and at the present time tension persists over the name of the Former Yugoslav Republic of Macedonia, which is deemed in Greece to represent a territorial claim to its own province of Macedonia. Some Macedonians (citizens of FYROM) claim that they are not Slavs at all, but direct descendants of Alexander.[45] Adoption by FYROM of the Macedonian sun-burst symbol for its national flag provoked outrage in Greece.[46] T-shirts proclaim 'Alexander the Great: 2000 Years Greek'; and the Minister for Northern Greece, Stelios Papathemelis, declared in 1992 that Macedonia is 'an inalienable and eternal possession of Hellenism, a piece of its soul'.[47] Such declarations might have surprised Alexander, who probably supposed that Greece was in fact one of *his* possessions. So the king of Macedon who became the tyrannical master of his Hellenic neighbours and carried their culture to the ends of the earth is celebrated as really a Greek. It is *paideia* ('culture') that makes a Greek, and Alexander's legacy to the world, despite the brutality of his historical career, is *paideia*. If only it were true that, as the Aegean mermaids sing, 'Alexander the Great lives and rules and keeps the world at peace'![48]

EPILOGUE

In the middle of my life . . . I drew the path of it upon a map and I studied it a long time. I tried to see the pattern that it made upon the earth because I thought that if I could see that pattern and identify the form of it then I would know better how to continue. I would know what my path must be. I would see into the future of my life.

. . . – How did you know it was the middle of your life?

– I had a dream. That was why I drew the map . . . .

These dreams reveal the world also, he said. We wake remembering the events of which they are composed while often the narrative is fugitive and difficult to recall. Yet it is the narrative that is the life of the dream while the events themselves are often interchangeable. The events of the waking world on the other hand are forced upon us and the narrative is the unguessed axis along which they must be strung. It falls to us to weigh and sort and order these events. Each man is the bard of his own existence.

Cormac McCarthy, *Cities of the Plain* (1998), 268–9, 283

The Alexander of legend has revealed himself in many guises in this book: as son of a god with immortal longings, as a redoubtable explorer who goes beyond the bounds of the world to defend that world against the terrors that lie outside, as a resourceful inventor who is never at a loss in any situation, even as a philosopher who can doubt the value of his career as a conqueror in the face of inevitable death – like T.E. Lawrence, he is a 'world changer who never lost the capacity to doubt'.[1] He enters the Middle Ages as a monster-fighter and moralist as well as a harbinger of the end of time, and becomes a journeyer to Paradise, a knight of God and an Everyman who sometimes comes close to being identified with Christ. But, like Everyman, he has to face death. When he enters the modern Greek tradition, he is a universal king who keeps the world at peace, a model for Byzantine emperors and a nationalist hero immersed in modern Balkan politics, as well as a force of Nature whose footprints (and whose horse's hoofprints) are imprinted on the rocks and shores of the Aegean. Even when he entered Muslim tradition through the Qur'ān, he began as a defender of the cosmos against Chaos and became a warrior and prophet of God as well as a Mirror for Princes.[2] The Persian Alexander, too, is an ideal king, a *javanmard* or youthful hero, a sage and a *memento mori*.

Such a cosmic destiny is far from anything that we can recover of the Alexander of history. The latter has been characterised as everything from a brutal conqueror whose only skill was killing[3] to a visionary who aspired to unite the whole world in brotherhood; a proud tyrant with a remarkable capacity for generosity to a drunken slob;[4] but, however heroic (or not) the Alexander of history may have been, there is little in his history to prepare one for the extraordinary development of his legend. How can it have come about?

Klaus Mann, in his novel *Alexander: Roman der Utopie* (*Alexander: A Novel of Utopia*, 1929) made a pregnant contribution to our understanding of the legend by taking the events of the *Alexander Romance* and treating them as a dream that Alexander dreams. It is a story of failure, as Alexander recognises when he makes his 'confession' in the final pages of the novel. His last ambition was to stand at the gates of Paradise, to go where no explorer had ever been before: 'What have we achieved, if we have *not* established the kingdom of happiness and of eventual blessedness on earth?' (p. 176). Yet as he lies on his deathbed (poisoned by Roxane, as it happens) an angel, not mincing his words, tells him 'You have failed in your mission.' The dreams remained only dreams.

Many of the events of the *Alexander Romance* are deeds which the historical Alexander could only long to do, deeds to which his *pothos,* his quasi-religious 'longing', impelled him: the exploration of the Nile, the march to the outer Ocean, the meeting with the Amazons. Even the conquest of the west, that featured in his Last Plans, makes a brief appearance in Book I of the *Romance*. So, like Cormac McCarthy's nameless traveller in *Cities of the Plain,* the Alexander of legend starts to create the narrative and the events of his own life through his dreams. Each successive rewriting of his legend adds more tales, more depth and resonance to his deeds and encounters. Not all the tales of the legend are dreams that Alexander dreamed, but all of them are dreams that most human beings can understand, have dreamed, or can sympathise with. To meditate on one's path through life, or to long for an increased span of life, are universal imperatives. The *Alexander Romance*, and the legends that it became, is a dream of the life of man.

In this respect his story bears comparison with the other great emblems of the human condition. Faust also learns to fly and to achieve his greatest desires. If he loses his soul he gains the immortality of legend. Such great tales are almost always about a quest of some kind. In the series of lectures organised by the British Library in 1996, 'The Mythical Quest', the five exemplars were Gilgamesh, the search for the Holy Grail, Jason and the Golden Fleece, Sindbad the Sailor – and Alexander. (All these characters and motifs have made their appearances in this book too.) A poem by James Elroy Flecker, 'The Ballad of Iskender', adapts the Greek and oriental legends of Alexander into a tale that turns him into a kind of Flying Dutchman. The 'King of Everywhere and Everything' sends out a ship to 'inquire for men unknown to man'. Carrying on board the two Greek sages of Arabic tradition, Aflatun and Aristu (Plato and Aristotle), the ship sails 'for seven years and seven years' to 'that Lone Sea Whose shores are near Eternity'. In the end their black, bedraggled ship meets a silver, phantom ship:

Theirs is the land (as well I know)
Where live the Shapes of Things Below
Theirs is the country where they keep
The Images men see in Sleep.

On sight of the vision the black ship crumbles into air.

Flecker saw in this story of Alexander's mission the same lesson of the impossibility of human longing as is expressed in the *Romance*. Not only is Alexander not permitted immortality, he is not vouchsafed the day of his death, except that it will come – as he always fears – too soon. So for all his absorption into Christian (and Muslim) tradition, it is no surprise that Alexander, even though he reached the Paradise of Christian tradition and talked with angels on the Muslim Mount Qaf, saw immortality slip from his grasp. He is not Christ, nor was meant to be; nor could he even achieve the immortality of the prophet Khidr, who balked him at the Well of Life. In death he can take nothing with him. If the medieval Christian saw Christ as a paradigm but himself could be no more than Everyman, the same is true of the Alexander of both pagan and Christian tradition. He embodies the aspirations, he is a metaphor for the dreams, of Everyman; and, like every man, he must die. What was it all for?

That is the question the Alexander legend proposes in its many forms, and therein, perhaps, lies the secret of its still potent appeal.

APPENDIX I

THE FORMATIVE ALEXANDER ROMANCES, THEIR MAIN DERIVATIVES, AND THE MAIN ILLUSTRATED VERSIONS

This appendix tabulates most of the texts referred to in the body of the book and should serve as a quick reference on their dates and main features if the reader finds it difficult to maintain the distinctions of these many works in his/her head. It does not pretend to completeness and the reader is referred to the works of Cary 1956 and Ross 1963b for more comprehensive surveys of the western manuscripts, and to those of Veloudis 1977/1989, Mitsakis 1970 and Moennig 1987 for the medieval Greek ones. There is no comprehensive treatment of the eastern works or manuscripts so I have tried to point to works that will take the reader further: this is the easier as they are less numerous than the medieval western ones.

Greek

A

The only MS of the oldest recension, alpha, is in the Bibliothèque Nationale in Paris (Parisinus gr. 1711). It dates from between 1013 and 1124 and forms the last portion (from fol. 395) of a very large codex containing several other historical works. The scribe seems to have been tiring by the time he reached the *Alexander Romance*: the writing is slovenly and he was obviously working from a poor exemplar from which he at times copied meaningless strings of letters. All subsequent copyists of the Greek *Romance*, as well as Julius Valerius in Latin, seem to have been working from this text, or something like it, and many of their alterations can only be seen as attempts to restore sense to something that made no sense in A. This MS contains at III. 7–16 the whole of Palladius *On the Brahmans,* which is not part of the *Romance* and does not appear in recensions beta and lambda. It also contains the fullest version of the description of Nectanebo's astrological calculator, one of the most corrupt passages in any ancient author. All subsequent scribes and translators gave up on this passage and omitted most of it.

Editions: Kroll 1926; Stoneman 2007 (Book I; II and III forthcoming).
Translations: Haight 1955 (Engish), Pfister 1978 (German), Tallet-Bonvalot 1994 (French), Franco 2001 (Italian).

The beta recension

The author of beta wrote some time after the Latin translation of A was made by Julius Valerius (by 340), but before the composition of the Armenian version, some time around

AD 500. Beta wrestles with the text of A and frequently rewrites and rephrases its model to make better (or any) sense of it, but it also includes new material. The end of Book I and the first six chapters of Book II (the debate in Athens) are missing from beta.

The four main MSS are Parisinus gr. 1685 (B), a finely written MS completed in Otranto in 1468; Vaticanus 1556 (V: fifteenth–sixteenth century); Laurentianus 70.37 (F: a palimpsest of the thirteenth century); and Mosquensis 436 (298) (K, fourteenth–fifteenth century). The earliest MS is Parisinus suppl. 690 (S: eleventh century), which contains only III.30–35. Some MSS contain additional material, for example K, which has part of the epsilon recension also.

Edition: Bergson 1965, with full details of all the MSS.

The lambda recension

A variant of beta preserved in five MSS: Bodl. Barocc 23 (O, fourteenth century, incomplete), Vaticanus 171 (W, sixteenth century), Bodl. Holkham Gr. 99 (H, fifteenth century), Ambrosianus O 117 sup (N, a faithful copy of H, sixteenth century) and Bodl. misc. 283 (P, 1516). The most substantial additions are in Book III.

Edition: van Thiel 1959.

L

This (Leiden Vulcanius 93, fifteenth century Sicily) is a unique variant of beta. This version of the story, written before the eighth century, expands the beta version with several new adventures, most notably the diving bell and the flying machine. It has therefore been a popular choice for translators.

Editions: van Thiel 1983. Translations: van Thiel 1983 (German), Dowden 1989 (English), Stoneman 1991 (English); Centanni 1991 (Italian), Bounoure and Serret 1992 (French).

The epsilon recension

(MS Bodl. Barocc. 17, thirteenth century: Q). The importance of this abridged rewriting of the story was only recognised by Jürgen Trumpf who edited it in 1974. Trumpf argued for a seventh-century date, but it uses material from the *Apocalypse* of Pseudo-Methodius which was written about 692, so the traditional date of eighth century remains likely. It does not follow the order of events and structure of the other recensions, but it was of importance for the development of the medieval Greek tradition and especially the *Phyllada*.

Edition: Trumpf 1974. Translation: none.

The gamma recension

This is the longest of the Greek recensions and tells the story in fuller form, with more additional material than the earlier ones, including the enclosure of the Unclean Nations in Book III (from Pseudo-Methodius or, more directly, from epsilon). It contains much that is clearly of Jewish origin, such as the visit to Jerusalem and the preaching of the one God in Alexandria, and some elements also seem to be Christianised. There is some absurd overwriting, not least the episode after Alexander's death where his horse, Bucephalus, enters the room where Alexander lies, identifies the murderer, and tears him to pieces: 'bits of him flew all over everyone like snow falling off a roof in the wind'.

There are three MSS: Parisinus suppl. 113 of 1567 (C); Bodl. Barocc. 20 (R: fourteenth century); and Venice, Hellenic Institute gr. 5 (D; fourteenth century), a beautifully illustrated MS whose pictorial tradition probably goes back to late antiquity

Editions: Lauenstein 1962 (Book I), Engelmann 1963 (Book II) and Parthe 1969 (Book III). Stoneman 2007 (Book I; II and III forthcoming).
Translation: none.
Facsimile edition: Trahoulias 1997. See also Xyngopoulos 1966.

Pseudo-Methodius, *Apocalypse*

The Greek translation was made from the Syriac soon after its completion *c.* 692: see under *Syriac*, p. 250 below.
Of the fifteen MSS, four are fundamental: Cod. Vat. Gr. 1700, Cod. Laud. Gr. 27, Pii II Gr. 11, Vindob. Med. 23: see Pseudo-Methodius, ed. Aerts and Kortekaas 1998, 38.

Editions: Aerts and Kortekaas 1998 (Greek and Latin recensions); Pseudo-Methodius, ed. Lolos 1976 (Greek).

Palladius, *On the Brahmans*

This originally independent treatise (see Chapter 5), which is a fifth-century Christian rewriting of a Cynic *diatribe* written before the second century AD (the date of the papyrus), was incorporated into the alpha and gamma versions of the *Romance* (III. 7–17) because of its similarity in theme to the episode of Alexander's interview with the Brahmans or naked philosophers.

Editions: Palladius, ed. Derrett 1960; Palladius, ed. Berghoff 1987; Stoneman (2007 and forthcoming).
Translation: Stoneman 1994a.

Armenian

A text related to A was translated into Armenian about the year 500, possibly by the great historian Movses of Khoren: the earliest MS is of the twelfth century. The translator worked from a much better text than A: the Armenian not only often makes clear what the original Greek actually said, but offers several additional episodes, including the correspondence with Zeuxis in Book I and the *Letter to Aristotle about India* in III.
Two of the MSS are beautifully illustrated and the iconography probably goes back to the late antique tradition: one is in the John Rylands Library (Armenian 3, fourteenth century), the other San Lazzaro, Venice cod. 424, thirteenth–fourteenth century.

Edition: (Armenian) by the Mekhitarists in Venice, 1842.
Greek retroversion (translation from Armenian into ancient Greek): Raabe 1896. English translation: Wolohojian 1969.

Syriac

The Greek *Alexander Romance* was translated into Syriac probably in the seventh century, the golden age of Syriac writing, centred around the churches of Syria (Brock 1983). The Greek source text was related to A but differs so considerably that it has generally been reckoned a witness for a lost Greek recension known as delta*. It includes the episode of Alexander's visit to the Emperor of China which became a standard feature of the Persian versions. Other episodes only in Syriac are Aristotle's advice to Alexander about the building of Alexandria; Nectanebo's and Olympias' discussion of Philip's disaffection from his wife (I. 14); the metaphor of the golden eggs (I. 23); and the jokes about the mustard seeds (I. 36 and 39). The commissioning of a painting of Alexander by the ambassadors from Darius is properly motivated only in Syriac, where it is shown to Darius' daughter. But there is a large lacuna at II. 6–14, presumably the result of a defective Greek original.

It used to be thought that this translation was made from a Pehlevi (Middle Persian) version, but Ciancaglini 1998 has disproved this and shows that it was made directly from the Greek.

Edition and translation: Budge 1889, based on British Museum Add. MS 25, 875 (AD 1708), with readings from four other MSS.

The 'Poem' attributed to Jacob of Serugh; the 'Christian Legend'; and the *Apocalypse* of Pseudo-Methodius

Budge 1889 collects a cluster of other Syriac works relating to Alexander: the 'Poem' attributed to the ecclesiastical writer Jacob of Serugh, the 'Christian Legend' and the *Apocalypse* of Pseudo-Methodius. The first two, both dating from the early seventh century, treat Alexander's enclosure of the Unclean Nations. (Edition of 'Poem': Reinink 1983a; German translation: Hunnius 1904). This episode was taken from them by the author of the *Apocalypse* (*c.* 692), which pretends to be the work of Methodius, Bishop of Patara in 311. The *Apocalypse* presents a history of the world from Adam and Eve to the present, based on the presupposition that the end of the world is imminent: Alexander's role in enclosing the Unclean Nations, who will be released on the coming of Antichrist, is a crucial part of this progression.

Pseudo-Methodius was translated into Greek within twenty years, and into Latin about the same time; the Latin version was then translated into most western languages by 1500, and there are 220 MSS of the European versions.

MS: Cod. Vat. Syr. 58; see further Pseudo-Methodius ed. Aerts and Kortekaas 1998, 37. Translations: Pseudo-Methodius ed. Reinink 1993 (German). The only modern English translation is Budge 1889; for the Middle English version see D'Evelyn 1918.

Persian

Firdausi

Firdausi (first half of tenth century–early eleventh century) incorporates portions of the narrative of the *Romance* into his *Shahnameh*, or Book of Kings. His source was certainly the Syriac version, presumably through earlier translations, to which he added material from the Persian oral tradition. See Chapter 2.

Firdausi's version formed the basis of the Mongol Alexander legends: see Cleaves 1959, Boyle 1965, Hillenbrand 1996.

Editions for those who can read Persian, there are many editions. See De Blois 2004, 100–38.
English translations (see under Firdausi): Warner and Warner 1905; Levy 1967 (abridged); Davis 2004 (portions); Davis 2007 (complete).

Most MSS of the *Shahnameh* are wonderfully illustrated and a regular cycle is devoted to Alexander. Many such paintings are reproduced in Davis 2004.

Examples: Chester Beatty Library, Dublin: Persian cat. 157 and 158; Pierpont Morgan Library, New York: M 540, M 847; New York Public Library: Turk. MS 1; Bodleian Library: Ouseley 344, Ouseley Add. 176, Elliott 325. See further Robinson 1980, Grabar and Blair 1980, Schmitz 1992.

Nizami (1140–1208?)

The *Iskandarnameh* (pre-1197) is a very long account of the life of Alexander, largely based on the *Romance* and including many more episodes than are in Firdausi. The first part is devoted to Alexander's adventures, the second to his wisdom and kingly achievements. See Chapter 2.

Editions: see De Blois 2004, 363–409.
Translations: Bacher 1871 (German); Wilberforce Clarke 1881 (English); Bürgel 1991 (German).
    As with Firdausi, most of the MSS are wonderfully illustrated. Examples: Chester Beatty Library, Dublin: Persian cat. I 124, 137, 141, 162, 171, 182, 195, 196, 276; Pierpont Morgan Library, New York: M 445, 470, 468, 469, 471; New York Public Library: Persian MS 47; Bodleian Library: Elliott 186, 192, 194, 339, 340; British Library : Oriental MS 12208, Add MS 25900; Berlin MS Diez A. A few of the illustrations are reproduced in Bürgel 1991. See also the works cited in the entry on Firdausi.

For the remaining Persian versions see the discussion in Chapter 2.

Arabic

The most problematic part of the Romance tradition. The story of Alexander as told in Pseudo-Methodius enters the Qur'ān, there are several Arabic MSS narrating portions of the Alexander story, and the existence of the Ethiopic version can only be explained by its being based on an Arabic original; in addition, several early Arabic *Romances* draw on the narrative of the Greek version but diverge widely from it. However, no complete Arabic translation has yet been found. Recent discoveries have opened up fresh hopes that a full Arabic translation may soon be identified. See the full discussion in Chapter 8; Doufikar-Aerts 2003a and 2003b; Zuwiyya 2001.
    The Arabic romances are those of Wahb ibn Munabbih (*c*. 680), 'Umara ibn Zaid (786–815) and 'Abd al-Rahman b. Ziyad, *Qissat Dhu'l-qarnain* (later than 'Umara). On Wahb, see Nagel 1978; on 'Umara, see Friedländer 1913; on *Qissat Dhu'l-qarnain*, Zuwiyya 2001. There is a brief account of the legendary life of Alexander by Mubaššir ibn Fatik, *Ahbar al-Iskandar* (pre-1053): see Mubaššir, ed. Meissner 1895.

La leyenda de Alejandro/ Historia de Dulcarnain

This is the name given to a text written in western Arabic, in Spain or perhaps Sicily, presumably in the twelfth century, and deriving from the same sources as the Ethiopic *Romance*, or perhaps from the contemporary *Historia de proeliis*, with the addition of the Qur'ānic story of the enclosure of Gog and Magog, some stories about the marvels of Alexandria (cf. Mas'udi), a conversation with an angel on Mount Qaf, Dulcarnain's letter to his mother and the sayings of the philosophers at the tomb. It was among the influences on the Hebrew version attributed to Ibn Tibbon.

Spanish translation and edition: Garcia Gomez 1929.

There are other Arabic versions, such as Berlin cod. Arab. 9118 (AD 813–33, fragmentary: see Weymann 1901). Ibn Suweidan 1666 derives from the Byzantine prose romance. As-Suri

1446 (see Doufikar-Aerts 2003b) was the source of the Malay version (van Leeuwen 1937, Schönegger 1989). Arabic versions also influenced the Mongol version (Cleaves 1959, Boyle 1965).

Needless to say, there are no illustrated Arabic versions.

Mas'udi and Qazvini both contain Alexander-related material and the Persian MSS of the latter are often illustrated. Examples: Chester Beatty Library, Dublin: Persian cat. 212; New York Public Library: Persian MS 45.

Ethiopic

The MS of the Ethiopic *Romance* dates from the fourteenth century AD but probably represents a much older tradition. Special features: see Chapter 8.

Translation: Budge 1896 with Ethiopic text, also in Budge 1933.

Hebrew

There are several stories about Alexander in the Talmud: Tamid 3b–32a – the Elders of the South, the Amazons, the Wonderstone; Avodah Zarah III.1. 42c – the Flight, which infiltrated both the western and the Islamic traditions. The first consecutive account of Alexander in Hebrew is that in Yosippon, a medieval rewriting of Josephus' history in Hebrew (*c.* AD 953). There are three recensions of Yosippon and the Alexander story was interpolated in it by about AD 1000 (Levi 1894) or later, from the Latin version of the *Historia de proeliis* (J^2). In the second and third two different accounts of the Alexander story are incorporated. In the second the interpolation consists of the story from the death of Philip onwards, based essentially on the Greek recension beta. This was translated into Arabic with the addition of the first part of the Alexander story, taken from the second recension of *HP*. Then, in the third recension of Yosippon, both interpolations are included, in the correct order. See van Bekkum 1992, 16 ff. There is a Latin translation by Breithaupt (Josephus Hebraicus, (1710) but no English translation. Edited by D. Flusser, Yosippon, (1978–80).

In addition there are four *Alexander Romances* in Hebrew, but all except possibly the oldest are based on the *Historia de Proeliis*.

i   *Alexandros ha-Mokdoni* (*c.* 1100–1300): Found in three MSS in Modena (MS LIII, Bibl. Estense), Oxford (Bodl. MS Cod. Heb. 2797.10) and Damascus (unpublished but studied by A.Y. Harkavy in 1892: see Kazis 1962, 27). Gaster believed it antedated the Yosippon text. Its content is very different from that and from the three *Romances* listed below. Olympias becomes Cleopatra, Nectanebo becomes the magician Bildad, and is not the father of Alexander. The flight and the diving bell (Talmudic episodes) are included. Translations: Gaster 1897; Reich 1972.

ii   *Ma'aseh Alexander* (mid-twelfth century): Found in a fourteenth-century MS in Parma (MS Heb. 1087): an amalgam of beta and alpha, with material from a Byzantine chronicle and the addition of the Palladius text. Edited by D. Flusser 1956; no English translation.

iii *Sefer Toledoth Alexandros* (1150–1230, attributed to Ibn Tibbon): Found in two MSS in Paris and London: Paris BN MS 671 is edited and translated by Levi 1887, and again by van Bekkum 1992, and London Jews' College MS 145, van Bekkum 1994. It is based on *HP* J^2 via an Arabic translation of the latter; it was obviously written in the west since it refers to Lombardy, and Armenia is reinterpreted as 'Alemania' (Germany).

iv   *Sefer Toledoth Alexandros ha-Mokdoni*, composed by Immanuel ben Jacob Bonfils (active AD 1349–56): he had left Spain as a result of the Almohad conquest of 1140 and moved to Orange. Paris, BN MS Cod. Heb. 750.3. This adds the *Sayings of the Philosophers*, known from Syriac and Arabic, after the death of Alexander. Edited and translated by Kazis 1962.

Latin

The alpha version of the *Romance* was translated into Latin by Julius Valerius Alexander Polemius, almost certainly to be identified with the Flavius Polemius who was consul in AD 338 and *comes* of the east in 345. The MSS entitle it 'Deeds of Alexander translated from Aesop the Greek'. This translation is into flowery and mannered post-classical Latin: it refers to the Aurelian Walls, built in 270, and describes Rome as the capital of the Empire, which it ceased to be in 330, so those dates provide the time frame in which it was written. It thus belongs to a time when Alexander was becoming a symbol for the late antique 'pagan revival', in opposition to the newly dominant Christian religion.

Edition: Rossellini 2004 (2nd edn).
Literature: Stoneman 1999a.

Itinerarium Alexandri

This is a broadly historical work based on Arrian's authoritative history, but it also makes use of Julius Valerius' *Res gestae*. It can be dated to 340–45 since it is addressed to Constantius on the eve of his departure for an eastern campaign. It survives in one MS in the Ambrosiana in Milan. It was in turn used by the author of one MS of the *Res gestae* (Parisinus 4880), so it is possible that both it and the variant version of the *Res gestae* are also by Julius Valerius, as argued by Romano 1974, and Lane Fox 1997.

Edition: *Itinerarium* ed. Tabacco 2000.

The Metz Epitome

In the fourth or fifth century a breviary of Alexander's career was made. This probably derived ultimately from Clitarchus, one of the earliest Alexander historians, and was combined with a separate work known as the *Liber de morte Alexandri testamentoque eius*, and preserved in a single MS in Metz, hence known as the Metz Epitome (MS Mettensis 500). This MS was destroyed by fire following a bombing raid on Metz in the Second World War, but fortunately two copies (apographs) had been made and published by the scholars Volkmann, in 1886, and Wagner, in 1891; a third, which was made by the French scholar Quicherat, was not published. It was discovered in the 1960s in the Bibliothèque Nationale. The Epitome contains some historical information not known from elsewhere, such as the death in infancy of a son born to Roxane in the Far East. The *Liber de morte* is a Latin version of a lost Greek original, which also provided the substance of Book III. 31–3 of the Greek *Romance*.

Edition: Thomas 1966 (2nd edn).
Literature: Cary 1956, 59 and 355–7; Ruggini 1961; Heckel 1988; Baynham 1995.

The Zacher Epitome of Julius Valerius

Made not later than the ninth century and known as the Zacher Epitome from its first editor. MS: Hagensis 830 (ninth century), and 65 others: Cary 1956, 25 n. 2. It is drastically abridged and seems to have been designed as a prologue for the *Letter to Aristotle*, with which it often appears. It provides the main source for Thomas of Kent and Vincent of Beauvais, and was translated into French in the fourteenth century. There were two other similar epitomes (Oxford–Montpellier and Liegnitz–Historia, both ed. Hilka 1911), but from the twelfth century onwards the popularity of these was eclipsed by the *Historia de proeliis*.

Edition: Zacher 1867. See Cary 1956, 24–6.

Leo the Archpriest

In the tenth century a cleric named Leo was sent by the Duke of Naples on a diplomatic mission to Constantinople. He brought back a MS of the Greek *Romance* (perhaps A) and made a new translation, being unaware of the earlier version by Julius Valerius. This work ended up in the cathedral library at Bamberg, founded by the Emperor Henry II in 1007 (Bambergensis E.111.4, *c.* 1000): presumably he brought it back from his campaigns in southern Italy, along with many others. This MS also contains the *Commonitorium Palladii*; Dindimus on the Brahmans; the *Collatio Alexandri cum Dindimo*; and the *Letter of Alexander to Aristotle about India*. There is a second, partial copy of Leo in Lambeth Palace Library, MS 342. This work, through its successive rewritings as the *Historia de Proeliis*, is the foundation stone of the whole medieval European tradition.

Editions: of Leo: Pfister 1913 (Bamberg MS); Ross 1959 (Lambeth MS).
Of the other works in the Bamberg MS: Pfister 1910.
Translation: Stoneman 1994a (of the minor works, not Leo). Kratz 1991 includes translation of Leo.

The *Historia de proeliis* (*HP*)

The oldest MS of this work is Bodleian Rawlinson B 149, which bears the title *Liber Alexandria Philippi Macedonum qui primus regnavit in Grecia et de proeliis eiusdem*, hence its usual designation as *Historia de proeliis* or *HP*. There are three recensions:

> HP J^1, before AD 1100. This is a combination of Leo's text with elements from Josephus, Jerome, Orosius, Solinus, Isidore, the *Letter of Pharasmanes*, the Indian treatises and the Letter to Aristotle.
> MSS: Graz, Universitätsbibliothek MS 1520 (twelfth century), Innsbruck Universitätsbibliothek 525 (AD 1304).
> Editio princeps Cologne *c.* 1471; two Dutch editions probably Utrecht *c.* 1475.
> Edition: Hilka and Steffens 1979. English translations: Pritchard 1992; Kratz 1991 (with portions of J^2 and J^3, the *Letter to Aristotle*, the Journey to Paradise and Leo).

> HP J^2. The 'Orosius recension', so called because of its heavy use of Orosius. It also borrows material from Valerius Maximus, Pseudo-Methodius, Josephus (the visit to Jerusalem), Pseudo-Epiphanius and the Indian works. It was the source of the Old French Prose Alexander (Hilka 1920) and of two Middle English poems.
> Edition: Hilka, Bergmeister and Grossmann 1976–77.
> German translation: Kirsch 1991, with miniatures taken from the Leipzig MS.

> HP J^3. Completed by 1236, when it became the basis of the Latin verse version by Quilichinus of Spoleto. It is a reworked version of J^1 and also includes the episode of the Sages at the Tomb of Alexander. There are very many MSS and it was printed at Strasburg in 1486, 1489 and 1494.
> Editions: Kirsch, in, the edition of Quilichinus, 1971; Steffens 1975.

Synoptic edition of all three recensions (Books I–II only); Bergmeister 1975.

The Letter to Aristotle about India

The Greek original of this is lost, though it is preserved in abridged or truncated form in all the Greek versions of the *Romance*. The first Latin translation belongs to the seventh century (or earlier); a second was made, into a Latin which is already becoming Italian, in the tenth century. It purports to be written by Alexander and to describe his adventures after the conquest of Porus. It is thus the source for most of the wonder stories so familiar in the tradition. In the later Greek recensions (epsilon and gamma) the contents are told in the third person as part of the continuous narrative of the *Romance*, which causes some dislocation of the chronological relations.

There are 67 MSS of the Latin text in European libraries, dating from the ninth to the fifteenth century, and a further five in the USA.

This was the first 'fabulous' Alexander text to be translated into a medieval western language: the translation into Old English forms part of the unique codex (British Library Cotton Vitellius A XV) which also contains *Beowulf* and *The Wonders of the East*. (The scribe, or patron, was interested in monsters.) See Sisam 1953, Tolkien 1983. The Irish *Romance* is not an exception to this generalisation as it is not based on the Romance tradition but on Quintus Curtius (Meyer 1949, Peters 1967).

Editions: Boer 1973; Feldbusch 1976.
Of the Middle English translation: DiMarco and Perelman 1978.
Translation: Gunderson 1980 (of the first Latin version). Stoneman 1994 (of the second); Stoneman also translates *The Wonders of the East* (*Letter of Pharasmanes*) and other works.

The Sayings of the Philosophers

The Latin work of this title, written in the thirteenth century, has a complicated prehistory. It goes back to the short Syriac work written in the seventh century, *The Sayings of the Philosophers at Alexander's Tomb* (Brock 1970), which consists of various sententious observations about the impact of the hero's death. This became the source of an Arabic work by Hunain ibn Ishaq (d. 873), *Kitab adab al-falasifa* (*The Book of the Sayings of the Philosophers*). This does not survive but is known from an Arabic reworking by Muhammad ibn 'Ali al-Ansari (before 1198). It was also translated into Hebrew by Jehuda al-Harizi (1170–1235) and into Spanish (*El Libro de los buenos proverbios*: see Knust 1879). It was also the chief source of Mubaššir ibn Fatik's *Mukhtar al-hikam*, translated into Spanish as *Los Bocados de oro* (1257): see again Knust 1897. (The Arabic text with a German translation can be found in Mubaššir, ed. Meissner 1895, 601f. and 618f.) In this form the sayings at the tomb are the culmination of a section devoted to Alexander which narrates his life in a version loosely related to the *Romance* and concludes it with a series of Alexander's own wise sayings, including his letter of consolation to his mother: the sayings at the tomb then follow. In Mubaššir the philosophers are Hermes Trismegistus, Aesculapius, Homer, Solon, Hippocrates, Pythagoras, Plato, Aristotle, Socrates, Diogenes, Ptolemy and Galen.

The sayings entered the *Disciplina clericalis* of Petrus Alfonsi, and thence the third recension of the *Historia de proeliis*. An English version (*The Dictes and Sayings of the Philosophers*, 1450) was made by Stephen Scrope, William Worcester and Earl Rivers, and was printed by William Caxton; there also survive 13 MSS of the translation from the third quarter of the fifteenth century.

Edition: Scrope, ed. Bühler 1941. See Metlitzki 1977, 115. There is also a French translation.

The Secret of Secrets (Secretum secretorum)

This work, which in its Latin form was enormously popular in the Middle Ages, started out as an Arabic text written about AD 800 by a Christian Arab, Yahya ibn Batriq, in the reign of the Caliph al-Ma'mun: he claimed to have translated it from 'Rumi', though if this means Greek he probably used a Syriac intermediary. (There is an edition by A.R. Badawi, 1954.) It takes the form of a letter of advice on statecraft addressed to Alexander from his tutor Aristotle. The requirements of the good ruler include not only the obvious political skills, but a knowledge of medicine and of physiognomy. The work belongs in that tradition which also includes Aristotle's *Book of Stones* (Ruska 1912) and *Aristotle on the World State* (Stern 1968). None of these has identifiable Greek forebears, though Grignaschi (1967) has boldly argued that the basis of the *Secret of Secrets* was one chapter of a very long epistolary romance which was made by Salim Abu al-'Ala' from a putative Greek original. Williams (2003, 19) is sceptical of any Greek source for Yahya's work.

Parts of the SS were translated into Latin by Johannes Hispalensis (1135–50), who only included the portions on health. There was also a twelfth-century Spanish translation. The first complete Latin translation was made in 1232 by Philip of Tripoli (who may have been the man Pope Alexander III proposed to send as an emissary to Prester John in 1177: Thorndike 1922–23, 270).

About the same time the Arabic was translated into Hebrew by Jehuda al-Harizi (1170–1235), who had also translated the *Sayings of the Philosophers* of Hunayn. An English translation of the Hebrew by Moses Gaster is in *JRAS* 1907.

The number of MSS of the Arabic (about 50, from AD 941 onwards – two different recensions) is dwarfed by that of the Latin *SS*, of which there are at least 500 MSS from the twelfth century onwards. It was translated into many languages. Manzalaoui 1977 is an edition of nine English versions. There is also a versified version by John Lydgate (d. 1449) and Benedict Burgh, *Secrees of Old Philisoffres* (Ed. Robert Steele 1894, EETS e.s. 66). The Dutch version, *Heimelijkheid der Heimelijkheiden,* is by Jacob van Maerlant (*c.* 1266), who was also the author of an Alexander book, *Alexanders Geesten* (a translation of Walter of Châtillon), as well as incorporating the Alexander story in his *Spiegel Historiael*, a translation of Vincent of Beauvais' *Speculum Historiale* (van Oostrom 1996). There is an Anglo-Norman version of *c.* 1275 and an Old French one of *c.* 1300. For a full survey of the European translations, see Williams 2003, and Ryan and Schmitt 1982. By the end of the thirteenth century its influence was waning as fuller sources became available on the topics it covered, and people gradually became aware that it was not a genuine work of Aristotle; but it was nevertheless printed by Robert Copland as late as 1528, and the last printed edition of the Latin was in 1555.

Latin text: *Secretum secretorum*, ed. Steele 1920. Latin and Middle High German: *Secretum secretorum*, ed. Möller 1963.
Literature: Williams 2003, Ryan and Schmitt 1982.

Alexander's Journey to Paradise

This twelfth-century Latin text is perhaps the work of a Jewish author, as it derives from the Talmudic story.
Text: Hilka 1935. English translation: Stoneman 1994a.

French

Alberic of Besançon

Written in the early twelfth century; only a fragment survives, of 105 lines on Alexander's early life and education, which is based on the seven liberal arts and courtly skills such as chess, hunting and flirting (*parler a dames cortoisement d'amors*). It was soon translated into German by Pfaffe Lamprecht, whose work survives in total, though in variant versions. It was based on *HP* J[1] with an admixture of Julius Valerius and Quintus Curtius. It is the first

French biography of a non-religious figure and formed one of the nuclei of the French *Roman d'Alexandre*.

Literature: Simons 1994.

Alexander of Paris, *Roman d'Alexandre*

In the years following 1180 Alexander of Paris brought together several different poems of the 1170s, that of Alberic, Eustache's *Fuerre de Gadres*, Lambert li Tort's *Alexander*, and probably another as well, and welded them together into a long romance of 16,000 verses, each of the three main source works constituting a separate 'branch' of the poem. See Chapter 11.

Edition: Harf-Lancner 1994. There is a facsimile edition of MS Bodl. 264 (Lambert li Tort) by M.R. James, 1933.

The French Prose Alexander

There are 16 MSS of this fifteenth–century prose version of the *Romance*, and there were also 11 printings between 1506 and 1630. One of the finest of all illustrated Alexander MSS is that made for Margaret of Anjou, British Library Royal 15 E VI: see Otaka, Fukui and Ferlampin-Acher 2003.

Perceforest

This vast *Romance*, composed between 1337 and 1344 at the instigation of William I of Hainaut, is a continuation of the adventures of Alexander as told in the *Roman d'Alexandre*. It tells how Alexander's fleet, as he sailed on beyond India, was blown severely off course by a storm and arrived on the shores of Britain. Alexander made himself ruler of the island and set up his lieutenants, Betis and Gadifer, as kings respectively of England and Scotland. They thus became the ancestors of the royal houses of these lands. The upshot of the story is to establish a link between the cycles of Alexander and of Arthur and the Grail.

Edition: *Perceforest*, ed. Taylor 1979.

Jehan Wauquelin, *Les Faicts et les conquestes d'Alexandre le Grand*

This prose version of the *Alexander Romance* was composed in Burgundy in the mid-fifteenth century and also incorporates the episode told in the separate romance *Les Voeux du paon* (*The Vows of the Peacock*).

Edition: Wauquelin, ed. Hériché 2000.

German

Pfaffe Lamprecht

The earliest German Alexander-poem, *c.* 1150: three widely varying MSS exist: Vorau-Alexander, Strassburger Alexander (written 1187, destroyed 1870) and Basel Alexander – part of a world chronicle. The book is a translation from the French of Alberic of Besançon, which formed one of the nuclei of the French *Roman d'Alexandre*.

Edition (Strassburger Alexander): Lamprecht, ed. Ruttmann 1974.

English translation J. W. Thomas 1989.
Literature: D. H. Green 1975.

Rudolf von Ems

Rudolf was writing between 1220 and 1250, and died in 1252 or 1253. He was a nobleman in the service of the Count of Montfort, and may have established the collection of MSS in the count's castle at Hohenems near Bregenz. He is the author of several works, including an unfinished *Weltchronik*. His *Alexander*, also unfinished, is a portrait of an ideal ruler. The story follows the pattern of *HP* J^3, with the visit to Jerusalem, marriage with Roxane, the enclosure of the Unclean Nations, and a meeting with the queen of the Amazons (here called Thalestris). But many other episodes of the *Romance* are omitted, including Candace, and the fabulous Indian adventures.

Edition: Rudolf, ed. Junk 1928, 1929.

Seifrit, *Alexander*

A translation of *HP* J^2 made in 1352.

Edition: Kühnhold 1939.

Johann Hartlieb, *Alexanderbuch*

Hartlieb (d. *c.* 1468–74) was the personal physician to succeeding Dukes of Bavaria. His several translations from Latin include the *Alexanderbuch*, which was written about 1444; there are 19 MSS from the 1460s in Germany, Vienna and the USA, of which three contain a substantial number of illustrations and one other has illuminated initials. There were also 18 printings from 1472 to 1670. Hartlieb's Alexander book is a translation of the Latin Alexander book, Parisinus 310 (second half of twelfth century: edition: Schnell 1989), which derived ultimately from Leo's work. Pfister argued that there was first a Bavarian recension of Leo on which this and the Munich MS, Clm 23489, were based. This Bavarian recension incorporated material also from the Epitome of Julius Valerius, Orosius, the Correspondence of Alexander and Dindimus and the *Letter to Aristotle*, Justin, Peter Comestor and the First Book of Maccabees. The aim was thus to make a rather complete compilation of Alexander texts. One result is that some episodes appear twice: the Brahmans appear both as 'gymnosophists' (1147ff.) and as 'Brahmans' (1349ff.).

Hartlieb's book was dedicated to Duke Albrecht III of Bavaria and its circulation is associated with the Mülich family of Augsburg, connected by marriage with the Fuggers and collectors of a number of historical works. It was used as material for a tragedy by Hans Sachs and was also translated into Danish in 1584.

The finest of the illustrated MSS are Bayrische Staatsbibliothek Cgm 581 (33 illustrations) and New York, Pierpont Morgan Library Ms 782 (230 illustrations).

Edition: Hartlieb, ed. Pawis, 1991.

Ulrich von Etzenbach

Ulrich was a Bohemian active at the court of Ottokar II (d. 1278). His *Alexander* is based on Walter of Châtillon's *Alexandreis* (which in turn belongs to the Curtian tradition, not the *Romance* tradition), and set out to glorify Ottokar, who, however, was killed long before the poem was completed in *c.* 1287.

Edition: von Etzenbach, ed. Toischer 1888.

Der Jüngere Titurel

This long poem of 6,000 stanzas, written about 1272 by Albrecht von Scharfenberg, is based on the fragments of Wolfram von Eschenbach's unfinished *Titurel*, which recounts the love between Schionatulander and Sigune. *Der Jüngere Titurel* follows their adventures and includes a retelling of the Grail and Parzival stories, and journeys and battles in the Orient. Notable is the search for the Earthly Paradise, which reprises a great deal of Alexander material.

Edition: Wolf, ed. von Scharfenberg 1955–92.

Spanish

Libro de Alexandre

This classic of Spanish literature, which stands alongside the *Poema de Mio Cid*, the *Libro de Buen Amor* and the *Libro de Apolonio*, was composed in the thirteenth century and consists of 2,675 four-line stanzas. Its central structure is based on the twelfth-century poem of Walter of Châtillon, which in turn derives from Quintus Curtius and not from the *Romance* tradition. For example, there is no trace of the Nectanebo story, or, of that of Candace, and almost the whole body of the poem is occupied with the historical events of the conquest of Persia. There are however various digressions on Greek history and mythology. The author also takes from the *Historia de proeliis* a few of the legendary adventures, including the famous episodes of the diving bell (2141) and the flying machine (2349) and the meeting with the headless men (2331). He was also familiar with one of the versions of the French *Roman d'Alexandre*.

Edition: *Libro*, ed. Murillo 1978. Translation into modern Spanish: *Libro*, trans. Catena 1985. Literature: Michael 1970, Marin 1991.

El Rrekontamiento del Rrey Ališandre

This is an *aljamia* text (Spanish written in Arabic characters), probably from the sixteenth century and not later than 1588. The author may have been 'one of the half-learned *alfaquis*' (Nykl 1929) who flourished among the Moriscos (converted, Spanish-speaking Muslims) who remained in Spain after the conquest of Granada in 1492. (A number of such texts survive and remain unpublished: Marin 1991, n.2.) Consisting of about 90 pages of printed Spanish, it is an eclectic text based on the *Romance* tradition, probably through the intermediary of Mubaššir and perhaps other Arabic versions, perhaps including the *Leyenda de Alejandro* (Garcia Gomez 1929: see above under Arabic versions).

Edition: Nykl 1929.

English

Thomas of Kent, *Roman de Toute Chevalerie*. This Anglo-Norman verse text was composed between 1170 and 1200 by an author who cannot be further identified. Its main sources are the Epitome of Julius Valerius and the *Letter to Aristotle about India*, with an admixture of Solinus and Aethicus Ister; it incorporates the *Fuerre de Gadres* of Eustache, which was also incorporated into the French *Roman d'Alexandre*.

Edition: Thomas of Kent, ed. Foster 1976.

Kynge Alisaundre

Written in rhymed octosyllabic couplets and dating from the fourteenth century, it survives in three MSS. It main source is Thomas of Kent. In the Lincoln's Inn MS (MS150, *c.* 1400) the narrative proceeds directly from the death of Darius to the episode of Gog and Magog, omitting all the other fabulous adventures; in the other MSS much of the *Letter to Aristotle* is incorporated in addition.

Edition: *Kynge Alisaundre*, ed. Smithers 1952/1957.

The Alliterative Romance of Alexander

This consists of two fragments, 'Alexander A' (Oxford, Bodleian MS Greaves 60) and 'Alexander B' or *Alexander and Dindimus* (preserved in MS Bodley 264, which also contains the French *Roman d'Alexandre* and is sumptuously illustrated). Both fragments probably belong to the alliterative revival of the fourteenth century, but they differ in style and may be by separate hands and not part of the same work at all. The first contains the beginning of the story as in *HP*, with the Nectanebo story, and breaks off with Philip's siege of Byzantium; the second recounts the episode of the gymnosophists based on *HP* J², plus the five letters of the *Collatio*.

Edition: Skeat 1867 (of *Alexander and Dindimus*: Skeat 1878); Magoun 1929.

The Wars of Alexander

Early fifteenth century, in alliterative verse; its main source is *HP* J³.

Edition: *Wars of Alexander*, ed. Duggan and Turville-Petre 1989.

The Scots Buik of Alexander

A translation in octosyllabic couplets of the *Fuerre de Gadres* and *Les Voeux du Paon,* dated 1438 in its epilogue and printed by Alexander Arbuthnet in about 1580: a single copy survives. It has sometimes been attributed to John Barbour, author of *The Bruce.*

Edition: *Buik of Alexander*, ed. Ritchie 1921.

Sir Gilbert Hay, Buik of Alexander

This poem in pentameters was completed in 1499 and presents itself as a translation from the French: its main sources, besides the *Roman d'Alexandre*, are the *HP* J² and the *Secretum secretorum*, which Hay had also translated from French in 1456. It contains some unusual material such as Alexander's meetings with Diogenes and with a pirate, his infatuation with Campaspe, and – uniquely in English literature – the story of Alexander's journey to Paradise.

Edition: Hay, ed. Cartwright 1990.
An extract in modern English (the journey to Paradise) is in Stoneman 1994a.

The Thornton Prose Life of Alexander

Preserved in two MSS (Lincoln Cathedral Library MS 91 and BM Add. MS 31042) from the collection compiled *c.* 1440 by a Yorkshire gentleman, Robert Thornton. The Lincoln

MS also contains the unique copy of the alliterative *Morte Arthure*. It is a fairly close translation of the *HP* J³, but the treatment of Gog and Magog is much more extensive, based on Peter Comestor.

Edition: Westlake 1913.
Literature: Bunt 1994, chs 2–3, is a brief survey of all the early English Alexander texts.

Other Western European Languages

See Cary 1956. Some particular treatments are – Italian: Storost 1935. Romanian: Marinescu-Himou in Laourdas and Makaronas 1970. Czech: Kreft 1981. Swedish: Ronge 1957. Bulgarian: Köhler 1983. Serbian: Christians 1991.

Medieval and Early Modern Greek

The Byzantine Poem: A single MS, Marcianus 408, dated 1388. The poem, in the *politikos stichos*, is based on the beta tradition but includes some material deriving from alpha.

Editions: Wagner 1881; Reichmann 1963.
Literature: Gleixner 1961.

The Late Byzantine Prose Romance

This prose romance was probably first composed in about 1430–53. Its basis is epsilon: Gleixner 1961, 67 ff. There are 11 MSS dating from the sixteenth and seventeenth centuries: they are described and discussed by Moennig 1987. There are considerable variations between them. Three versions of the work have been edited separately under the following titles:

1. 'Middle Greek Prose Romance'. A reference to the fall of Constantinople shows that this cannot have been completed earlier than 1453. The edition by Lolos 1983 (Part I) and Konstantinopoulos 1983 (Part II) is based on two complete MSS (Florence, Laurentius Ashburnham 1444 and Eton College cod. 163) and two partial MSS.
2. 'Alexander Romance in Codex Vindobon. Theol. Gr. 244'. The edition by Mitsakis 1967 is based on a single MS, which is not especially representative. See the review by Trumpf 1967 and discussion in Moennig 1987. There is a paraphrase in Gleixner 1961, 71–85.
3. 'Tale (Diegesis) of Alexander and his great wars'. The edition of Mitsakis in Mitsakis 1970 is based on the MS Athous 3309 (Kutlumussiu 236).

Rimada

This is a verse account of Alexander's story in rhyming couplets of *politikos stichos*. It was published in Venice in 1529 – there were 14 editions – and there is a single MS, Meteora Codex 445 (Metamorphosis). The printed editions are illustrated with a small but variable number of woodcuts. The last printing was in 1805. The epilogue to the poem states that it was published 'by the efforts of Demetrios Zenos' of Zakynthos; however, this is not the name of the author, but probably that of the man who prepared the sheets for the press. It is largely based on the alpha tradition, with some beta elements. (Like beta, it omits I. 45–II.8.) Its immediate source is a MS in Oxford (Bodl. Misc. 283 (P)) written in 1516 which incorporates elements of beta, lambda and the modern Greek translation of alpha.

Edition: Holton 1974.

The Phyllada tou Megalexandrou

This immensely popular work of Greek folk literature, based on the epsilon version of the *Romance*, was first published in 1680. According to Veloudis (1968, 26 and 1989, 15), its nearest predecessor is an unpublished MS, Meteora (Metamorphosis) 400, dated to 27 July 1640. There have been 43 subsequent editions, and several are in print at the present time.

Editions: Veloudis 1977/1989, a scholarly study edition: includes some illustrations from various sources; *Phyllada*, ed. Pallis 1935, reprinted Athens, 1990–91: includes a few illustrations from Persian MSS.
French translation: La Carrière 2000.
Literature on the Greek tradition: Gleixner 1961, Mitsakis 1970, Holton 1973, Moennig 1987, Veloudis 1968, 1969 and in Veloudis 1977/1989.

APPENDIX II
TABLES

Table 1: The *Alexander Romance*: The Greek Versions, Translations, and Derivative Texts

Date	Greek	Syriac	Arabic	Hebrew	Persian	Latin
AD 300	A by 338; Alpha (source of A); translated into **Armenian** by 550					338 Julius Valerius tr. A; 340–50 *Itinerarium Alexandri*? Origins of *Collatio*
400				Eye parable, diving bell and flying machine stories in Talmud		
500	Palladius *c.* 500; beta recension by 550	Syriac tr. of Ps-Call.; 521 d. of Jacob of Serugh;				
600		626 Prose 'Legend of Al'; poem of 'Jacob of Serugh'; 692 Ps.-Methodius	*c.* 680 Wahb ibn Munabbih			C7 at latest: *Letter to Aristotle about India*; Latin tr. of Ps-Methodius
700	700–710: Greek translation of Pseudo-Methodius; Yosippon epsilon recension; lambda recension		786–815 'Umara ibn Zaid; Arabic source of			Late C8: *Collatio* referred to by Alcuin

Date	Greek	Syriac	Arabic	Hebrew	Persian	Latin
800	Gamma; 866 George the Monk		*Qissat Dhu'l-qarnain* (later than 'Umara); 813–33 Berlin cod. Arab 9118 809–73 Hunayn ibn Ishaq, *Sayings of the Philosophers*; Tabari		895/6 d. of Dinawari	C9 Metz Epitome and *Testamentum*; Aethicus Ister
900			900–950 Yahya ibn Batrik, *Sirr al-asrar* 948 Mas'udi	953 Yosippon	941–1019 Firdausi, *Shahnameh*	C10 Late Latin *Letter to Aristotle about India*; 951–69 Leo the Archpriest tr. *AR*; Bamberg MS
1000	Zeta* translated into Serbian		pre-1053 Mubaššir, *Ahbar al-Iskandar*, 1053 Mubaššir *Sayings of the Philosophers*; pre-1063 Arabic tr. of Yosippon			C11 *Iter ad Paradisum*; *Historia de Proeliis*; *Letter of Pharasmanes*
1100			*Historia de Dulqarnain*	*1100–1300: Alexandros ha-Mokdoni c. 1150: Ma'aseh*	1170 Nizami; C12–14 *Iskandarnameh*;	*Secretum secretorum*; *Hist. de Proeliis* J² (Orosius recension);

1200	c. 1200 Middle Greek Alex. book (Diegesis, Mitsakis, based on gamma; Serbian tr. C15) 1275 Rimada	1201–73 al-Makin, *Universal History*; 1283 Qazvini	pre-1235 Sod ha-Sodot (Yehuda al-Harizi 1170–1235)	1200–36 *Hist. de Proeliis* J³ 1236–8 Quilichinus of Spoleto 1250–1300 *Liber Philosophorum* (deriving from *Bocados de Oro*); C13: Wonder Stone; *Gesta Romanorum*
			Alexander 1150–1230: *Sefer Toledoth Alexandros* (attrib. Ibn Tibbon)	1150–1200 *Liber Alexandri Magni* (Paris MS); c. 1160 Peter Comestor and Godfrey of Viterbo 1178 Walter of Châtillon *Alexandreis*
1300	Lambda (5 MSS); composition of L; 1388 Byzantine Alexander poem		1340–56: *Sefer Toldoth Al ha-Mokdoni* by Jacob Bonfils, derives from HP J³	1336 Nuweiri; 1390 **Turkish** version of *AR* by Ahmedi of Kermiyan

Date	Greek	Syriac	Arabic	Hebrew	Persian	Latin
1400	First MSS of L *Alexander and Semiramis*		1446: as-Suri C15: **Ethiopic** version of *AR*		1469 Mirkhond 1492 d. of Jami	Liegnitz MS; 1471 first printed *Hist. de proeliis*
1500	1529 *Rimada* published by D. Zenos					
1600	1669 *Phyllada tou Megalexandrou*		1669–71 Yuwasif ibn Suwaidan tr. of Mid. Gr. (C12–13); *c.*1600: Malay version of *AR*			

Table 2: Medieval European Versions and Derivatives of the *Historia de Proeliis*

Date	English, Scots and Irish	French	German and Dutch	Spanish	Slavic and Nordic	Italian
900	Pre-1000, OE 'Letter to Aristotle'			Liber Alehandrei		
1000	Irish Alexander (uses Chronicles, Orosius, and Letter to Aristotle				C11–12 Russian Chronographer, based on beta Pre-1200 Old Bulgarian *Aleksandria*	
1100		C. 1100 Alberic of Besançon; 1160 decasyllabic *AR*; 1160–75 *Fuerre de Gadres*; 1175 Lambert li Tors; 1180 *Venjeance Al*; 1185 Alexandre de Paris; by end of C12	C. 1100 Fritolf of Michelsberg, *Chronicle* 1125 Pfaffe Lamprecht; 1175 Strasburg *Alexander*			1185–90 Godfrey of Viterbo, *Pantheon*

Date	English, Scots and Irish	French	German and Dutch	Spanish	Slavic and Nordic	Italian
1200	1250 Thomas of Kent	*Roman d'Alexandre* 1206–52 OF; Prose Alex, from *HP J²*; 1256 Vincent of Beauvais *Voyage au Paradis*	1220–54 Rudolf von Ems, from Curtius and *HP J²*; 1235–40 Ebstorf Map Wernigeroder MS (tr. of Quilichinus) 1255 Jacob van Maerlant *Al.s Gesten* (based on Walter) 1270–87 Ulrich von Etzenbach 1272 *Der jüngere Titurel* 1283 Hereford *Mappa Mundi* 1285 J.J. Enikel *Weltchronik*	C13 *Bocados de Oro* (from Mubaššir Sayings) *Los buenos proverbios* (from Hunayn ibn Ishaq) *Libro do Alejandre*	1260 Icelandic *AR* (based on Walter of Châtillon)	
1300	Early C14 *Kynge Alisaundre*; 1340 ME		1352 Seifrit (from *HP J²*); pre-1358 *Seelentrost*		1380 Middle Swedish	1355 (MS) Domenico Scolari tr. Quilichinus C14 *I Nobili Fatti*

				$d'A = HP\ J^2$	$C15$ tr. of J^3
1400	Al. and Dindimus; mid-C14 Alliterative Romance of Al.; 1370–1449 Lydgate; 1330–1408 Gower 1356 John Mandeville 1364 Ranulph Higden d. Wars of Alexander (from *HP* J³); 1428 Scots *Buik of Al.*; Thornton *Prose Al.* (from *HP* J²); 1450 Stephen Scrope and Caxton's *Dictes and Sayings* 1460 Gilbert Hay, *Buik of Al.*	C15: 4 MSS of *Perceforest* (printed 1528, 1531) Jean Wauquelin	(tr. of Leo) Dutch *Boek van de wraak Gods*		
			1439–63 Johann von Hartlieb C15 Meister Babiloth, *Al-Chronik* (from *HP* J³ and J²) 1425–50: German and Dutch History Bibles	Serbian *AR* from Mid-Gr. (transl. into Romanian and Georgian); 1433 Czech prose J³; 1469 Czech abridged J³; Serbian tr. of Epsilon; 1442 Pachomy Logofet (conflates Chronograph and Serbian)	

Date	English, Scots and Irish	French	German and Dutch	Spanish	Slavic and Nordic	Italian
1500			1512 Plattenberger, *Excerpta Chronicorum*	1500–88 *Rrekontamiento* (tr. from Arabic)	Serb chronicles 1550 Polish: Cracow et al. Czech: Walkenberg C17 Byelorussian *HP*	1512 *Alexandreida in rima* (printed)

NOTES

Preface

1. *A Literary Companion to Travel in Greece* (Penguin 1984; 2nd edn J. Paul Getty Museum 1994): see pp. 225–31.

Introduction

1. Ehrenberg 1938.
2. The appendix attempts to bring together details of the very numerous versions of this work and its rewritings.

Chapter 1. Nativity: Egyptian Origins (356 BC)

1. Cf. Ephorus, *FGrH* 70F217.
2. Saatsoglou-Palindeli 1991.
3. *Alexander the False Prophet* 7.
4. Livy 26.18.7, with Walbank 1967/1985; Suetonius, *Aug.* 94.
5. Bosworth 1988, 283.
6. Ephippus, *FGrH* 126F5.
7. Arr. *Anab.* 7.8.3.
8. Identified with Amun as Amun-Re since the New Kingdom: Kemp 2006, 262, see p. 20 below.
9. Jasnow 1997.
10. For a contrary view see Burstein 1995.
11. Thomas Boslooper, *The Virgin Birth* (London: SCM 1962) discounts any connection of the Gospel story with Greek hero stories. In general see Rank 1909.
12. Leiden: Voss 44F.3A. f. 157v.
13. Chéhab 1958–9; Ross 1963a.
14. I have examined the one in the John Rylands Library, Arm 3. For the others see appendix p. 249.
15. The scene is depicted very similarly in the Venetus MS, D, fol. 14v.
16. Alföldi 1943; see also Chapter 11.
17. DS 15.93, 16.51.1; cf. Plut. *Ages* 36–9; Eide et al., 1994–98, II. 501–3. The date is set in 341 (versus Diodorus, who conflates the campaigns of 350/49 and 343 onwards) by A.B. Lloyd in Trigger et al., 1983, 346 and in *Cambridge Ancient History* VI (1994), 357–9.

18. Manetho fr. 10 = Jos. *cAp* 243–53.
19. Doniger 2000. The classic study is Weinreich 1911. The motif 'seduction by posing as a god' is number K 1315.1 in Stith Thomson's *Motif Index of Folk Literature*.
20. Gardiner 1917, Koenig 1994.
21. Boswinkel and Sijpestein 1968.
22. Pinch 1994, 88ff., Ritner 1993, 64 n. 289, 219 n. 1020. For further details see my commentary on *AR* I. 3, Stoneman 2007, 482–3.
23. Lichtheim 1973–80, III.138, Betz 1992, 323–30.
24. Raven 1983; Pinch 1994, 94–9; Plato, *Laws* 933b.
25. Cf. *PGM* IV. 210–15, Graf 1997, 104–5. Usually the hawk has to be killed first, according to Aelian, *NA* 11.39: 'The Egyptians say that the hawk ... when it has departed this life and shed its body and become a disembodied spirit, it prophesies and sends dreams'. See Koenig 1994, 76.
26. Braun 1938.
27. Burstein 1995.
28. Perry 1966, 329.
29. First edited by W. Spiegelberg in 1914; the standard treatment is Koenen 1968, with updates in *ZPE* 3 (1968); 13 (1974); 54 (1984); see also Eddy 1961, 292–4.
30. Leiden pap. d'Anastasy 67, Pack² 2476, Wilcken 1922 I.81, Koenen 1985, etc. There is a translation in Maspéro 1967, 285–9. See Eddy 1961, 287 ff.
31. POxy XI 1381 (2nd century AD).
32. Comparetti 1895, 283.
33. For a brief summary see Pritchard 1992.
34. The indispensable survey is Cary 1956, supplemented by Ross 1963b and 1971 on the illustrations to the MSS.
35. The king himself was an instantiation of Amun: Kemp 2006, 272; Assmann 2001, 189–92.
36. Brunner-Traut 1986²; cf. Assmann 2001, 116–19.
37. Translation in Kemp 2006, 262–3.
38. Egypt may have been the source of many of the motifs that characterise the Greek romance. See Barns 1956; also Berg 1973, Hill 1981.
39. Divisions of the year into ten-day periods, each represented by a divinity.
40. Cauville 1997.
41. Several of these stones recur in the lapidaries with sometimes analogous functions: *Les Lapidaires grecs* 2003, 203. For example, lychnites gives protection against 'nyctalopes', Damigeron 28.
42. There was even a form of the god Horus as Harendotes, Horus-avenger-of-his-father: D. Meeks in *Lexikon der Ägyptologie* II (1977), 964–6.
43. It was more common to time *intercourse* to achieve a favourable conjunction (Augustine, *CD* 5.5), but Horos in a poem by Propertius (IV.1.89 and 99–103) boasts of having set auspicious moments for mothers to give birth.
44. Boll 1950, 351–6.
45. I have made some attempt at an interpretation, *exempli gratia*, in my commentary on this passage (Stoneman 2007, 498–505). A useful general survey is Barton 1994. The most approachable of the ancient texts on astrology is that of Firmicus Maternus.
46. A similar point is made in the story of Tiberius and his prophet Thrasyllus told by Suetonius, *Tib.* 14 and Tacitus, *Annals* 6.20–21: taking his prophet for a walk along a cliff-edge, Tiberius merrily asks him to prophesy his own current situation. 'I see that I am in great danger,' cries the prophet, whereupon the emperor, impressed by his skill, refrains from pushing him over the edge.
47. The English verse translation by A.G. and E. Warner (1905) and the abridged version by Levy 1967 remain valuable, but have been largely superseded by the new prose

translation by Dick Davis (2004), which is magnificently illustrated; it has been reissued as a Penguin (2007) without the illustrations.

Chapter 2. Golden Vines, Golden Bowls and Temples of Fire: The Persian Versions

1. E.G. John Rylands MS Pers. 856, *Khamsa* of Nizami f. 163b; (Shiraz *c.* 1575).
2. John Rylands Pers. 910 f. 334b, book 772.
3. Burstein 1976. See Introduction.
4. 'A probable impossibility is more convincing than an improbable possibility': *Poetics* ch. 25, 1461b11–12, cf. ch. 9, 1451a35–b6, 'Poetry is more philosophical than history'.
5. Davis 2002, 75–82 argues for a possible influence of Persian storytelling on the Greek *Romance*, and suggests that the death of Nectanebo might be modelled on the murder of Zahhak's father in the *Shahnameh*. However, the lines of possible transmission are not easy to discern.
6. A modern reader is irresistibly reminded of the scene in Eisenstein's *Alexander Nevsky* where the invading Teutonic Knights are trapped on the frozen River Neva, whose ice then breaks beneath them.
7. Tabari transl. Perlman 1987, 699.
8. Budge 1889, 109ff.
9. Ibid., 107; Budge 1896, 116–19. There is a dragon fight already in Julius Valerius' Latin translation of the *Romance*, during the foundation of Alexandria (I. 32). The modern Greek story from the Karagiozis puppet play of Alexander's fight with the dragon is a different matter.
10. On *The Laments of the Philosophers* see Chapter 10.
11. Boyce 1957. In the early twentieth century there are said to have been between 5,000 and 10,000 dervish reciters in Iran; in 1970 there were a mere four storytellers left in Shiraz, defending a last bastion against television: Yamamoto 2003.
12. The Persian taste for romance went back a long way. Alexander's historian Chares mentions the popularity in Persia of the romance of Zariadres and Odatis. In Firdausi's own time the poert Unsuri (*c.* 947–1040) wrote a romance, *Vamiq u Adhra*, which is a free translation of the Greek *Metiochus and Parthenope*: Hägg and Utas 2003. (Strohmaier 1995 asks why such a 'trivial' work should have had such a great reception in the Orient.) The author refers several times to Iskandar, for example when he receives information about the two Buddhas of Bamiyan, which are said to be statues of Vamiq and Adhra. See also Davis 2002. It is usually assumed that Unsuri found the Greek source of his novel in an Arabic translation, perhaps made in al-Mamun's 'House of Wisdom' in eighth-century Baghdad, but Bo Utas thinks he might have used the Greek directly. Is it possible that there was a Syriac intermediary here too?
13. Southgate 1978, 86–9, following Nöldeke, thinks not.
14. Agathias, *Histories* II.31. Unfortunately they did not like it, finding the crime rate and the incidence of adultery too high, the arrogance of the powerful intolerable, and 'the opportunity of conversing with the king proved a further disappointment. It was that monarch's proud boast that he was a student of philosophy but his knowledge of that subject was utterly superficial . . . . Finally the vicious promiscuity which characterised Persian society was more than the philosophers could stand. All these factors combined to send them hurrying home as fast as they could go' (tr. J.D. Frendo).
15. Nöldeke 1930/1979 and 1890.
16. Ciancaglini 1998. The key step had already been taken by Frye 1985, who observed that a Pahlavi version would have removed the Nectanebo story, as later Persian versions did.
17. The oldest work about which we have any information is the Pahlavi *Book of the Hero Zarer* (*c.* AD 500), followed by the *Book of the Deeds of Ardashir* (*Arda-Viraf-namak*) around

600, which borrows the story of the birth of Cyrus for its hero. There were king-lists – the Greek historian Agathias refers to them in the time of Chosrow I – and a chronicle from Gayumart to Chosrow II compiled in 651 by the *dihqan* (feudal lord) Danishvar. Both were certainly used by Firdausi. See Davidson 1994.

18. De Blois 2004, 107–10.
19. Horace, *Ep.* II.1.156.
20. Frye 1975, 153. The tenth-century Baghdad bookseller Ibn al-Nadim also refers in his *Fihrist* ('Catalogue') to romances of kings, and of chess, the tales of Sindbad, of Vamiq and Adhra, of Bilandar and Yudasaf (originally a Buddhist story, which emerges in Greek as *Barlaam and Josaphat* attributed to John Damascene). It is notable that these titles include works of entertainment as well as of learning.
21. Firdausi also drew, he says, on the poem of 'a brilliant youth well skilled in poetry' named Dakiki; but 'vicious habits were his friends .... And death, approaching unexpectedly, Imposed its gloomy helmet on his head' (Prelude, 9). Dakiki, who was probably a Zoroastrian, was murdered by a boy slave who was also his lover, when his poem had only got as far as the life of Zoroaster; so he cannot have had any impact on Firdausi's account of Iskandar.
22. Renard 1993, 89. This book is also the source of the following details from Tarsusi. See also Briant 2003, 475–7.
23. Herodotus 1.96 describes how Cyrus was exposed as a baby and brought up by peasants; cf. Ctesias F8*d*, a variant.
24. W.L. Hanaway, s.v. Eskandar in *Encyclopaedia Iranica*.
25. Hanaway 1974, 6–7.
26. Hillenbrand 1996, 222–3.
27. Boyle 1965.
28. Cleaves 1922, cf. Boyle 1977.
29. See Eccles, Franzmann and Lieu 2005. I thank Sam Lieu for bringing these inscriptions to my attention.
30. The fullest treatment is the unpublished PhD thesis by Andrew Mango 1955. On Nizami, Chelkowski 1977 is a basic introduction.
31. Part 1 is translated by H. Wilberforce Clarke (1881), a Victorian *tour de force* of oddity; there is a German translation of the whole work by J.C. Bürgel (1991).
32. Brend 1995, 39ff. gives a useful summary.
33. Boodberg 1938. The use of Taugast/Tabgach for western Turkistan is standard in Muslim sources, while Persians call both China and the region of Samarkand Chin: Haussig 1953.
34. It is told also in his *Haft Paykar* 6.29.
35. Bürgel 1988, 139–40.
36. *Republic* VII, 514a–516b: the contemplative path takes one from shadows and reflections to 'the appearances in the heavens', until finally 'he would be able to look upon the sun itself and see its true nature, not by reflections in water or phantasms of it in an alien setting, but in and by itself in its own place'.
37. E.g. John Rylands Library, Pers. 856, f. 207a; illustrated in Robinson 1980.
38. E.g. New York, Metropolitan Museum 13.228.30.
39. Bürgel 1991, 435, my translation.
40. See Chapter 9.
41. Alexander likewise appears as a model of the civilising king in the 'Mirror of Alexander' of Amir Khosrow of Delhi (AD 1251–1325, completed 1299), dedicated to Ala al-Din Muhammad Shah. Its atmosphere is more sufi than in Nizami and the section on China is particularly expansive. There are also many anecdotes in al-Ghazzali's *Counsel for Kings*, composed in Persian in 1105–11 and also translated into Arabic. See Bagley 1964, 82, 92, 96; at 61 Anushirvan divides a treasure as Alexander does in a familiar Jewish

story (see p. 121); and at 108 Solomon takes flight like Alexander in a flying throne (see Chapter 8); cf. 157.

42. Mango 1955, 123.
43. Four more courtly works deserve a brief mention: *Iskandarnameh*s by Zayn al-'Abedin 'Ali 'Abdi Bey Navidi Shirazi (1515–18); by Badr al-Din Kashmiri (16th century); by Tana'i Mashadi (16th century); and by Hasan Beg 'Etabo Takallu (d. *c.* 1611–12): see Hanaway in *Encyclopaedia Iranica*, s.v. Eskandar-nama.
44. Ciancaglini 1997.
45. Hillenbrand 1996, 23.
46. N. Davis 2007, 61.
47. Southgate 1978.
48. Ibid., p. 46.
49. Meisami 1999, 79. See also Wiesehöfer 1994, 19–22.
50. Mirkhond, transl. E. Rehatsek 1892, II. 249.
51. Briant 2003, 452.
52. The *Avesta* is the sacred book itself, the *Zand* the commentary on it.
53. Two grades of Zoroastrian priest.
54. Translated from the Italian of Ciancaglini 1997 (67ff.), on which my argument in these paragraphs is closely based.
55. Boyce 1968; Briant 2003, 452–9; Southgate 1978, 186–9. The work was translated into Persian by Abdullah ibn al-Muqaffa' (d. 760), but his translation is lost and the surviving translation is the thirteenth-century Persian one by Muhammad ibn al-Hassan ibn Isfandiyar.
56. It may be in this context that the tradition arose that misattributed Darius I's murder of the Magi to Alexander: Eddy 1961, 69; cf. 72.
57. Boyce 1979, 78.
58. Bailey 1943, 149ff.; Ciancaglini 1997, 68. See also Darmesteter 1892.
59. Clemen, *Fontes historiae religionis persicae*, Bonn 1929, 186.
60. Hall 1989, 87.
61. Herodian 6.2.1–2, Dio. 80.4.1, Amm. Marc. 17.5.5–6: 'that my forefathers' empire reached as far as the River Strymon and the boundaries of Macedonia even your own ancient records bear witness', says Shapur II to Constantius.
62. A recently discovered Aramaic text refers to Alexander as Shahanshah: Shaked 2004.
63. Levy 1967, 236ff., Davis 2004, 47ff.
64. Mørkholm 1991, 74.
65. Briant 2003, 460–3.
66. Record of Dareios' palace at Sousa: Old Persian text with Latin translation, OUP n.d.: my English translation. Another translation is Brosius 2000, 40–1.
67. Philostratus' golden wrynecks seem to be a variant of this story.
68. Liudprand of Cremona 1993, 153.
69. There were similar wonders at the Abbasid palace in Baghdad (gold lions that roared, birds in a bronze tree, and an organ), and at Theophilus' Magnaura palace at Brusa in Bithynia: Brett 1954 provides a survey.
70. Mandeville, *Travels* ch. 23 1983, 143; also in the palace of Prester John, ch. 30 (ibid. 171): 'there were different kinds of birds, worked by mechanical means, which seemed quite alive as they sang and fluttered'. The topic is picked up by Umberto Eco, *Baudolino* (2002), 333.
71. On Mandeville's sources see Letts 1949, ch. 2.

Chapter 3. Cities of Alexander:
Jews and Arabs Adopt the Hero

1. 'The juice that oozes out of the incision is called opobalsamum; it is extremely sweet in taste, but exudes in tiny drops, the trickle being collected by means of tufts of wool in small horns and poured out of them into a new earthenware vessel to store . . . . When Alexander the Great was campaigning in that country, it was considered a fair whole day's work in summer to fill a single shell' [say, a dessert-spoonful].

2. The attitude of the Macedonians as described does not seem to suit an army ambushing a small group of spies from a safe position. However, it could well describe the suicidal determination shown by the Jews on some occasions, notably the siege of Masada in AD 73 or 74.

3. See appendix .

4. Translated by J.J. Collins in Charlesworth 1983, I. 370.

5. The discussion is surveyed by R.A. Marcus in appendix C to the Josephus of 1967 (Loeb), vol. 6, 512–32. See also my article, Stoneman 1994d, on which this section is broadly based.

6. Momigliano 1979.

7. Another story about Alexander and the Samaritans is in the rabbinic tract *Megillath Ta'anith*: when the Samaritans asked Alexander for permission to build a schismatic temple on Mount Moriah, he responded by handing them over to Jewish justice: they were dragged behind horses and Mount Gerizim was ploughed over. In fact the action is that of John Hyrcanus, *c.* 110 BC (Jos. *AJ* 13.281, *BJ* 1.65). Josephus elsewhere (*cAp* 2.42ff.) says that Alexander gave Samaria to the Jews, though the gift was really made by Demetrius in 145 BC (1 Macc. 11.34).

8. Delling 1981.

9. See Appendix for details.

10. See Chapter 6 and nn. 43–44.

11. Fraser 1996. The identifications listed are discussed on pp. 109–13, 132–40, 154–6 and 152. Uncertain is Alexandria by the Caucasus (Opian or Begram: Fraser, 140–50). Alexandria by Issus (Fraser, 23) is an error, and Bucephala is lost (Fraser, 161ff.).

12. Curt. 4.8, DS 17.52 and Justin 11.11.13.

13. Arr. *Anab.* 3.4.5, Plutarch *Life of Alexander* 26.

14. Welles 1962.

15. Arr. *Anab.* 1.1.

16. Arr. *Anab.* 3.3.5–6.

17. 1980, 263.

18. Visser 1958, 5–7 and 65–6.

19. Schwarzenberg 1976.

20. Koenen 1968.

21. Jouguet 1940.

22. Also at III. 35.2, where it corresponds to the date known from other sources.

23. See my commentary on I. 32.10.

24. *Prophetarum vitae fabulosae*, ed. Th. Schermann (1907), 9.12; Torrey 1946, 35.

25. Ibid. 61.11ff = 44.16 (a text attributed to the Christian writer Dorotheus, who was active around AD 303, was exiled under Diocletian and martyred at the age of 107).

26. Pfister 1914/1975.

27. Ginzberg 1928–39, VI 452–3.

28. Ibid. 282–3, quoting the sources. Cf. J. ben-Gorion, *Der Born Judas* (Leipzig n.d.) 3.210.

29. Gutas 1998, 40, 43–4.

30. Yosef A. ben-Yochannan, *Africa, Mother of World Civilization* (Baltimore 1971) 483, 493. Cited in Mary Lefkowitz, *Not Out of Africa* (New York 1996), 151; cf. 2–3. Aristotle, it should be noted, died in 322 BC, and the Library of Alexandria was created a genera-

tion later by Ptolemy II (308–246 BC). Such impossible synchronisms are characteristic of legends of this type, but it is not always as easy to perceive the political agenda of the creators as it is in this case.

31. Jos., *cAp* I. 204; discussion in Bar-Kochva 1996, 57–71.
32. Vasunia 2001, 182; and ch. 4 in general on Greek views of Egyptian writing.
33. Fraser 1996, 36–7.
34. See esp. Wilcken 1922, I. 25–37; Fraser 1960 and Fraser 1972, I 246–76; Jouguet 1949; Hornbostel 1973 – on iconography.
35. Arr. *Anab.* 7.26.2.
36. Stambaugh 1972, 6–8.
37. The Egyptian population apparently remained hostile: Eddy 1961, 275–7.
38. 'A small window was orientated on the sunrise in such a way that, on the day when the idol of the sun was to be brought in to salute Sarapis, by careful observation of the time, a ray of the sun would fall through the window just at the moment when the idol entered the temple and illuminate the mouth and lips of Sarapis, so that, to the watching people, it would seem that Sarapis had been greeted by the kiss of the sun. There was also another trick of this kind. The nature of the stone called Magnet is said to be such that it pulls and draws to itself iron. The image of the sun was made, by the subtlest art of the sculptor, out of iron, so that a stone of this type being fixed to the ceiling, when the image was lowered gently to its position below its rays, the iron would draw it to itself by its natural force, and the image would seem to the people to rise up and hover in the air.' [The text in *PL* is somewhat corrupt, but this seems fairly certainly to be the sense.] Compare Pliny *NH* 34.42.148 on the aerial statue of Arsinoe.
39. Brodersen 1996, 11.
40. Clayton and Price 1988: the six are the Temple of Artemis at Ephesus, the temple of Zeus at Olympia, the Hanging Gardens of Babylon, the Pyramids, the Colossus of Rhodes, the statue of Athena by Phidias in Athens, and a seventh is often the Mausoleum at Halicarnassus.
41. Brodersen 1996, 107–110.
42. Text ibid. 104–5.
43. Butler 1978, 376–80.
44. Mas'udi 1965, paras 836–7; the translation from the French is my own. On Mas'udi see Khalidi 1975, ch. 6. See further Doufikar-Aerts 1996. Mas'udi was preceded by several other writers: Ya'qubi (9th century), Ibn Khordadbeh (849–85), Ibn Rustah and Ibn al Fakih (both early 10th century) who all told the same story. Altogether 37 Arab writers write about the Pharos, but the later ones leave out the story about the crabs: Ibn Battutah only mentions the internal passages (Thiersch 1909).
45. Strabo 17.1.6. The Pharos was built on an island and inaugurated by Ptolemy II in 283 BC. A causeway, the Heptastadion, was constructed to lead to it. Over time the causeway silted up: at the present day it has become a substantial piece of land. See Empereur 1998, 32 and plan p. 47.
46. Mas'udi 1965, 838. Alexander's magic mirror reappears in Benjamin of Tudela, and a similar one was operated by Prester John according to the German epic *Titurel*: Comparetti 1895, 303–4. J.L. Borges borrowed the conceit of Alexander's mirror: *The Aleph* 1998, 133: 'In 1867, Captain Burton was the British consul in Brazil; in July of 1942, Pedro Henriquez Ureña discovered a manuscript by Burton in a library in Santos, and in this manuscript Burton discussed the mirror attributed in the East to Iskandar dhu-al-qarnayn, or Alexander the Great of Macedonia. In this glass, Burton said, the entire universe was reflected.'
47. *Parastaseis* 1984, 22, 5a; Stoneman 1984, 15–18. Stories like this are common in Arab tradition: another example is Washington Irving, *The Alhambra* (1860), 171.
48. Midrash Tehillim, *Ps.* 93.5, referring to the Emperor Hadrian; Yalkut Shim'oni *Ps.* 93, 848: Kazis 1962, 19–20, *Der Born Judas* III. 306 and 135. See also Chapter 6 n. 18.

Chapter 4. The Marvels of India (329–326 BC)

1. Ehrenberg 1938.
2. Anderson 1928a.
3. Arr. *Anab.* 5.1.
4. Curt. 9.10.24ff.
5. DS 2.16–19; Agathias 2.25.4–5.
6. Plut. *De tranqillitate animi* 446D.
7. Düring 1957. Pliny *NH* 8.16.44 tells us that Alexander supported Aristotle's zoological researches in Greece; Theophrastus, *Hist. Plant.* 4.4.5 cites Alexander for the properties of a certain plant, thus suggesting the source of much of his Indian information.
8. *Meteor.* I.13.15.
9. On Greek knowledge of India, see Dihle 1964. The sources are surveyed in the older publications of McCrindle (1901 and 1926), Puri 1963 and Banerjee 1920. See also Halbfass 1988 ch. 1 and Velissaropoulos 1990.
10. Tzetzes, *Chiliades* 7. 629–36; Romm 1992, 84–5; Panchenko 1998.
11. *FGrH* F45–53, conveniently translated by N.G. Wilson (Photius 1994).
12. Fr. 45 Photius 45a ff.
13. Philostr. *Vit. Ap. Ty.* 2.45. Paus. 9.21.4 identifies it with the tiger; Solinus 52.37. There is an illustration in T.H. White 1954, 247 from Topsell 1607; and see p. 52 where White mentions that in 1930 a certain Mr Stanley was mistaken for a manticore somewhere in Andalusia.
14. Fr. 45 in Wilson 1994, 47b–48a. On dog-heads see D.G. White 1991.
15. Philostr., *Vit. Ap. Ty.* 3.45–49 (below), Agatharchides, *On the Erythraean Sea* 5.84a (topaz); Heliodorus, *Ethiopica* 4.8; see Stoneman 1992b, 104–6. Ps.-Aristotle, *De lapidibus* 6.49 mentions such a luminous stone: Ruska 1912, 9–10. Compare also the stones that glow in the Land of Darkness, developed in Firdausi, *Shahnameh* 20.29, where Alexander and Khidr each carry a luminous ring through the Land of Darkness. According to *AR* II. 41 (gamma), the luminous stone is found in the belly of a fish (p. 124 in my Penguin translation): there is a related folk-tale in John Moschus, *Spiritual Meadow*, ch. 185, *PG* 87.3.3060–1.
16. *Paradise Lost*, Book II, ll. 2.943–7.
17. Megasthenes in Strabo 15.1.44.
18. Romm 1992, 82–120; Karttunen 1989 and 1997.
19. Aristotle, *Sense and Sensibilia* 445a17: 'the theory held by certain of the Pythagoreans, that some animals are nourished by odours alone, is unsound'.
20. Cf. J. Petherick, an explorer of the Sudan, against E. Behm in *Petermanns Mitteilungen* 17 (1871), 151.
21. Aulus Gellius, *NA* 9.4–13 repeats the information, with expressions of disgust at its improbability. Pliny's account is the *locus classicus*: see Friedman 1981.
22. Pliny cites among his sources Crates, Artemidorus of Ephesus, Cleitarchus, Baeton, Ctesias, Eudoxus and also Antigonus of Carystus, the father of Hellenistic paradoxography. On this topic see Phlegon, ed. Hansen 1996, introduction.
23. *Les Lapidaires grecs* 2003, xxxiii.
24. Friedman 1981, Romm 1992, Wittkower 1942. See below in this chapter (p. 82) on the problems the monstrous races posed for Christian doctrine.
25. Arr. *Ind.* 15.4; Strabo 15.1.44 = *FGrH* 133F8.
26. Gunderson 1980 and Stoneman 1994a provide translations of two different versions. See also the editions by Boer 1973 and Feldbusch 1976, and the appendix to this book.
27. Boer 1973 lists 67.
28. Tolkien 1983, ch. 1; Sisam 1953. The other two texts in this codex are the story of St Christopher and another immensely popular work, *The Wonders of the East*. The owner of the codex seems to have been interested in monsters.

29. Compare Eco 2002, 341ff.
30. Goossens 1927–28.
31. Cf. Lassen 1827 I, 634.
32. Karttunen 1989, 189.
33. Zacher 1867, 153–8.
34. Gunderson 1980, 102–3.
35. Cosmas XI.7; Ps. 21.21.
36. Southgate 1978, 22.
37. *Letter* 39 (12 in L. Gunderson 1980). Cf. *Liber monstrorum* II. 2, Pliny *NH* 8.27.
38. On what follows see the discussion in Stoneman 1994c. Also Anderson 1928b, Standish 1970, Braund 1986, Kolendo 1987; Bosworth 1988, 94–5, Brunt's appendix to the Loeb Arrian, I. 522–5. Cf. Mayerson 1993 on the 'confusion of Indias'.
39. See Chapter 9.
40. Pliny *NH* 6.15.40.
41. And Marco Polo 1921, 38.
42. Strabo 11.5.5; Brunt in the Loeb Arrian I. 524.
43. Hdt. 4.110, Arrian, *Periplus* 15.3, Mela 1.19. A doxography on the location of the Amazons is given by Plutarch *Alexander* 46; see Hamilton's note ad loc. See also Blok 1995, Dowden 1997.
44. Brunt in Loeb Arrian I. 525.
45. Cod. Vindob. 34; facsimile edn Graz 1976; see Hartley and Woodward 1987, 238–41.
46. On Eratosthenes' map see Beazley 1949, 377ff., Hartley and Woodward 1987; cf. Dilke 1985, 33 and Wartena 1972, 9 ff. with Strabo 15.1.11. I have tried to depict the 'Alexander' world view in the map at the beginning of this book.
47. On the Hereford Map see Jancey 1987, Crone 1948, Wiseman 1992, Harvey 1996, Kline 2001. On the Ebstorf Map see Hahn-Woerle 1987. Also Harvey 1991, Edson 1997, Edson and Savage-Smith 2004, Scafi 2006 – the most comprehensive survey of such maps. On the Arab adaptation of this cosmology by Qazvini and others see Lane 1857, I. 19ff.
48. Berggren and Jones 2000, 119: Ptolemy (8.1) argued that the doctrine that Ocean surrounds the world arose from errors of drawing going back as early as Herodotus and Hecataeus.
49. Friedman 1981, 178 ff.
50. Löwe 1951.
51. His diary mentions (Sunday 4 November 1492) reports of one-eyed men and men with dog's snouts, which he claims to have seen himself on Friday 23 November; on Saturday 17 November 'he found large nuts like those of India, and large mice like those of India too, and very large crabs'. The island of women (Saturday 24 November) will concern us again in Chapter 7.
52. The story became widespread through Mandeville's *Travels*, where it occupies ch. 30. See Slessarev 1959, Silverberg 1972.
53. Quoted from Silverberg 1972, 42 ff.
54. DS 1.30.4–9, cf. 1.31.4 on rivers which disappear into sand; Plut. *Antony* 3.6; my commentary on II. 30 (forthcoming).
55. Cited from Bialik and Ravnitzky 1992, 492.66; cf. for the ten tribes 134.147; 135.148; 384.56. Also, Ginzberg 1928–39, IV. 316–18, VI 407–9. It reappears in several Arab sources: Ibn Khaldun I. 22 dismisses it as 'a silly story'.
56. Conti Rossini 1925; Adler 1930/1987, 4–21.
57. Epiphanius, ed. Blake and de Vis 1934, 116–18; *Les Lapidaires grecs*, xxxi–ii. The story was already in Herodotus 3.111ff., where it was applied to the collection of cinnamon, not diamonds.
58. This detail seems to come from a different episode of the Alexander story, in the *Letter to Aristotle* (20). 'From there we advanced to the valley of Jordia, where there were

serpents which had on their necks stones known as emeralds. These serpents will not allow anyone to approach this valley. They live on asafoetida and white pepper . . . . From there we took away only a few emeralds, but quite large ones.'

59. Cited from *The Thousand and One Nights*, E.W. Lane 1859/1981, III. 88ff.
60. Kieckhefer 1989, 182.
61. Cited from N.M. Penzer 1952, 3. The standard treatment of the subject is Hertz 1905a, 156–277.
62. The one exception may be an allusion in the *Harsacharita* of Bana (AD 630: Bana 1961): 'Alasa-Chandakasa having conquered the earth did not penetrate into Sirirajya or the Kingdom of Women'. See Sylvain Levi 1936 – who also mentions that coral, unknown to Vedic literature, is called Alakandaka in the *Arthashastra*.
63. Mayor 2003, 142 suggests he did.
64. See appendix for an account of this work, and the literature cited there.
65. Penzer 1952, 23ff. gives some other medieval versions of the tale. The motif reappears in Nathaniel Hawthorne's story 'Rappacini's Daughter' and (from the traditions of the American Indians) in Louis L'Amour's *Haunted Mesa* (1978).
66. Southgate 1978, 74.
67. Marco Polo, ch. I. 29; 1871, I. 157.
68. Tarn 1951, 408.
69. Burnes 1839, II. ch. 7, 191–2; III. ch. 4, 186.
70. Schuyler 1876, I. 237 and 277.
71. See also Holt 2005, 70.
72. His story is told by Macintyre 2004.
73. Ibid. 183.

Chapter 5. 'How Much Land Does a Man Need?': Alexander's Encounter with the Brahmans 326 BC

1. Repeated by Eusebius, *Life of Constantine* 4.30.
2. The main discussions of this important episode and the related texts are Becker 1889, Wilcken 1923, Hansen 1964, Berg 1970, van Thiel 1972, Stoneman 1995a and 1994b.
3. *The Oeconomy of Human Life*, a collection of aphorisms in biblical style. 'A small system of morality, written in the language and character of the ancient Gymnosophists or Bramins . . . . Those who admire it the most highly, are very fond of attributing it to Confucius . . . . Some will have it to be the institutes of Lao Kiun . . . . There are others, who, from some particular marks and sentiments which they find in it, suppose it to be written by the Bramin Dandamis, whose famous letter to Alexander the Great is recorded by the European writers.' I am grateful to John Bray for bringing this passage to my knowledge.
4. Presumably Prakrit–Sanskrit; Sanskrit–Persian; Persian–Greek.
5. Plutarch, *Life of Alexander* 65: he was a pupil of Diogenes, the original 'Dog'. Brown 1949, 38–53.
6. The practice of suicide by fire has seemed to be un-Brahman, and it is enjoined only for those who have killed a priest by the Laws of Manu (11.74). However, Indian philosophers had a propensity for burning themselves in public ways in antiquity. One Zamorus or Zarmonochegas had himself initiated in the Eleusinian Mysteries and then promptly immolated himself (Str. 15.1.730; other examples: Cicero *TD* V. 27; Stoneman 1994b, 506.)
7. Arr., *Anab.* 6.16.5, they support Sambus' revolt and are executed; 6.17, they support Musicanus.
8. See the discussion in Huizinga 1949, 133, who says they are 'variants of the sacred Vedic riddles'.

9. A near-doublet of Plutarch's version, without the dénouement, is preserved in an independent text of uncertain date: Boissonade, *Anecdota graeca* i. 45–6 (Codex Regius, Paris 1630), a collection of aphorisms and wisdom texts.

10. Crates, Fr. 1–2 attacked Megarian 'timewasting in the verbal pursuit of virtue', and Timon censured Euclides for 'deranged casuistry'.

11. Davids 1890, 1894; Derrett 1967.

12. *Mahabharata*, transl. Johnson 2005, 297 ff., cf. van Buitenen 1975, 800–5, Narayan 1978, 90–2. There is a similar dialogue also at *Mahabharata* 3 (37), Colloquy of a Brahmin and a Hunter; see also Bhishna's address to Yudhisthira in vol XI of P.C. Roy's translation (Calcutta n.d.).

13. Pythagorean School, 58 C 4 Diels-Kranz = Iamblichus, *On the Pythagorean Life* 82–3.

14. Van Thiel 1972; Muckensturm 1993.

15. Plut. *Alex.* 14: 'if I were not Alexander, I should be Diogenes'. This story is in the *Romance*, but only in epsilon 12.7 and gamma I.27, having been brought in from the 'historical' tradition.

16. Stoneman 2003b.

17. 3.15.1–2, in the new Loeb translation by C.P. Jones. See also Eusebius' mocking comments in his attack on the *Life of Apollonius*, printed in the Jones' 3rd volume (2006), 147ff (191).

18. II. 3, X. 2, 6, 10.

19. P. Genev. Inv. 271; the text is published by Martin 1959 and discussed in detail by Photiades 1959. See also Berg 1970 and Stoneman 1994b, with further references. See in addition Maresch and Wills 1988.

20. This family relationship was first observed by Jacob Bernays in his study of the *Letters of Heraclitus* published in 1869: see Momigliano 1994, 135.

21. Editions of Palladius: Derrett 1960, Berghoff 1987. Translation: Stoneman 1994a. The most comprehensive study is Weerakkody 1997.

22. Again we see the confusion of India with Africa, for Axum is Ethiopia. Weerakkody 1997 shows that the details are unhistorical: no king of Sri Lanka ruled any part of India in the fourth/fifth centuries AD.

23. It is however omitted from the most comprehensive history of utopias yet compiled, Manuel and Manuel 1979, as well as from Ferguson 1975 and Dawson 1992, which are nevertheless indispensable for the study of the other works discussed below.

24. FGrH 134F24; Brown 1949, 54–61. Megasthenes also emphasises Indian simplicity of life: Str. 15.1.53. See Bosworth 1996, 84–9.

25. Winston 1976, Graf 1993.

26. Schwartz 1983; the literature on Iambulus is surveyed by Winiarczyk 1997.

27. Karttunen 1989, 138–9, 186ff. In Ptolemy the land is called Ottorokorra and placed on the border of China. Already Lassen 1827, 83 had argued that the Greeks got the idea of the Hyperboreans from India. See also Romm 1992 60–67; Bridgman 2005.

28. Such a *Schlaraffenland* is also the subject of Pleij 2001, in which Alexander makes a few appearances.

29. Reardon 1989, 619–49.

30. Ael. *VH* 3.18: Theopompus, *Philippica* viii, 'On Wonders' = FGrH 115F75c.

31. Shrimpton 1991, 144–5 scorns the notion; but see Romm 1996, 134–5.

32. Diog. Laert. 6.85.

33. Similarly, Taprobane in Pliny, *NH* 6.81–91 is a kind of anti-Rome.

34. Nussbaum 1994, 103, 198; Warren 2005, *passim*.

35. Flintoff 1980; Dillon 2000.

36. A similar point is made in a different context in Jami's *Iskandarnameh*, where the Khaqan sends Iskandar a girl, a servant, a suit of clothes and a tray of food, the moral being that if he conquered the whole world he could not enjoy more. Mango 1955, 127.

37. Cynics were not vegetarians, and in fact Diogenes is supposed to have died while trying to eat a raw octopus. But vegetarianism is clearly on a continuum with ideas about a 'life according to nature'. On ancient vegetarianism see Dombrowski 1984/1985, Sorabji 1993, and the brief discussion in Stoneman 1994b.
38. Berg 1970, Derrett 1960, Stoneman 1994b.
39. Translation (of the Syriac) in Charlesworth 1985, II, 443–61; see Knights 1994 and 1995.
40. The philosopher Clearchus, in his book 'On the Indians' (Fr. 6 Wehrli), thought that the Jews were descended from the Brahmans, whom they resembled in their piety and rules of purity. He may have been talking to Megasthenes, since he certainly visited Bactria, where he erected an inscription of philosophical maxims at Kandahar: Robert 1968. Philo's Therapeutae are a good example of a Jewish 'sect' who live a Brahman-like existence. See also Wallach 1941.
41. See appendix.
42. Kazis 1962, 13ff.
43. Pfister 1941 = 1975, 73–4.
44. Kazis 1962 is a translation and edition of this work.
45. Pfister 1910; Cary 1956; tr. in Stoneman 1994a.
46. Printed in Stoneman 1994a.
47. Aristotle observes that the suppression of appetite produces self-control, not virtue (*EN* 1188b28–33, 1119b15–16); one must learn to *manage* appetite). Nussbaum 1994, 82.
48. This brilliant writer was the son of Thomas Mann, who emigrated from Germany in 1933 and took his own life in 1949.

Chapter 6. From the Heights of the Air to the Depths of the Sea: Alexander as Inventor and Sage

1. See van Bekkum 1992, 11–12; Schmidt 1995, 10; Bialik and Ravnitzky 1992, 759.4.
2. The same form of aphorism appears at III. 35 (gamma): 'if Philo, the friend of the king, were to die, the king would find another Philo for a friend; but if something untoward were to happen to Alexander, the whole world would be plunged into grief'. See also Plutarch, *Life* 42.8.
3. Ziegler 1998, Dahmen 2007, 124–6.
4. Polyaenus 4.19 and Frontinus 2.4.1: Papirius Cursor and dust; Polyaenus excerpt. 15.6, 15.9 (dust), 15.5 (fires); Frontinus 4.7.20: Ptolemy versus Perdiccas; Plutarch, *Eumenes* 15.5.–6 (fires); and compare Alexander's tactics at the Hydaspes, Arr. *Anab.* 5.10, also Hdt. 4.135, Polyb. 3.93.
5. Legend also tells of Semiramis' use of dummy elephants: DS 2.16.9, 19.2.
6. Arr. *Anab.* 2.25.2–3, Plut. *Life of Alex.* 29. 8–9, Curt. 4.11, DS 17.54.1–5. The Byzantine poem flattens the point: 'You are right, Parmenio, so would I'; cf. the Armenian version, Wolohojian 1969, 191.
7. Stoneman 1995b.
8. See Chapter 3, n.32.
9. Procopius, *Bell. Vandal.* 1.7.7–10.
10. It is also a topic of encomium: Menander Rhetor 87.
11. See Chapter 3, p. 56.
12. Possibly of the second century AD: see the edition of Perry 1952; translations in Sir Roger L'Estrange's version of Aesop's *Fables* (1692) and in Wills 1997, 10–215. See Stoneman 1992b, 108–9. The work has many affinities with the *Alexander Romance*.
13. Δ is the Greek symbol for 4, *tessara*.
14. Stoneman 1995b.
15. Maspero, 1967, 290–303). See Stoneman 1992b.
16. A similar story is told of Croesus' escape from the anger of Cambyses in Herodotus 3.36.

17. West 1969, 113–34. On Ahiqar see Meissner 1894b and 1917; Conybeare, Harris and Lewis 1913. The story was well-known to fifth-century Greeks, for Democritus studied it (68B 299DK), as did Theophrastus later (DL 5.50), and to the Jews of fifth-century Egypt, where it appears in the Aramaic Elephantine papyri (Cowley 1923). It is also in the Book of Tobit (14.10–11). See further Wilsdorf 1991, Luzzatto 1992.

18. Pal. Talmud Avodah Zarah 3.1.42c; Midrash Bamidbar Rabba 13.14; Pirqe d'rabbi Elieser 11. See *Der Born Judas* III. 306; Gaster, *Exempla of the Rabbis* no. 5, pp. 52 and 186; Donath 1873. See Chapter 3 n. 48.

19. An interesting variant in Midrash Tehillim b93.6 tells the same story of the Emperor Hadrian.

20. Hill and al-Hassan 1986, 244–5.

21. Schmidt 1995, 162; Thorndike 1922–23, 654–5.

22. Ross 1967; *Annolied*, ed. Nellmann 1972, strophe 14.

23. *De naturis rerum* II.21; Thorndike 1922–23, 263.

24. Cf. Levi 1886.

25. Van Bekkum 1992, 15.

26. Schmidt 1995. See also Settis-Frugoni 1973; Jouanno 2002, 273–6.

27. Avodah Zarah III. 1.42c; see van Bekkum 1992, 11–12; Schmidt 1995, 10.

28. The scene is also widely known in Byzantine art (Gleixner 1961, 120ff.), appearing on stone reliefs (see Plate 39), textiles, bronze tableware (a twelfth-century dish in the Hermitage collection, inv. w 1501: see *The Road to Byzantium* (exhibition catalogue) 2006, 114 and 169) and so on. Given the Greek influence on south-eastern Italy, the image may have become familiar through this route also.

29. For a discussion of such interpretations see Stoneman 1992b.

30. See n. 17 above.

31. Cowley 1923. It is also alluded to in the Book of Tobit, 14.10–11.

32. E.g. New York Public Library, Spencer Indo-Pers. MS 13 f. 98v, Spencer Pers. MS 62 f. 131v, M & A Pers. MS 2, f. 78, Spencer Indo-Pers. MS 40, f. 82; Chester Beatty Library, Persian Cat. 157, f. 81b.

33. Irwin 1994, 21–2.

34. Rufinus, *PL* 21, 295. See Chapter 3, n. 38. Pliny, *NH* 34.42 (148): 'the architect Timochares had begun to use lodestone for constructing the vaulting in the Temple of Arsinoe at Alexandria, so that the iron statue contained in it might have the appearance of being suspended in mid air; but the project was interrupted by his own death and that of King Ptolemy who had ordered the work to be done in honour of his sister'.

35. Hasluck 1929, 17 n. Also Digenis Akritas I. 101 on the floating stone in a mosque in Palermo.

36. Settis-Frugoni 1973.

37. Gianfreda 1995.

38. Smalley 1952.

39. Mulder-Bakker 1983, 183–240.

40. See Chapter 11.

41. Merzdorf 1870.

42. Farmer 1926, and 1931, 79, 119ff., with illustration p. 134.

43. Palestinian Talmud *Baba Mezia* (ed. Krotoschin 1866) II.5.8c; also in Bialik and Ravnitzky 1992, 167.35: see Kazis 1962, 20–22, Stoneman 1994d. Al-Ghazzali (Bagley 1964, 61) transfers the story to the Persian legendary hero Chosrow Anushirvan.

44. Two more versions of the story appear in Philostr. *Vit. Ap. Ty.* 3. 39 and 6. 39, where it is Apollonius' wisdom that resolves the conundrum.

45. Brocker 1966, esp. 82–128.

46. Al-Nadim 1970, 737, 853; Young, Latham and Serjeant 1990, 292.

47. Gutas 1975.

48. Rosenthal 1975, 38, 226.

49. Al-Nadim 1970; cf. Brocker 1966, 117.

50. Foerster (1888), 22.

51. Alexander also appears in the preface to one sixteenth-century Latin manuscript of the *Kyranides*, as the author of a book on the seven herbs and seven planets. (The *Kyranides* was purportedly a Greek translation of an Arabic work 'delivering not only the Naturall but Magicall propriety of things, a work as full of vanity as variety, containing many relations, whose invention is as difficult as their beliefs, and their experiments sometimes as hard as either' – Sir Thomas Browne, *Pseudodoxia Epidemica* I. 8; see Thorndike 1922–23, 229–33.).

52. Ruska 1912. Klein-Franke 1970. See also Thorndike 1922–23, 260–3.

53. Other writings on magical stones were, in late antiquity, attributed by Greek and Roman writers to the legendary Persian Magus Astrampsychos, who was also the author of the *Oracle of Pythagoras* (there are papyri from the third century AD onwards), which Alexander is supoposed to have taken with him to help him conquer the world. See Astrampsychos, ed. Brodersen 2006, 7–9.

54. Williams 2003, 304.

55. Halleux and Schamp 1985 collect the texts.

56. Paras 36, 41, 42, 98, 114, 159, 167, 174: 'On Mt Tmolus it is said that a stone is produced like pumice-stone, which changes its colour four times in the day; and that it is seen only by maidens who have not yet attained to years of discretion.' Much information of this kind, as well as more rational material, is absorbed into Books 36 and 37 of Pliny's *Natural History*.

57. Gutzwiller 2005, Petrain 2005.

58. See *Paradoxographorum graecorum reliquiae*, ed. A. Giannini (Milan 1965); Phlegon, ed. Hansen 1996.

59. Georgius Monachus I. 19.

60. Peter the Deacon (1107–40) said in his autobiography that he translated Evax/Damigeron; but how? He did not know Greek. The book of Damigeron was the main model for Marbod of Rennes' poem, though it had already been interpolated with parts of the Pseudo-Aristotle in some MSS (Halleux and Schamp 1985, 211ff.).

61. Tert., *De anima* lvii, 1; Halleux and Schamp 1985, 225.

62. Mas'udi has another story about Alexander and gems. He tells us that the precious stones found around the Pharos are the remains of his drinking cups, thrown into the sea by his mother when he died: *Meadows of Gold* 2007, 46.

63. It has an ancestor in the similar story in Herodotus 3.111. See p. 85 above.

64. It is the *pantarbe* stone of Ctesias, *Ind.* 2 and Philostratus, *Vit. Ap. Ty.* 3.46. Chapter 4 n. 15.

65. Cf. Ps.-Arist. *De mirab. auscult.* 166 on the stone that silences dogs.

66. The story seems to be an outgrowth of that in the *Romance*, II. 39 and 41, where a wise old man advises Alexander's men to pick up anything they find on the ground in the Land of Darkness. When they return to the light, these turn out to be lumps of gold and pearls. 'Then the others regretted that they had not brought back more, or in some cases had brought nothing.'

67. Norris 1972, 52–3. See also Marin 1991.

68. Alexander's sojourn in the Sahara resulted in his fathering the dynasty of the Cissés of Wagadou (Ghana): Niane 1965, 32, 35, 82ff. It was prophesied that the hero Sundiata would exceed Alexander's greatness, ibid. 37.

69. Budge 1896, 437–553 = Budge 1933, 236–56; the tale occurs at pp. 457–62/240–4.

70. An aquatic version of the story of the City of Brass is recounted in Buschor 1944: gathered in Pomerania, of all places, it tells how the captain of a ship that has lost its way follows a stork in the hope of reaching land. Eventually the ship comes in sight of an island entirely surrounded by a high wall. The captain drops anchor, and sends one of his men to spy out the land: he scales the wall, looks over – and, with a great leap,

vanishes from sight. A second emissary suffers the same fate. When the third climbs up, his companions hold on to his feet and drag him back after he has looked over. For three days he cannot speak. Eventually he finds his voice and announces that behind the wall lies Paradise, and there he had seen angels singing and playing music.

71. See n. 34 above.
72. Lane 1857–9, I. 161 with note 72 on p. 217; Lane says that it comes from Qazvini, but I have not been able to trace it there.
73. Procopius, *Pers.* 1.19 already knew that this was untrue: Hourani 1995, 95.
74. Marco Polo 1871, 117.
75. Mandeville 1949, Chs 18 and 30: see Letts 78 and 84, noting that the source may also be Vincent of Beauvais 8. 21.
76. Pritchett 1991, 109–16.

Chapter 7. Amazons, Mermaids and Wilting Maidens

1. Stephens and Winkler 1995, 23ff. and 246ff.
2. *The Persian Boy* (1922).
3. Plut. *Alex.* 22.
4. Hdt. 4.110–17, DS 2.45.–6, also e.g. Pherecrates, *FGrH* 3F15, Aesch. *PV* 723–5. The most systematic modern survey of their 'ethnography' is Carlier 1979; see also Blok 1995 and Dowden 1997.
5. Tyrrell 1984; Hall 1989, 53; Du Bois 1982.
6. Arr., *Anab.* 4.15.4. Pharasmanes' name became attached to a work on the wonders of the east (Pharasmanes ed. Lecouteux 1979), which was probably written in the reign of Trajan, but which contains no mention of Amazons.
7. DS 17.77, Curt. 6.5.24–32, Justin 12.3.5ff., Strabo 11.5.1 and the lost authors cited by Plutarch, 46.
8. The story is perhaps modelled on the historical encounter with Cleophis in Swat, Curt. 8.10.22.
9. Wilde 1999; Blok 1995, 93–104.
10. Curt. 8.1.7–10, cf. Arr. *Anab.* 4.15.1–6 (misattributed to Bactra); Holt 2005, 83.
11. Hisuan Tsang, a Chinese traveller in India in AD 630–44, also encountered a 'kingdom of women of the West' on an island to the south-west of Fu-Lin. 'The king of Fu-Lin sends them every year men to unite with them, but if they give birth to male children the custom of the country does not permit them to bring them up.' See S. Levi 1936. Hisuan Tsang seems to have been reading the Greek sources!
12. The etymology *a-* = 'without', *mazos* = 'breast' is a false one.
13. Slessarev 1959, 70, Silverberg 1972, 143ff., 153.
14. Kleinbaum 1983, 22 and 51–8.
15. Adam of Bremen 1959 III. xvi (15).
16. Columbus 1990, 183 and 201; Kleinbaum 1983, 104.
17. Kleinbaum 1983, 118–21.
18. 1614, IV 2. xv.
19. Ralegh, ed. Whitehead 1997, 146. Apparently these 'women alone' or 'women without men' really existed, though the sharing of offspring may be an invention: Whitehead ibid., 94–7. The Amazons had perhaps migrated to South America after the Trojan War, according to Andre Thevet's *New Founde Worlde* of 1568: Kleinbaum 1983, 112.
20. Moennig 1992.
21. Veloudis 1968, 169, 176, 292. The wish to add to the erotic aspect of Alexander seems also to lie behind his appearance a few years ago in the Doonesbury cartoon strip, where Boopsie, a Hollywood starlet with paranormal tendencies, remarks to a companion, 'Alexander the Great once told me that for years after the battle of Issus he

used to have terrible nightmares.' Her companion replies, 'Damn, you're crazy, girl!' and Boopsie responds 'I know, Alex used to tease me about it.'

22. The portrait motif occurs in a number of stories from later antiquity: one appears in the Byzantine *Life* of Irene, Abbess of Chrysobalantion, and yet another in the *Acts of Silvester*, where Peter and Paul are recognised by comparing them with their icons. It is also found in the Ethiopian *Kebra Nagast*, where Sheba shows Menedik his father in a mirror. As she is here given the name Makeda (?= Macedonian) one wonders if there is any influence from the *Alexander Romance*, which was known in Ethiopia from an early date, though the MS of the Ethiopian version is of the fourteenth century AD.

The story of Candace, and the portrait motif, is told twice in the late thirteenth- century Arabic *Livre des ruses* (Khawan 1976, 225ff. and 309ff. from Ibn al-Muqaffa'): the second time, she has ten cupboards with ten portraits, and Alexander is accompanied by Khidr.

23. Van Thiel 1959, 58.27; Trumpf 1966.
24. Pennachietti 2000; Jouanno 2002, 322–4; cf. Qur'ān 18.44 and W.M. Watt in Pritchard 1974. The motif is borrowed by Tabari, ed. Zotenberg 1867 (760), in his account of Zenobia revealing herself to Jadhima: Stoneman 1992a, 157.
25. This convergence of Alexander and Solomon, which we have encountered elsewhere, seems to occur because in Islam these two are the world conquerors who are believers (where Nimrud and Nebuchadnezzar are the unbelievers). Lassner 1993, 239–450 n.11.
26. On Meroe, see above all Török 1988, 107–341. Still useful is Shinnie 1967. See also Zach 1992 and Burstein 2001. Brief illustrated surveys are offered in two exhibition catalogues: Priese 1992–93 and Haynes 1992. The ancient sources are collected at *FGrH* 111C.666–73 and in Eide, Hägg and Török 1994–98.
27. There are some suspect references to works of Democritus dealing with Meroe (DK 68(55)A33 and B299a). Diogenes Laertius (9.35) says that Democritus visited Persia, the Chaldaeans, the Red Sea and 'some say' the gymnosophists in India, and Ethiopia.
28. Török 1988, 129ff., 269, 272.
29. *FGrH* 90F103m with IIC Komm. 255f. Török 1988, 136. Cf. Zach 1992, who concludes that the term *kntkj* in Egyptian hieroglyphs, *ktke* in Meroitic – should be interpreted 'she who holds the office of sister'. Török 1988, 161 interprets it as 'wife of the king', which comes to much the same thing.
30. The treatment reflects contemporary conditions, not ancient ones: Bowersock 1994, 50.
31. M.R. James, *The Apocryphal New Testament* (Oxford 1924), 466.
32. The information comes from John Lydus (*De mens*, 4.107), quoting a lost passage of Seneca's *Natural Questions*. Cf. Lucan 10. 272–5. See Burstein 1976.
33. But see Graf 1993, where he discusses sun-cities as an element of utopian writing of the period.
34. For a possible source for the *katabasis* episode see Pfister 1915/1976.
35. See Gleixner 1961.
36. Veloudis 1968 and 1969. The latter abridgement of his thesis also forms the basis of his introduction (in modern Greek) to *Diegesis Alexandrou tou Makedonos* (Veloudis 1977/1989).
37. Moennig 1993.
38. Grottaferrata v. 2190–452: cf. Mavrocordato's edition, *Digenis Akritas* 1956, 2229–384: Veloudis 1969, 268.
39. Konstantinopoulos 1983, II. 22.19.
40. Ctesias, *FGrH* 681, *ap.* DS 2, 1–28. The main elements reappear in the Byzantine historian Agathias, 2.18.4–5, 24.2–3. 25.4–5.
41. Eilers 1971.
42. Eddy 1961,121ff.; Braun 1938, 13–18.
43. This becomes the standard view: cf. Agathias 2.25.4–5. It also occurs in Orosius and other world histories.
44. For Ninus, see Stephens and Winkler 1995, 23–71.

45. Brock 1989, 268 ff. (269).
46. Cizek 1978, 189–211 (199).
47. Moennig 2004. The contents were first described and summarised by Christos I. Dimitroulopolos 1989, and 1995/1999; cf. Veloudis 1968, 256.
48. Some other examples are mentioned by Gikas 1973.
49. The story is probably of Persian origin, appearing in the tale of the Red Dome in Nizami's *Haft Paykar*, and some other works discussed by Moennig 2004. The direct source of *Turandot* is 'Calaf and the Princess of China' in the *1001 Days*. See also Aarne and Thompson 1961, 851 on the story-pattern of overcoming trials to win a woman.
50. Carner 1984, 7–18; Irwin 1994, 101.
51. Lappas 1993, 60–61; cf. 35, where Fatmé poses riddles to Karagiozis. Stephanides 1980 does not include this passage.
52. Leigh Fermor 1958, 187; N. G. Politis 1904, nos 551, 552.
53. Stratis Myrivilis, *The Mermaid Madonna* (1955); Elias Venezis, *Beyond the Aegean*, tr. E.D. Scott-Kilvert 1956, 92–4. On the iconography of the two-tailed mermaid see Politis 1904, 1166–95.
54. Dawkins 1955, 5.
55. Lawson 1964, 185; see further Dawkins 1937 and 1955, and Romaios 1973, 104–9.
56. Reinink 1990.
57. The episode derives from the experience on the Indus where the army marches at night because of the heat (Curt. 9.4.18, Str. 15.2.6, Arr. *Anab.* 6.23.1, 25.3). Mandeville, *Travels* ch. 28, has a new tale about the Land of Darkness: God sent it to cover Shapur in Abasgia [Abkhazia] and prevent him from reaching Paradise. See also Ramayana IV. 42.
58. Acts of Peter, ch. 13. But it is also in Herodotus 9.120. Stoneman 1992b, 98–100.
59. Alexiou 1974, 75; Payne 1991, 176–81.
60. Sometimes it is a sea-squill (Dawkins 1937, 184), which is called 'immortal'. In a version from Armenia, Alexander *makes* the Water of Life from onion seeds.
61. Megas 1970, 200–2; Dawkins 1937, 183–4.
62. But she is his lover in Flecker's poem and also in a story from Samsun (Dawkins 1933, 186), where it is her curiosity that causes her to drink it all up.
63. Weever 1990.
64. The Flower Maidens of *Parsifal* seem to be a combination of the ones from the Alexander legend with Blanchefleur and her castle in Chrétien de Troyes.
65. Lamprecht, ed. Ruttmann 1974, 5157–358. See Chapter 11 and appendix.
66. It is also in the Syriac and Armenian, but has evidently dropped out of A.
67. Patch 1970, 282ff.

Chapter 8. The Search for Immortality

1. Ehrenberg 1938; Seibert 1972, 183–6. Curtius' term is *ingens cupido*.
2. Ael. *VH* 2.19, Plut. *Mor.* 219E.
3. Following the translation of Dalley 1989.
4. Meissner 1894b. See also Wheeler 1998, which takes no account of Stoneman 1992b.
5. Millet 1923; Dalley 1989, 189; Stoneman 1992b.
6. Reinink 1990.
7. Ctesias, *FG&H*, F47a,b; Pliny, *NH* 31.21, Karttunen 1989, 186ff.
8. Uttarakuru enters consciousness in the fabulous people, the classical Attacorae, mentioned by Pliny *NH* 6.20.55. See Chapter 5 n. 27.
9. Ctes., at *FG&H*, F45 ke = Val. Max. 8.13 ext. 5.
10. Slessarev 1959, 72.
11. Thomson, *Motif Index*, II. 185; Olschki 1941.
12. A good short survey of the main topics is Abel 1955.

13. The story recurs, apparently as an emblem of Christ's resurrection, in the Greek Acts of Peter, written not later than AD 200. 'Peter turned and saw a herring hung in a window, and took it and said to the people: If ye now see this swimming in the water like a fish, will ye be able to believe in him whom I preach? And they said with one voice: Verily we will believe thee. Then he said – now there was a bath for swimming at hand: In thy name, O Jesu Christ . . . . in the sight of these live and swim like a fish. And all the people saw the fish swimming, and it did not do so at that hour only . . . and seeing this, many followed Peter and believed in the Lord' (ch. 13, transl. M.R. James, Oxford 1924, 316).

14. Budge 1889, 172–4.

15. Khidr's name, 'the green one', was connected by Friedländer 1913 with the similarly named Greek hero Glaucus (sea-green), a fisherman who one day observed his catch of fish, as they lay expiring on the shore, bite into a certain herb that grew there and immediately return to life and leap back into the water. Glaucus, following suit, was transformed into a sea demon and became the patron of fisherfolk and seafarers. Ovid, *Metamorphoses* 13.898–14.69.

Pleij 2001, 144 refers to a converse tale of Alexander in which fish cook themselves for him as he journeys closer to Paradise, but I have not been able to trace this text, unless he is thinking of Tamid 32a–b where Alexander 'washes salt fish in water and the sweet smell tells him it comes from Eden': Bialik and Ravnitzky 1992, 168.

16. Wheeler 1998 argues that it was 'the commentators' who caused the identification of Dhu'l-qarnain with Alexander in the first place, and that it is baseless. In Tabari (d. 923) the two have been fully separated, and Tabari's account of Alexander follows the *Romance* while omitting the Qur'ānic episodes: Zuwiyya 2001, 8–9. Al-Tha'alabi (d. 1036), however, writes as if the two were identical.

17. Stewart 1993, 318–19, Plates 117–22; Anderson 1927; Dahmen 2007, 42, 63.

18. For a fuller discussion see Stoneman 2003a and the literature cited there, esp. Brocker 1966, 84ff., Macuch 1991. Another brief but informative survey is Zuwiyya 2001.

19. Translation in Budge 1896 and 1933. See Weymann 1901. Anderson 1927 and Norris 1972, 70 repeat the view that it must have an Arabic original. In the main it follows the outline of the Greek and Syriac versions: 1. Birth, 2–7 Darius, 8 Porus, 9 The Brahmans, 10 Letter to Aristotle, 11 Candace and the Amazons; from here on it includes the Wall against the Unclean Nations, the Land of Darkness, the events in Babylon, and the letters of consolation, but *not* the *Sayings of the Philosophers* familiar from many Arabic texts.

20. The point is also made by Gero 1993, 5; Southgate 1978; Frye 1985. An exception is the work discussed by Grignaschi 1993, 228.

21. Macuch 1991, 262–3.

22. Zuwiyya 2001, 9–10 confidently states that none could ever have existed because it would have contradicted Qur'ān 18.83–98. Cf. Macuch 1991, who points out that only a Christian Arab could have made a straight translation of the Greek–Syriac original.

23. O'Leary 1949; Gutas 1998.

24. Samir 1998, 242.

25. Anderson 1927; Garcia Gomez 1929; Doufikar-Aerts 2000, 38.

26. Spanish written in Arabic letters.

27. Nykl 1929: in this Alexander is a militant *mujahid*.

28. The same is true of the text by Ibn Suweidan of 1666, which is a translation of the Byzantine prose version: Trumpf 1974, Lolos 1983, Konstantinopoulos 1983; Samir 1998, 243. Another Arabic tale of Alexander is found in Istanbul, MS Aya Sofia 3003, probably from the thirteenth century (the actual MS is dated AH 871, AD 1446). There is a detailed summary in Doufikar-Aerts 2003b, 256–320. Interestingly, it begins with the Darab story from the Persian version. In it Iskander (as he is here called) bridges the Strait of Gibraltar and undertakes the conversion of Andalusia, which was conquered by the Arabs in the early eighth century. This text is closely related to Istanbul MS Aya Sofia 1466, which was the direct source of the Malay *Romance of Alexander*, which belongs to

the sixteenth century: van Leeuwen 1937 is a translation. See Winstedt 1940, 63–5; also Boyle 1977.

29. Abbott 1957 thought that 'Umara was a translation from the Greek: she had not looked at the Greek. Samir 1998 ends in aporia. For some other straws in the wind see Stoneman 2003a, 10.

30. Weymann 1901.

31. Doufikar-Aerts 2003a. Another scrap is an account of Alexander's city-foundations by Ibn al-Fatik, which seems to derive from the Syriac. Could it be another fragment of the same Arabic translation? See Bulgakov 1965.

32. Mubaššir ed. Meissner 1895.

33. Doufikar-Aerts 2003b; the key discussion is that on pp. 50–65, of the MS of the scribe Quzman, Paris BN 3687. See also Doufikar-Aerts 2003a. Grignaschi 1967 hypothesised *another* Arabic (originally Greek) epistolary romance, of which the *Secret of Secrets* would have been the final chapter. Another chapter might be Aristotle's advice to Alexander on the administration of empire, again preserved in Arabic: Plezia 1971.

34. On 20 February 1871 William Beckford wrote from Paris: 'This is the land of oriental literature and I am once more running over my favourite poems: the expedition of Alexander in search of the Fountain of Immortality and the affecting tale of Mejnun and Leilah.' He was presumably reading Firdausi and Nizami.

35. BM Add. MS 5928; see Friedländer 1913; the story is told in similar form in MS Aya Sofya 3003: see n. 28 above. For further discussion of the Arab texts see Stoneman 2003a. Two further similar texts have been published by Zuwiyya 2001.

36. The story influenced a Romanian folk-tale about the alleged custom of the killing of the Khazar kings. See Gaster 1919. In this story a son hides his father in a cellar to prevent his killing (like in the Aesop story), and sets off to kill a monster. His father advises him to 'kill a foal and bury it at the mouth of the monster's cave; thus the mare will lead him back to safety'. When the hero emerges safe at the end of his mission, he reveals to his friends his secret: that he had not killed his father but taken advice from him. At this proof of the superior wisdom of the old, the Khazars abandon their distasteful custom. The story is also in Marco Polo, *Travels* III. 45. The origin may be Persian: Aelian *NA* 6. 48.

37. It is the *pantarbe* stone of Philostr. *Vit. Ap. Ty.* 3.46: cf. Chapter 7, n. 24 and Chapter 4, n. 15. But the lantern stone used by Alexander in the Land of Darkness in *AR* III. 41 gamma is found in the belly of a fish.

38. Firdausi, transl. Davis 2004, III, 99. Cf. Mango 1955, 43.

39. See Chapter 6, n. 44.

40. See Nagel 1978. Also Doufikar-Aerts 1994, 335. A fuller summary of the story in Stoneman 2003a.

41. For this identification to work, as early scholars pointed out, Dhu'l-qarnain would have had to live some 1,600 years. Zuwiyya 2001, 8.

42. I am grateful to Julia Bray for allowing me to see her translation of the relevant portion of al-Tha'alabi. Interestingly, it also contains the story that Alexander burnt the books of Zoroaster.

43. It is translated by E.W. Lane in his edition of *The Thousand and One Nights* (1857/1979), II. 303–8. Lane transliterates the name as Sheddad, but Shaddad seems now to be current. His story begins at Qur'ān 89. 5–7, and is also told by Tabari (ed. Zotenberg 1867, I. 53–4).

44. Lane 1857/1979, II. 306.

45. Mas'udi 1965, II. 421, vol. 2. 313. A brief account of the magic city that appears and disappears, until it is replaced by the Alhambra itself, is given by Washington Irving, *The Alhambra* (1860), 182–9. Aben Habuz, king of Granada, is about to enter the magic city created by his private astrologer, but when he tries to cheat the latter of his reward, both city and astrologer disappear. 'Either the boasted Elysium was hidden from sight by

enchantment, or it was a mere fable of the astrologer . . . . The Alhambra has been built on the eventful mountain, and in some measure realizes the fabled delights of the Garden of Iram.'

46. Nizami, transl. Bürgel 1991, 504–7.
47. In Jami's Alexander Romance (Chapter 2, pp. 38–9) the Khaqan of India sends Iskandar a girl, a servant and a suit of clothes and a tray of food, with the admonition that if he conquered the whole world he could not enjoy more than this. Mango 127. Jami's work is a continuation of Nizami with a predominantly moralising and homiletic tone.
48. See in general Delumeau 1995, esp. ch. 3 (the French edition (Delumeau 1992) also includes many illustrations) and Tardiola 1993. Of the older literature, Graf 1878 and Ringbom 1958 may be singled out. See also Chapter 4, p. 81–3.
49. Anderson 1932, 62.
50. Scafi 2006 is an exhaustive and impressive discussion of ideas about the location of Paradise from Genesis to modern times.
51. J.L. Borges plays with this tradition in his story, 'The Immortal', where the City of the Immortals lies beyond the Ganges (Borges 1998, 3–19).
52. For bibliography see Chapter 4, n. 47.
53. The instruction from flying creatures to Alexander to turn back was common knowledge by the first century AD; Seneca *Suas* 1.2, schol. Luc. *Phars* 3.233. This admonition is located on the Indus by the Ravennas 1.5ff. (Beazley 1949, 310).
54. Scafi 2006, 160 ff.
55. *Topographia Christiana*, ed. in 3 vols by W. Wolska-Conus, Cosmas 1968–73. See also Wolska 1962.
56. Cosmas, transl. McCrindle 1897. It is thus particularly piquant that in Umberto Eco's *Baudolino* (2002, 326 ff.) the travellers make use of the map of Cosmas to follow in the footsteps of Zosimus towards Paradise.
57. Scafi 2006, 179, 193.
58. Ibid., ch. 8. Thomas Malory in the late fifteenth century (*Morte d'Arthur*, V.x) took it for granted that Paradise could be reached: Sir Piramus and Sir Gawaine are severely wounded in battle. 'And Piramus took from his page a phial full of the four waters that come out of Paradise, and with a certain balm anointed their wounds, and washed them with that water, and within an hour they were both as whole as ever they were.'
59. Tamid B1 32. See Hartmann 1922.
60. Ed. Hilka 1935. Translation in Stoneman 1994a.
61. The mossy walls are also mentioned in Chaucer's *Parlement of Foules* 121.
62. Proverbs 27.20: 'Hell and destruction are never full: so the eyes of man are never satisfied.'
63. See Chapter 12.
64. Lascelles 1936, cf. Pleij 2001, 255ff. But it is not in the Greek tradition: it is absent, for example, from the *Phyllada*.
65. Stoneman 1994a, 104.
66. Tardiola 1993, 55–77; see also in general Pleij 2001, ch. 25.
67. O'Meara 1976.
68. Silverberg 1972, 221; he goes on to mention some other such tales, including that of the Infante Dom Pedro.
69. Columbus 1930–33, II. 38, quoted in Scafi 2006, 241.

Chapter 9. The Unclean Nations and the End of Time

1. Stephens 2003, 176, 178.
2. On the identity of the odontotyrannus, 'tooth-tyrant', see Goossens 1927–28.
3. There is a similar passage in Hanno's account of his voyage around West Africa in about 480 BC (*Periplous* 56r, 90ff.): 'In this bay was an island . . . filled with wild savages. The

biggest number of them were females, with hairy bodies, which our interpreters called "gorillas" . . . . We caught three females who bit and scratched their captors and did not want to follow them. So we had to kill them and flayed them and we brought their skins to Carthage.'

4. Cizek 1981.

5. Prachyaka, i.e. India. Julius Valerius I. 32 already has a dragon fight during the foundation of Alexandria.

6. The mixture resembles that used by Bellerophon to kill the Chimaera.

7. Firdausi, transl. Davis 2004, 93ff.; X. 30 in the Warners' translation.

8. *O Megalexandros kai to katarato fidhi*. See Stephanidis 1980, 16–18. In general, Lappas 1993.

9. Ps.-Callisthenes, III. 26A (gamma). The story is also in the Byzantine poem (5712–99), which otherwise largely follows beta. On the whole episode see Anderson 1932.

10. The name is certainly a corruption of Bersilae, the name of a Khazar people: Moravčsik 1958, 89.

11. On the location see Anderson 1928b and the other articles cited in Chapter 4 n. 38.

12. *Asynchyton*. On the definition of this mysterious substance, see Aerts 1996a, and the same scholar's note on Ps.-Methodius in Pseudo-Methodius 1998, II. 22–3. The word *synchytike* appears in Ps.-Maximus Confessor, *Loci Communes* 80.151c (*PG* 91), meaning 'complete union'. Aethicus 127.4 says that *asynchyton* is used for caulking ships. I have wondered if there could be a connection with the expression used to describe the magnet, *symphytos dynamis*, meaning something like 'the power to grow together'.

13. The list takes a different form in the Ethiopic *Romance* (Budge 1896, 138), where the names are Arabic in form, and the characters' habits are even more repulsive: their women have only a single breast and carry knives; they wear skins and eat their food raw, they live in tents; and when they go to war they strip naked a pregnant woman and place her before a fire until the child in her womb is roasted; then they rip out the child, boil it in a pan and sprinkle the flesh over their weapons of war to make themselves invincible. Such are these servants of Satan.

14. Merzdorf 1870. I have examined a number of the Bibles in the Koninklijke Bibliothek in the Hague, 78D38II (1425), 128C2 (1450), and the Pierpont Morgan Library, New York, M268 (fifteenth century). The source is the Seelentrost Alexander, a text deriving directly from Leo: Pfister 1913, 29.

15. The most comprehensive study is Anderson 1932; see also Alexander 1985, 185–92, and Stoneman 1994c.

16. The Breasts of the North may have their origin in Midrash Rabbah: see Anderson 1932, 43, who interprets the episode as Jewish through and through.

17. For Josephus, *AJ* 1.6.1, they are the Scythians.

18. Commodian 1877, 802–5. Also Godfrey of Viterbo 16.24; Higden, *Polychronicon* 1.17.

19. Anderson 1932, 63; he gives a complete list at 12 ff.

20. Boek van de Wraak, *Gods* 1994.

21. English translations in Budge 1889 (repr. Amsterdam 1976), 144–58, 163–200. Edition of the Syriac text of the poem, with commentary, by G.J. Reinink: Pseudo-Methodius 1993; of the Greek text, by Lolos: Pseudo-Methodius 1976 and 1983.

22. Kaegi 1992, 205–30; G.J. Reinink, in Pseudo-Methodius 1993; Aerts and Kortekaas in Methodius 1998; Palmer 1993.

23. Cf. Kaegi 1992, 286; Gero 1993, 7.

24. Kaegi 1992, 213–15.

25. 'Sebeos', 1999, ch. 47, sect. 161–2.

26. Its historical structure derives from a Syriac work known as the Cave of Treasures: see Pseudo-Methodius 1993, vi, and index, s.v. *Schätzhöhle*. The parts about Alexander derive, as we have seen, from the Syriac Alexander texts with, apparently, some admixture of Ethiopian tradition; and some of the material reappears in another Syriac work

of the eighth century, the *Chronicle* of Ps.-Dionysius of Tel-Mahre: Sackur 1898, Palmer 1993; Witakowski 1987; also Hedenskog 1868.

27. See Kmosko 1931, 291; Alexander 1985, 151–84, Tanner 1993, 120–8.
28. Aethicus Ister 1993, 137ff.
29. Robert Lerner in McGinn 1999, 326ff.; for the English translations, Bunt 1993; D'Evelyn 1918.
30. Whealey 1946.
31. See the edition by Giuseppe Frasson, with Latin translation of the Armenian text, Venice 1976.
32. Dr Chanca, in Columbus 1930–33, I. 70.
33. Norris 1983, 253 incorrectly says that it is taken from the Pseudo-Callisthenes.
34. At the same date, this adventure is mentioned by Hassan ibn Thabit, 'who was contemporary with Muhammad, to whose cause he devoted what poetical talent he possessed': Nicholson 1907, 18.
35. Tabari, *Chronique*, ed. Zotenberg 1867, part I, ch. 23 (this is not in Perlman's 1987 translation of Tabari, but is from a Persian version of *c.* AD 963 containing much extra material from the Old and New Testaments and antiquity); see Bousset 1896, 116ff.
36. *Prairies d'Or* III. 66–7; Lewis 1982, 139.
37. Mercator sees them as aerial trumpets guarding the entrance to Tartarus: Anderson 1932, 83ff., 101, 103.
38. Kampers 1901; Alexander 1985, esp. 151–84.
39. Mulder-Bakker 1983, 236; Tanner 1993, ch. 6.
40. Bousset 1896, 63.
41. Gaster 1924, 1.
42. Cohn 1961 and 1993.
43. McGinn 1994.
44. Potter 1990, 140; cf. Potter 1994.
45. Cameron 1991, 119; cf. 225 on the use of words and images to articulate the vision.
46. Ed. Prinz 1993, 120, 137, 158–60, 168.
47. See pp. 79–81 above and bibliography cited there, n. 47.
48. See pp. 77–8. W. Freygang, *Letters from the Caucasus and Georgia* (1823), 141 describes the wall, as does Dr Reineggs, *Description of Mount Caucasus* (1807), I. 128–38. See especially 135–7: 'Those walls [of Derbend] rise out of the sea, and run a considerable distance over its rocky bed, before they reach the land; from whence they continue, in a western direction, of alternate thickness, over a steep high ridge of mountains; and almost at the top unite with other walls, where stands the real fortress . . . . A single, large, antique iron gate, forms the only ingress at present, through both walls, from the north and south sides; and hence has properly arisen the denomination Porta Ferrea [i.e, in Turkish, Demir Kapi]. It is everywhere known by that name, and the Turks particularly think of it with dread; because, according to an old prophecy, they may look upon the destruction of their empire as certain, as soon as a hostile infidel nation, with yellow faces, penetrated into their territory by that passage.'
49. Another Wall of Alexander, east of the Caspian, is mentioned by Christina Dodwell, *A Traveller on Horseback in Eastern Turkey and Iran* (1987), 14.
50. There is a synoptic treatment of the subject of Alexander's wall in the remarkable book of Demetrios Gobdelas 1822 (in Greek), 68–74.
51. Gobeldas 1822, 69.
52. Gibbon 1909, IV 278.
53. J.L. Borges' story 'Averroes' Search' (Borges 1998, 73) suggests an even earlier interest!
54. Norris 1983, 254. He also visited the Cave of the Darkness of the Seven Sleepers: Qur'ān 18.5–20.
55. Wilson 1922, recast in French in Miquel 1975, II, 498. Also told in Tha'alabi 366 (Chapter 8, n. 42).

56. This was to be expected, since Alexander too had reached the regions of Gog and Magog through the vicinity of the Foetid Sea, a peculiarly Arab geographical fantasy which is described in detail in the Ethiopic *Romance* (134–41: Budge 1896).
57. Qamus al-a'lam thought the two were the same: Macuch 1991, 247; cf. Wilson 1922, Waldron 1990, 202–3. See also Burton 1934, III. 1893–94. Alexander had of course already been to China in the Syriac *Romance*, and in Theophylact Simocatta 7.9.6ff. (see above, Chapter 2., p. 35), so the confusion was not perhaps so remarkable.
58. As argued by de Goeje: Anderson 1932, 95.
59. Dunlop 1971, 167ff.
60. Waldron 1990, 203–4.
61. White 1991.
62. Anderson 1932, 103. Actually the achievements of the navigators may have caused their demise a little sooner: their last appearance may be the Genoese world map of 1457, Scafi 229, 2006, fig. 8.21.

Chapter 10. Death in Babylon (323 BC)

1. Nice 2005.
2. 'The 13th (20 Sept. 331 BC), moonset to sunrise . . . lunar eclipse in its totality covered . . . . That month (Ululu), on the 11th (18 Sept. 331 BC), panic broke out in the camp of the king . . . . On the 24th (1 Oct. 331 BC), in the morning, the King of the World . . . the standard (?). They fought with each other, and a severe defeat of the troops of . . . . The troops of the king deserted him . . . . They fled to the land of Gutium.' Babylonian oracle from Sachs and Hunger 1988.
3. Magicians in the Talmudic period, however, might offer ways of discovering the dismal truth. 'If you wish to know in which month you will be taken from the world . . . purify yourself from all impiety for three weeks . . . (etc. etc.)': Sepher ha-Razim 5.19–37, quoted in R. Kraemer, *When Aseneth met Joseph* (1998), 98.
4. Apollonius of Tyana also visited a speaking tree which addressed him 'in an articulate but feminine voice': Philostr. *Vit. Ap. Ty.* 6.10 (p. 31 in Conybeare's Loeb), with Eusebius, *in Philostr.* xxx (p. 565 in Conybeare's Loeb).
5. Already in Ctesias, 46a.
6. Olympias was murdered in spring 316 by Cassander: DS 17.118.2, Justin 14.6.11–13. Alexander's sister Cleopatra was killed in 308 (DS 20.37.3–6, Paus. 9.7.2) and his half-sister Thessalonike in 296 (Justin 16.1, Plut. *Dem.* 36.1). His wife Roxane was put to death on Olympias' orders in 310 BC: Hammond 1998, 208. Since the Latin *Letter to Aristotle* specifies that his sisters will have long happy lives (*sororesque tuae felices erunt fato diu*), it must have been composed between 316 and 308: Gunderson 1980, 118ff.
7. Lane 1857–9, III. 480–1 says that these islands are most commonly identified with Borneo. (Lunde and Stone in Mas'udi 2007, 66 opt for Madagascar.) The accounts in Qazvini and Ibn al-Wardi, in Lane's translation, described the habits of the people. 'Here too is a tree that bears fruits like women . . .; they have beautiful faces, and are suspended by their hair. They come forth from integuments like large leathern bags; and when they feel the air and the sun, they cry out "Wak! Wak!" until their hair is cut; and when it is cut, they die; and the people of these islands understand this cry, and augur ill from it.' See also Baltrušaitis 1954.
8. White 1991, 22–46.
9. Mubaššir ed. Meissner 1895, 617. Its ultimate source is probably the prophecy of Moses to those who disobey the law, Deut. 28.23: 'Thy heaven that is over thy head shall be brass, and the earth that is under thee shall be iron', though the reasons for the transference to Alexander are obscure.
10. Chapter 8.

11. Cf. Lucian, *Demonax* 25; Plutarch in his *Consolation to Apollonius* quotes Euripides' line from *Merope*, 'Many thousands have drunk life's dregs as I have' (110D). The Ethiopic *Romance* (Budge 1896, 531–20) has Alexander instructing Olympias to fetch water from a house where no one has ever died.

12. Burlingame 1921, part II book viii story 13, pp. 257–60. There is a similar Burmese story in Maclean 2000, 47. See also Koehler 1894, 129; Thomson 1955–8, N135.31 = H.1394. Other examples include the Indian tale of Kisagotami; the Renaissance text of Ser Giovanni, *Pecorone*; and Hans Christian Andersen, 'The Cripple'.

13. Doufikar-Aerts 2003a; Grignaschi 1993. For the Hebrew tradition, see *Der Born Judas*, II, 191ff.

14. Lang 1951.

15. Quoted from Mango 1955, 123.

16. This work does not survive in its original form, but in a reworking by Mohammad ibn 'Ali al-Ansari and in Hebrew and Spanish translations. See Brock 1970.

17. Doufikar-Aerts 2003a and 2003b.

18. Knust 1879. The first English translation appeared in 1450 (Scrope 1450) and became the source for many reworkings. The Persian versions do not include the sayings of the philosophers in this form, though in Nizami the death of Alexander is followed by accounts of the deaths of Aristotle, Plato, Porphyry and others. Firdausi takes from Eutychius the details of Alexander's laying out but leaves out the philosophers episode. See Hertz 1905b for a general study, and Doufikar-Aerts 2003b, 109–17. The *Sayings* also appear in Jacob Bonfils' Hebrew translation of *HP* J^2, from a lost Arabic intermediary: Kazis 1962, 159–73.

19. Budge 1896, 376–9.

20. Told in Gregory Barhebraeus' *Laughable Stories* of Kaikubad: 'Yesterday the king spoke volubly, but today he being silent admonisheth us with greater effect.' Brock 1970, n. 2. An early Irish poet, Fearghal Og Mhac an Bhaird, told the story again: 'After his burial there came to the grave of the emperor four of the wisest men. Although he who was yesterday one of ourselves today is no-one under the sun, who would not properly revere the man who had the crowds of the earth all around him . . . . He was the king of life who used to give golden gifts, said one of them in the midst of great sorrow, and the gold lives on instead of him, as does his reputation by which we are enlightened' (adapted from a literal translation kindly made for me by Maeve O'Brien).

21. Parian Marble, *FGrH* 239B11. The Parian Marble is a chronology of historical events from the reign of Cecrops (1581/0 BC), inscribed on marble on the island of Paros, probably in 264/3 (the final year covered). Part is in the Paros Museum, part in the Ashmolean.

22. Thompson 1988, 212; Chugg 2004/5, 59–62; Saunders 2006.

23. See Frankfurter 1998, 241–8 on the use of Egyptian/Greek literature to forge a new Egyptian/Greek identity. Dillery 1999, 104 compares the story at Herodotus 2. 137–41, where one king flees Egypt and a son returns to complete his work. On Manetho's role, Saunders 2006, 193–4.

24. Erskine 2002, Chugg 2004/5.

25. Fraser 1972, II.11–12 and 32.

26. Saunders 2006, 59–62.

27. Fraser 1972, II. 365.

28. Saunders 2006, 63–76.

29. Dio Cassius 51.16.5; contrast Suetonius *Augustus* 18.

30. 26th Homily on II Corinthians, *PG* 61, p. 581.

31. Forster 1923, 89. Clitophon is the hero of Achilles' novel.

32. N.Z. Davis 2007, 232–4.

33. Empereur 1998, 148.

34. Chugg 2004/5, 188.

35. Saunders 2006, ch. 11.

Chapter 11. Universal Emperor: The Christian Hero

1. Otto of Freising 1928, 179–84.
2. The contemporary John of Salisbury (1115–80) likewise drew mainly on Cicero (possibly via Augustine, but probably directly) for his allusions to Alexander: Cary 1956, 95ff.
3. It is certain that he did not use Orosius alone, since he knows the story that Alexander was the son of Nectanebo, which is not in Orosius.
4. *Simulacra*. Mierow incorrectly translates 'phases'.
5. I have not tried to do the same for the Islamic legends, which would require a vaster knowledge than I have of those texts and languages. This will, perhaps, be a topic for another scholar. Cf. Doufikar-Aerts 2003b, Zuwiyya 2001, Mango 1955, F. de Polignac in Bridges and Bürgel 1996.
6. Bohm 1989, Spencer 2002, Stoneman 2003b.
7. Alföldi 1943.
8. Sande 1993 and 1999; Saunders 2006, 109; Dahmen 2007, 152–3.
9. Chéhab 1957, Ross 1963a.
10. Except of course its translator, Julius Valerius.
11. Stöcker 1979.
12. An Old English translation of Orosius is attributed, with little plausibility, to King Alfred (ed. H. Sweet 1889, EETS 79). The Middle Irish *Alexander*, belonging possibly to the eleventh century, derives mainly from Orosius, with the addition of some material from the *Letter to Aristotle* and the *Collatio*. See Meyer 1949. For the text of the Middle Irish work, with a German translation, see Stokes and Windisch 1887; another German translation in Peters s1967.
13. Boer 1973, DiMarco and Perelman 1978.
14. Cary 1956, 14.
15. On the *Itinerarium Alexandri* see Lane Fox 1997, and the edition by Tabacco: *Itinerarium* 2000; and on the late Latin works in general the brief summary in Stoneman 1999a, which I avoid repeating here.
16. Thomas 1966 is an edition of the work; see also Ruggini 1961; Baynham 1995.
17. Cary 1956, 25 n. 2.
18. The source of the information about Alexander given in the Middle High German *Annolied* (c. 1075) is imponderable. The author selects only the fact of Alexander's visit to India, the episode of the Oracular Trees, the flight, and the story of the diving bell, told in a version which has no known precedents: Ross 1967 (also in Ross 1985). Possibly he drew on Leo's translation, now available in Bamberg. (The author of the *Annolied*, however, lived far away from Bamberg, in Siegburg in the region of Cologne.)
19. The partial MS is in Lambeth Palace, no. 342. Edition of the Bamberg MS: Pfister 1913; of the Lambeth MS, Ross 1959. On Henry II see Haskins 1927, 21; and the comprehensive publication of Kirmeier, Schneidmuller, Weinfurter and Brockhoff 2002.
20. Ed. Pfister, 1910. See Schnell 1989, 31.
21. It does not include the text of Palladius which forms ch. III. 7–16 in A. But, like beta, it stops halfway through Book II. The *Letter to Aristotle* is given in the first person, as in A and beta. The story of the diving bell and the flying machine appear, but in the first person, in the course of the *Letter to Olympias* (III. 27–9), not as part of the narrative, as in the Greek version of L. The story of the trees of the sun and moon does not appear.
22. There is an interesting symbiosis of the Latin versions with those in Hebrew. Though stories about Alexander had become established in the Talmud, there does not seem to have been any full-scale narrative about Alexander in Hebrew before the tenth century. The key text here is the rewriting of Josephus' *Antiquities of the Jews* that goes by the name of Yosippon. It was completed in 953 in southern Italy or Sicily. Inspired, perhaps, by Yosippon, several independent Hebrew *Alexander Romances* were created: see

appendix. One of them, a translation of J² of *HP*, was made by R. Immanuel b. Jacob Bonfils (1150–1230), who lived in Orange in southern France, whither he had removed as a result of the expulsion of the Jews from Spain in the Almohad conquest of 1140 (ed. Kazis 1962). Thus the Hebrew versions represent an additional line of transmission, difficult to trace in any detail, from the original Greek version back to the west. Who can say which of the troubadours Jacob Bonfils may have talked to in twelfth-century Provence, to make the name of Alexander known in the cradle of chivalric literature?

23. One MS, from the ninth century, provided the archetype for the 123 existing MSS: Baynham 1995, 2–3.

24. Cary 1956, 62.

25. Walter's poem was the source of several other Alexander texts, namely the old Czech, Icelandic and Middle Irish Alexander books (Cary 1956, 63–4, cf. Meyer 1949). Ulrich von Etzenbach's Alexander poem in Middle High German (*c.* 1250–1300) likewise derived from Walter, as did Jacob van Maerlant's *Alexanders Geesten* (which incorporated also the *Journey to Paradise*).

26. Haskins 1929 calls it 'The renaissance of the twelfth century'.

27. The formulation is that of R. W. Southern 1953, 174.

28. Reilly 1993, 127.

29. Haskins 1927, 155–93.

30. Ibid., ch. 12.

31. Ibid., 1927, ch. 9.

32. Norwich 1991, 474ff.

33. Gleixner 1961, 16.

34. Van Cleve 1972, 301. Abulafia 1988, 263–4 is, however, very dismissive of any claims of Frederick to scholarship.

35. Haskins 1927, 254.

36. Quilichinus' poem was in turn the source of the Italian poem by Domenico Scolari: Storost 1935, 42–5.

37. See Burnett 1997, 38 on the establishment of Arabic studies in England in Henry's reign, and on the role of Petrus Alfonsi. John of Salibury, one of the greatest intellects of the age, was part of this movement, and books reached England from Toledo around the 1170s: Burnett 1997, 60–1.

38. Haskins 1927, 260. But Walter Map's view of Alexander was a Senecan one: describing Llywelyn ap Gruffudd (*De nugis curialium*, dist. ii. C. 23), he writes: 'he resembled Alexander of Macedon and all others in whom covetous lust destroys self-control, liberal, vigilant, quick, bold, courteous, affable, extravagant, pertinacious, untrustworthy, and cruel'. Cf. the passage from Shakespeare's *Henry V* quoted in the epigraph to the chapter.

39. Burnett 1997, 74, 79.

40. This is the only part of the Alexander story in the MSS of Godfrey that is heavily illustrated: for example the Sandomierz Chapter Library MS 114 includes, in 28 miniatures, 27 of the wondrous creatures of India, and one of Gog and Magog: besides his apocalyptic role, Alexander here functions largely as a vehicle for geography. See Secomska 1975.

41. Mulder-Bakker 1983, 236 argues that Barbarossa may have seen himself as a forerunner of the Last Emperor.

42. Mulder-Bakker 1983, 238.

43. Van Oostrom 1996.

44. D. Constantine, *Mappa Mundi* 1984.

45. Le Goff 1988, 57.

46. See Williams 2003.

47. Ibid., 112.

48. Williams 2003, 304.
49. Keen 1984, 107ff.
50. Turner 1851, 187, 236.
51. It has even been suggested that there was an English edition of *HP* J[3] which directly influenced the *Prose Alexander*, the *Wars of Alexander* and the *Gesta Herewardi*, though Ross (1963b, 65) is sceptical.
52. See the clear account of Laurence Harf-Lancner in her introduction to her edition of Alexander de Paris, *Roman d'Alexandre* (Livre de Poche 1994).
53. The first French vernacular non-religious biography – see Simons 1994. It derives from the interpolated Curtius: Cary 1956, 62–3.
54. Green 1975, 247 and 260.
55. Bunt 1994, 19ff.
56. Harf-Lancner 1994. See also the studies by Gosman 1994, Gaullier-Bougassas 1998, Maddox and Sturm-Maddox 2002.
57. Cary 1954, 234.
58. Keen 1984, 41 and 44–6. Albrecht Altdorfer's great painting in Munich's Alte Pinakothek, *Alexander's Battle*, models the conflict at (probably) Issus on a crusader battle.
59. Cary 1956, 46–8: there are 16 MSS and there were 11 printings between 1506 and 1630.
60. British Library, Royal 15 E vi. Ed. Otaka, Fukui and Ferlampin-Acher 2003. Two hundred years later, Wauquelin's *Faicts et conquestes* (*c*. 1448: five MSS) offered another prose retelling of the *Roman d'Alexandre*.
61. Hübner 1933, 41.
62. Wisbey 1966; cf. Hübner 1933.
63. Chaucer told the story of Alexander and the Pirate in 'The Manciple's Tale', 226–34, probably known from Augustine. It was also in John of Salisbury *Policraticus* II. xiv, and in Higden's *Polychronicon* 1865 Book 46. Cary 1956, 95 and 252.
64. *Dittamondo* II. 26.61 (in a context of the Sack of Constantinople in 1204 and of the preaching of Saints Dominic and Francis): '*Ancora in questo tempo ch'io riesco / Gog e Magog, ch'Alessandro racchiuse / col suon, che poi più tempo stette fresco, / uscir de' monti con diverse muse / e col fabbro Cuscan, lo qual fu tale / che più paesi conquise e confuse.*'
65. Storost 1935.
66. Ronge 1957. Sweden had been Christian since the twelfth century.
67. Hübner 1933, 44.
68. Bunt 1994, 61–8.
69. Otto Springer in Loomis 1959, 234; Kratz 1973, excursus.
70. Montpellier H 31 (13th century); Bamberg MS Hist 3 (13th century); Madrid 9783 (mid-13th century). See Schnell's edition of the *Liber* (1989), and pp. 31–2 on these MSS.
71. Storost 1935.
72. Polish and Russian, based on *HP* J[2] (Ross 1963b 64); also Czech (Kreft 1981). The Serbian version, made by 1389, however, is based on the Greek tradition (but adds the information that Alexander read all of Homer, and Aristotle's *Organon*, in his two years of education: Jouanno 1995, 273) and is the source of the Romanian and Georgian versions: Moennig 1992, 31; cf. Christians 1991. There are two Bulgarian versions, the first (10th–11th century) based on beta and a second (14th century) based on the Serbian: Köhler 1983.
73. Merzdorf 1870. See above, p.120.
74. *Perceforest*, ed. Taylor 1979. Studies by Szkilnik in Maddox and Sturm-Maddox 2002 and Lods 1951. An earlier example of such syncretism is Aimon de Varennes' *Florimont* (1188; ed. A. Hilka 1933), in which the hero is the grandfather of Alexander. It tells the story of Philip's lion-fighting and his marriage to an African princess; he rejects the king

of Hungary's request to marry his daughter Romadanaple, and founds the city of Philippopolis.

75. Keen 1984, 248.
76. Bennett 1969, 242–319.
77. Steinberg 1955, 102.
78. Ibid., 47.
79. Williams 2003, 304.
80. Bolgar 1954, 278, 511, 529.
81. See e.g. Stoneman 2003b.
82. Ralegh 1997: see Chapter 7.
83. Stoneman 1995a, 93–101.

Chapter 12. King of the World: Alexander the Greek

1. Gleixner 1961 (reviewed by Trumpf 1962), Holton 1973, Trumpf 1967, Veloudis 1968 and 1969.
2. *Parastaseis*, eds Cameron and Herrin 1984, 69.
3. Veloudis 1968, 235, 237, Veloudis 1969 57ff. Even the Suez Canal was his doing, according to a later tale: Veloudis 1977/1989, 67.
4. *Ad illuminandos catechesis* 2.5, *PG* 49.240.
5. Procopins *Buildings of Justinian,* 6.2.16.
6. Frugoni 1978, 43, Frugoni 1988, 165.
7. Trumpf 1962.
8. Gleixner 1961, 58–60.
9. Charlesworth 1983, I. 755ff.
10. *Chronicon Paschale* 115a–116; Gleixner 1961, 37.
11. Gleixner 1961, 37ff.
12. Ibid., 37; Stoneman 1995a.
13. Gleixner 1961, 43ff.
14. See further, Jouanno 2000–1.
15. Angold 1984, 88; Roueché 1988, 126–7.
16. And what can be the connection with the mysterious document known as 'Alexander's Cappadocian Testament', in which Alexander expresses his wish to be buried in that region? See Trumpf 1959.
17. Weitzmann 1951, 59–60, 186–8, and Figs 70, 250, 253.
18. Schmidt 1995, Plate 14.
19. Beck 1971, 94.
20. Saunier in Beaton and Ricks 1993, 147.
21. Cf. Chapter 7. (The source is perhaps George the Monk, who refers to just these episodes, rather than the *Romance* directly.)
22. Politis 1973, 33ff.
23. *Drosilla and Charicles, Hysmines and Hysminias, Rhodanthe and Dosicles,* and perhaps *Callimachus and Chrysorrhoe.*
24. Angold 1988, 206ff., 212–20.
25. Beck 1971, 132–5.
26. Köhler 1983.
27. Jouanno 2002, 342ff., 361–5.
28. Wagner 1881, Reichmann 1963.
29. Holton 1973.
30. Some examples are reproduced in Veloudis 1977/1989.
31. Moennig 1987. See appendix for fuller details.
32. Veloudis 1977/89, *Phyllada*, ed. Pallis (1935).

33. Moennig 1992.
34. The Byzantine poem of 1388, however, follows the order of events of Pseudo-Callisthenes, as does the *Rimada* of 1529.
35. The episode was well-known to churchmen because of its importance to Christian doctrine. Pseudo-John Damascene cites this episode of the visit to the Cave of the Gods in a letter to the Emperor Theophilus (829–42): Pfister and Riedinger 1955.
36. Gleixner 1961, 111–15.
37. P. Collart, *Philippes* (Paris 1937), 188 n. 1, 326 n. 5, 327 n. 12.
38. Karakasidou 1997, 36.
39. Veloudis 1977/1989, 58.
40. Gleixner 1961, 105.
41. I, 202–9.
42. Saunders 2006, 185.
43. Karakasidou 1997, 96.
44. Herzfeld 1986, 155.
45. Danforth 2003, 351.
46. Karakasidou 1997, 228.
47. Danforth 2003, 350.
48. Leigh Fermor 1958, 187; see Chapter 7 n. 52.

Epilogue

1. P. Conradi, *Iris Murdoch: A Life* (London: HarperCollins 2001), 151.
2. 'Arabic literature in the period between 750 and 1450 portrays the Macedonian king in his multiple guises: an explorer and ruler of the world, a king of kings, a wise and spiritual prince, and, eventually, an invincible monarch who willy-nilly became a messenger to the nations of the earth.' Doufikar-Aerts 2003b, 364; cf. Polignac 1996.
3. Bosworth 1996; the opposite extreme from the noble ruler of W. W. Tarn in his classic *Alexander the Great* of 1948.
4. On the Roman view of Alexander see Spencer 2002 and Stoneman 2003b.

BIBLIOGRAPHY

Classical authors and journals are cited according to the conventions used in the *Oxford Classical Dictionary* and Liddell–Scott, *Greek–English Lexicon*. Other references are given in full below.

I. Editions and Translations of the *Alexander Romance* and Related Texts

Ausfeld, A. 1907. *Der griechische Alexanderroman*. Leipzig (translation of A)

Bergmeister, H.-J. 1975. *Die Historia de Preliis Alexandri Magni. Synoptische Edition . . . Buch I und II*. Meisenheim am Glan

Bergson, L.1965. *Der griechische Alexanderroman rezension Beta*. Stockholm

Bergson, L. 1989. *Carmina praecipue choliambica apud Pseudo-Callisthenem reperta*. Stockholm

Boer, W.W. 1973. *Epistola Alexandri ad Aristotelem ad codicum fidem edita*. Meisenheim am Glan

Bounoure, G. and Serret, B. 1992. *Le roman d'Alexandre*. Paris (transl.)

Braccini, T. 2004. *Carmen choliambicum quod apud Ps.-Callisthenis* Historiam Alexandri *reperitur*. Munich

Budge, E.A.W. 1889. *The History of Alexander the Great* (edn and transl. of Syriac texts). London, repr. Amsterdam 1976

Budge, E.A.W. 1896. *Life and Exploits of Alexander the Great* (transl. of Ethiopic texts)

Budge, E.A.W. 1933. *The Alexander Book in Ethiopia*. (The content is the same as in the previous item, but the pagination is different.)

Buik of Alexander, The 1921. ed. R.L. Graeme Ritchie. Edinburgh, 2 vols

Centanni, M. 1991. *Il Romanzo di Alessandro*. Turin

Christians, D. 1991. *Die serbische Alexandreis*. Cologne, etc.

DiMarco, V. and Perelman, L. 1978. *The Middle English Letter of Alexander to Aristotle*. Amsterdam

Dimitroulopoulos, Ch. 1999. *Diegesis Alexandrou meta Semirames vasilissas Syrias*. Athens

Dowden, K. 1989. 'The Alexander Romance'. In Brian Reardon (ed.), *Collected Ancient Greek Novels*. Berkeley, 650–735 (transl. of L)

Engelmann, H. 1963. *Der griechische Alexanderroman Rezension Gamma, Buch II*. Meisenheim am Glan

Feldbusch, M. 1976. *Der Brief Alexanders an Aristoteles über die Wunder Indiens. Synoptische Edition*. Meisenheim am Glan

Flusser, D. (ed.) 1956. 'Ma'aseh Alexandros Lefi Ketab-yad Parma', *Tarbiz* 26.2 (December)

Franco, C. 2001. *Vita di Alessandro di Macedone*. Palermo

Garcia Gomez, E. 1929. *Historia de Dulcarnain. Un texte arabe occidental de la Leyenda de Alejandro.* Madrid

Gaster, Moses. 1897. 'The Book of Alexander of Macedon' = *Alexander ha-Mokdoni* (transl.) *JRAS*, 29, 485–99

Gunderson, L. 1980. *Alexander's Letter to Aristotle about India.* Meisenheim am Glan (transl.)

Haight, E.H. 1955. *The Life of Alexander of Macedon by Pseudo-Callisthenes.* New York

Harf-Lancner, L. (ed). 1994 *Le Roman d'Alexandre.* Livre de Poche (the medieval French Romance)

Hartlieb, J. 1991. *Alexander,* ed. R. Pawis. Munich

Hay, Sir G. 1990. *The Buik of King Alexander,* ed. J. Cartwright. Aberdeen, 3 vols

Hilka, A. 1911. 'Liegnitz Historia Alexandri Magni' *Romanische Forschungen* 29, 1.30.

Hilka, A. 1920 *Der altfranzösische Prosa-Alexanderroman nebst dem Lateinischen Original der Historia de Preliis (Recension J²)* Halle

Hilka, A., Bergmeister H.-J., and Grossman R. 1976–77 *Historia Alexandri Magni (Historia de Preliis): Rezension J² (Orosius-Rezension)* Meisenheim am Glan

Hilka, A. and Steffens, K. 1979. *Historia Alexandri Magni: Rezension J¹* Meisenheim am Glan

Holton, D. 1974. *The Tale of Alexander. The Rhymed Version.* Thessaloniki (Greek text)

Hunnius, C. 1904. *Das syrische Alexanderlied.* Göttingen

Itinerarium Alexandri. 2000. Ed. Rafaella Tabacco. Turin

James, M.R. 1933. *The Romance of Alexander. A Collotype Facsimile of MS Bodley 264.* Oxford

Julius Valerius 2004. *Res gestae Alexandri Macedonis,* ed. M. Rosellini, 2nd edition

Kazis, I.J. ed. 1962. *The Book of the Gests of Alexander of Macedon.* Cambridge, Mass.

Kirsch, W. 1991. *Das Buch von Alexander.* Leipzig (illustrated translation of *HP* J²)

Konstantinopoulos, V.L. 1983. *Ps.-Kallisthenes: Zwei mittelgriechische Prosa-fassungen des Alexanderromans II* Meisenheim am Glan

Kratz, D.M. 1991. *The Romances of Alexander.* New York

Kroll, W. 1926. *Historia Alexandri Magni (Pseudo-Callisthenes). Recensio vetusta.* Berlin (edition of A)

Kynge Alisaundre, 1952/1957. Ed. G.V. Smithers. EETS 227, 237

La Carrière, J. 2000. *La légende d'Alexandre.* Paris (transl. of *Phyllada*)

Lauenstein, U. von. 1962. *Der griechische Alexanderroman rezension gamma Buch I aus der HS R herausgegeben.* Meisenheim am Glan

Libro de Alexandre. 1978. Ed. J. Cañas Murillo. Madrid

Libro de Alejandro. 1985. Transl. E. Catena. Madrid

Lolos, A. 1983. *Ps.–Kallisthenes: Zwei mittelgriechische Prosa-fassungen des Alexanderromans I.* Meisenheim am Glan

Mitsakis, K. 1967. *Der byzantinische Alexanderroman nach dem Codex Vindob. Theol. Gr. 244.* Munich: Institut für Byzantinistik und neugriechische Philologie der Universität

Mitsakis, K. 1968. 'Der byzantinische Alexanderroman nach dem cod. Gr. 236 des Athosklosters Kutlumussi: *Diegesis peri tou Alexandrou kai ton megalon polemon'. Byz. Neugr. Jahrb.* 20, 228–302 and 344–84

Moennig, U. 1992. *Die spätbyzantinische Rezension zeta* des Alexanderromans.* Neograeca medii aevi VI: Cologne

Moennig, U. 2004. *Die Erzählung von Alexander und Semiramis.* Berlin

Nykl, R.A. 1929. *Aljamiado literature: El Rrekontiamento del Rrey Ališandre.* Paris

Otaka, Y., Fukui, H. and Ferlampin-Acher, C. (eds) 2003. *Roman d'Alexandre en prose.* Colour reproductions of BL, MS Royal 15 E VI

Palladius ed. Berghoff. 1987. *De gentibus Indiae et Bragmanibus,* ed. W. Berghoff

Palladius ed. Derrett. 1960. 'The History of "Palladius on the Races of India and the Brahmans",' ed. J.D.M. Derrett. *Classica et Medievalia* 21, 77–135

Parthe, F. 1969. *Der griechische Alexanderroman Rezension gamma, Buch III.* Meisenheim am Glan

Peters, E. 1967. 'Die Irische Alexandersage'. *Zeitschrift für celtische Philologie* 30, 71–264

Pfister, F. 1910. *Kleine Texte zum Alexanderroman: Commonitorium Palladii, Briefwechsel zwischen Alexander und Dindimus, Brief Alexanders über die Wunder Indiens.* Heidelberg

Pfister, F. 1913. *Der Alexanderroman des Archipresbyters Leo.* Heidelberg

Pfister, F. 1978. *Der Alexanderroman mit einer Auswahl aus den verwandten Texten – übersetzt –.* Meisenheim am Glan

Phyllada tou Megalexandrou, I. 1935. Ed A.A. Pallis. Athens 1990–91. See also Veloudis 1977/1989

Pritchard, R.T. 1992. *The History of Alexander's Battles. The Historia de Proeliis J¹.* (English transl.)

Quilichinus of Spoleto 1971. *Historia Alexandri Magni nebst dem text der Zwickauer HS der Historia de Proeliis Alexandri Magni Rezension J3,* ed. W. Kirsch. Skopje: Živa Antika 4

Raabe, R. 1896. *Historia Alexandrou. Die armenische Übersetzung der sagenhaften Alexander-Biographie ('Pseudo-Callisthenes') auf ihre mutmassliche Grundlage zurückgeführt.* Leipzig

Reardon, B.P. 1989. *Collected Ancient Greek Novels.* Berkeley

Reich, R. 1972. *Tales of Alexander the Macedonian.* New York

Reichmann, S. 1963. *Das byzantinische Alexandergedicht.* Meisenheim am Glan

Reinink, G.J. 1983a. *Das syrische Alexanderlied: Die drei Rezensionen.* Louvain

Ross, D.J.A. 1959. 'A New MS of Archpriest Leo of Naples: *Nativitas et Victoria Alexandri Magni*'. *Cl. et Med.* 20, 98–158; also in Ross 1985

Schnell, R. (ed.) 1989. *Liber Alexandri Magni. Die Alexandergeschichte der Handschrift Paris, B.N. n.a.l. 310. Untersuchungen und Textausgabe.* Munich

Skeat, W.W. 1867. *William of Palerne.* EETS e.s.1. (includes also the alliterative *Romance of Alisaunder*)

Skeat, W.W. 1878. *Alexander and Dindimus.* EETS e.s. 31

Steffens, K. 1975. *Historia Alexandri Magni (Historia de preliis Rezension J³).* Meisenheim am Glan

Stephanides, Th. 1980. 'Alexander the Great and the Dreadful Dragon'. *The Greek Gazette* (December)

Stoneman, R. 1991. *The Greek Alexander Romance.* Harmondsworth (transl. of L with additional material)

Stoneman, R. 2007. *Il Romanzo di Alessandro: Testo, Commentario ed Introduzione.* Mondadori (volume 1; volumes 2–3 forthcoming)

Tallet-Bonvalot, A. 1994. *Le Roman d'Alexandre.* Paris

Thomas of Kent 1976. *Roman de toute chevalerie,* ed. Brian Foster. London, Anglo-Norman Text Society

Thomas J.W. 1989. *The Strassburg Alexander and the Munich Oswald. Pre-courtly adventures of the German Middle Ages.* Columbia, SC

Thomas, P.H. (ed.) 1960 and 1966². *Epitoma rerum gestarum Alexandri et Liber de morte eius.* Leipzig

Trahoulias, N.S. 1997. *The Greek Alexander Romance. Facsimile edition of Venice, Hellenic Inst. Cod. 5.* Athens

Trumpf, J. 1974. *Vita Alexandri regis Macedonum* [= epsilon recension]. Stuttgart

Van Bekkum, W.J. 1992. *A Hebrew Alexander Romance according to MS London, Jews' College no 145.* Louvain

Van Bekkum, W.J. 1994. *A Hebrew Alexander Romance according to MS Heb. 671.5, Paris, Bibliothèque Nationale.* Groningen

Van Leeuwen, P.J. 1937. *De maleische Alexanderroman.* Utrecht (diss).

Van Thiel H. 1959. *Die Rezension Lambda des Pseudo-Kallisthenes.* Bonn

Van Thiel, H. 1983. *Leben und Täten Alexanders von Makedonien: Der griechische Alexanderroman nach der Handschrift L.* Darmstadt: WBG (edn and transl. of L)

Veloudis, G., ed. 1977/1989. *Diegesis Alexandrou tou Makedonos.* Athens

Wagner, W. 1881. *Alexandreis,* in *Drei byzantinische Gedichte.* repr. Athens 1990

Walter of Châtillon. 1996. *Alexandreis*, transl. D. Townsend. Philadelphia
Wars of Alexander, The. 1989. Ed H.N. Duggan and T. Turville-Potre EETS s.s. 10
Wauquelin, J. 2000. *Les Faicts et les conquestes d'Alexander le Grand*, ed. S. Hériché. Droz
Westlake, J.S. 1913. *The Prose Life of Alexander from the Thornton MS* EETS 143
Wolohojian, A.M. 1969. *The Romance of Alexander the Great by Pseudo-Callisthenes, translated from the Armenian.* New York

II. Other Primary Texts and Modern Editions

Adam of Bremen. 1959. *History of the Archbishops of Hamburg-Bremen*, ed. F.J. Tschan. New York
Aethicus Ister. 1993. *Cosmographia*, ed. O. Prinz. Monumenta Germania Historica 14
Al-Nadim. 1970. *Fihrist*, transl. B. Dodge. New York
Annolied, Das. 1972. Ed. Eberhard Nellmann. Stuttgart
Astrampsychos ed. and transl. K. Brodersen. 2006. *Der Pythagoras-Orakel*. Darmstadt
Bana. 1961. *Harsacharita* Transl. E.B. Cornell and F.W. Thomas. Delhi (reprint of OTF translation 1897)
Boek van der Wraak. 1994. *Gods*, transl. W. van Anrooij. Amsterdam
Boniface, St. 2000. trans. E. Emerton *Letters*. New York
Borges, J.L. 1998. *The Aleph*. Harmondsworth
Born Judas, Der. N.d. Leipzig. See also the abridged one-vol. edn, Suhrkamp 1959
Chronicon Paschale, ed. W. Dindorf 1832
Commodian. 1877. *Carmen propheticum*, ed. E. Ludwig
Cosmas Indicopleustes, transl. J.W. McCrindle. 1897. *The Christian Topography*. Hakluyt Society vol. 98
Cosmas Indicopleustes, 1968–73. *Topographie Chrétienne* I–III, ed. W. Wolska-Conus. Paris
Ctesias. 2004. *L'Inde et la Perse*. ed. Dominique Lenfant Paris
Dalley, S. 1989. *Poems from Mesopotamia* Oxford
Davids, T.W. Rhys. 1829. *Dialogues of the Buddha*. Sacred Books of the Buddhists II. London: Henry Frowdle
Davids, T.W. Rhys 1890, 1894. *The Questions of King Milinda*. Sacred Books of the East vols 35–36. Oxford
Digenis Akritas. 1956. Ed. J. Mavrocordato. Oxford
Eco, U. 2002. *Baudolino*. London: Secker and Warburg
Eide, T., Hägg, T., Pierce, R.H. and Török, L. 1994–98. *Fontes Historiae Nubiorum, I–III.* Bergen
De gemmis. Epiphanius. 1934. Ed. R.P. Blake and H. de Vis
Eutychius ed. L. Cheikho 1962. *Patriarchae Alexandrini Annales*. Louvain: CSCO I–II (Arabic text)
Eutychius. *Annales. PL* vol. 111. (Latin transl.)
Firdausi. 1905. *Book of Kings*, transl. A.G. and E. Warner. London
Firdausi. 1967. *The Epic of the Kings*, transl. R. Levy. London
Firdausi. 2004. *Sunset of Empire: Stories from the Shahnameh of Ferdowsi*. transl. Davis, Dick Washington, DC. Reissued without illustrations, in one vol., Penguin 2007
Georgius Monachus. *Chronicle*. Partial transl. in Stoneman 1994a
Georgius Syncellus. *Chronography*. transl. W. Adler and P. Tuffin 2002. Oxford
Gesta Romanorum. 1876. transl. C. Swan and W. Hooper. London
Gervase of Tilbury. *c.* 1200. *Otia imperialia*, transl. eds S.E. Banks and J.W. Binns, 2002. Oxford
Higden, R. 1865. *Polychronicon* ed C. Babington, London
Hilka, A. (ed.) 1935. *Itinerarium Alexandri ad Paradisum*, in L.P.G. Peckham, and M.S. La Du, *La Prise de Defur*. Princeton

Hunnius, C. 1904. *Das syrische Alexanderlied*. Göttingen. Inaugural dissertation

Ibn Khaldun. 1958. *The Muqaddimah: an introduction to history*, transl. and ed. F. Rosenthal. London

James, M.R. 1893. *Apocrypha Anecdota*. Texts & Studies 2.3. Cambridge

James, M.R. 1924. *The Apocryphal New Testament*. Oxford

Jones, C.P. 2006–7. Loeb, 6.10.3 and *Eusebius in Hieroclem* 34. Harvard, Cambridge, Mass

Josephus 1967. *Antiquities of the Jews*. Loeb Classical Library, vols 4–10. London

Josephus Hebraicus. ed. J.F. Breithaupt 1710. *Libri VI Hebraice et Latine*

Jüngere Titurel, Der, von Albrecht von Scharfenberg 1955–92, ed. Werner Wolf. Berlin

Khawan, René. 1976. *Le Livre des ruses*. Paris

Knust, H. 1879. *El libro de los buenos proverbios*. Stuttgart

Kühnhold, I. 1939. *Seifrits Alexander*. Dresden

Lamprecht, Pfaffe. Ed. I. Ruttmann. 1974. *Das Alexanderlied*. Darmstadt

Lane, E.W. 1857–59 (1979–1981). *The Thousand and One Nights*, 3 vols. London

Lapidaires grecs, Les. 2003. Ed. J. Schamp and R. Halleux. Paris

Levi, I. 1887. *Sammelband kleiner Beiträge aus HSS* II 1886 = *Le Roman d'Alexandre*. Paris

Liber monstrorum. ed. F. Porsia. 1976. Bari

Lichtheim, M. 1973–80. *Ancient Egyptian Literature*. Berkeley. 3 vols

Liudprand of Cremona. 1993. *The Embassy to Constantinople and Other Writings*. transl. F.A. Wright, ed. J.J. Norwich

Maerlant, J. van. 1882. *Alexanders Geesten*. ed J. Franche Groningen

Maerlant, J. van. 1997. *Spiegel Historiael* (selection, illustrated). Leuven

Magoun, F.P. 1929. *The Gests of King Alexander the Great. Two Middle English Alliterative Fragments*. Harvard

Mahabharata, The. 1975. Transl. J.B. van Buitenen. Chicago

Mahabharata, The. 1978. Transl. R.K. Narayan. London

Mahabharata, The. 1987. J-C. Carrière and P. Brook. New York

Mahabharata, The. 2005. Book III, vol. 4, transl. W.J. Johnson. New York

Mandeville, Sir John. 1968. *Travels*, ed. M.C. Seymour. Oxford

Mandeville, Sir John. 1983. *Travels*, ed. C.W.R.D. Moseley. Harmondsworth

Mann, K. 1929. *Alexander. Roman der Utopie*. Berlin

Manu, Laws of 1991. Transl. W. Doniger and B. K. Smith. Harmondsworth

Map, Walter. 1983. *De nugis curialium*. ed. C. Brooke and R.A.B. Mynors. Oxford

Mas'udi. 1965. *Les Prairies d'Or* II, transl. B. de Meynard et P. de Courteille. Paris

Mas'udi. 2007. From *Meadows of Gold* transl. Paul Lunde and Caroline Stone. Harmondsworth

Mubaššir ibn Fatik. 1895. *Ahbar al-Iskandar*. Ed. and transl. B. Meissner. *ZDMG* 49, 583–627

Niane, D.T. 1965. *Sundiata: An Epic of Old Mali*. London

Nizami. 1991. *Das Alexanderbuch. Iskandarnameh*. Transl. J. Bürgel. Zurich

Nizami. 1881. *Sikandar Nama, e Bara*. Transl. H. Wilberforce-Clarke. Delhi

O'Meara, J.J. 1976. *The Voyage of St Brendan*. Drumcoudra, Ireland

Orosius. 1883. *King Alfred's Orosius*. ed. H. Sweet. EETS 79

Otto of Freising. 1928. *The Two Cities*, transl. C. Mierow. Columbia

Parastaseis syntomoi chronikai. 1984. ed. A. Cameron and J. Herrin. Leiden

Perceforest. ed. J. Taylor. 1979. Geneva

Perry, B.E. 1952. *Aesopica*. Illinois

Pharasmanes, Letter of. ed. C. Lecouteux 1979 (*De rebus in oriente mirabilibus*). Meisenheim am Glan

Phlegon of Tralles. ed. W. Hansen 1996. *Book of Marvels*. Exeter

Photius transl. N.G. Wilson 1994. *Bibliotheca*. London: Duckworth

Pizan, Christine de. *The Book of the City of Ladies*. Transl. E.J. Richards, 1982. London

Polo, Marco. 1921. *The Book of Ser Marco Polo*, ed. H. Yule and H. Cordier. London

Prophetarum vitae fabulosae. 1907. Ed. Th. Schermann

Pseudo-Methodius. 1976 and 1983. *Die Apokalypsis des Pseudo-Methodios.* Ed. A. Lolos. Meisenheim am Glan
Pseudo-Methodius. 1993. *Die syrische Apokalypse des Pseudo-Methodios.* ed. G.J. Reinink. Louvain
Pseudo-Methodius. 1998. *Die Apokalypse des pseudo-Methodios: Die ältesten griechischen und lateinischen Übersetzungen.* Ed. W.J. Aerts and G.J.A. Kortekaas. Louvain
Ralegh, Walter. 1614. *History of the World.* London
Ralegh, W. 1997. *The Discoverie of the Large, Rich and Beautiful Empyre of Guiana.* Ed. N.L. Whitehead. Manchester
Rudolf von Ems. 1928–29. *Alexander.* Ed. V. Junk
Rufinus. *Historia ecclesiastica. PL* 21.
Scrope, S. 1941. *The Dicts and Sayings of the Philosophers.* Ed. C.F. Bühler. EETS 211
'Sebeos'. transl. R.W. Thomson. 1999. *The Armenian History.* Ed. J. Howard-Johnston with T. Greenwood. Liverpool
Secretum secretorum. Ed. R. Steele. 1920. In *Works of Roger Bacon.* vol. 5
Secretum secretorum. Ed. R. Möller. 1963. Hiltgart von Hürnheim. *Mittelhochdeutsche Prosaübersetzung des Secretum Secretorum.* Berlin
Secretum secretorum. Ed. M.A. Manzalaoui 1977. *Nine English Versions of the Secretum Secretorum.* EETS 276
Southgate, M. 1978. *Iskandarnameh.* New York
Stephens, S. and Winkler J.D. 1995. *Ancient Greek Novels: The Fragments.* Princeton
Tabari. Ed. J. Zotenberg. 1867. *Chronique.* Paris
Tabari. Transl. M. Perlmann 1987. *History vol. IV: The Ancient Kingdoms.* Albany
Teles. Ed. O. Hense. 1909. *Teletis Reliquiae.* Tübingen
Theophylact Simocatta. transl. M. and M. Whitby. 1986. *History.* Oxford
Torrey, C.C. 1946. *Lives of the Prophets.* Philadelphia
Ulrich von Etzenbach. 1888. *Alexander* l. ed. W. Toischer. Tübingen
Wolf, W. 1955–92. *Der Jungere Titurel.* Ed. A. von Scharfenberg. Berlin
Yosippon. 1978–1980. *Sefer Yosippon.* Ed. D. Flusser. Jerusalem. See also Josephus Hebraicus ed. Breithaupt 1710

III. Secondary Literature

Aarne, A. and Thompson, S. 1961. *The Types of the Folktale.* Helsinki
Abbott, N. 1957. *Studies in Arabic Literary Papyri I: Historical Texts.* Chicago
Abel, A. 1955. *Le Roman d'Alexandre.* Brussels
Abulafia, D. 1988. *Frederick II. A Medieval Emperor.* Oxford
Adler, E.N. 1930/1987. *Jewish Travellers in the Middle Ages* London: Routledge/New York: Dover
Aerts, W.J. 1996a. 'Alexander's Wondercoating'. In R.I.A Nip et al., *Media Latinitas.* Turnhout
Aerts, W.J. 1996b. 'Die Bewertung Alexanders des Grossen in den Beischriften des byzantinischen Alexandergedichts'. In Bridges and Bürgel 1996, 69–86
Aerts, W.J. and Gosman, M. 1988. *Exemplum et Similitudo. Alexander the Great and Other Heroes as Points of Reference in Medieval Literature.* Groningen
Aerts, W.J. and Smits, E.R. 1986. *Vincent of Beauvais and Alexander the Great.* Groningen
Alessandro Magno: Storia e Mito 1995. Exhibition catalogue. Rome. Leonardo Arte
Alexander, P.J. 1985. *The Byzantine Apocalyptic Tradition.* ed. D. DeF. Abraamse. California
Alexiou, M. 1974 *The Ritual Lament in Greek Tradition.* Cambridge
Alföldi, A. 1943. *Die Kontorniaten*; 2nd edn *Die Kontorniaten-Medaillons.* 1976 and 1990
Anderson A.R. 1927. 'Alexander's Horns'. *TAPA* 58, 100–22
Anderson, A.R. 1928a. 'Heracles and his Successors'. *HSCP* 39, 7–58
Anderson, A.R. 1928b. 'Alexander at the Caspian Gates'. *TAPA* 59, 130–63

Anderson, A.R. 1931. 'The Arabic History of Dulcarnain and the Ethiopian History of Alexander'. *Speculum* 6, 434–45

Anderson, A.R. 1932. *Alexander's Gate, Gog and Magog, and the Inclosed Nations.* Cambridge, Mass.

Angold, M. 1984. *The Byzantine Empire 1025–1204: A Political History.* London

Assmann, J. 2001. *The Search for God in Ancient Egypt,* transl. D. Lorton. Cornell

Bacher, W. 1871. *Nizamis Leben und Werke.* Leipzig

Baffioni, C. ed. 2000. *La diffusione dell'eredità classica nell' età tardoantica e medioevale,* vol. 3. Alessandria

Bagley, F.R.C. 1964. *Ghazzali's Book of Counsel for Kings.* Oxford.

Bailey, H.W. 1943. *Zoroastrian Problems in the Ninth-Century Books.* Oxford

Baltrušaitis, J. 1954. 'Une Survivance mediévale, la plante à têtes'. *La Revue des Arts,* no. Q 81–92

Baltrušaitis, J. 1955. *Le Moyen Age fantastique.* Paris

Banerjee, G.N. 1920. *Hellenism in Ancient India.* Calcutta

Bar-Kochva, B. 1996. *Pseudo-Hecataeus: On the Jews.* Berkeley, etc.

Barns, J.W.B. 1956. 'Egypt and the Greek Romance'. *Mitteilungen aus der Papyrussammlung der österreichischen Nationalbibliothek,* n.s. 5, 29–36

Barton, T. 1994. *Ancient Astrology.* London

Baynham, E. 1995. 'An Introduction to the Metz *Epitome*: Its traditions and value'. *Antichthon* 29, 60–77

Beaton, R. and D. Ricks. eds. 1993. *Digenis Akrites: New Approaches to Byzantine Heroic Poetry.* London

Beazley, C.R. 1949. *The Dawn of Modern Geography.* New York

Beck, H.G. 1971. *Geschichte der byzantinischen Volksliteratur.* Munich

Becker, H. 1889. *Die Brahmanen in der Alexandersage.* Königsberg

Beeston, A.F.L., Johnstone, T.M. Serjeant, R.B. and Smith, G.R. 1983. *Arabic Literature to the End of the 'Umayyad Period.* Cambridge

Bennett, H.S. 1969. *English Books and Readers 1475–1577.* Cambridge

Berg, B. 1970. 'Dandamis: An early Christian portrait of Indian asceticism'. *Classica et Medievalia* 31, 269–305

Berg, B. 1973. 'An Early Source of the Alexander Romance'. *GRBS* 14, 381–7

Berggren, J.L. and Jones, A.S. 2000. *Ptolemy's Geography: An Annotated Translation of the Theoretical Chapters.* Princeton

Bernhard, Thomas. 1991. *Yes.* Transl. Ewald Osers. Chicago

Betz, H.D. 1992. *The Greek Magical Papyri in Translation.* Chicago

Bialik, H.N. and Ravnitzky, Y.H. 1992. *The Book of Legends: Sefer ha-Aggadah.* New York

Blok, J. 1995. *The Early Amazons: Modern and Ancient Perspectives on a Persistent Myth.* Leiden: Brill

Bohm, C. 1989. *Imitatio Alexandri.* Munich

Bolgar, R.R. 1954. *The Classical Heritage and its Beneficiaries.* Cambridge

Boll, F. 1950. *Kleine Schriften zur Sternkunde des Altertums.* Leipzig

Boodberg, P.A. 1938. 'Marginalia to the History of the Northern Dynasties I: Theophylactus Simocatta on China'. *Harvard Journal of Asiatic Studies* 3, 223–43

Bopearachchi, O. and Flandrin, P. 2005. *Le Portrait d'Alexandre le grand. Histoire d'une découverte pour l'humanité.* Paris

Boswinkel E. and Sijpestein P.J. 1968. *Greek Papyri, Ostraca and Mummy Labels.* Amsterdam

Bosworth, A.B. 1980/1995. *Commentary on Arrian's History of Alexander,* I and II. Oxford

Bosworth, A.B. 1988. *Conquest and Empire.* Cambridge

Bosworth, A.B. 1996. *Alexander and the East.* Oxford

Bosworth, A.B. ed. 2000. *Alexander the Great in Fact and Fiction.* Oxford

Bousset, W. 1896. *The Antichrist Legend.* London

Bowersock, G. 1994. *Fiction as History.* California

Boyce, M. 1957. 'The Parthian Gosan and the Iranian Minstrel Traditions'. *JRAS* 18, 10–45

Boyce, M. 1968. *The Letter of Tansar.* Rome. IsMEO: Persian heritage series no. 9

Boyle, J.A. 1965. 'The Alexander Romance in Central Asia'. *Zentralasiatische Studien* 9, 265–73

Boyle, J.A. 1977. 'The Alexander Romance in East and West'. *Bulletin of the John Rylands Library* 60, 13–27

Braun, M. 1938. *History and Romance in Graeco-Oriental Literature.* Oxford

Braund, D.C. 1986. 'The Caucasian Frontier: Myth, exploration and the dynamics of imperialism'. In P. Freeman and D. Kennedy, *The Defence of the Roman and Byzantine East.* BAR: 31–49

Brend, B. 1995. *The Emperor Akbar's Khamsa of Nizami.* London

Brett, G. 1954. 'The Automata in the Byzantine "Throne of Solomon"'. *Speculum* 29, 477–87

Briant, P. 2003. *Darius dans l'ombre d'Alexandre.* Paris: Fayard. See also the review by Stoneman in *Classical Review* 56, 2006

Bridges, M. and Bürgel, J. Ch. eds. 1996. *The Problematics of Power. Eastern and Western Representations of Alexander the Great.* Bern, etc.

Bridgman, T. 2005. *Hyperboreans.* New York

Brock, S. 1970. 'The Laments of the Philosophers over Alexander in Syriac'. *7ss* 15, 205–18 = *Studies in Syriac Christianity*, Hampshire 1992, viii

Brock, S. 1983. 'Towards a History of Syriac Translation Technique'. *Orientalia Christiana Analecta* 221. Rome = *Studies in Syriac Christianity*, Hampshire 1992, x

Brock, S. 1989. 'Syriac Culture in the Seventh Century'. *ARAM* 1, Hampshire 268 ff.

Brocker, M. 1966. *Aristoteles als Alexanders Lehrer in der Legende.* Bonn

Brodersen, K. 1996. *Die sieben Weltwunder.* Munich

Brosius, M. 2000. *The Persian Empire from Cyrus II to Artaxerxes I.* London Association of Classical Teachers

Brown, T.S. 1949. *Onesicritus: A Study in Hellenistic historiography.* Berkeley California

Brunner, H. 1964 (2nd edition 1986). *Die Geburt des Gottkönigs*

Bulgakov, P. 1965. [The Arabic parallel to the 2nd chapter of the 3rd book of the Syriac *Romance of Alexander*]. *Palestinskij Sbornik* 2 (64/5), 53–57 (in Russian)

Bunt, G.V.H. 1993. 'The Middle English Translations of Ps.-Methodius'. *Polyphonica Byzantina* 131–43

Bunt, G.V.H. 1994. *Alexander the Great in the Literature of Medieval Britain.* Groningen

Bürgel, J.C. 1988. *The Feather of Simurgh: The 'Licit Magic' of the Arts in Medieval Islam.* New York

Burlingame, E.W. 1921. *Buddhist Legends Translated from the Dhammapada Commentary.* Cambridge

Burnes, A. 'Bokhara'. 1839. *Travels into Bokhara.* London

Burnett, C. 1997. *The Introduction of Arabic Learning into England.* London

Burstein, S. 1976. 'Alexander, Callisthenes and the Sources of the Nile'. *GRBS* 17 = *Graeco-Africana: Studies in the History of Greek Relations with Nubia.* New Rochelle. 63–76

Burstein, S. 1991/1995. 'Pharaoh Alexander: A scholarly myth'. *Ancient Society* 22 = *Graeco-Africana: Studies in the History of Greek Relations with Nubia.* New Rochelle: Caratzas, 53–62.

Burstein, S.M. 1995. 'Alexander in Egypt: Continuity and change'. In *Achaemenid History* VIII = *Graeco-Africana*, 43–52

Burstein, S. 2001. 'The Kingdom of Meroe'. In E. Yamauchi. ed., *Africa and Africans in Antiquity.* East Lansing. 132–58

Buschor, E. 1944. *Die Musen des Jenseits.* Munich

Butler, A.J. 1978. *The Arab Conquest of Egypt*, 2nd edn. Oxford

Cameron, A. 1991. *Christianity and the Rhetoric of Empire.* California

Campbell, M. 1989. *The Witness and the Other World. Exotic European Travel Writing 400–1600.* Cornell

Carlier, J. 1979. 'Voyage en Amazonie grecque'. *Acta Antiqua Academiae Scientiae Hungaricae* 27, 381–405

Carner, M. 1984. *Turandot: English National Opera Guide*. London

Cary, G. 1956. *The Medieval Alexander*. Cambridge

Cauville, S. 1997. *Le Zodiaque d'Osiris*. Louvain

Charlesworth, J.H. 1983. *The Old Testament Pseudepigrapha*. London

Charlesworth, M. 1987. 'Preliminary Report of a Newly-Discovered Extension of "Alexander's Wall"'. *Iran* 25, 160–5

Chéhab, M 1957. 'Mosaiques de Liban'. *Bulletin du Musée de Beyrouth* 15, 46–50 and Plates 22–25

Chelkowski, P.J. 1977. 'Nizami's Iskandarnameh'. In *Colloquio sul poeta Nizami e la legenda iranica di Alessandro Magno*. Rome. Accademia Nazionale dei Lincei, 11–53

Christians, D. 1991. *Die serbische Alexandreis nach der Sofioter illustrierter Handschrift Nr. 771*. Cologne, etc.

Chugg, A. 2002 [2003]. 'The Tomb of Alexander the Great in Alexandria'. *AJAH* n.s. 1.2, 75–108

Chugg, A. 2004/2005. *The Lost Tomb of Alexander the Great*. London

Ciancaglini, C. 1997. 'Alessandro e l'incendio di Persepoli'. In Valvo 1997, 59–81

Ciancaglini, C. 1998. 'Gli antecedenti del romanzo siriaco di Alessandro'. In Finazzi and Valvo 1998, 55–93

Ciancaglini, C. 2001. 'The Syriac Version of the Alexander Romance', *Le Muséon* 114, 121–40 (updated and abridged version of Ciancaglini 1998)

Cizek, A. 1978. 'Alexander the Great as God's Champion in the South-east European Folkbooks'. *Orientalia Lovanensia Periodica* 9, 189–211

Cizek, A. 1981. 'Ungeheuer und magische Lebewesen in der *Epistula Alexandri*'. In J. Gossens and T. Sodman. eds. *Third International Beast Epic, Fable and Fabliau Colloquium (Münster 1979): Proceedings*. Cologne, 78–94

Cleaves, F.W. 1959. 'An Early Mongolian Version of the Alexander Romance'. *Harvard Journal of Asiatic Studies* 22, 1–99

Cohn, N. 1961. *The Pursuit of the Millennium*. 2nd edn. London

Cohn, N. 1993. *Cosmos, Chaos and the World to Come*. Yale, New Haven

Cölln, J., Friede, S. and Wolfram, H. eds. 2000. *Alexanderdichtungen im Mittelalter*. Göttingen

Columbus, C. 1930–33. *Select Documents illustrating the Four Voyages of Christopher Columbus*, transl. and ed. Cecil Jane. Warminster

Columbus, C. 1990. *Journal of the First Voyage, 1492*. transl. and Ed. B.W. Ife. Warminster

Comparetti, D. 1895. *Virgil in the Middle Ages*. English transl. E.F.M. Benecke. London and New York

Conti Rossini, C. 1925. 'Leggende Geografiche Giudaiche nel 9. secolo (il sefer Eldad)'. *Bolletino. della reale società geografica italiana*, I–VI

Conybeare, F.C., Harris, J.R. and Lewis, A.S. 1913. *The Story of Ahikar. From the Aramaic, Syriac, Arabic, Armenian, Ethiopic, Old Turkish, Greek and Slavonic Versions*. 2nd edn, London

Cowley, A. 1923. *Aramaic Papyri of the Fifth Century BC*. repr. Osnabrück. 1967

Criscuolo, L. and Geraci, G. 1989. *Egitto e Storia Antica*. Bologna

Crone, G.R. 1948. *The Hereford World Map*. London: Royal Geographical Society

Dahmen, K. 2007. *The Legend of Alexander the Great on Greek and Roman Coins*. Abingdon

Danforth, L.M. 2003. 'Alexander the Great and the Macedonian Conflict'. In Roisman 2003.

Darmesteter, J. 1883. 'La Légende d'Alexandre chez les Parses'. In *Essais Orientaux*, 227–50

Darmesteter, J. 1892. 'Alexandre le grand dans le Zend-Avesta'. *Revue des Etudes Grecques* 2, 189–96

Darmesteter, J. 1894. 'La Lettre de Tansar au roi de Tabaristan'. *Journal Asiatique* 9, 185–250, 502–55

Davidson, O. 1994. *Poet and Hero in the Persian Book of Kings*. Cornell

Davis, D. 2002. *Panthea's Children: Hellenistic Novels and Medieval Persian Romances.* New York

Davis, N.Z. 2007. *Trickster Travels: in search of Leo Africanus.* London

Dawkins, R.M. 1937. 'Alexander and the Water of Life'. *Medium Aevum* 6, 173–92

Dawkins, R.M. 1955. *More Greek Folktales.* Oxford

Dawson, D. 1992. *Cities of the Gods.* Oxford

De Blois, F. 2004. *Persian Literature: A Bio-Bibliographical Survey. Volume IV: Poetry of the Pre-Mongol Period.* London

Delling, G. 1981. 'Alexander der Grosse als Bekenner des jüdischen Gottseglaubens'. *JSJ* 12, 1–51

Delumeau, J. 1992. *Une Histoire du Paradis.* Paris; English transl. (without the colour plates), *History of Paradise.* New York 1995

Derrett, J. Duncan M. 1967. 'Greece and India: The Milindapanha, the Alexander-romance and the Gospels'. *Zeitschrift für Religions und Geistesgeschichte* 19, 33–64

Desanges, J. 1969. 'D'Axum à l'Assa, aux portes de la Chine: Le voyage du "scholasticus de Thèbes" (entre 360 et 500 après J-C)'. *Historia* 18, 635–39

D'Evelyn, C. 1918. 'The MS Metrical Version of the Revelations of Ps.-Methodius; with a study of the influence of Methodius in medieval writings'. *PMLA* 33, 135–203

Dihle, A. 1964. 'The Conception of India in Hellenistic and Roman Literature'. *PCPS* n.s. 10, 15–23

Dilke, O.A.W. 1985. *Greek and Roman Maps.* London

Dillery, J. 1999. 'The First Egyptian Narrative History: Manetho and Greek historiography'. *ZPE* 127, 93–116

Dillery, J. 2004. 'Alexander's Tomb at "Rhacotis": Ps.-Callisthenes 2.34.5 and the Oracle of the Potter'. *ZPE* 148, 253–8

Dillon, M. 2000. 'Dialogues with Death: The last days of Socrates and the Buddha'. *Philosophy East and West* 50, 525–58

Dimitroulopoulos, C.I. 1989. 'Ena anekdoto protoneoelliniko poiima gia to Mega Alexandro'. *Parnassos* 31, 31–8

Dimitroulopoulos, C.I. 1995/1999 *Diegesis Alexandrou meta Semirames vasilissas Syrias . . . Ekdosi Kritiki me eisagoge.* Athens

Dodwell, C. 1987. *A Traveller on Horseback in Eastern Turkey and Iran.* London

Dombrowski, D.A. 1984/1985. *Vegetarianism: The Philosophy Behind the Ethical Diet.* Amherst and Wellingborough

Donath, L. 1873. *Die Alexandersage in Talmud und Midrasch.* Fulda

Doniger, W. 2000. *The Bed Trick: Tales of Sex and Masquerade.* Chicago

Doufikar-Aerts, F. 1994. 'A Legacy of the Alexander Romance in Arab Writings: Al-Iskander, founder of Alexandria'. In Tatum 1994, 323–43

Doufikar-Aerts, F. 1996. 'Alexander the Great and the Pharos of Alexandria in Arabic Literature'. In Bridges and Bürgel 1996, 191–20

Doufikar-Aerts, F. 2000. 'Epistola Alexandri ad Aristotelem Arabica'. In Baffioni 2000, 35–52

Doufikar-Aerts, F. 2003a. '"The Last Days of Alexander" in an Arabic Popular Romance of Al-Iskandar'. In Panayotakis, Zimmermann and Keulen 2003

Doufikar-Aerts, F. 2003b. *Alexander Magnus Arabicus. Zeven eeuwen Arabischer Alexandertraditie: van Pseudo-Callisthenes tot Suri.* Leiden

Dowden, K. 1997. 'The Amazons: Development and Functions'. *RhMus* 140, 97–128

Du Bois, P. 1982. *Centaurs and Amazons.* Ann Arbor

Dunlop, D.M. 1971. *Arab Civilization to AD 1500.* London

Düring, I. 1957 *Aristotle in the Ancient Biographical Tradition.* Göteborg

Eccles, L., Franzmann, M. and Lieu, S. 2005. 'Observations on Select Christian Inscriptions in the Syriac Script from Zayton'. In I. Gardner, S. Lieu and K. Parry. eds. *From Palmyra to Zayton: Epigraphy and Iconography* = Silk Road Studies X. Turnhout: Brepols, 247–78

Eddy, S.K. 1961. *The King Is Dead: Studies in the Near Eastern Resistance to Hellenism, 334–31 BC.* Lincoln, Nebr.

Edson, E. 1997. *Mapping Time and Space. How Medieval Mapmakers Viewed their World*. London

Edson, E. and Savage-Smith, E. 2004. *Medieval Views of the Cosmos*. Oxford

Ehrenberg, V. 1938. 'Pothos'. In *Alexander and the Greeks*. Oxford, 52–61

Eilers, W. 1971. 'Semiramis. Entstehung und Nachhall einer altorientalischen Sage'. *Sitzungsberichte der Kaisserlichen Akademie der Wissenschaften in Wien, philologisch-historische Klasse* 274.2

Empereur, J.-Y. 1998. *Alexandria Rediscovered*. London

Erskine, A. 2002. 'Life after Death. Alexandria and the body of Alexander the Great'. *G&R* 49, 163–79

Farmer, H.G. 1926. 'The Horn of Alexander'. *JRAS*, 500–3

Farmer, H.G. 1931. *The Organ of the Ancients*. London

Ferguson, J. 1975. *Utopias of the Classical World*. London

Finazzi, R.B. and Valvo, A. eds. 1998. *La diffusione dell' eredità classica nell' età tardoantica e medioevale: Il 'Romanzo di Alessandro' e altri scritti*. Alessandria

Flintoff, E. 1980. 'Pyrrho and India'. *Phronesis* 25, 88–108

Flusser, D. 1987. 'Josippon – a medieval Hebrew version of Josephus'. In L.H. Feldman and G. Hata. eds. *Josephus, Judaism and Christianity*. Leiden, 386–97

Foerster, R. 1888. *De Aristotelis quae feruntur secretis secretorum commentatio*. Kiel

Forster, E.M. 1923. *Pharos and Pharillon*. London

Frankfurter, D. 1998. *Religion in Roman Egypt*. Princeton

Fraser, P.M. 1960. 'The Cult of Sarapis in the Hellenistic World'. *Opuscula Atheniensia* 3, 1–54.

Fraser, P.M. 1972. *Ptolemaic Alexandria*. Oxford, 3 vols.

Fraser, P.M. 1996. *Cities of Alexander the Great*. Oxford

Friedländer, I. 1913. *Die Chadhirlegende und der Alexanderroman*. Leipzig

Friedman, J.B. 1981. *The Monstrous Races in Medieval Art and Thought*. Harvard, Cambridge, Mass.

Frugoni, C. 1978. *La fortuna di Alessandro Magno dall' antichità al medioevo*. Florence

Frugoni, C. 1988. 'La leggenda di Alessandro'. In F. Sisti (ed.), *Alessandro Magno: Storia e Mito*. Florence

Frye, R.N. 1975. *The Golden Age of Persia*. London

Frye, R.N. 1985. 'Two Iranian Notes'. In *Papers in Honour of Mary Boyce*. Leiden. vol. I, 185–90

Gardiner, A.H. 1917. 'Professional Magicians in Ancient Egypt'. *PSBA*, 31–43

Gaster, M. 1919. 'The Killing of the Khazar Kings'. *Folklore* = *Studies and Texts* II. 30, 1131–4

Gaster, M. 1924. *Exempla of the Rabbis*. London

Gaullier-Bougassas, C. 1998. *Les Romans d'Alexandre. Aux frontiers de l'épique et du Romanesque*. Paris

Gero, S. 1992. 'The Alexander Legend in Byzantium: some literary gleanings'. *Dumbarton Oaks Papers* 46, 83–7

Gero, S. 1993. 'The Legend of Alexander the Great in the Christian Orient'. *Bulletin of the John Rylands Library* 75.1, 3–4

Gianfreda, G. 1995. *Otranto e il primato dell' umanesimo Occidentale*. Lecce

Gibbon, E. 1909. *Decline and Fall of the Roman Empire*, ed. J.B. Bury. London

Gikas, G.P. 1973. *Zei kai vasilevei: mythistorimatiki viografia*. Athens

Ginzberg L. 1928–39. *Legends of the Jews*. Philadelphia

Gleixner, H.J. 1961. 'Das Alexanderbild der Byzantiner'. Munich

Gobdelas, D. 1822. *The History of Alexander the Great in the Oriental Writers*. Warsaw (in Greek). Repr. Larisa 2000

Goossens, R. 1927–28. 'L'Odontotyrannos, animal de l'Inde'. *Byzantion* 4, 29–52

Gosman, M. 1994. *La Légende d'Alexandre le Grand dans la littérature française du 12e siècle. Une réécriture permanente*. Amsterdam

Grabar, O. and Blair, S. 1980. *Epic Images and Contemporary History. The Illustrations of the Great Mongol Shahnama*. Chicago

Graf, A. 1878. 'La leggenda del paradiso terrestre'. In *Miti, leggende e suprestizioni del medio evo*, 2 vols. Turin 1892–93; 1 vol. Turin 1925. repr. Mondadori 1984, 33–149

Graf, A. 1883. 'La leggenda di Gog e Magog'. In *Roma nella memoria e nelle immaginazioni del medioevo*. Turin. vol. 2, 507–63

Graf, D.F. 1993. 'Early Hellenistic Travel Tales and Arabian Utopias'. Athens. *Graeco-Arabica V*, 111–17

Graf, F. 1997. *Magic in the Ancient World*. Harvard, Cambridge, Mass.

Green, D.H. 1975. 'The *Alexanderlied* and the Emergence of the Romance'. *German Life and Letters* 28, 246–62

Grignaschi, M. 1967. 'Le Roman épistolaire classique conservé dans la version arabe de Salim Abu-l-'Ala". *Le Muséon* 80, 211–64

Grignaschi, M. 1993. 'La Figure d'Alexandre chez les arabes et sa génèse'. *Arabic Science and Philosophy* 3, 205–34

Gunderson, L. 1970. 'Early Elements in the Alexander Romance'. In Laourdas and Makaronas

Gutas, D. 1975. *Greek Wisdom Literature in Arabic Translation*. Yale, New Haven

Gutas, D. 1998. *Greek Thought, Arabic Culture: The Graeco-Arabic Translation Movement in Baghdad and Early Abbasid Society (2nd–4th/8th–10th Centuries)*. London

Gutzwiller, K. 2005. *The New Posidippus. A Hellenistic Poetry Book*. Oxford

Hägg, T. and Utas, B. 2003. *The Virgin and Her Lover. Fragments of an Ancient Greek Novel and a Persian Epic Poem*. Leiden

Hahn-Woerle, B. 1987. *Die Ebstorfer Weltkarte*. Ebstorf

Halbfass, W. 1988. *India and Europe*. Albany

Hall, E. 1989. *Inventing the Barbarian*. Oxford

Hammond, N.G.L. 1998. *History of Macedonia*. Oxford

Hanaway W.L. 1974. *Love and War: Adventures from the Firuz Shah Nama of Sheikh Bigami*. New York

Hansen, G.C. 1964. 'Alexander und die Brahmanen'. *Klio* 43–45, 351–80

Harf-Lancner, L., Kappler, C. and Suard, F. eds. 1999. *Alexandre le Grand dans les littératures occidentales et proche-orientales. Actes du colloque de Paris, 27–29 novembre 1999*. Centre des sciences de la littérature, Université de Paris X–Nanterre, Paris

Harley, J.B. and Woodward, D. 1987. *The History of Cartography I: Cartography in Prehistoric, Ancient, and Medieval Europe and the Mediterranean*. Chicago

Hartmann, R. 1922. 'Alexander und der Rätselstein aus dem Paradies'. In *Oriental Studies Presented to E.G. Browne*, Cambridge 179–85

Harvey, P.D.A. 1991. *Medieval Maps*. London

Harvey, P.D.A. 1996. *Mappa Mundi: The Hereford World Map*. London

Haskins, C.H. 1927. *Studies in the History of Medieval Science*. Cambridge, Mass.

Haskins, C.H. 1929. *Studies in Medieval Culture*. Oxford

Hasluck, F.W. 1929. *Christianity and Islam under the Sultans*. Oxford

Haussig, H.W. 1953. 'Theophylacts Exkurs über die skythischen Völker'. *Byzantion* 23, 275–462

Haynes, J.L. 1992. *Nubia: Ancient Kingdoms of Africa*. Boston, Mass.

Heckel, W. 1988. *The Last Days and Testament of Alexander the Great: A Prosopographic Study*. Stuttgart = (Historia Einzelschrift 74)

Hedenskog, C.A. 1868. *Berättelse om Alexander den Store*. Lund

Hertz, W. 1905a. 'Die Sage vom Giftmädchen'. In *Gesammelte Abhandlungen*. Stuttgart and Berlin, 156–277

Hertz, W. 1905b. 'Aristoteles beim Tode Alexanders'. In *Gesammelte Abhandlungen*. Stuttgart and Berlin, 130–53

Herzfeld, M. 1986. *Ours Once More. Folklore, Ideology and the Making of Modern Greece*. New York

Hill, B. 1981. 'The Alexander Romance: The Egyptian connection'. *Leeds Studies in English* 12, 185 ff.

Hill, D.R. and al-Hassan, A. 1986. *Islamic Technology.* Cambridge

Hillenbrand, R. 1996. 'The Iskandar Cycle in the Great Mongol *Šahnama*'. In Bridges and Bürgel 1996, 203–30

Holt, F.L. 2005. *Into the Land of Bones.* Berkeley

Holton, D. 1973. 'I elliniki paradosi tou mythistorimatos tou Megalexandrou, i synecheia kai i exelixi tis'. Athens: Keimena kai meletai neoellinikis filologias, 83

Hornbostel, W. 1973. *Sarapis.* Leiden

Hourani, G.F. 1995. *Arab Seafaring.* 2nd edn. Princeton

Hübner, A. 1933. 'Alexander der Grosse in der deutschen Dichtung des Mittelalters'. *Die Antike* 9, 32–48

Huizinga, J. 1949. *Homo Ludens.* London

Irwin, R. 1994. *The Arabian Nights: A Companion.* London

Jancey, M. 1987. *The Hereford World Map.* Hereford Cathedral

Jane, C. 1930–33. *Select Documents Illustrating the Four Voyages of Christopher Columbus.* Hakluyt Society. London

Jasnow, R. 1997. 'The Greek Alexander Romance and Demotic Egyptian Literature'. *JNES* 56, 95–103

Jouanno, C. 1995. 'Le Roman d'Alexandre ou l'enfance d'un héros.' In D. Auger. ed., *Enfants et enfance dans les mythologies.* Paris, 265–89

Jouanno, C. 2000–1. 'La Réception du Roman d'Alexandre à Byzance'. *Ancient Narrative* 1, 301–21

Jouanno, C. 2002. *Naissance et métamorphose du Roman d'Alexandre. Domaine grec.* Paris

Jouguet, P. 1940. 'La date alexandrine de la fondation d'Alexandrie'. *REA* 42, 192–7

Jouguet, P. 1949. 'Les premiers Ptolémées et l'hellénisation de Sérapis.' In *Hommages Bidez-Cumont* (Coll. Latomus II), Brussels' Collection Latomus, 2, 159–66

Kaegi, W. 1992. *Byzantium and the Early Islamic Conquests.* Cambridge

Kampers, F. 1901. *Alexander der Grosse und die Idee des Weltimperiums in Prophetie und Sage.* Freiburg

Kantorowicz, E. 1931. *Frederick the Second 1194–1250,* transl. E.O. Lorimer. London

Karakasidou, A.N. 1997. *Fields of Wheat, Hills of Blood. Passages to Nationhood in Greek Macedonia 1870–1990.* Chicago

Karttunen, K. 1989. *India in Early Greek Literature.* Helsinki

Karttunen, K. 1997. *India and the Hellenistic World.* Helsinki

Keen, M. 1984. *Chivalry.* Yale, New Haven

Kemp, B. 2006. *Ancient Egypt.* 2nd edn. Abingdon

Khalidi, T. 1975. *Islamic Historiography: The Histories of Mas'udi.* Albany

Khalidi, T. 1994. *Arabic Historical Thought in the Classical Period.* Cambridge

Kieckhefer, R. 1989. *Magic in the Middle Ages.* Cambridge

Kirmeier, J., Schneidmuller, B. Weinfurter, S. and Brockhoff, E. Eds. 2002. *Kaiser Heinrich II 1002–1024.* Stuttgart

Klein-Franke, F. 1970. 'Aristotle's Lapidary during the Latin Middle Ages'. *Ambix* 17, 137–42

Kleinbaum, A.W. 1983. *The War against the Amazons.* New York

Kline, N.R. 2001. *Maps of Medieval Thought*

Kmosko, M. 1931. 'Das Rätsel des Pseudo-Methodios'. *Byzantion* 6, 273–96

Knights, C. 1993. 'The Story of Zosimus or the History of the Rechabites?' *JSJ,* 24, 235–45

Knights, C. 1995. 'Towards a Critical Introduction to the History of the Rechabites'. *JSJ,* 26, 324–42

Köhler, I. 1983. *Der neubulgarische Alexanderroman. Untersuchungen zur Textgeschichte und Verbreitung.* Amsterdam

Koehler, R. 1894. *Aufsätze über Märchen.* Berlin

Koenen, L. 1968. 'Die Prophezeiungen des Töpfers'. *ZPE* 2, 178–209

Koenen, L. 1985. 'The Dream of Nektanebos'. *Bulletin of the American Society of Papyrologists* 22, 171–94

Koenig, Y. 1994. *Magie et magiciens dans l'Egypte ancienne*. Paris

Kolendo, J. 1987. 'Sur le Nom de *Caspiae Portae* appliqué aux cols de Caucase'. *Folia Orientalia* 24, 141–8

Kragl, F. 2005. *Die Weisheit des Fremden. Studien zur mittelalterlichen Alexandertradition.* Bern, etc.

Kratz, H. 1973. *Wolfram von Eschenbach's Parzival.* Bern

Kreft, W. 1981. *Ikonographische Studien zur altčechischen Alexandreis.* Amsterdam

Lane Fox, R. 1997. 'The Itinerary of Alexander: Constantius to Julian'. *CQ* 47, 239–52

Lang, R. 1951 *A Mirror for Princes. The Qabus nama of Kai Ka'us.* London

Laourdas, B. and Makaronas, Ch. Eds. 1970. *Arkhaia Makedonia: anakoinosis kata to proton diethnes symposion en Thessalonikei 26–28 April 1968.* Thessaloniki: Inst. of Balkan Studies

Lappas, T. 1993. *Karagkiozis.* Athens

Lascelles, M. 1936. 'Alexander and the Earthly Paradise in Medieval English Writings'. *Medium Aevum* 5, 31–47, 79–104, 173–88

Lassen, C. 1827. *Indische Altertumskunde.* Bonn

Lassner, J. 1993. *Demonizing the Queen of Sheba.* Chicago

Laufer, B. 1919. *Sino-Iranica.* Chicago

Lawson, J.C. 1964. *Modern Greek Folklore and Ancient Greek Religion.* New York

Lefkowitz, M. 1996. *Not Out of Africa.* New York

Le Goff, J. 1988. 'The Marvelous in the Medieval West'. In *The Medieval Imagination,* Chicago, 27–44

Leigh Fermor, P. 1958. *Mani.* London

Letts, M. 1949. *Sir John Mandeville.* London

Levi, I. 1881a. 'La Légende d'Alexandre dans le Talmud'. *Revue des Etudes Juives* 2, 293–300

Levi, I. 1881b. 'Les Traditions hébraïques de l'histoire légendaire d'Alexandre'. *Revue des Etudes Juives* 3, 238–75

Levi, I. 1883. 'La Légende d'Alexandre dans le Talmud et le Midrasch'. *Revue des Etudes Juives* 7, 78–93

Levi, I. 1886. 'Le Voyage d'Alexandre au Paradis'. *Revue des Etudes Juives* 12, 117–18

Levi, I. 1887. *Le Roman d'Alexandre.* Paris

Levi, I. 1894. 'Le Yosippon et le Roman d'Alexandre'. *Revue des Etudes Juives* 28, 147–8

Levi, S. 1936. 'Alexander and Alexandrias in Indian Literature'. *Indian Historical Quarterly,* 126 ff.

Lewis, B. 1982. *The Muslim Discovery of Europe.* London

Lidzbarski, M. 1892. 'Wer ist Chadir?' *Zeitschrift für Assyriologie* 7, 104–18

Lidzbarski, M. 1893. 'Zu den arabischen Alexandergeschichten'. *Zeitschrift für Assyriologie* 8, 263–312

Löwe, H. 1951. *Ein literarische Widersacher des Bonifatius. Virgil von Salzburg und die Kosmographie des Aethicus Ister.* Abhandlungen Mainz, Geistes und sozialwiss. Kl, nr. 11, 903–83

Lolos, A. Ch. 1984. 'I araviki metafrasi tou metegenesterou pezou mythistorimetos tou Pseudo-Kallistheni gia to Mega Alexandro'. *Graeco-Arabica* 3, 191–202

Loomis, R.S. 1918. 'Alexander the Great's Celestial Journey'. *Burlington Magazine* 38, 136–40, 177–85

Loomis, R.S. ed. 1959. *Arthurian Literature in the Middle Ages.* Oxford

L'Orange, H.P. 1953. *The Iconography of Cosmic Kingship.* Oslo

Lovejoy, A.O. and Boas, G. 1965. *Primitivism and Related Ideas in Antiquity.* New York

Luzzatto, M.J. 1992. 'Grecia e vicino Oriente: tracce della "Storia di Ahiqar" nella cultura greca tra VI e V secolo a.C'. *Quaderni di Storia* 36, 5–84

McCarthy, C. 1998. *Cities of the Plain.* New York

McCrindle, J.W. 1901. *Ancient India as Described in Classical Literature*. Delhi

McCrindle, J.W. 1926. *Ancient India as Described by Megasthenes and Arrian*. Delhi

McGinn, B. 1994. *Antichrist: Two Thousand Years of the Human Fascination with Evil*. San Francisco

McGinn, B. ed. 1999. *Encyclopaedia of Apocalypticism*. New York

Macintyre, B. 2004. *Josiah the Great: The True Story of the Man Who Would Be King*. London

Maclean, R. 2000. *Under the Dragon*. London

Macuch, R. 1989. 'Egyptian Sources and Versions of Pseudo-Callisthenes'. In Criscuolo and Geraci, 503–11

Macuch, R. 1991. 'Pseudo-Callisthenes Orientalis and the Problem of Dhu l-qarnain'. *Graeco-Arabica* 4, 223–64

Maddox, D. and S. Sturm-Maddox eds. 2002. *The Medieval French Alexander*. Albany

Magoun, F.P. 1929. *The Gests of King Alexander of Macedon*. Harvard, Cambridge, Mass.

Mango, A. 1955. 'Studies on the Legend of Iskandar in the Classical Literature of Islamic Persia, with Special Reference to the Work of Firdausi, Nizami and Jami'. Unpublished doctoral dissertation, London, SOAS Library

Manuel, F. and Manuel, F. 1979. *Utopian Thought in the Western World*. Harvard, Cambridge, Mass.

Manzalaoui, M. 1965. 'The Pseudo-Aristotelian *Sirr al-Asrar* and Three Oxford Thinkers of the Middle Ages'. In G. Makdisi ed., *Arabic and Islamic Studies in Honour of H.A.R. Gibb*. Leiden

Manzalaoui, M. 1974. 'The Pseudo-Aristotelian *Kitab Sirr al-Asrar*'. *Oriens* 23–24, 147–254

Maresch, K. and Wills, W.H. 1988. 'The Encounter of Alexander with the Brahmans: New fragments of the Cynic diatribe *P. Genev. Inv 271*', *ZPE* 74, 59–83

Marin, M. 1991. 'Legends on Alexander the Great in Muslim Spain'. *Graeco-Arabica* 4, 71–90

Marinescu-Himou, M. 1970. 'La Légende d'Alexandre le Grand dans la littérature roumaine'. In Laourdas and Makaronas 1970, 407–16

Martin, V. 1959. 'Un Recueil de diatribes cyniques: Papyrus Genève inv. 271'. *MusHelv* 16, 77–115

Martinez, F.J. 1987. 'The Apocalyptic Genre in Syriac: the world of Pseudo-Methodius'. In H.J.W. Drijvers, R. Lavenant, C. Molenberg and G.J. Reinink eds., *IV Symposium Syriacum*. Rome

Maspéro, F. 1967. *Popular Stories of Ancient Egypt*. New York (transl. of *Contes populaires égyptiennes*, 1882)

Mayerson, P. 1993. 'A Confusion of Indias: Asia, India and Africa in the Byzantine sources'. *Journal of the American Oriental Society* 113, 169–74

Mayor, A. 2003. *Greek Fire, Poison Arrows and Scorpion Bombs. Biological and Chemical Warfare in the Ancient World*. London

Megas, G. 1970. *Folktales of Greece*. Chicago

Meisami, J.S. 1987. *Persian Court Poetry*. Princeton

Meisami, J.S. 1999. *Persian Historiography to the End of the Twelfth Century*. Edinburgh

Meissner, B. 1894a. 'Quellenuntersuchungen zur Haikargeschichte.' *ZDMG* 48, 171–97; largely repeated in *Alte Orient* 16 (1917)

Meissner, B. 1894b. *Alexander und Gilgamesch*. Leipzig. Repr. Berlin 1928

Meissner, B. 1917. *Das Märchen vom weisen Ahiqar*. Leipzig

Merkelbach, R. 1977. *Die Quellen des griechischen Alexanderromans: Zweite neubearbeitete Auflage unter Mitwirkung von Jürgen Trumpf*. Munich

Merzdorf, J.F.L.T. 1870. *Die deutschen Historienbibeln des Mittelalters*. Tübingen

Metlitzki, D. 1977. *The Matter of Araby in Medieval England*. Yale, New Haven

Meyer, P. 1886. *Alexandre le Grand dans la littérature française du moyen âge*. Paris. Repr. Geneva 1970

Meyer, R.T. 1949. 'The Sources of the Middle Irish Alexander'. *Modern Philology* 47, 1–7

Michael, I. 1970. *The Treatment of Classical Material in the Libro de Alexandre.* Manchester

Millet, G. 1923. 'L'Ascension d'Alexandre', *Syria* 4, 85–133

Miquel, A. 1975. *La Géographie humaine du monde musulman jusqu'au milieu du deuxième siècle.* The Hague

Mitsakis, K. 1967. 'Beobachtungen zum byzantinischen Alexandergedicht'. *Jahrbuch der österreichischen byzantinischen Gesellschaft*, 16, 119–26

Mitsakis, K. 1970 'The Tradition of the Alexander Romance in Modern Greek Literature'. In Laourdas and Makaronas 1970, 376–86

Moennig, U. 1987. 'Zur Überlieferungsgeschichte des mittel- und neugriechischen Alexanderromans'. Cologne

Moennig, U. 1993. 'Digenis = Alexander? The relationships between *Digenis Akrites* and the Byzantine *Alexander Romance* in their different versions'. In Beaton and Ricks 1993, 103–15

Momigliano, A. 1979. 'Flavius Josephus and Alexander's Visit to Jerusalem'. In *Settimo contributo alla storia degli studi classici e del mondo antico*, 319–29. Rome = *Pagine ebraiche* (Turin 1987), 85–93

Momigliano, A. 1994. *Studies on Modern Scholarship*, ed. G.W. Bowersock and T.J. Cornell. Berkeley

Mookerji, R.K. 1943. *Chandragupta Maurya and his Times.* Madras

Moravcsik, J. 1958. *Byzantinoturcica* II. Budapest: Magyar-Görög Tanulmányok 21

Morgan, J.R. and Stoneman, R. eds. 1994. *Greek Fiction. The Greek Novel in Context.* London

Mørkholm, O. 1991. *Early Hellenistic Coinage.* Cambridge

Muckensturm, C. 1993. 'Les Gymnosophistes étaient-ils des cyniques modèles?' In M-O. Goulet-Cazé and R. Goulet eds, *Le Cynisme ancien et ses prolongements*. Paris, 225–39

Mulder-Bakker, A.B. 1983. *Vorstenschool. Vier Geschiedschrijvers over Alexander en hun Visie op het Keizerschap.* Groningen

Nagel, T. 1978. *Alexander der Grosse in der frühislamischen Volksliteratur.* Walldorf-Hessen

Niane, D.T. 1965. *Sundiata: An Epic of Old Mali.* London

Nice, A. 2006. 'The Reputation of the Mantis Aristander'. *Acta Classica* 48, 87–102

Nicholson, R.A. 1907. *Literary History of the Arabs.* Edinburgh

Noble, P., Polak, L. and Isoz, C. 1982. *The Medieval Alexander Legend and Romance Epic: Essays in Honour of D.J.A. Ross.* Millwood, NY

Nöldeke, T. 1890. 'Beiträge zur Geschichte des Alexanderroman'. *Denkschriften der Kaiserlichen Akademie der Wissenschaften, Phil. Hist. Klasse* 38. Vienna

Nöldeke, T. 1930/1979. *The Iranian National Epic.* Bombay

Norris, H.T. 1972. *Saharan Myth and Saga.* Oxford

Norris, H.T. 1983. 'Qisas elements in the Qur'an'. In Beeston, Johnstone, Serjeant and Smith

Norwich, J.J. 1991. *The Normans in Sicily.* Harmondsworth

Nussbaum, M. 1994. *The Therapy of Desire: Theory and Practice in Hellenistic Ethics.* Princeton

O'Leary, De L. 1949. *How Greek Science Passed to the Arabs.* London

Olschki, L. 1941. 'Ponce de Leon's Fountain of Youth: History of a Geographical Myth'. *Hispanic American Historical Review* 21, 361–85

Palmer, A. 1993. *The Seventh Century in West Syrian Chronicles.* Liverpool

Panayotakis, S., Zimmerman, M. and Keulen, W., eds, 2003. *The Ancient Novel and Beyond.* Leiden

Panchenko, D. 1998. 'Scylax' Circumnavigation of India and its Interpretation in Early Greek Geography, Ethnography and Cosmography I'. *Hyperboreus* 4, 211–42

Papathomas, A. 2000. 'Der erste Beleg für die "historische Quelle" des Alexanderromans'. *Philologus* 144, 217–26

Patch, H.R. 1970. *The Other World, according to Descriptions in Medieval Literature.* New York

Payne, M. 1991. 'Alexander the Great: Myth and the Polis and Afterwards'. In D. Pozzi and J. Wickersham, eds, *Myth and the Polis.* Cornell, 164–81

Pennachietti, F.A. 2000. 'The Queen of Sheba, the Glass Floor and the Floating Tree-trunk'. *Henoch* 22, 223–46

Penzer, N.M. 1952. *Poison-Damsels and Other Essays in Folklore and Anthropology.* London

Perry, B.E. 1966. 'The Egyptian Legend of Nectanebo'. *TAPA* 97, 327-33.

Perry. B.E. 1967. *The Ancient Romances.* Berkeley, etc.

Peters, E. 1967. 'Die irische Alexandersage'. *Zeitschrift für celtische Philologie* 30, 71–264

Petrain, D. 2005. 'Gems, Metapoetics and Values: Greek and Roman responses to a third-century discourse on precious stones'. *TAPA* 135, 329–57

Pfister, F. 1913/1975. 'Chadhir und Alexander' [review of Friedländer]. *Berlin philol. Wochenschrift* 912–91 = *Kleine Schriften zum Alexanderroman.* Meisenheim. 1976, 143–50

Pfister, F. 1914/1975. 'Eine jüdische Gründungsgeschichte Alexandrias' *Sitzungsberiate Heidelberg* 1914 Abh 11 = *Kleine Schriften zum Alexanderroman.* Meisenheim. 1976, 80–103. Alexanderroman. Meisenheim. 1976

Pfister, F. 1915/1976. 'Das angebliche Mithraeum in Galiläa und Alexanders Besuch in der Götterhöhle'. *Orientalistische Literaturezeitung* 1549–52 = *Kleine Schriften zum Alexanderroman.* Meisenheim 1976, 173–4

Pfister, F. 1941. 'Das Nachleben der Überlieferung von Alexander und den Brahmanen'. *Hermes* 76, 143–69 = *Kleine Schriften zum Alexanderroman.* Meisenheim. 1976. 53–79

Pfister, F. 1956. *Alexander der Grosse in den Offenbarungen der Griechen, Juden, Mohammedanern und Christen.* Berlin

Pfister, F. 1976. *Kleine Schriften zum Alexanderroman.* Meisenheim am Glan

Pfister, F. and Riedinger, U. 1955. 'Ein Zitat aus dem Alexanderroman des Pseudo-Kallisthenes in einer untergeschobenen Schrift des Johannes von Damaskos'. *BZ* 48, 86–88

Photiades, P. 1959. 'Les Diatribes cyniques de papyrus de Genève 271, leurs traductions et élaborations successives'. *MusHelv* 16, 116–39

Pinch, G. 1994. *Egyptian Magic.* London

Pleij, H. 2001. *Dreaming of Cockaigne: Medieval Fantasies of the Perfect Life.* New York

Plezia, M. 1971. 'De novo Pindari fragmento arabico'. In *Philomathes. Studies and Essays in the Humanities in Memory of Philip Merlan.* The Hague, 270–80

Polignac, F. de 1996 'Cosmocrator: l'Islam et la légende antique du souverain universel'. In Bridges & Bürgel 1996, 149–64

Politis, L. 1973. *A History of Modern Greek Literature.* Oxford

Politis, N.G. 1904. *Meletai tou biou kai tis glossis tou ellinikou laou. Paradoseis I.* Athens

Potter, D.S. 1990. *Prophecy and History in the Crisis of the Roman Empire.* Oxford

Potter, D.S. 1994. *Prophets and Emperors.* Harvard

Priese, K.H. 1992–93. *The Gold of Meroe.* New York; Mainz

Pritchard, J.B. 1974. *Solomon and Sheba.* Phaidon

Pritchett, F.W. 1991. *The Romance Tradition in Urdu.* New York

Puri, B. 1963. *India in Classical Greek Writings.* Ahmedabad

Rank, O. *et al.* 1909. Revised edn 2004. *The Myth of the Birth of the Hero.* Baltimore, Maryland

Raven, M.J. 1983. 'Wax in Egyptian Magic and Symbolism'. *Oudheidkundige Mededelingen uit het Rijksmuseum van Oudheiden te Leiden* 64, 7–48

Reilly, B. 1993. *The Medieval Spains.* Cambridge

Reinink, G.J. 1983b 'Der Verfassername "Modios" der syrischen Schatzhöhle und die Apokalypse des Pseudo-Methodios'. *Oriens Christianus* 67, 46–64

Reinink, G.J. 1990. 'Alexander der Grosse und die Lebensquelle im syrischen Alexander-Lied'. *Studia Patristica,* ed. E.A. Livingstone, 18.4, 282–8

Renard, J. 1993. *Islam and the Heroic Image.* South Carolina

Ringbom, L.I. 1958. *Paradisus terrestris: Myt, Bild och Verklighet.* Helsinki

Ritner, R.K. 1993. *The Mechanics of Ancient Egyptian Magical Practice.* Chicago

Robert, L. 1968. 'Inscriptions grecques nouvelles de la Bactriane'. *Comptes rendus de l'Académie des Inscriptions,* 416–57

Robinson, B.W. 1980. *Persian Paintings in the John Rylands Library*. London

Rogers, T. 1870. *Buddhaghosha's Parables*. London

Roisman, J., ed. 2003. *Brill's Companion to Alexander the Great*. Leiden

Romaios, K. 1973. *To athanato nero*. Athens

Romano, Domenico, 1974. *Giulo Valerio*, Palermo, Palumbo

Romm, J. 1992. *The Edges of the World in Ancient Thought*. Princeton

Romm, J. 1996. 'Cynicism before the Cynics?' In B. Branham and M.O. Goulet-Cazé, eds, *The Cynics: The Cynic Movement in Antiquity and Its Legacy*. Berkeley, 121–35

Ronge, H.H. 1957. *Konung Alexander. Filologiska Studier i en Fornsvensk Text*. Uppsala

Rosenthal, F. 1975. *The Classical Tradition in Islam*. London: Routledge

Ross, D.J.A. 1963a. 'Olympias and the Serpent'. *Journal of the Warburg and Courtauld Institute* 16, 1–21

Ross, D.J.A. 1963b. *Alexander Historiatus. A Guide to Medieval Illustrated Alexander Literature*. London: Warburg Institute Surveys, I

Ross, D.J.A. 1967. 'Alexander the Great and the Faithless Lady: A Submarine Adventure'. London. Repr. in Ross 1985, 382–401

Ross, D.J.A. 1971. *Illustrated Medieval Alexander Books in Germany and the Netherlands. A Study in Comparative Iconography*. Cambridge

Ross, D.J.A. 1985. *Studies in the Alexander Romance*. London

Roueché, C. 1988. 'Byzantine Writers and Readers: storytelling in the eleventh century'. In R. Beaton, ed., *The Greek Novel AD 1–1985*. Beckenham, 123–33

Ruggini, L. 1961. '*L'Epitoma rerum gestarum Alexandri Magni* e il *Liber de Morte Testamentoque eius*'. *Athenaeum* 39, 285–337

Ruska, J. 1912. *Das Steinbuch des Aristoteles mit literargeschichtlichen Untersuchungen*. Heidelberg (incorporates his much shorter 1911 Habilitationsschrift, published as *Untersuchungen über das Steinbuch des Aristoteles*)

Ryan, W.F. and Schmitt, C.B. 1982. *Pseudo-Aristotle, the Secret of Secrets: Sources and Influence*. London: Warburg Institute Surveys IX

Saatsoglou-Palindeli, C. 1991 'Serpenti à Pella'. *To arkhaiologiko ergo sti Makedonia kai Thraki* 5, 12–16

Sachs, A.J. and Hunger, H. 1988. *Astronomical Diaries and Related Texts from Babylonia I*. Vienna

Sackur, E. 1898. *Sibyllinische Texte und Forschungen*. Halle

Samir, K. 1998. 'Les Versions arabes chrétiens du Roman d'Alexandre'. In Finazzi and Valvo 1998, 227–47

Sande, S. 1993. 'The Golden Alexander'. In J. Carlsen *et al.*, eds, *Alexander the Great: Reality and Myth = Analecta Romana Instituti Danici*. suppl. 20; Rome, 189–96

Sande, S. 1999. 'Famous Persons as Bringers of Good Luck'. In D. Jordan, ed., *The World of Ancient Magic*. Bergen, 227–38

Saunders, N.J. 2006. *Alexander's Tomb. The 2000 Year Obsession to Find the Lost Conqueror*. New York

Scafi, A. 2006. *Mapping Paradise. A History of Heaven On Earth*. London

Schmidt, V. 1995. *A Legend and its Image*. Groningen

Schmitz, B. 1992. *Islamic Manuscripts in the New York Public Library*. New York

Schönegger, D. 1989. 'Kopfjäger, Schiffstücher und der Alexanderroman'. *Balkan Studies* 30, 197–212

Schuyler, E. 1876. *Turkistan*. London

Schwartz, F.F. 1983. 'The Itinerary of Iambulus – Utopianism and History.' In *Indology and Law: Festschrift J.D.M. Derrett*. Heidelberg

Schwarzenberg, E. 1976. 'The Portraiture of Alexander'. In *Entretiens Hardt: Alexandre le Grand*, Vandoeuvres, 223–67

Secomska, K. 1975. 'The Miniature Cycle in the Sandomierz Pantheon and the Iconography of Alexander's Indian Campaign'. *Journal of the Warburg and Courtauld Institute* 38, 53–71

Sedlar, J.W. 1980. *India and the Greek World*. Totowa, NJ

Seibert, J. 1972. *Alexander der Grosse. Erträge der Forschung*. Darmstadt

Settis-Frugoni, C. 1973. *Historia Alexandri elevati per griphos ad aerem. Origine, iconografi e fortuna di un tema*. Rome: studi storici, 80–2

Shaked, S. 2004. *Le Satrape de Bactriane et son gouverneur. Documents araméens du quatrième siècle avant notre ère provenant de Bactriane*. Persika, 4

Shinnie, P.L. 1967. *Meroe: A Civilization of the Sudan*. London

Shrimpton, G.S. 1991. *Theopompus the Historian*. Montreal

Silverberg, R. 1972. *The Realm of Prester John*. New York

Simons, P. 1994. 'Theme and Variations: The Education of the Hero in the *Roman d'Alexandre*'. *Neophilologus* 78, 195–208

Sisam, K.E. 1953. 'The Compilation of the Beowulf MS'. In *Studies in the History of Old English Literature*, 65–96. Repr. in *Oxford Review of English Studies* 10 (1934), 342ff)

Slessarev, V. 1959. *Prester John, the Letter and the Legend*. Minnesota

Smalley B. 1952. *The Story of the Bible in the Middle Ages*. Oxford

Sorabji, R. 1993. *Animal Minds and Human Morals*. London

Southern, R.W. 1953. *The Making of the Middle Ages*. London

Spencer, D. 2002. *The Roman Alexander*. Exeter

Spiegel, F. 1851. *Die Alexandersage bei den Orientalen*. Leipzig

Sprague de Camp, L. 1960. *The Ancient Engineers*. Garden City

Stambaugh, J. 1972. *Sarapis under the Early Ptolemies*. Leiden

Standish, W.F. 1970. 'The Caspian Gates'. *G&R* 17, 12–24

Steinberg S.H. 1955. *Five Hundred Years of Printing*. Harmondsworth

Stephens, S.A. 2003. *Seeing Double: Intercultural Poetics in Ptolemaic Alexandria*. Berkeley

Stern, S.M. 1968. *Aristotle on the World State*. Oxford

Stewart, A. 1993. *Faces of Power. Alexander's image and Hellenistic politics*. California

Stewart, Z. 1958. 'Democritus and the Cynics'. *HSCP* 63, 179–91

Stöcker, C. 1979. 'Alexander der Grosse bei Fulgentius und die Historia Alexandria Macedonis des Antidamas'. *Vigiliae Christianae* 33, 55–75

Stokes, W.H. and Windisch, E. 1887. *Irische Texte*. Leipzig

Stoneman, R. 1984. *Land of Lost Gods*. London

Stoneman, R. 1991. *The Greek Alexander Romance*. Harmondsworth

Stoneman, R. 1992a. *Palmyra and its Empire*. Ann Arbor

Stoneman, R. 1992b. 'Oriental Motifs in the Alexander Romance'. *Antichthon* 26, 95–113

Stoneman, R. 1994a. *Legends of Alexander the Great*. London

Stoneman, R. 1994b. 'Who Are the Brahmans?' *CQ* 44, 500–10

Stoneman, R. 1994c. 'Romantic Ethnography'. *Ancient World* 25, 93–107

Stoneman, R. 1994d. 'Jewish Traditions on Alexander the Great'. *Studia Philonica Annual* 6, 37–53

Stoneman, R. 1994e. 'The Alexander Romance: from history to fiction'. In Morgan and Stoneman

Stoneman, R. 1995a. 'Naked Philosophers'. *JHS* 115, 99–114

Stoneman, R. 1995b. 'Riddles in Bronze and Stone'. *Groningen Colloquia on the Novel* 6, 159–70

Stoneman, R. 1999a. 'The Latin Alexander'. In H. Hofmann (ed.), *Latin Fiction*. London 1999, 167–86

Stoneman, R. 1999b. 'The Medieval Alexander'. In H. Hofmann (ed.), *Latin Fiction*. London 1999, 238–52

Stoneman, R. 2003a. 'Alexander the Great in the Arabic Tradition'. In Panayotakis, Zimmermann and Keulen 2003, 3–21

Stoneman, R. 2003b. 'The Legacy of Alexander in Ancient Philosophy'. In Roisman 2003

Storost, J. 1935. *Studien zur Alexandersage in der älteren italienischen Literatur. Romanistische Arbeiten* XXIII. Halle

Strohmaier, G. 1995. 'Al-Biruni und der griechische Parthenope-Roman'. *Graeco-Arabica* 6, 72–8

Szkilnik, M. 2002. 'Conquering Alexander: *Perceforest* and the Alexandrian tradition'. In Maddox and Sturm-Maddox 2002, 203–17

Tanner, M. 1993. *The Last Descendant of Aeneas: The Hapsburgs and the Mythic Image of the Emperor.* Yale, New Haven

Tardiola, C. 1993. *Viaggiatori al Paradiso.* Florence

Tatum, J., ed. 1994. *The Search for the Ancient Novel.* Baltimore

Tcheraz, M. 1901. 'La Légende d'Alexandre le Grand chez les Armeniens'. *Revue de l'histoire des religions* 43–4, 345–51

Telle, J. 1994. 'Aristoteles an Alexander über den philosophischen Stein – die alchemische Lehre des Ps.-Aristoteles Secretum Secretorum in einer deutschen Versübersetzung des 15. Jhdts'. In *Licht der Natur, Festschrift G. Keul.* Göppingen

Thiersch, H. 1909. *Pharos: Antike, Islam und Occident.* Leipzig and Berlin

Thompson, D.J. 1988. *Memphis under the Ptolemies.* Princeton

Thomson, S. *Motif Index of Folk Literature,* 6 vols 1955–8. Copenhagen

Thorndike, L. 1922–23. *A History of Magic and Experimental Science, I–II.* New York

Tolkien, J.R.R. 1983. *The Monsters and the Critics.* London

Török, L. 1988. 'Geschichte Meroes. Ein Beitrag über die Quellenanlage und den Forschungsstand.' *ANRW* 11.10.1 (Berlin), 107–341

Torrey, C. 1946. *The Lives of the Prophets.* Philadelphia

Trigger, B. *et al.* 1983. *Ancient Egypt: A Social History.* Cambridge

Trumpf, J. 1959. 'Alexanders Kappadokisches Testament'. *BZ* 52, 253–6

Trumpf, J. 1962. Review of Gleixner 1961. *BZ* 55, 82–7

Trumpf, J. 1966. 'Alexander und die Königin von Saba'. *Athenaeum* n.s. 44, 307–8

Trumpf, J. 1967. 'Zur Überlieferung des mittelgriechischen Prosa-Alexander und der *Phyllada tou Megalexandrou'. BZ* 60, 3–40

Turner, T.H. 1851. *Some Account of Domestic Architecture in England.* Oxford

Tyrrell, W.B. 1984. *Amazons, a Study in Athenian Mythmaking.* Baltimore, Maryland

Ullendorff, E. 1974. 'The Queen of Sheba in Ethiopic Tradition'. In Pritchard 1974

Valvo, A. 1997. *La diffusione dell'eredità classica nell'età tardoantica e medioevale: Forme e modi di trasmissione.* Alessandria

Van Bekkum, W.J. 1981. 'Alexander the Great in Medieval Hebrew Literature'. *Journal of the Warburg and Courtauld Institute* 4, 218–26

Van Cleve, T. 1972. *The Emperor Frederick II Hohenstaufen, Immutator Mundi.* Oxford

Van der Spek, R.J. 2003. 'Darius III, Alexander the Great and Babylonian Scholarship'. *Achaemenid History* 13, 289–346

Van Oostrom, F. 1996. *Maerlants Wereld.* Amsterdam

Van Thiel, H. 1972. 'Alexanders Gespräch mit den Gymnosophisten'. *Hermes* 100, 343–59

Vasunia, P. 2001. *The Gift of the Nile. Hellenizing Egypt from Aeschylus to Alexander.* Berkeley

Velissaropoulos, D.K. 1990. *Ellines Kai Indoi.* 2 vols. Athens

Veloudis, Georg 1968. *Der neugriechische Alexander.* Munich. Miscellanea Byzantina Monacensia 8

Veloudis, G. 1969. *Alexander der Grosse. Ein alter Neugrieche.* Munich

Visotzky, B. and Fishman, D. 1991. *From Mesopotamia to Modernity.* Boulder, Colorado

Visser, E. 1958. *Götter und Kulte in ptolemäischer Alexandria.* Amsterdam

Walbank, F. 1967/85. 'The Scipionic Legend'. *PCPS* 13, 54–69 = *Selected Papers.* Cambridge, 120–37

Waldron, A. 1990. *The Great Wall of China.* Cambridge

Wallach, L. 1941. 'Alexander the Great and the Indian Gymnosophists in Hebrew Tradition'. *Proceedings of the American Academy of Jewish Research* 11, 47–83

Ward, H.L.D. 1961–62. *Catalogue of Romances in the Department of Manuscripts.* London *(British Museum)* I–III

Wartena, J.R. 1972. *Inleiding op een uitgave der Tabula Peutingeriana.* Amsterdam

Weerakkody, D.P. M. 1997. *Taprobane: Ancient Sri Lanka as Known to the Greeks and Romans.* Turnhout

Weever, J. de 1990. 'Candace in the Alexander Romance'. *Romance Philology* 48.4, 529–46

Weinreich, O. 1911. *Der Trug des Nektanebo.* Leipzig and Berlin

Weitzmann, K. 1951. *Greek Mythology in Byzantine Art.* Princeton

Welles, C.B. 1962. 'The Discovery of Serapis and the Foundation of Alexandria'. *Historia* 11, 271–98

West, M.L. 1969. 'Near Eastern Material in Hellenistic and Roman Literature'. *HSCP* 73, 113–34

Weymann, K.F. 1901. *Die aethiopische und arabische Übersetzung des Pseudocallisthenes. Eine literarische Untersuchung.* Kirchhain

Whealey, A. 1946. '*De Consummatione Mundi* of Pseudo-Hippolytus: Another Byzantine apocalypse from the early Islamic period'. *Byzantion* 66, 461–9

Wheeler, B. 1998. 'Moses or Alexander? Early Islamic exegesis of Qur'ān 18.60–65'. *Journal of Near Eastern Studies* 57, 191–215

White, D.G. 1991. *Myths of the Dog-Man.* Chicago

White, T.H. 1954. *The Book of Beasts.* London

Wiesehöfer, J. 1994. *Die dunklen Jahrhunderte der Persis.* Munich. Zetemata 90

Wilcken, U. 1922. *Urkunden der Ptolemäerzeit (UPZ),* vol. 1. Berlin/Leipzig

Wilcken, U. 1923. 'Alexander der Grosse und die indischen Gymnosophisten'. *Sitzungsberichte der preussischen Akademie, Berlin (philologisch-historische Klasse),* 150–83

Wilde, L.W. 1999. *On the Trail of the Women Warriors.* London

Williams, S. 2003. *The Secret of Secrets.* Ann Arbor

Wills, L.A. 1997. *The Quest of the Historical Gospel.* London

Wilsdorf, H. 1991. 'Der weise Achikaros bei Demokrit und Theophrast. Eine Kommunikationsfrage'. *Philologus* 135, 191–206

Wilson, C.E. 1922. 'The Wall of Alexander against Gog and Magog and the Expedition Sent Out to Find it by the Khalif Wathiq in 842 AD', *Asia Major,* 575–612

Winiarczyk, M. 1997. 'Das Werk des Jambulos'. *RhMus* 140, 128–53

Winstedt, R.O. 1940. *A History of Malay Literature.* London

Winston, D.F. 1976. 'Iambulus' Islands of the Sun and Hellenistic Literary Utopias'. *Science Fiction Studies* 3, 219–27

Wisbey, R. 1966. *Das Alexanderbild Rudolfs von Ems.* Berlin

Wiseman, T.P. 1992. 'Julius Caesar and the Hereford World Map'. In *Talking to Vergil.* Exeter

Witakowski, W. 1987. *The Syriac Chronicle of Pseudo-Dionysius of Tel-Mahre. A Study in the History of Historiography.* Uppsala

Wittkower, R. 1942. 'Marvels of the East. A study in the history of monsters'. *Journal of the Warburg and Courtauld Institute* 5, 159–97

Wolska, W. 1962. *Recherches sur la topographie chrétienne de Cosmas Indicopleustes: Théologie et science au vi^e siècle.* Paris: Bibliothèque Byzantine, études 3

Wright, D.H. 2001. *The Roman Virgil and the Origins of Medieval Book Design.* London

Wright, J.K. 1925. *The Geographical Lore of the Time of the Crusades.* New York

Xyngopoulos, A. 1966. *Les Miniatures du roman d'Alexandre le Grand dans le codex de l'Institut Hellénique de Venise.* Athens and Venice

Yamamoto, K. 2003. *The Oral Background of Persian Epic.* Leiden

Yamauchi, Edwin 2004 *Africa and the Bible.* Grand Rapids

Young, M.J.L., Latham, J.D. and Serjeant, R.B. 1990. *Religion, Learning and Science in the 'Abbasid Period.* Cambridge

Zach, M. 1992. 'Meroe: Mythos und Realität einer Frauenherrschaft im antiken Afrika.' In E. Specht, ed., *Nachrichten aus der Zeit: Ein Streifzug durch die Frauengeschichte des Altertums.* Vienna

Zacher, J. 1867. *Pseudo-Callisthenes. Forschungen zur Kritik und Geschichte der ältesten Aufzeichnung der Alexandersage.* Halle

Ziegler, R.1998. 'Alexander der Grosse als Städtegründer: Fiktion und Realität'. In U. Peter, ed., *Stephanos Numismatikos. Festschrift E. Schönert-Geiss.* Berlin, 679–97

Zuwiyya, Z.D. 2001. *Islamic Legends concerning Alexander the Great Taken from Two Medieval Arabic MSS in Madrid.* Binghamton

INDEX